Understanding Psychology

Understanding Psychology

RESOURCE CONTRIBUTORS

Edmund J. Fantino, Ph. D.,
*University of California
at San Diego*

Kurt Fischer, Ph.D.,
University of Denver

Dennis Krebs, Ph.D.,
Harvard University

George S. Reynolds, Ph.D.,
*University of California
at San Diego*

Zick Rubin, Ph.D.,
Harvard University

EDITORIAL REVIEW BOARD

George D. Fuller, Ph.D.,
City College of San Francisco

Thomas E. McCloud, Ph.D.,
*Wayne County Community
College, Detroit*

Wm. Lloyd McCraney, M.L.A.,
Community College of Baltimore

GENERAL ADVISER
AND CONTRIBUTOR

Alastair McLeod, Ph.D.

CRM BOOKS
Del Mar, California

Introduction

Since around the beginning of the twentieth century, the body of psychological knowledge has grown immensely. In the last three-quarters of a century, psychologists have discovered a vast number of facts and developed a variety of theories about human development, mental processes, behavior, and interaction. The purpose of this book is to pass along to you some of the knowledge that has been gained. To accomplish this purpose, we have made a special effort to explore as many facets of psychology as possible, without emphasizing a particular subject area or point of view to the exclusion of any others.

To enhance this approach, we prepared this book with three broad objectives in mind: first, to provide an introduction to the terms and concepts psychologists use; second, to illuminate the special fascination of the topics that draw people to the field of psychology; and third, to explain the significance of psychological findings for the reader's own life.

This text will serve as your handbook to the understanding of psychology, and as such it contains a number of aids designed to make the information it presents as clear and as useful as possible. These aids include:

1. *Organization.* The book is divided into sixteen chapters, which are grouped into six units. Each unit roughly corresponds to a major field of psychology. The unit openings give you an overview of what each section and chapter contains.

2. *Text and Illustrations.* The text, captions, and illustrations work together to present the research, theories, and ideas central to psychology. Chapters are divided by numerous subheadings that describe the subject of each section, and key terms and concepts are italicized when they are first introduced to draw them to your attention. The illustrations and captions are designed to clarify important ideas, to add interesting information, and to provoke thought.

3. *Outlines and Summaries.* Brief outlines at the beginning of each chapter prepare you for what you are about to read. Summaries at the end of the chapters help you to locate the important points and to review them.

4. *Activities.* The activities that follow each chapter are intended to help you relate the ideas in the chapter to experiences of your own.

5. *Suggested Readings.* The last element of each chapter is a description of several interesting and readable books related to the topics presented in the chapter.

6. *Bibliography.* After Chapter 16 you will find a list of books and articles that provide in-depth coverage of some of the subjects explored in the chapters. These sources are useful for pursuing an interest in a particular topic.

7. *Glossary/Index.* Definitions of key terms and concepts have been included in the index to give you easy access to any idea in the book.

All these aids have been developed to help make the field of psychology come alive for you. This is a book you can study from, but it is also one you can browse through, read for enjoyment, and refer to when trying to understand psychological aspects of the world you live in, the people you know, and your own personality.

Contents

Understanding Psychology

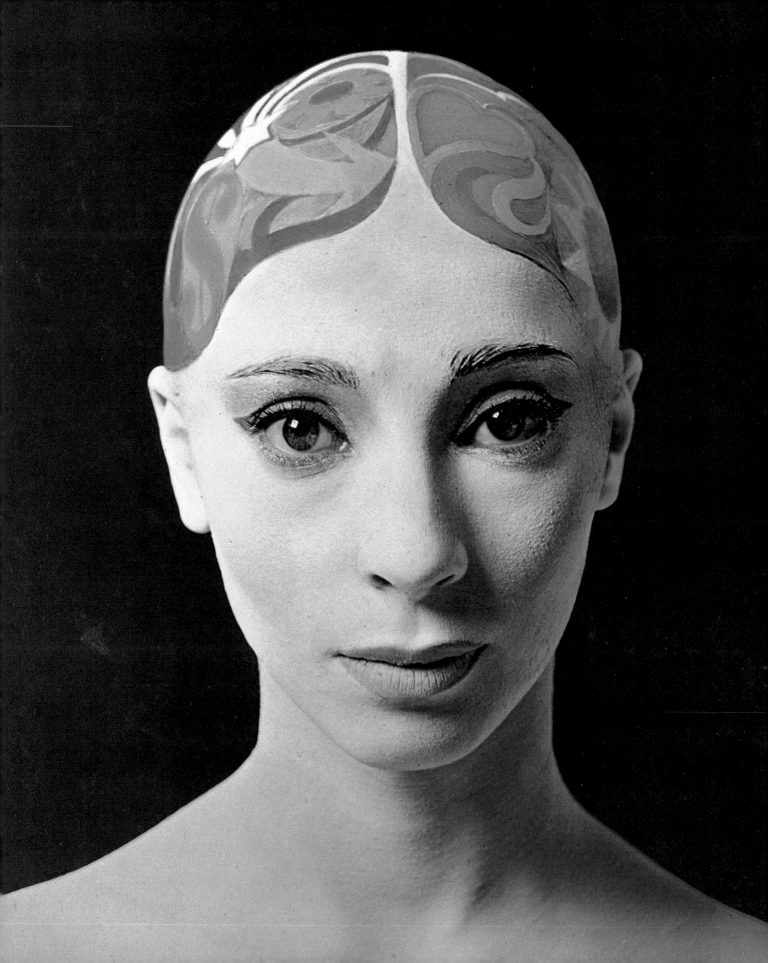

1
What Psychology Is About

Figure 1.1

This photograph suggests a some of
the major concerns of psychology: the
relation of the mind to the body, the
nature of thought and creativity, and the
individuality of personality,
to name a few.

It has been said that the field of psychology has a short history but a long past. Its history is short because psychology has been known as a separate field of study for less than one hundred years. But people have been examining, talking about, and writing on psychological subjects for thousands of years.

Some of the earliest thinkers on the subject of psychology were philosophers. The ancient Greek philosophers Plato and Aristotle both tried to answer the question: What is the soul or the mind? In doing so, they tried to discover what it means to reason, to love, to perceive, to remember, and to dream. Today psychologists are still grappling with these problems, as well as with many others.

But just what is psychology? The subject matter of psychology is not easy to define. One rather satisfying definition is, "Psychology is the science of mental life." This definition suggests a picture of the study of dreams, fantasies, memories, thought processes, anxieties, sensations, and so on. Certainly psychologists are interested in such things, but they are also interested in what people *do*. Because it is possible to study what people do in an objective, clear way, many psychologists prefer the definition: "Psychology is the science of *behavior.*"

Unfortunately, neither of these definitions means much to a person who has not already done some thinking about the subject matter of psychology. As is the case with many words, the only people who really understand what "psychology" means are the ones who have experience with what lies behind it. For this reason, this chapter will not give you a definition. Instead, it will explore some of the interesting ideas and incidents in the past that provided a foundation for what psychologists study today.

As you go through the chapter, you will notice that the historical examples each concentrate on a major area of psychology: perception, the relation between the body and behavior, child development, social interaction, personality, mental illness, and research. (This presentation follows the sequence in which these subjects are

Figure 1.2
Plato and Aristotle. Both of these famous Greek philosophers were interested in the nature of the soul. Plato believed that the soul was made up of three parts: an impulsive, instinctive part that resided in the abdominal viscera, an emotional, spiritual part that came from the heart, and an intellectual, reasoning part that was seated in the brain. Plato suggested that personality depended on the proportions of these three qualities in the individual's soul. Plato's student, Aristotle, is often credited as being the founder of psychology because he wrote the first book dealing with psychological matters: *De Anima (On the Soul)*. He explored such topics as sensation, perception, memory, thought, motivation, learning, and dreams.
(Detail from "The School of Athens" by Raphael.)

discussed in the book.) By the time you finish the chapter, you should have a reasonable idea of what psychology is all about. Perhaps then you can formulate your own definition of psychology.

EXPERIENCING ONE'S ENVIRONMENT

One question that has always intrigued thoughtful men is the problem of how things outside a person come to be experienced inside him. How do flowers in a garden come to be experienced as colors, shapes, and smells? How does a bee cause one to hear a buzzing sound or feel a sting? The early Greeks came up with some ingenious schemes to explain how man experiences his environment. Most Greek thinkers believed that objects in the world sent out particles and that it was these particles that were somehow perceived.

Some of these Greek thinkers felt that substances in the environment corresponded to substances in the body and that "like is perceived by like." Thus, they believed that warmth outside the body produced particles that were received by the warmth substances inside the body, causing the person to experience the particles as warm. Opposed to this view was the idea that perception involved opposites—that the "warmth" particles had to be received by the inner "cold" substances in order to be experienced.

One of the most interesting theories was provided by Democritus, a famous Greek philosopher who lived in the fifth century, B.C. Democritus was the first person to think that everything is made up of atoms. He believed that objects gave off particles in the form of tiny images of themselves. When these images came in contact with the human body, they set into motion the tiny "fire atoms" that Democritus thought made up the soul. It was this motion of the soul's fire atoms that he thought caused one to perceive the original object. To make an impression on the body, the original images had to be of a certain strength; otherwise they would not be experienced.

Democritus used his theory to explain a number of phenomena. For example, he saw dreams as the result of images that had caused such weak motion of the fire atoms that the motion was not expe-

Figure 1.3
Centuries after Democritus had developed his theories about the nature of perception, a great French philosopher, René Descartes, explored the problem. By Descartes' time, many scientists had dissected the human body, and much more was known about physiology than had been known by the Greeks. Descartes created this diagram to show the way in which he believed external objects excited "animal spirits" in the eye and brain and thus caused the soul to see. He considered the soul to be some sort of nonphysical substance that interacted with the physical substance of the brain.

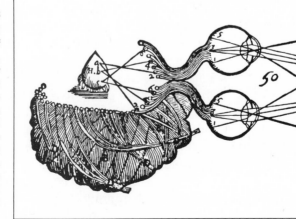

rienced until the person was asleep. He believed that thought was simply a very refined motion of the fire atoms. Sensations, such as taste, that cannot be experienced as images depended on the shape of their particles. Democritus described the atoms of sourness, for example, as being angular, thin, small, and winding.

Many of Democritus' ideas, such as the notion that dreams, thoughts, and sensations all result from the same process, turned out to be remarkably accurate in certain respects. His ideas formed the basis of various theories of perception that remained popular until modern times. What psychologists and scientists currently believe to be the nature of sensation, perception, thinking, and conscious experience is presented in the first unit of this book.

THE MIND AND THE BODY

To these early Greek thinkers the functions of the mind somehow made man unique, different from rocks and the sea, different from plants and animals. But they could see that man, like everything else, had a physical existence. They tried to see the entire world as a great, unified system composed of a few simple elements, and they tried to see man with his organs, fluids, bones, and his tissues as a part of this system. From their theories about the nature of the world emerged the first attempt to understand the properties of mind and personality in terms of physiology and the physical world. Such an understanding has been the goal of many scientists ever since.

Elements, Humors, and Temperaments

According to the Greeks, all things in the world, including man, were made up of combinations of four primary elements: fire, air, earth, and water. These elements had four corresponding qualities: warm, cold, dry, and moist, respectively. The elements and qualities were thought to be represented in the human body in the form of four *humors:* blood (a combining of warm and moist), black bile (cold and dry), yellow bile (warm and dry), and phlegm (cold and moist).

Disease was described in terms of excesses and deficiencies in the humors, and treatment consisted of creating conditions thought to bring the qualities back into balance with one another. For centuries, this theory applied solely to medicine. Then, in the second century A.D., a Greek physician related the humors to personality. This man, Galen, theorized that a greater proportion of one of the four humors in a person's body caused the person to have a distinct *temperament,* or set of personality characteristics. An excess of blood resulted in a *sanguine,* or cheerful, warm-hearted temperament. Predominance of black bile was related to the *melancholic,* or sad person. When a man was dominated by yellow bile, he was said to be *choleric,* or hot tempered, and if one had an excess of phlegm, he was considered *phlegmatic,* or apathetic.

Galen used the temperaments primarily to explain medical conditions, but this theory became a popular way for categorizing people,

5

Figure 1.4
The elements, humors, and temperaments. The ancient Greeks believed that four essential elements made up the world and that these elements combined in various ways to produce the four fluids, or humors, that were thought to make up the human body. Galen and other later Greeks described human personality, or temperament, in terms of balances and imbalances in the proportions of bodily humors.

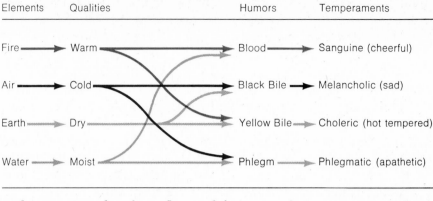

Elements	Qualities		Humors	Temperaments
Fire	Warm		Blood	Sanguine (cheerful)
Air	Cold		Black Bile	Melancholic (sad)
Earth	Dry		Yellow Bile	Choleric (hot tempered)
Water	Moist		Phlegm	Phlegmatic (apathetic)

and it continued to be influential for more than 1,400 years. Even today people describe one another as being "in a bad humor" or having an "even temperament."

Phrenology

Attempts to relate physical characteristics to psychological ones have been made repeatedly since Galen's time. One of the most influential of these attempts was made by two German physicians, Franz Joseph Gall and Johann Kaspar Spurzheim, in the early 1800s. They called their theory *phrenology* and claimed that anatomical and physical aspects of the brain were directly related to psychological abilities.

As a child, Gall had noticed what seemed to be a similarity between the shapes of his friends' heads and their personalities. As an adult, Gall examined the skulls of criminals, friends, and public figures, looking for bumps and indentations. Whenever he found two or more people who seemed to share a personality trait and who also had a bump in the same spot on their heads, he would name the trait and afterward associate it with that spot. In this way he mapped out the skull according to psychological abilities.

Spurzheim was intrigued by Gall's theory, and he formulated a list of thirty-seven independent powers or functions of the human brain. He considered about fourteen of these functions to be "intellective" (having to do with thought and memory) and the remainder to be "affective" (having to do with feeling). Among the latter were Amativeness (the various sexual urges or passions), Adhesiveness (the ability to form and maintain attachments to people), Ideality (the power or faculty of imagination), Reverence, Benevolence, and so on. The size of each of the faculties was believed to affect the size and shape of the skull at that particular part of the brain. It was believed that the physical characteristics of the brain could be changed by use or disuse, in much the same way that muscles could be enlarged by exercise or shrink through lack of it.

Although Gall and Spurzheim were both respected scientists, phrenological theory came into scientific disrepute when quacks and charlatans seized upon it and made it a popular fad. Phrenologists analyzed a person's character, his psychological strengths and weak-

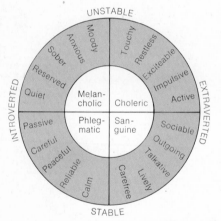

Figure 1.5
A contemporary British psychologist, Hans Eysenck, devised this chart to show how the ancient theory of the humors and temperaments can be understood in modern terms. Where the ancient theory described four *types* of people, modern approaches describe people as *varying* in two ways—from outgoing to inner-directed and from stable to unstable. These two factors in various degrees and combinations produce a number of personality characteristics that can be connected with the temperaments of ancient theory. For example, a person who is outgoing and stable is the sanguine type, with some of the characteristics shown in the lower right part of the circle.

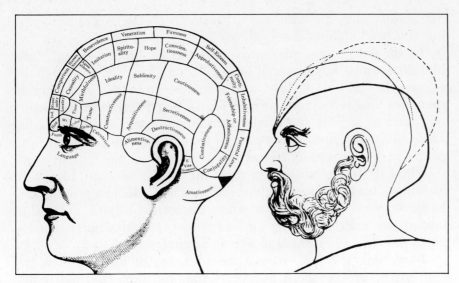

Figure 1.6
These phrenological diagrams should give you some idea of what personality characteristics were at one time associated with various head shapes. (*left*) Bulges at the back of the head were thought to indicate a warm and loving individual, whereas prominences on the very top of the head were associated with coolness and good moral character. Most of phrenology's claims have been discredited: Scientists have shown, for example, that functions associated with vision are located at the back of the brain, not around the eye. (*right*) Although practice and experience do cause physical changes in the brain, these changes are not of the kind that would produce the skull deformations illustrated here.

nesses, by examining the prominent areas and indentations on his head, consulting their charts to find out what these bumps and hollows signified. Some people came to rely on phrenology as a guide for living and for selecting friends and employees.

Scientific research (much of it in reaction to popularized phrenology) soon disproved most phrenological claims. Researchers found that the faculty of speech, for example, was not located behind the eyes but in another part of the brain entirely.

But even though the claims of Gall and Spurzheim turned out to be wrong in detail, their general ideas and goals were entirely correct. They were convinced that the faculties of the mind and the characteristics of personality could be classified, named, and related to the physical characteristics of the brain. In addition, they felt sure that the experiences and efforts of an individual resulted in lasting changes that took place in his brain. Since that time, research has confirmed these principles and made the nature of the relationships involved much clearer, though they are still far from being understood. Some of the things that psychologists do know about the body's relation to behavior are described in Chapter 5.

THE CHILD AS FATHER TO THE MAN

The mechanisms of body and brain are only one aspect of the questions that interest psychologists. Many of the subjects they study have little if anything to do with anatomy and physiology. Many psychologists, for example, are primarily concerned with how a child becomes an adult—with how people develop different ways of thinking, feeling, and behaving as they grow older. These psychologists are interested in discovering what factors promote human psychological development and what factors harm it. Some of the most interesting information in this area comes from accounts of *feral* children—children who have somehow survived in the wilderness without benefit of family, friends, or society and therefore have not developed in the same way as "normal" children. A famous case was the "wild child of Aveyron."

In the late 1700s, in Aveyron in the south of France, some hunters found a boy of about twelve, living like a wild animal in the woods. He was naked, dirty, and covered with scars. He seemed to spend his time scrounging around for roots and berries to eat. He did not react to sounds and made no noises himself. His eyes darted about constantly, never stopping to gaze at anything. He ran from people and bit or scratched anyone who touched him.

The French government brought him to Paris and put him in an institution for deaf-mute children. The leading doctors pronounced him a hopeless idiot. But one young doctor, Jean Itard, decided to take on the task of civilizing the wild boy—of teaching him to behave like a human child instead of like an animal.

Itard took the boy, now named Victor, to his house in the country, where he spent five years training him. He quickly discovered that Victor was not deaf, so there was hope of teaching him to talk. Itard's first task, however, was to teach Victor some human behavior.

By rewarding the boy with food, Itard was able to teach Victor to behave in ways expected of him—to eat with a fork, to dress himself, to keep himself clean, and to pay attention to other people. Victor was not mute, either. He learned a certain number of words, such as "milk" and "water." But Itard could not get him to use these words as *requests,* only as responses to the sight of the things he could name.

Figure 1.7

Stills from *The Wild Child*, a film about Jean Itard's attempt to civilize and educate the "wild child of Aveyron." It has been conjectured that in a sense everyone begins life as a wild child like Victor, but unlike Victor, other people are sucessfully civilized and educated.

Itard then tried to teach Victor the alphabet, first getting him to match letters made of wood with letters printed on a board. Victor finally came to learn words and to assemble the letters of the words he knew in order to ask for things. But he never really did learn to speak in normal sentences.

What was really wrong with Victor, if anything, will probably

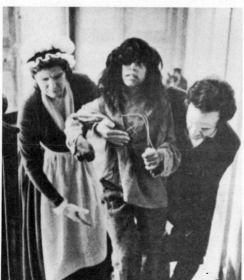

never be known. Victor may have had some kind of brain damage, or the terrors of his childhood may have driven him mad. It may be that a person who has had certain kinds of experiences in childhood can never be taught to live like people who have had very different experiences. Again, perhaps Itard's teaching methods were faulty; perhaps he tried to teach Victor the wrong things in the wrong way.

Whatever the truth of the matter was, this incident illustrates a large number of psychological questions. Most of these questions have to do with learning, education, and the effects of childhood experiences in later life. No questions could be more typical of the subject matter of psychology than these, and few could be of more practical importance. Some of the answers psychologists have given to questions about human development are discussed in Unit III.

THE INDIVIDUAL IN SOCIETY

An understanding of how and what an individual learns as a child would be an understanding of how an individual becomes part of a great body of individuals—his society. No person can be understood alone. The times, the people, the culture surrounding him must be seen if the individual's actions are to make sense. The following passage describes the actions of individuals in a society rather different from the society of the readers of this book:

> Beyond the sounds of the woodcutter, of the churn, of the distant dog, the chanting could barely be heard. It grew louder, and soon the villagers could see them, even make out the red crosses on their breasts. At the head of the ragged column was a man bent by the weight of the rough-hewn cross strapped to his back, the foot etching the path that others would follow. In spite of the dirt and the bloodstains, the fine fabric of his clothes stood out from the coarse tunics the others wore. He had not been with them long; he was a recent convert. As they moved into the church square, their chanting attracted the few villagers left, the few who had not fallen to the plague.
>
> The flagellants stood for a moment, swaying and chanting. Suddenly one of the younger men flung back his head and screamed. In his hand was a whip, knotted along its length, with iron tongs at the end. As it arched over his head, the tongs bit into his back and blood soaked through his torn tunic: the self-humiliating orgy began.

The flagellants described in this passage saw themselves as saviors. Believing that plagues were caused by man's sins, they roamed Europe, doing extreme penance and seeking converts to forgive. Today medieval flagellantism is generally considered an example of mass madness. What is one to make of such behavior? Is it any easier to understand such modern-day examples of group madness as four-hour traffic jams, race riots, and dance crazes?

In order to account for such mass behavior as religious fanaticism, fashion trends, fads, and social crazes, nineteenth-century

Figure 1.8
During medieval times, cases of mass madness were relatively common. This seventeenth-century French engraving depicts "moonstruck" women dancing in a town square A full moon was believed to cause madness, thus giving rise to the terms "lunacy" and "lunatic."

thinkers used the terms "imitation" and "suggestion." They saw *imitation* of others as an instinct or impulse in man. Such imitation begins in childhood, when the infant tries to reproduce the words and actions of his or her parents. But imitation, they said, continues into adulthood and can be seen when a cough or yawn is copied by a group of people. (This use of the word imitation may today correspond to conformity.)

Similarly, *suggestion* was used to describe the influence a group has over its members. Social theorists used the term suggestion in the same way it is used in hypnosis: In the hypnotic state, the subject is obedient and docile and does what the hypnotist commands. These thinkers believed that this effect accounted for the behavior of people on a mass scale. Through both imitation and suggestion, an idea could spread quickly through a crowd of people and cause them to behave in ways they ordinarily wouldn't.

Gustave Le Bon based his 1895 book *The Crowd* on the assumption that the gathering of people into a crowd creates a new mentality that is particularly receptive to suggestion. From this "group mind," he thought, came behavior that was irrational, impulsive, dangerous, and susceptible to easy manipulation by leaders. Psychologists have discounted Le Bon's theory of a group mind and have developed other theories of how and why people behave in groups and in crowds. Some of these theories are presented in Chapter 10.

FATE, PHYSIQUE, AND PERSONALITY

The way people behave in groups has been of interest to thoughtful people for as long as there have been dissatisfactions with life in society—for the entire history of civilization, in other words. But not every person hoping to change things for the better has felt that the answer lies in the study of groups. As many people, probably more, have looked instead at the inner life and character of the individual.

One of the first steps in the study of individuals has always been to classify them according to their personality traits, their mental capacities, and so on. Galen tried to do this, and so did the phrenologists. In both cases they were trying to tie personality characteristics to bodily ones. Other methods, such as astrology and Tarot, tie personality to the occult.

Body Types and Character

One of the most extensive and rigorous attempts to show a relationship between personality and physique was carried out by psychologist William Sheldon in the 1940s. Sheldon developed three primary components of physical variation. He called the first component *endomorphy,* which is characterized by a soft and spherical appearance. The abdominal area is highly developed, and the bones and muscles are underdeveloped. The person high in this component is fat.

The second component is *mesomorphy,* which is characterized by a hard, rectangular body, with a predominance of bone and muscle. The mesomorphic body is strong and tough. A person high in this component has an athletic build. The third component is *ectomorphy,* which is characterized by thinness, light muscles, fragility, and a large brain and central nervous system. A person high in this component is skinny.

Few individuals are pure endomorphs, mesomorphs, or ectomorphs. Most people are some mixture of all three. Sheldon developed a method called *somatotyping* for rating individuals on each of the primary components. The somatotype of an individual is expressed by three numbers, the first of which always refers to endomorphy, the second to mesomorphy, and the third to ectomorphy. The numerals range from 1 to 7, with 1 representing the absolute minimum of the component and 7 the highest possible amount. The rating of 4 is average. Thus, a person with a 462

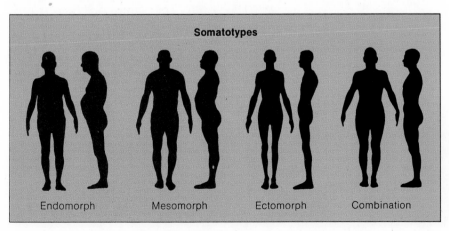

Figure 1.9
William Sheldon's three basic somatotypes. According to Sheldon, most people have physiques that represent a combination of these three extreme components. Sheldon related the composition of the body to specific personality traits, just as the Greeks related bodily humors to the four temperaments.

somatotype would be average in endomorphy, high in mesomorphy, and low in ectomorphy.

Sheldon also identified three primary dimensions of personality, or temperament, as he preferred to call the behavior of a person. Each of these three temperamental types he characterized with a particular cluster of personality traits. The first cluster included love of comfort, sociability, gluttony, relaxation, slow reactions, even temper, and tolerance. The second cluster contained aggressiveness, courage, vigorous activity, and domination. Among the traits in the third cluster were restraint, inhibition, secretiveness, self-consciousness, fear of people, overquick reactions, preference for solitude, and youthful appearance.

Sheldon then rated individuals according to these three temperamental types, once again using a 7-point scale. When he compared a person's somatotype to his temperamental type, he found a high relation between the two. That is, if an individual had a somatotype of 462, his temperamental type was likely to be 462 or close to it. Thus a predominantly endomorphic person would tend to have the temperamental characteristics of cluster one, and so on. In this way, Sheldon showed a relationship between physique and personality.

Many psychologists have since disputed Sheldon's findings and have attributed the relationships he found primarily to social factors—athletes are expected to be aggressive, fat people are encouraged to be sociable, and so on. Several theories of personality that are not dependent on physiology are described in Chapter 12.

Astrology

Looking to the stars and constellations for insights into the nature of things on Earth has been a popular activity since ancient times. People have frequently turned to such "mystical" sources to try to better understand themselves and to learn the hidden secrets of their personalities. Recently, astrology and other occult systems have once

Figure 1.10
The signs of the zodiac. Each sign corresponds to a constellation of stars in a certain part of the sky. Your sign indicates the part of the sky the sun was in, in relation to the earth, when you were born. According to astrologer John Jocelyn, people born in Aries are bursting with the energy of spring. Taurus is concerned with earthy, concrete forces and bondage, whereas Gemini represents the combination of spirit and intellect. Cancer is associated with the mystery of changing form, and Leo emphasizes the human heart. Virgo signifies purity and perfection. Libra represents balance and wholeness, and Scorpio has to do with awakening from death. Sagittarius is the sign of adventures and journeys; Capricorn is the sign of ambition and deep understanding; Aquarius is the sign of life-giving love; and Pisces signifies suffering of the spirit. The signs are also divided according to the four essential elements that the Greeks believed made up the universe. Taurus, Virgo, and Capricorn are earth signs; Gemini, Libra and Aquarius are air signs; the fire signs are Aries, Leo, and Sagittarius; and the water signs are Cancer, Scorpio, and Pisces.

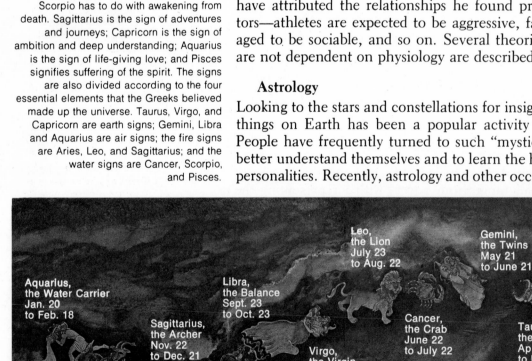

again become of particular interest to a large number of Americans.

According to astrology, a person is like a cell in a living body. Each movement of the body affects the cell, if only in some slight way. The cell is jolted when the body collides with another body, and positive and negative emotions in the body also affect each cell, again if only in some slight way. Astrologers believe that man has the same sort of relation to the planets and stars as his cells have to him. All living things experience motion, commotion, and emotion in the orbits and cyclic rhythms of the heavenly bodies.

The majority of astrologers think of the planets and signs of the zodiac (based on groups of stars) as metaphors for psychological processes. Astrology thus provides guidelines for psychological growth and development. Through the casting of an astrological chart, the individual becomes aware of certain personal qualities—some dominant, others less strong—within him. Once the individual realizes that he is a miniature version of the solar system he comes to be aware of the influences of the planets upon his life and can act accordingly.

Astrology is one attempt at coping with the psychological problems of living—it explains one's character and suggests ways to understand one's fate. The planets and constellations that form the signs of the zodiac indicate different personalities and different ways of being and acting. Although one may question the scientific basis of astrology, it has helped to make some people more sensitive to and aware of their own character and that of others around them, and to help them realize the limitless possibilities of action that are open to people.

Tarot Cards

Tarot cards, the tools of another mystical system, are thought to lead people on a journey through worlds beyond the one they look at every day. In the cards man sees himself transformed in the mirror of myth. The mirror shows man things within himself that he is afraid to think about because they are too bright for his "dim" mind.

The images on the Tarot cards include those of the magician, the high priestess, the empress, the emperor, the hanged man, death, strength, the devil, the hermit, the sun, the moon, and judgment. Each image suggests some influence, power, or mystery within the individual. The moon, for example, is given the interpretation provided in Figure 1.11.

In use, the cards are laid out in a certain order. The first card represents the immediate future, or what is coming. The second represents the past, or what is declining in influence. The third card symbolizes the present, or what is happening now. The fourth card represents what is in the present but hidden. The fifth, or key, card signifies what is needed to bring all these influences into balance. Although people are supposed to interpret the cards as yielding messages, Tarot is not just a way of telling fortunes. The cards show

Figure 1.11

The Moon, one of the seventy-eight cards in the Tarot deck. The interpretation is by Arthur Waite, an expert on the Tarot. According to Waite, this card is meant to show how man must use his rational mind to understand his animal nature as he grapples with the mysteries of human life.

The card represents life of the imagination apart from life of the spirit. The path between the towers is the issue into the unknown. The dog and wolf are the fears of the natural mind in the presence of that place of exit, when there is only reflected light to guide it.

The last reference is a key to another form of symbolism. The intellectual light is a reflection and beyond it is the unknown mystery which it cannot shew forth. It illuminates our animal nature, types of which are represented below—the dog, the wolf and that which comes up out of the deeps, the nameless and hideous tendency which is lower than the savage beast. It strives to attain manifestation, symbolized by crawling from the abyss of water to the land, but as a rule it sinks back whence it came. The face of the mind directs a calm gaze upon the unrest below; the dew of thought falls; the message is: Peace, be still; and it may be that there shall come a calm upon the animal nature, while the abyss beneath shall cease from giving up a form.

in images the factors that must be taken into account in order to achieve psychological balance. Similarly, it is often the psychologist's job to help people achieve psychological balance, as is discussed in Chapter 14.

DEALING WITH MADNESS

Mental disorders and insanity have played a tragic role in the history of mankind. The mentally disturbed have been tortured, beaten, hanged, starved, bloodlet, imprisoned, and subjected to ridicule and scorn even in the most "enlightened" cultures.

Ancient man attributed bizarre behavior to possession by demons. One of their "cures" for possession was to cut a hole in the person's skull to allow the evil spirits to leave. Another type of treatment was *exorcism,* which involved various techniques for drawing or driving the evil spirit out of the body of the possessed. These practices typically included prayer, sacrifice, starvation, noise-making, and bloodletting.

Witch Hunting and Asylums

In medieval times, mental disturbance became a religious concern. Disturbed individuals were considered to be witches, in league with the devil, and they were subjected to widespread religious persecution. Because it was thought that Satan's pride was his downfall, treatment of persons possessed by the devil often involved insults to the devil's pride in the form of obscene epithets and foul accusations. The cruel fate of the afflicted was punishment directed at the devil

Figure 1.12

In medieval times abnormal behavior was taken as evidence of the devil's work, and the detection and treatment of disturbed individuals fell to religious leaders. This late-fifteenth-century painting portrays Saint Catherine of Sienna casting the devil out of a possessed woman. The devil is pictured as a tiny elf fleeing from the woman's head, apparently to escape the forces of prayer and goodness.

14

within them. Extreme methods of exorcism such as flogging, starvation, and immersion in hot water were justified ways of making the body uninhabitable for the devil.

Witch hunting became a mania, both in Europe and in the United States. Large numbers of men, women, and children were hanged, burned alive, strangled, beheaded, or maimed. This period marked a low point in the victimization of emotionally disturbed individuals.

In France in the late 1600s, the first insane asylum was founded. There, the patients, although still not treated well by current standards, were regarded as sick people, not witches or devils in disguise. Several more asylums were established throughout Europe. Although the treatment of the inmates was still outrageous, the asylums took the insane out of sight of the ordinary people and reduced the fear that prompted them to think of insanity as a supernatural visitation.

Even in asylums, however, the situation of the insane remained worse than that of criminals in prison, which was pretty grim in comparison with today's standards. Inmates were left naked, practically swimming in filth, beaten, half-starved, held in chains, bled, and ducked into almost freezing water, either as a way to keep them under control or as a means for curing them.

Freeing the Insane

But such abuse was by no means the only treatment ever received by the mentally ill. As early as the 1500s a few enlightened men were

Figure 1.13
In the 1500s, the belief that mad people were possessed by evil spirits became justification for torture and execution instead of pity and prayer. People who behaved strangely, or who were disliked for some other reason, were branded as witches and were imprisoned, tried, tortured, and often executed by burning, as this engraving shows.

Figure 1.14
In the eighteenth century, insane asylums were often indistinguishable from prisons. (*left*) An engraving of a famous London robber visiting his mother in Bedlam, an English asylum. (*right*) A Cairo asylum that was, in fact, a prison. In these times the insane were sources of curiosity and amusement for sightseers.

advocating humane treatment of people thought to be insane. This new kind of thinking grew slowly, and it was a major victory for humanitarianism when in 1793 a French doctor named Phillippe Pinel obtained permission to unchain the inmates of the insane asylum at Bicêtre Hospital in Paris. Pinel had previously begun the unusual practice of talking with his patients, keeping records, and assembling case histories. He had also achieved some success with his experiment in treating the mentally ill with kindness and consideration. A few patients were unchained, were given rooms instead of dungeons, and were permitted to walk around the hospital grounds. As a result of his efforts, Pinel saw many of his patients recover. One of the first men Pinel released was so grateful he became Pinel's bodyguard for life.

Pinel's successes encouraged him to try to have *all* the inmates of his hospital unchained. The leader of the French government, from whom he had to get permission, greeted the idea with such comments as: "Why not proceed to the zoo and liberate the lions and the tigers?" Nevertheless, Pinel convinced him and invited the President to see it done. At Bicêtre, the President looked at the 300 inmates, screaming and rattling their chains, and said to Pinel: "Well, citizen, are you mad yourself that you want to unchain these animals?" Pinel replied: "Citizen, it is my conviction that these mentally ill are intractable only because they are deprived of fresh air and of their liberty."

Pinel proved to be correct, and the reforms that he started had considerable influence on the treatment of mentally disturbed people in other countries as well as his own. (Current attitudes toward and treatment of psychological disorder are described in Chapters 13 and 14.) But although Pinel's reforms were welcome changes in society's reaction to madness, they were not changes in science's understanding of it. In Pinel's day, psychology as a science still did not exist.

Figure 1.15
Phillippe Pinel supervising the unchaining of mental patients at the insane asylum at La Salpêtrière, a hospital he went to after his work at Bicêtre. The horrifying conditions depicted in this painting were typical in eighteenth-century asylums, but equally depressing scenes may still be found in the back wards of some modern mental institutions.

Medical doctors were the people who cared for the mentally disturbed. A science of the body was well established, but a science of the mind was only just beginning to stir.

THE METHODS OF SCIENCE

At the same time that Phillippe Pinel's inmates were gratefully shedding their bonds, that Jean Itard was hard at work trying to educate Victor, and that Franz Gall was looking at the contours of his friends' craniums, scientists who were interested in the mysteries of matter and energy rather than of souls and personalities were proceeding steadily. Newton's laws of motion had been discovered a century before, chemists were determining the atomic weights of various substances, physicists were beginning to think that heat was not a material substance, and the nature of electricity was being explored.

Careful measurements and rigorous experiments made the rapid advancement of the physical sciences possible. One of the first applications of such methods to the study of human behavior occurred quite by accident, however.

Measurement: The "Personal Equation"

In 1795, in Greenwich, England, the Royal Astronomer decided to fire his assistant for incompetence. It was the Royal Astronomer's job to check the standard clock of England against the constant speed of the stars. This he did by noting the movement of the stars past fine hairlines on the lens of a telescope and by checking the number of seconds the clock ticked off as the stars passed from one hairline to another. The astronomer and his assistant took turns making these

17

measurements, alternating from night to night. But the assistant began to obtain results different from the astronomer's. At first, his results were a half-second off, but the difference between their results gradually increased to eight-tenths of a second. So the astronomer let his assistant go.

Twenty years later a German astronomer, F. W. Bessel, read about the incident at Greenwich. He began comparing the timing of his own observations with those of his co-workers. He found consistent differences, often of more than a second. Bessel published his findings, and his work stimulated more research on "errors of observation" in noting the movements of the stars. Astronomers discovered that individuals appeared to be fairly constant in their differences and that these differences were not due to carelessness.

Obviously, some of the astronomers were faster than others in responding to the passage of a star image across a hairline on the telescope. Bessel tried to compare the errors that the different astronomers made and arrive at a "personal equation" for each one that would express just how fast or slow he was. Bessel failed in this endeavor but scientists who read about his work realized that what he was trying to measure was the "speed of thought" in various individuals. The time between the presentation of stimulus and the production of a response is now called *reaction time* and has been measured in many different ways by psychologists. But in the early 1800s it was one of the few psychological measurements being made, and the fact that it had been discovered in a science as precise as astronomy made it seem possible that psychology, too, could become a science.

Introspection

In 1879 in Leipzig, Germany, psychology did become a science. In that year Wilhelm Wundt, a German physician, single-handedly grabbed psychology away from philosophy and made it stand alone. He wrote the first major book on psychology, founded the first experimental laboratory, and began the first psychological journal. Because of these achievements, Wundt is usually regarded as the first psychologist.

Early in his life, Wundt set himself the task of bringing together scientific experimentation—which had developed in the physical sciences and medicine—with the study of the mind. He believed that the task of psychology was to study the living system from the inside, with the "mind's eye." This method of self-observation, called *introspection,* involves looking *into* one's self, paying close attention to one's own sensations, feelings, emotions, and thoughts. At Wundt's laboratory, trained observers studied what they were conscious of as it happened, asking themselves well-defined questions under carefully specified conditions.

Wundt's emphasis on careful observation and controlled experimentation became the basis of scientific psychology. His method of

Figure 1.16
Wilhelm Wundt, the founder of experimental psychology, was the stereotypical German professor. Each day, he would read, think, and write all morning, take a walk after noon, and then inspect the work of his students. Finally, he would give a lecture precisely at four o'clock, always on time and always to a large audience. Wundt was a prolific writer, and by the end of his life he had turned out 50,000 pages of material in addition to having influenced hundreds of students to carry his ideas and methods to all parts of the world.

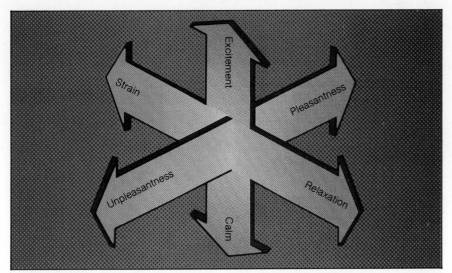

Figure 1.17
Wundt's three-dimensional map of feelings. Wundt discovered that in the experience of listening to various patterns of beats came feelings of pleasure or displeasure. As he listened to the clicking of a metronome at a slow rate, Wundt found that as he waited for the next click in a series, he felt tense. After the expected click came, he felt relieved. He also noticed that as he listened to the clicks at a faster rate, he felt mildly excited. As the clicks slowed down, he felt quieted. After further experiments, Wundt concluded that consciousness extended out in three different ways. He then suggested that every conscious feeling can be located somewhere in the three-dimensional "space" created by these three sets of opposites.

introspection, however, did not last as long. Scientists began to complain that introspection was a useless, unscientific method that allowed anyone to hold any theory he wanted to. To justify his particular theory, all an introspectionist had to do was to claim that he was only reporting the way things seemed to him when he introspected. Who could argue? Who else could observe the introspectionist's own consciousness?

The other sciences, however, were built on agreement about things that anyone could observe. Efforts were made to put psychology on the same basis. In 1913 John B. Watson stated that psychologists, like other scientists, must study only phenomena that are visible to everyone. Psychology became the science not of inner mental events but of observable behavior. "The time has come when psychology must discard all reference to consciousness," Watson proclaimed. "Its sole task is the prediction and control of behavior; and introspection can form no part of its method."

Most psychologists agreed with Watson and have continued to agree until fairly recently. But there have been those who disagreed, thinking Watson's proclamation too severe. An English psychologist, Sir Cyril Burt, commented humorously that psychology "having first bargained away its soul and then gone out of its mind, it seems now, as it faces an untimely end, to have lost all consciousness." Psychology has by no means reached any untimely end as yet, and it does not seem likely to do so. It has regained some consciousness and even a little mind, as you will see when you read this book. It has used scientific methods to study objectively, and it is steadily developing its own methods to suit its own unique subject matter.

PSYCHOLOGY TODAY

Since the early 1900s psychology has grown by leaps and bounds. Its concerns now cover an enormous range. There are psychologists in advertising, in education, in criminology; there are psychologists

studying death, art, and robots. Psychological themes and terminology have penetrated all areas of life and have become integral parts of novels, films, and television programs.

What do today's psychologists do? About one-third of all psychologists with a Ph.D. (doctorate) in psychology are *clinical* psychologists. They work in mental hospitals, prisons, schools, clinics, and private practice helping people with psychological problems. Clinical psychologists often call themselves *psychotherapists;* their work is described further in Chapter 14.

About one-fifth of all professional psychologists work in the area of *educational psychology.* They are concerned with effective methods of teaching, the construction of tests, intelligence and memory, and the use of instructional devices, such as films, tapes, television, and so on. A major contribution of psychology to education has been the teaching machine. These machines are used for *programmed learning,* in which the individual pursues a subject step by step at his own rate. The machine provides information, asks questions, and tells the student whether his answers are right or wrong.

A third major area in which psychologists are employed is *counseling* and *guidance.* About one-tenth of psychologists are involved in this type of work, providing advice and assistance for such people as college students, drug abusers, and those seeking careers. These psychologists are often employed by industrial firms, schools, and universities.

Industrial and *engineering psychology* is another major focus for psychologists. Psychological methods have been used to boost production, improve working conditions, place applicants in the job for which they are best suited, devise methods for training people, and reduce accidents. Psychologists have also been involved in making tools and machines more suited to the characteristics of the humans that use them—making instrument panels more readable, and so on.

Finally, about one-fourth of all psychologists are engaged in *experimental psychology.* They do the basic sort of experimentation and research that is described in this book. Most, but not all, researchers work in colleges and universities, and some do teaching and writing at the same time. They do everything from testing how electrical stimulation of a rat's brain affects its behavior, to studying how mentally disturbed people think, to observing how different socioeconomic groups tend to vote in elections.

Most psychologists are involved in several different kinds of activity. A busy psychologist might divide his time between doing research, teaching, providing therapy or counseling, administering various types of psychological tests, writing books and research papers, and working on such business affairs as serving on committees, figuring budgets, dealing with his employers, attending professional conventions, and so on.

The business lives of psychologists are not the subject of this book, however. This book describes what psychologists think about,

Figure 1.18 (*opposite*)
Psychologists at work.
(a) A psychotherapist talks with a woman, helping her sort out the difficulties she is having in her personal life. (b) Using an automated instructional system designed by educational psychologists, a child learns to make letter and word combinations as first steps in learning to read and write. (c) A psychologist administers a standard intelligence test to a young girl to find out how she compares intellectually to other children her age. (d) A mentally disturbed boy is coaxed, prompted, and rewarded by a psychotherapist who is trying to increase the boy's responsiveness to the world around him. (e) Psychologists have contributed to solving engineering problems related to man's behavior in the unique conditions present in a space vehicle. (f) Two psychological researchers gather information about sleep and dreaming by examining the brain-wave patterns of a person sleeping in another room. (g) Family interaction is videotaped and later observed by the family and by psychotherapists in order to help family members understand their problems. (h) A researcher operates on a rats' brain. Later, the rat is placed in a controlled situation where the effects of chemical brain stimulation on its behavior can be measured.

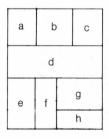

what they know, what experiments they have done, what observations they have made, what conclusions they have drawn, and what their work means to a person who is not a psychologist. Psychology is a science that is trying to answer some of the most interesting questions of everyday life:

What happens during sleep?
How can bad habits be broken?
Is there a way to measure intelligence?
Why do crowds sometimes turn into mobs?
What does the world look like to other animals?
Do dreams mean anything?
How does punishment affect a child?
How can memory be improved?
What causes madness?

Today, psychologists are approaching answers to such questions. They try to tie together all that has been discovered about human behavior in order to look at the total human being. The picture is far from complete, but much of what is known will be found in this book.

SUMMARY

1. Psychology has been a separate area of study only since the late nineteenth century. Until then, "psychological" matters were considered a part of philosophy.

2. Psychology has been defined as "the science of mental life." But as it has become more and more scientific, psychologists have preferred to define it as "the science of behavior."

3. The earliest psychological theories came from the early Greeks, such as Democritus, who believed that man's experience of the world is a result of the reception of particles sent out by objects in the environment.

4. Several early theories tried to tie personality to bodily factors. The Greek Galen thought that temperament was determined by a predominance of one of four humors. In the early 1800s, phrenologists explained behavior in terms of the size, shape, bumps, and indentations of the skull.

5. In the late 1700s, the French physician Jean Itard taught a "wild child" to make and use simple words. This work illustrates many typical psychological problems related to teaching methods and the effects of childhood experiences.

6. The nature of how people interact with one another was of interest to thinkers in the late nineteenth century. Gustave Le Bon believed that crowds have a "mass mind" and that through imitation

and suggestion an idea could spread quickly through a crowd and cause people to behave in ways they ordinarily wouldn't.

7. Somatotyping was a method developed by William Sheldon in the 1940s for rating individuals on each of three primary body types. Sheldon also rated people according to certain dimensions of temperament to show a connection between temperament and physique.

8. Astrologers believe that man has a sort of cellular relation to the planets and stars—the movements of one effect a change in the movements of the other. Many people believe that astrology provides guidelines for psychological growth and development and that it helps man to realize infinite possibilities of action.

9. Tarot cards are another form of mysticism that enables people to think about their possibilities in a new way. Their purpose is to indicate the direction of psychological balance.

10. Man has always invented some explanation for, and ways of dealing with, mental disorders. Some early forms of "treatment" included exorcism and witch hunting. The first insane asylum was founded in the late 1600s and represented a shift in traditional ways of thinking about insanity.

11. One of the first experimental studies was conducted by Bessel, an astronomer who compared reaction times of his co-workers as they plotted the movements of the stars.

12. Wilhelm Wundt was the first person to apply scientific experimentation to the study of the mind. He relied on the method of introspection, emphasizing carefully controlled observation and experimentation. Later the method of introspection was rejected by Watson, who insisted that psychology use the methods of other sciences and study only observable behavior.

13. The field of psychology has many distinct areas. These areas include clinical, educational, counseling and guidance, industrial and engineering, and experimental. Although each of these areas is self-contained and well-defined, most psychologists are involved in several of these fields simultaneously.

ACTIVITIES

1. Write your own definition of psychology. How different is your definition from one you would have written before reading the chapter? Put the definition in a place for safekeeping and at the end of the course take it out and re-read it.

2. Obtain a paperback copy of an astrology book that contains interpretations of characteristics for all the zodiac signs. Find a person who is not familiar with astrology but who expresses some curiosity about it. Ask him what sign he is (determined by his birth date) and read him an interpretation for a sign not his own. During the reading, note his responses. Do many suggestions create an affirmative response? Does he seem even partially convinced? After-

ward, ask him if he thinks he fits "his" sign. Then tell him about the test and let him read the interpretations for his own sign. What conclusions can you draw from this experiment?

3. How accurate is Sheldon's body type theory? Make a list of ten people you know fairly well and classify them on a chart according to Sheldon's components of physique. (Try to select people with different body types). To what extent do the people on your list conform to Sheldon's personality characteristics for each type of physique?

4. The *I Ching* is an ancient Chinese text, known also as "The Book of Changes." It is one of the earliest known types of divination, or means of foretelling the future, but more importantly, the *I Ching* is a prescription for how to live well, that is, in accordance with the laws of nature. Obtain a copy of the book (available in paperback) and determine your "fortune" by following the instructions located in the back of the book. Ask a friend or relative to do the same. Why do you suppose this book has enjoyed popularity for nearly 2,000 years?

5. Reaction time, one of the earliest psychological measurements made, can be measured with a yardstick. Hold the yardstick against a door jamb and have your subject hold his hand over the bottom of the stick (without touching it) so that his or her middle finger is at the zero point (see illustration at left). Tell your subject to watch your hand and to try to stop the yardstick as soon as possible after you have let it fall. After he has stopped the yardstick, note the number of inches that have passed his middle finger. The inches can be converted into a reaction time for the person, using the table at the lower left. Measure the reaction time of each subject several times to see how much his or her scores vary.

6. How is psychology involved in your life? Considering the information at the end of the chapter regarding the various areas of psychology, make a list of all the ways that psychology affects your life. (Hint: Traffic signs and classroom interiors are often designed by psychologists.)

7. Psychology is generally thought of as being a benevolent science, and it is expected to produce such results as happier people, accident-free and more productive workers, and greater understanding in interpersonal relationships. But well-meaning people throughout history have also applied what they considered to be sound "psychological" techniques that have actually served to increase the torment or to totally destroy their intended beneficiary. Can you see any possibilities today that psychological knowledge could be used *against* the best interests of an individual or society?

Inches	Seconds	Inches	Seconds
1	0.072	10	0.227
2	0.102	11	0.238
3	0.125	12	0.250
4	0.144	16	0.288
5	0.161	20	0.322
6	0.176	24	0.352
7	0.190	30	0.394
8	0.203	36	0.432
9	0.216		

SUGGESTED READINGS

BAKER, ROBERT A. (ed.). *Psychology in the Wry.* New York: Van Nostrand, 1963 (paper). A collection of amusing, satirical articles in which psychologists make fun of their own pomposity and other shortcomings.

EYSENCK, H. J. *Fact and Fiction in Psychology*. Baltimore: Penguin, 1965. Eysenck delves into popular notions of psychology and applies the scientific method to come up with some witty and entertaining conclusions. Topics range from criminal personality and the four temperaments to accident proneness. Also of interest are two other books by Eysenck that, together with this one, make up a trilogy: *Uses and Abuses of Psychology* (1953) and *Sense and Nonsense in Psychology* (1957).

GOLDENSON, R. M. *Mysteries of the Mind*. Garden City, N.Y.: Doubleday, 1973. Goldenson has gathered together a wide variety of unusual case studies in human behavior. He discusses such things as child prodigies, voodoo deaths, photographic memory, mass hysteria, and multiple personalities and tries to find explanations for these fascinating phenomena.

JUNG, CARL. *Man and His Symbols*. New York: Doubleday, 1964. A history of human archetypes and symbols through the ages. Jung wrote this book with the intention of reaching as many people as possible; therefore, the writing style is highly readable. Lots of beautiful graphics.

MACKAY, CHARLES. *Extraordinary Popular Delusions and the Madness of Crowds*. New York: Farrar, Straus, & Giroux, 1932, originally published, 1841. A remarkable book describing in vivid detail cases of human folly throughout the ages. Special emphasis is given to mass movements and the psychology of crowds, which will be discussed in detail in Chapter 10.

MILLER, GEORGE. *Psychology: The Science of Mental Life*. Baltimore: Penguin, 1962 (paper). This is a brief history of psychology from the late nineteenth century to the middle 1950s. The book highlights major personalities, events, and experiments in the field for this period.

PsychoSources: A Psychology Resource Catalog. New York: Bantam, 1973. This large-format paperback is a treasure-house of information about psychology. It contains book and film reviews, access information, and comments and essays about current trends on everything from identity crisis to health care in China.

SARGENT, D. S., and K. R. STAFFORD. *Basic Teachings of the Great Psychologists*. New York: Dolphin, 1965 (paper). A good introduction to the major areas of psychology. The authors trace the historical and present-day explorations of such questions as: How can human abilities be measured? What is instinct? How does the nervous system work? What is personality? and many others.

WILSON, J. *The Mind*. New York: Time-Life Books, 1964. A beautifully illustrated and easy-to-read book about the past, present, and possible future of psychological investigation.

*. . . whether man can describe
his own mind in an intellectually useful
way is uncertain and complex; but the
effort is certainly worth making.*

Paul Kolers (1968)

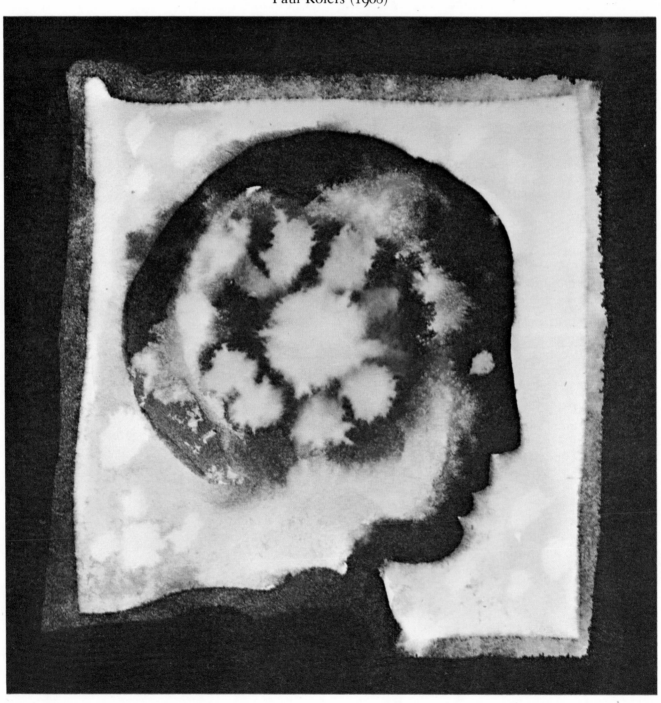

Unit *I*

Workings of the Mind

Usually, scientists study objects or processes from the outside. For example, astronomers who study an exploding star can only try to imagine what must be taking place inside the star; they can never know what it is like to *be* an exploding star. Psychologists, however, find themselves in a different position from other scientists: their object of study is themselves.

Psychologists study from the outside processes they are already experiencing from the inside, and this first unit presents some of the results of their observations. Chapter 2 is about such perceptual processes as seeing and hearing—processes you take for granted and use all the time, even as you read this page. Chapter 3 is about such mental processes as paying attention, remembering, and thinking—processes that you must use even as you try to understand them. Chapter 4 explores the nature of consciousness—the fact that humans can be conscious of being conscious is why it occurred to someone to write Chapter 4 in the first place.

Trying to study the very processes that one must use to study anything at all is a difficult task, but certainly a fascinating one. Psychologists have already gained a great deal of knowledge about these processes: They know how the senses work, what kinds of mistakes can occur in perception, and how much the senses can be trusted. They know something about how memories are stored and retrieved and about what distinguishes a creative thinker from a conventional one. They know why people with different interests see the world differently, and, finally, they know that it is possible for people to be conscious of themselves and of the world in many different ways and on many different levels, from the deepest sleep to yet unexplored heights.

2
Awareness of the World

Figure 2.1

Visitors to the 1967 World's Fair
in Montreal wander between the giant figure
of a woman and the stainless-steel sheet
from which it was cut. The play of images
in this photograph demonstrates the
complex nature of normal perception.
Seeing seems so simple most of the time,
but the injection of a few unexpected and
ambiguous elements can make it
confusing and difficult.

In the next few seconds, something peculiar will start hap pening to the material youa rereading. Iti soft ennotre alized howcom plext heproces sofrea ding is. Afe w sim plerear range mentscan ha vey oucomp lete lycon fused!

As you can see, your success in gathering information from your environment, interpreting this information, and acting on it depends considerably on its being organized in ways you already expect. By the end of this chapter, you should have some understanding of why this is so.

Your knowledge of the external world—and of your internal state as well—comes entirely from chemical and electrical processes occurring in the nervous system, particularly in the brain. (This process is described in detail in Chapter 5.) Basically, some physical change in the external or internal environment triggers chemical-electrical activity in sense receptors. After a complex sequence of message relays in the nervous system, a particular pattern of activity is produced in certain areas of the brain. You experience this electrical activity as a *sensation*—awareness of colors, forms, sounds, smells, tastes, and so on. Usually you experience some object, some meaningful whole, rather than a collection of sensations. The organization of sensory information into meaningful wholes is known as *perception*.

This entire process can be seen in the simple act of eating. Receptors in your eyes are stimulated to send messages to the brain as to the size, shape, and color of the food. Receptors in your nose and mouth inform the brain as to the food's taste and odor. Receptors in your hands provide additional input as to the texture and heat of the food. The brain combines all these inputs into the perception of the particular food, whether a hamburger, a carrot, or clam chowder.

This chapter will look at each of these steps more closely, focusing on how each organ converts the energy of physical changes into chemical-electrical signals and on how perceptions are built from this information. Finally, it will discuss the possibility of gaining information without the senses—by the process of extrasensory perception.

SENSATION

The world is filled with physical changes—sunlight streams down, radar beams bounce off cars, clouds of smoke billow into the air, and footballs collide with feet. *Sensation* is the result of converting these changes into *sensory experiences*—of brightness, loudness, smells, tastes, and so on. Any physical change that can be converted into experience is called a *stimulus.* Sunlight, smoke, and moving footballs are all stimuli for human beings. Radar beams are not.

A stimulus can be measured in some way—by its size, its duration, its intensity, its wavelength, and so on. A sensory experience can also be measured, but a sensory experience and a stimulus are not the same. For example, the same tomato (stimulus) might taste (sensory experience) one way to you after eating thirty other tomatoes and quite a different way after eating nothing for a week. On the other hand, the same sensory experience (flashing lights, for example) might be produced by different stimuli (a blow to the head or a fireworks display).

Psychologists are interested in the relationship between stimuli and sensory experiences. In vision, for example, the chief stimulus is light. People exposed to this stimulus experience the sensations of color and brightness. The sensation of color corresponds to the *wavelength* of the light, whereas brightness corresponds to the *intensity* of this stimulus.

What is the relationship between color and wavelength? How does changing a light's intensity affect one's sensation of its brightness? The psychological study of such questions is called *psychophysics.* The goal of psychophysics is to understand how sensory experiences (such as color and brightness) correspond to stimuli (such as lights of different wavelengths and intensities).

Threshold

In order to establish some laws about how people sense the external world, psychologists first try to determine how much of a stimulus is necessary in order for a person to sense it at all. How much energy is required for a person to hear a sound or to see a light? How much of a scent must be in the room before one can smell it? How much pressure must be applied to the skin before a person will feel it?

To answer such questions, a psychologist might set up the following experiment. First, a person (the subject) is placed in a dark room and is instructed to look at the wall. He is told to say, "I see it" when he is able to detect a light. The psychologist then uses an extremely precise machine that can project a low-intensity beam of light against the wall. The experimenter turns on the machine to its lowest light projection. The subject says nothing. The experimenter increases the light until finally the subject responds, "I see it." At this point, the experimenter has determined the subject's *threshold*—the smallest amount of energy that will produce a sensation. The threshold is the amount of energy that makes the subject say, "Yes, I experience the sensation," most of the time it is presented.

After reaching the threshold, the experimenter continues to slowly increase the light. At first the subject detects no change, but as the light is increased, he finally responds, "I see a difference." The experimenter can now establish how much increase in light energy is necessary for the subject to experience a change in sensation. The smallest change in the light that produces a change in sensation ("I see a difference") is called the *just-noticeable difference.*

Threshold measurements show that humans are extremely sensitive to some things. For example, psychologists have found that by delivering very faint sounds through headphones to people in soundproof rooms, people can almost hear the molecules bouncing around randomly against their eardrums. They say, "Yes, I hear a sound," even when the energy entering the headphones is so small it can hardly be measured.

Sensory Ratios

By conducting such experiments, psychologists have found that a particular sensory experience depends more on *changes* in the stimulus than on the absolute size or amount of the stimulus. For example, if you add three pounds to a small package you are carrying, the sensation of weight will be greatly increased, but if you add the same amount to a hundred-pound backpack, the sensation will hardly increase at all. This is because sensation of weight reflects how much the load has changed, and three pounds is not much change at all in a one-hundred-pound load.

In psychophysics, this idea is known as *Weber's law:* the larger or stronger a stimulus, the larger the change required for an observer to

Figure 2.2

This sequence of colored circles gradually decreases in brightness until the last circle cannot be distinguished from the surrounding blackness. In the next-to-last frame, there is a just-noticeable difference between the brightness of the circle and its surroundings, and you can just barely tell that the circle is there. In the final frame the circle is said to have gone below threshold. Its brightness is no longer sufficient for you to distinguish it.

Figure 2.3

These lines help to demonstrate Weber's law. Most people can detect the difference between the two short lines more readily than they can between the two long lines. Yet the difference between the two long lines is actually greater. If you have a three-way light bulb, you can try another demonstration. Compare the difference in sensory experience between 50 and 100 watts to the difference between 100 and 150 watts. The wattage difference is the same in both cases, but is your judgment of the brightness difference also the same? According to Weber's law, which difference should appear to be greater?

notice that anything has happened to it (to experience a just-noticeable difference).

The amount of stimulus change necessary to produce some increase in sensory experience is different for different senses, but it is always proportional. Suppose, for example, that you have a glass of unsweetened lemonade. In order to make it sweet, you add two spoonfuls of sugar. Now to make the lemonade taste "twice as sweet," you must add six spoonfuls—three times the original amount of sugar. Then you discover that in order to make the lemonade "four times as sweet," you must add a total of eighteen spoonfuls. Each time the sweetness doubles, the amount of sugar triples. The increase in sweet sensation is proportional to the increase in the amount of the stimulus, sugar.

By experimenting in this way with variations in sounds, temperatures, pressures, colors, tastes, and smells, psychologists are developing a complete knowledge of how each sense responds to stimulation. Some senses produce huge increases in sensation in response to small increases in energy. For example, the pain of an electric shock can be increased more than eight times by doubling the voltage.

Sensory Adaptation

Psychologists have focused on the sensation of changes in stimuli because they have found that the senses are tuned to change—that they are responsive to increases and decreases, to new events rather than to ongoing, unchanging stimulation. They can respond in this way because they have a general ability to *adapt,* or to adjust themselves, to a constant level of stimulation. They get used to a new level and respond only to changes away from it.

A good example of this process of adaptation is the increase in visual sensitivity that you experience after a short time in a darkened movie theater. At first you see only blackness, but after a while your eyes adapt to the new level and you can see seats, faces, and so on. Adaptation occurs in some form for the other senses as well: Receptors in your skin adapt to the hot water when you take a bath; a disagreeable odor seems to disappear after awhile; humming noises cease to bother you. Without sensory adaptation, you would feel the constant pressure of the clothes on your body, and other stimuli would seem to be bombarding all your senses at the same time.

Effects of Motivation

Psychologists have discovered that sensory experience does not depend on the stimulus alone. A person's ability to detect a stimulus also depends on his motivation. The individual does not simply receive a signal—he makes a decision as to its presence.

Thus, if you are anxious to receive a phone call, you may think you hear the phone ring, even when it has not. On the other hand, you may be so anxious about the phone call that you do not notice a knock at the front door. In this way, feelings and motivation can influence whether or not you experience a sensation, independent of the presence or level of the stimulus.

THE SENSES

Although people are traditionally thought to have five senses, there are actually many more. In addition to vision, hearing, taste, and smell, there are several skin senses and two "internal" senses: vestibular and kinesthetic.

Each type of sensory receptor takes some sort of external stimulus—light, chemical molecules, sound waves, pressure—and converts it into a chemical-electrical message that can be understood by the brain. So far these processes are best understood in vision and hearing; the other senses have received less attention and are a bit more mysterious in their functioning.

Vision

Vision is the most studied of all the senses, reflecting the high importance man places on his sense of sight. Vision provides a great deal of information about one's environment and the objects in it—the sizes, shapes, and locations of things, and their textures, colors, and distances.

Scientists have learned a great deal about how vision works. Light enters the eye through the *pupil* (see Figure 2.4a) and reaches the *lens*, a flexible structure that changes thickness to focus light on the *retina*, which contains the light-sensitive receptor cells. The retina contains two types of light-sensitive receptors: the *rods* and the *cones* (see Figure 2.4b). These are the cells responsible for changing the light energy into electrical impulses, which then travel over the *optic nerve* to the brain.

The cones require more light than the rods before they begin to respond, so they work best in daylight. The rods are sensitive to

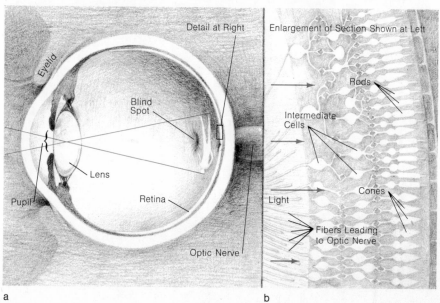

a   b

Figure 2.4

The process of vision.
(a) A cross-section of the human eye, showing the passage of light. Note that the eye receives an inverted image of the external world, although people are never aware of this inversion. The place where the optic nerve leaves the eye is called the blind spot because it is the only spot on the retina where no sensation takes place. Only under special circumstances (see Figure 4.3 on page 81) does a person become aware of this blind spot. (b) The cell structure of the retina. Note that the light-sensitive cells (the rods and cones) are those furthest from the light, not the closest as one might expect. Light arriving at the retina must pass through various other cells before striking the rods and cones, which convert it into nervous impulses. The impulses then pass through these other cells to be coded and organized before traveling over the optic nerve to the brain.

much lower levels of light than the cones and are particularly useful in night vision. There are many more rods (75 to 150 million) than there are cones (6 to 7 million), but only the cones are sensitive to color. The rods and cones can be compared to black-and-white and color film: Color film takes more light and thus works best in daylight; sensitive black-and-white film works not only in bright light but in shadows, dim light, and other poor lighting conditions.

Color Blindness   When all or some of a person's cones do not function properly, he is said to be color-blind. There are several kinds of color blindness; most color-blind people do see *some* colors. For example, some people are blind only to red and green. They see the world as something like what is shown in Figure 2.5b. Other people are able to see red and green but cannot see yellow and blue; they might see things as pictured in Figure 2.5c. A very few people are totally color-blind. They depend on their rods, so to them the world looks something like black-and-white television programs—nothing but blacks and whites and shades of gray, as depicted in Figure 2.5d.

Color blindness affects about 8 percent of American men and less than 1 percent of American women. It is thought to result from a hereditary defect in the cones. This defect is carried in the genes of

Figure 2.5

Representations of how people with various types of color blindness might experience the visual world. (a) The scene as viewed by a person with normal color vision. (b) The scene as it might appear to a person with red-green color blindness. Such a person does not necessarily see all reds and greens as grays; however, he is unable to distinguish between red and green, even though they appear to him to be different from blue and yellow. (c) The way the scene might be viewed by a person who can distinguish red and green but cannot tell the difference between yellow and blue. (d) How a totally color-blind person might experience the scene. Such people have no cones in their retinas, so they have less-accurate daytime vision as well as living in a world that lacks the colors most people have come to take for granted.

a

b

c

d

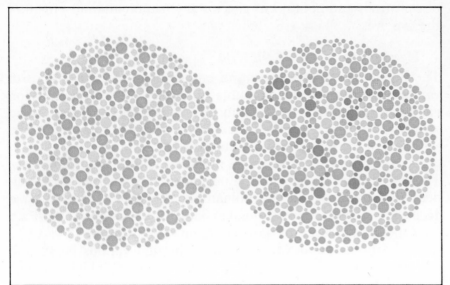

women whose vision is usually normal; these women pass the color blindness genes on to their sons, who are born color-blind.

Binocular Fusion Because human eyes are some distance apart, they receive slightly different images. But instead of providing a double image, the eyes give a fused picture of the world. If you take a close object, such as a ruler held in front of your eyes, and look at it with first one eye, then the other, it will seem to jump around. In this case you are alternating from one eye image to another, but when you use both eyes, you are taking advantage of *binocular fusion.*

Binocular fusion contributes to man's ability to see depth. A device that demonstrates this phenomenon is the stereoscope, which fuses the images of two photographs taken from slightly different angles so that the picture looks three-dimensional (see Figure 2.7). Thus vision involves not only the reception of light by the right kinds

Figure 2.7
To experience stereoscopic depth perception, take a tall, thin piece of cardboard and place it perpendicular to the page on the line that marks the separation of the two pictures. Then, with the edge of the cardboard resting between your eyes (as shown in the drawing), look at the left photo with your left eye and the right photo with your right eye and try to let the two images come together as one. (It helps to concentrate on the white dot.) If you are successful in fusing the images, the scene will suddenly jump out in depth. Children's Viewmaster slides work on the same principle: Two slightly different images of the same scene fuse to produce a single, three-dimensional image. This process of binocular fusion contributes continuously to your ability to perceive depth.

of cells (rods and cones) but also the interaction and movement of the two eyes.

Hearing

The human ear is sensitive to an enormous number of sounds of various frequencies and amounts of energy. Vision depends on vibrations of light energy. Hearing depends on air vibrations, called sound waves, that enter the ear and push against the eardrum. The sensation of the *loudness* of a sound depends mainly on the strength of these vibrations. This strength, or energy, is measured in *decibels*. The sounds that humans encounter range upward from zero decibels, the softest sound the human ear can detect, to about 140 decibels, which is roughly as loud as a jet plane taking off. Figure 2.8 gives the decibel levels of some common sounds.

In hearing, sound vibrations pass through various bones and fluids (see Figure 2.9) until they reach the inner ear, which contains tiny hairlike cells that move back and forth, much like a field of wheat waving in the wind. These hair cells have the function of changing the vibrations into chemical-electrical signals that travel through the *auditory nerve* to the brain.

The main functions of hearing are the detection, identification, and location of sounds. Sound sources and distances are detected mainly on the basis of their loudness. Sounds are identified chiefly through *pitch*—the sensation of a sound's frequency. Frequencies range from low to high; the corresponding pitches detectable by humans range from deep bass to high squeaks. When you hear a sound composed of a combination of different frequencies, you can hear the separate pitches even though they occur simultaneously. For example, if you strike two keys of a piano at the same time, your ear can detect two distinct pitches.

Sounds are located through the interaction of the two ears. When

---

160 — Wind Tunnel

140 — Jet at Takeoff

120 — Thunder

100 — Subway Train

80 — Vacuum Cleaner

60 — Conversation

40 — Residential Neighborhood at Night

20 — Leaves Rustling in a Breeze

0 — Threshold of Hearing

Sound Pressure (decibels)

Figure 2.8
The decibel ratings for various common sounds. Sound actually becomes painful at about 130 decibels. Decibels represent ratios: A 20 decibel difference between two sounds indicates that one sound is ten times more intense than the other. Thus a vacuum cleaner puts ten times as much pressure on your eardrums as conversation does, and a subway train puts ten times as much pressure on them as a vacuum cleaner.

Figure 2.9
The hearing process. Sound vibrations in the air strike the eardrum and set a chain of three tiny bones into motion. These bones are attached to another drum, the oval window, which sets up vibrations in the fluid of the cochlea, a long, coiled tube with a long, skinlike membrane running down the center of it. Stimulation of the hair cells on this membrane causes them to convert the vibrations into electrical impulses, which are relayed by the auditory nerve to the brain.

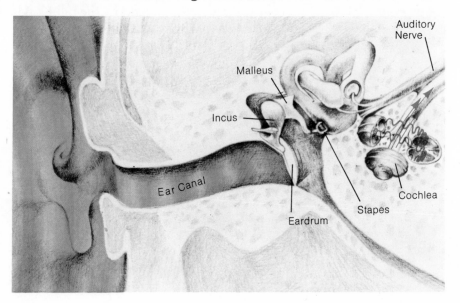

Auditory Nerve

Malleus

Incus

Ear Canal

Eardrum

Stapes

Cochlea

a noise occurs on your right, for example, the sound comes to both ears, but it reaches your right ear a fraction of a second before it reaches the left. If the sound is located directly in front of or behind you, however, it reaches both ears at the same time and you will have some difficulty locating the source.

To summarize, the physical stimuli involved in hearing are the size and frequency of sound waves. Among the sensations they produce are loudness and pitch. Locating a sound is accomplished by the interaction of the two ears.

Smell and Taste

Smell and taste are known as the chemical senses because their receptors are sensitive to chemical molecules rather than to light energy or sound waves. For you to smell something, the smell receptors in your nose must come into contact with the appropriate molecules. These molecules enter your nose in vapors, which reach a special membrane in the nasal passages on which the smell receptors are located. These receptors send messages about smells over the *olfactory nerve* to the brain.

For you to taste something, appropriate chemicals must stimulate receptors in the taste buds on your tongue. Taste information is relayed to the brain along with data about the texture and temperature of the substance you have put in your mouth.

Some scientists have proposed that all smells are made up of six qualities: flowery, fruity, spicy, resinous, putrid, and burned (see Figure 2.10). Other scientists have come up with a similar scheme for taste, which they say is made up of four primary qualities: sour, salty, bitter, and sweet (see Figure 2.11).

Much of what is referred to as taste is actually produced by the sense of smell. In fact smell receptors may be as much as 10,000 times more sensitive than taste buds. You have undoubtedly discovered that when your nose is blocked by a cold, foods taste different, usually blander and less interesting.

Sensations of warmth, cold, and pressure also affect taste. Try to imagine eating cold tomato soup or drinking a hot soft drink, and you will realize how important temperature is to the sense of taste. Now imagine the textural differences between a spoonful of pudding and a crunchy chocolate bar, and you will see how the pressure of food also influences taste.

The chemical senses play a relatively unimportant role in human sensation when compared to the functioning of lower animals. Insects, for example, often depend on smell to communicate with one another, especially in mating. In humans, smell and taste have become more a matter of aesthetics than of survival.

The Skin Senses

Receptors in the skin are responsible for providing the brain with at least four kinds of information about the environment: (1) pressure,

Figure 2.10
Henning's smell prism. This three-dimensional map was designed to encompass every possible smell. Supposedly, each smell can be located on one of the surfaces of this prism shape. For example, it should be possible for something to smell somewhat putrid, flowery, burnt, and spicy, but it should be impossible to have a smell that is spicy, resinous, and putrid. Where on Henning's smell prism would you place the smell of fresh cantaloupe?

Figure 2.11
A map of the human tongue, indicating the areas that seem more sensitive to one kind of stimulation than to others. Interestingly, it is possible to be taste-blind as well as color-blind. There is a chemical called phenylthiocarbamide (PTC) that tastes extremely bitter to some people and is quite tasteless to others.

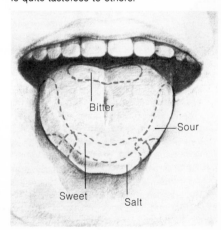

(2) warmth, (3) cold, and (4) pain. All these functions can be interpreted as ways of detecting possibly dangerous changes in one's physical environment.

Sensitivity to pressure varies from place to place in the skin. Some spots, such as your fingertips, are densely populated with receptors and are therefore highly sensitive. Other spots, such as the middle of your back, contain relatively few receptors. Pressure sensations can serve as protection. For example, feeling the light pressure of an insect landing on your arm is enough to warn you of the danger of being stung.

Some skin receptors are particularly sensitive to hot or cold stimuli. In order to create a hot or cold sensation, a stimulus must have a temperature greater or less than the temperature of the skin. If you plunge your arm into a sink of warm water on a hot day, you will experience little or no sensation of hot or cold. If you put your arm in the same water on a cold day, however, the water will feel quite warm. The sensations of warmth and cold are protective in that they provide warnings of possible burning or freezing.

About 3 million skin receptors are particularly sensitive to pain. Many kinds of stimuli—scratches, punctures, severe pressure, heat, cold—can produce pain. Their common property is real or potential injury to bodily tissues. Pain makes it possible for you to prevent damage to your body—it is an emergency system that demands immediate action.

Because pain acts as a warning system for your body, it does not easily adapt to stimulation—you rarely get "used to" pain. Pain tells you to stop the stimulation, that it is harmful to you. Without this mechanism, you might "adapt" to a fire when you stand next to it. After a few minutes you would literally begin to cook, and your tissues would die.

Although pain is primarily a protective sense, the other skin

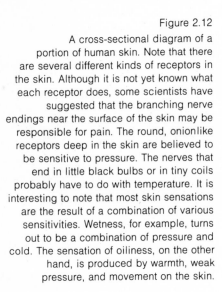

Figure 2.12

A cross-sectional diagram of a portion of human skin. Note that there are several different kinds of receptors in the skin. Although it is not yet known what each receptor does, some scientists have suggested that the branching nerve endings near the surface of the skin may be responsible for pain. The round, onionlike receptors deep in the skin are believed to be sensitive to pressure. The nerves that end in little black bulbs or in tiny coils probably have to do with temperature. It is interesting to note that most skin sensations are the result of a combination of various sensitivities. Wetness, for example, turns out to be a combination of pressure and cold. The sensation of oiliness, on the other hand, is produced by warmth, weak pressure, and movement on the skin.

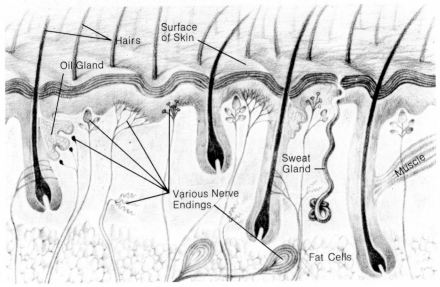

senses serve many nonprotective functions. Touch is particularly important in interpersonal relations, for example.

Balance

The body's balancing sense is regulated by the *vestibular system* inside the inner ear. Its prominent feature is the three *semicircular canals,* as shown in Figure 2.13. When your head starts turning, the movement causes the liquid in the canals to move, bending the endings of receptor hair cells. The cells connect with the *vestibular nerve,* which joins the auditory nerve into the brain.

The stimuli for vestibular responses include movements such as spinning, falling, and tilting of the body or head. Overstimulation of the vestibular sense by such movements can result in dizziness and "motion sickness," as you probably have experienced by going on amusement-park rides or by spinning around on a swivel stool. Although you are seldom directly aware of your sense of balance, without it you would be unable to stand or walk without falling or stumbling.

Body Sensations

Kinesthesis is the sense of movement and body position. It cooperates with the vestibular and visual senses to maintain posture and balance. The sensation of kinesthesis comes from receptors in and near the muscles, tendons, and joints. When any movement occurs, these receptors immediately send messages to the brain.

Without kinesthetic sensations, your movements would be jerky and uncoordinated. You would not know what your hand was doing if it was behind your back, and you could not walk without looking at your feet. Furthermore, complex physical activities, such as surgery, piano playing, and acrobatics, would be impossible.

Another type of bodily sensation comes from receptors that monitor internal body conditions. These receptors are sensitive to pressure, temperature, pain, and chemicals inside the body. A full stomach stretching these internal receptors informs the brain that the stomach has ingested too much.

Little is known about pain from the interior of the body except that it seems to be deep, dull, and much more unpleasant than the sharply localized pain from the skin. In some cases internal pain receptors may send inaccurate messages. They may indicate, for example, that a pain is located in the shoulder when in reality the source of irritation is in the lower stomach. Such sensation of pain in an area away from the actual source is called *referred pain.*

PERCEPTION

A person does not usually experience a mass of colors, noises, warmths, and pressures. Rather, he sees cars and buildings, hears voices and music, and feels pencils and desks. He does not merely have sensory experiences; he *perceives objects.* The brain receives

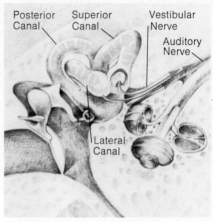

Figure 2.13

The vestibular system. The organs of balance consist of three semicircular canals arrayed at right angles to one another and filled with a freely moving fluid. Continuous motion in a straight line produces no response in this system, but starting, stopping, turning, speeding up or slowing down makes the fluid in at least one of the canals move, stimulating the hair cells attached to the canal walls. These hair cells convert the movement into electrical impulses that are sent to the brain via the auditory nerve.

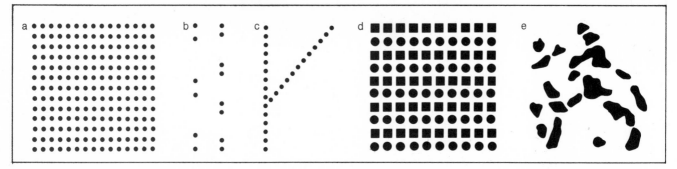

Figure 2.14

Principles of perceptual organization. A group of psychologists in the 1920s, 1930s, and 1940s became interested in the fact that human beings see patterns and groupings in their environments rather than disorganized arrays of bits and pieces. These Gestalt psychologists noted, for example, that it is impossible to look at the array of dots in (a) without seeing shifting patterns of squares and lines. They tried to identify the rules whereby disordered elements are organized into stable patterns. Proximity, or closeness of elements, as shown in (b), is one obvious factor. Elements that are close to one another seem to belong together. However, as (c) shows, continuity can be more important than proximity: Although the bottom dot in the inclined series of dots is closer to the vertical series of dots, it is not seen as belonging to the vertical row. It is seen as a continuation of the inclined row and therefore as part of it. (d) Similarity also organizes elements. The similar elements seem to belong to one another and therefore one sees the array as a set of horizontal rows rather than vertical columns as one might if all the elements were the same. Finally, in (e) a principle known as closure is demonstrated. The human brain has a tendency to fill in the gaps once an organization has emerged. The breaks are ignored; what is seen is a "whole."

information from the senses and organizes and interprets it into meaningful experiences. This process is called *perception*.

Principles of Perceptual Organization

Through the process of perception, the brain is always trying to build "wholes" out of the confusion of information that bombards the senses. The "whole" experience that comes from organizing bits and pieces of information into meaningful objects and patterns is called a *Gestalt*. The Gestalt, or "whole," experience is named after the German word *Gestalten*, which means patterns, or configurations.

Gestalt psychologists have tried to identify some of the principles the brain uses in constructing perceptions. Many of the principles they have discovered are demonstrated in Figure 2.14. For example, they have found that people tend to see the dots in patterns and groups. In Figure 2.14a, for example, you see shifting patterns of lines and rectangles, not just an array of dots.

Two principles that people use in organizing such patterns are *proximity* and *similarity*. If the elements of the pattern are close to one another or are similar in appearance, they tend to be perceived as belonging to one another. These principles are demonstrated in Figures 2.14b, 2.14c and 2.14d.

The Gestalt principles of organization help to explain how people group their sensations and fill in gaps in order to make sense of the world. In music, for instance, you tend to group notes on the basis of their closeness to one another—you hear phrases. Similarity and continuity are also important. They allow you to follow the sound of a particular voice or instrument even when many other sounds are occurring—to follow the bass guitar through a song, for example.

Figure and Ground

The simplest form of perceptual organization is the division of experience into *figure* and *ground*. Look at Figure 2.15—what do you see? Sometimes the figure looks like a white vase against a black background, yet at other times it appears to be two black faces against a white background.

When you look at a three-dimensional object against the sky or some other unstructured background, you have no trouble deciding which areas represent objects and which represent spaces between objects. It is when something is two dimensional, like Figure 2.15, that you may have trouble telling the figure from the ground. Nevertheless, such figure-ground problems give clues as to the active nature of perception. They show, for instance, that a single pattern can be perceived in more than one way.

Figure and ground are important in hearing as well as in vision. When you follow one person's voice at a noisy party, that voice is a figure and all other sounds become ground. Similarly, you may have had the experience of listening to a piece of music you did not recognize when suddenly a familiar melody leaped out at you. The melody became the figure, and the rest of the music, merely background.

Perceptual Inference

When you put a book on a table, you do not check beforehand to make sure the table is hard or solid. Before you sit down, you probably do not test a chair to see if it will bear your weight; you assume that its four legs are planted firmly on the floor, even though some of them may be hidden from view. The reason for this trust is that perception relies on past experience. A person needs to see only part of a chair to be able to conclude that the chair has four legs. This process is called *perceptual inference.*

Perceptual inference is possible because of the role of past experience in perception. Because you have dealt with certain objects and stimuli in the past, you know what to expect from them in the present.

One way to understand perceptual inference is to see what happens when it backfires. If your sensory information is faulty, your ability to perceive objects in light of past experience is limited. Suppose a child visits a friend's house and notices a large bowl of fruit on the kitchen table. He reaches for a tasty looking apple, but as his hand grasps it, he is shocked to discover that it is plastic. Because the apple is the proper shape, color, and size, he has inferred that it is edible. Fortunately, such perceptual errors are infrequent. Normally, perceptual inference allows people to assume a great deal about their environment so they can devote their attention to novel stimuli and problems.

Learning to Perceive

Newborn babies live in a world composed mostly of sensory experiences. Perceiving is in large part something that infants learn to do. The perceptual whole of a human face, for example, does not exist for the infant. At first he will smile at any moving object that is approximately the size of a human head. It is not until about six weeks of age that an infant can begin to distinguish individual facial features.

At three months, a baby will smile on seeing a model of a face with realistic eyes. At twenty weeks, the face must have a mouth in

Figure 2.15
What did you see the first time you looked at this famous illustration? Whatever you saw, you saw because of your past experiences and current expectations. People invariably organize their experience into figure and ground. Whatever appears as figure receives the attention, is likely to be remembered, and has a distinctness of form that is lacking in the vague, formless ground. But, as this figure shows, what is meaningless ground one minute may become the all-important figure the next.

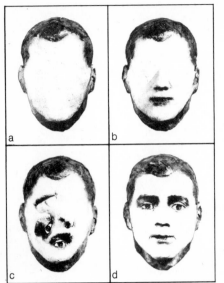

Figure 2.16
Clay masks used in an experiment on the perceptual abilities of infants. Psychologists learned that babies show a preference for complex patterns and human features almost from birth. Four-month-old babies pay much more attention to the masks in (c) and (d) than those in (a) and (b) and seem to slightly prefer the face with the regular features. By the age of two years, however, babies spend more time looking at the face with the mixed-up features. By this time they have a good conception of what a human face looks like and find exceptions to the rule interesting and arousing.

Figure 2.17
A cut-away view of the apparatus used to show that active involvement is necessary for perceptual learning. Both these kittens are receiving roughly the same visual input as they move in relation to the vertical stripes painted on the walls of the cylinder, but one kitten is producing the changes in what it sees by its own muscular movements. The other kitten sees similar changes because of the way it is harnessed to the first kitten, but what it sees has nothing to do with its own movements. This second kitten was found not to have developed the ability to see depth in this situation, while the active kitten developed depth perception normally.

order for the infant to smile. By twenty-eight weeks, he can tell a female face from a male one. Finally, at around eight months, he can distinguish between familiar and unfamiliar people.

Learning to perceive is a lifelong process. Psychologists have shown that people and animals must be actively involved in their environments for perception to be learned. An experiment on newborn kittens suggests one way in which perception can be learned. The kittens were raised in the dark until they were ten weeks old. Then the kittens were divided into two groups: actives and passives.

For three hours a day an active kitten and a passive kitten were linked together, as shown in Figure 2.17. The kittens were harnessed in such a way that every action of the active kitten moved the passive kitten an equal distance, forward, backward, up, down, and from side to side. The visual stimulation for the two kittens was approximately the same, but the active animal produced its *own* changes in stimulation (by walking, turning its head, and so on), whereas the passive kitten had its stimulation produced for it. When the kittens were tested later, the passive one was not able to discriminate depth—to tell how close or far away various objects were. The active kitten, however, developed this ability normally. Not until the passive kitten had been allowed to live normally for two days—to move around in a visual environment of its own—did it develop normal depth perception.

Experiments on human beings have also shown that active involvement in one's environment is important for accurate perception. People who have been blind from birth and who have had their sight restored by an operation (which is possible in only a few cases)

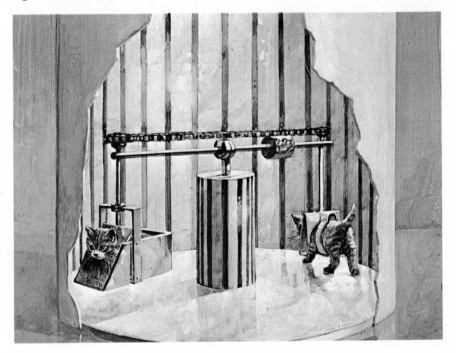

have visual sensations, but they cannot tell the difference between a square and a circle or see that a red cube is like a blue cube.

Depth Perception

Depth perception—the ability to recognize distances and three-dimensionality—is one of the first types of perception that people develop. If you place a baby on a large table, he will not crawl over the edge. He is able to perceive that it is a long distance to the floor. Such early depth perception in infants has been tested with the aid of a device called the visual cliff (see Figure 2.18). Visual-cliff experiments have shown that infants are fully able to perceive the cliff and the depth below.

People use many cues to perceive depth. One is the information provided by binocular fusion, as discussed early in the chapter. Another is *motion parallax*—the apparent movement of objects that occurs when you move your head from side to side or when you walk around. You can demonstrate motion parallax by looking toward two objects in the same line of vision, one near you and the other some

Figure 2.18

The visual cliff apparatus. A human infant of crawling age (about six months) will refuse to cross the glass surface over the "deep" side even if his mother is on the other side and is urging the child to join her. The infant is perfectly willing to cross the "shallow" side to reach his mother, however. Even though the child can feel the hard solid glass surface beneath him, he refuses to venture out over an edge that visually appears to be a sudden drop. A variety of animals such as chicks, lambs, and kittens respond in the same way. These animals can walk almost as soon as they are born. It seems, then, that animals are born with enough depth perception to avoid such hazards as walking off cliffs.

distance away. If you move your head back and forth, the near object will seem to move more than the far object. In this way, motion parallax gives you clues as to which objects are closer than others.

You are probably familiar with many other cues to distance. Nearby objects sometimes obscure parts of objects that are farther away. The more distant an object is, the smaller its image. Continuous objects such as railroad tracks, roads, rows of trees, and the walls of a room form converging lines, another cue to distance.

Constancy

When a person learns to perceive certain objects in the environment, he tends to see them in the same way, regardless of changing conditions. You probably judge the whiteness of the various portions of these pages to be fairly constant, even though you may have read the book under a wide range of lighting conditions. The object you perceive does not change, but the light, angle of vision, and distance do. Under changing physical conditions people are able to perceive objects as the same by the processes of size, shape, and brightness *constancy.*

An example of *size constancy* will illustrate how people have an automatic system for perceiving an object as being the same size whether it is far or near. A friend walking toward you does not seem to change into a giant even though the images inside your eyes become larger and larger as he approaches. To you, his appearance stays the same size because even though your visual image is increasing, you are perceiving an additional piece of information: Distance is decreasing. The enlarging eye image and the distance information combine to produce a perception of an approaching object that stays the same size.

The size-constancy system uses distance information to compensate for the enlarging eye image. If information about distance is eliminated, your perception of the size of the object begins to correspond to the actual size of the eye image. For example, it is difficult for most people to estimate the size of an airplane in the sky because they have little experience judging such huge sizes and distances. Experienced pilots, however, can determine whether a flying plane is large or small because they are experienced in estimating the sizes and distances of planes.

Illusions

When constancies are misinterpreted, one often perceives an *illusion.* Illusions are perceptions that are misrepresentations of reality. For example, look at the lines in Figure 2.20. Which lines are longer? Measure the lengths of the pairs of lines with a ruler, than look again. Do the lines look the same now that you know they are the same? For most people, the answer is no.

A possible explanation of this type of illusion is that even though the patterns are two-dimensional, your brain treats them as three-

Figure 2.19
This figure can be used to demonstrate two striking features of vision. Stare steadily at the lower right-hand star for about forty-five seconds, or until the colors start to shimmer. Then look at a blank piece of white paper. The flag in its usual colors will appear as a *negative afterimage,* which occurs as a result of tiring out the receptors in the retina. Now shift your glance to a blank wall some distance away. Suddenly the flag will appear huge. This happens because of the principle of constancy—the brain interprets the same image as large when it is far away (apparently on the wall) and small when it is close (apparently on a piece of paper in your hand).

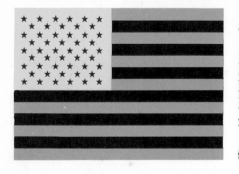

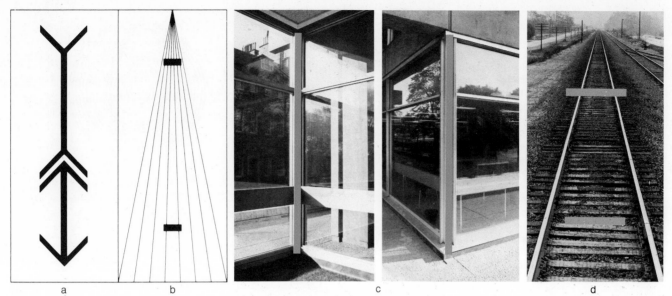

a   b   c   d

Figure 2.20

The Muller-Lyer illusion (a) and the Ponzo illusion (b) are two of the most famous illusions in psychology. The lines between the arrow heads in (a) are exactly the same length, as are the heavy black lines in (b). It is believed that the reason these lines appear to be different in length is that the brain interprets the diagrams in (a) and (b) as though they are scenes such as those in (c) and (d).

dimensional. These illusions have features that usually indicate distance in three-dimensional space. The top line in Figure 2.20a, for example, can be thought of as a far corner of a room, and the bottom one is like a near corner of a building. In Figure 2.20b, the converging lines are interpreted as a cue to distance, so the lower bar appears to be nearer than the upper one.

Figure 2.21a shows two women in a room. Their sizes look dramatically different because you perceive the room as a rectangle. In fact, as Figure 2.21b shows, the back wall is smaller on the right than it is on the left. The wall appears to be rectangular because it is set at an angle, with its right-hand edge closer to the viewer.

These illusions show that people are often forced to decide

a

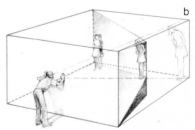

b

Figure 2.21

These two women appear to be a giant and a midget in an ordinary room. In fact, they are ordinary-sized women in a very peculiar room. This room, the true design of which is shown in the accompanying diagram, was constructed by psychologist Adelbert Ames. Again, the illusion is produced by tricking the brain into accepting an unusual situation as usual.

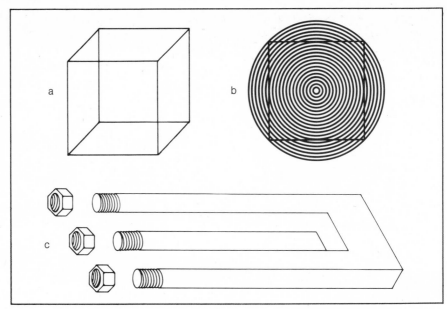

Figure 2.22
The unusual visual effects seen in these figures are all produced by leading the interpretative processes of perception into error. (a) The famous Necker Cube is impossible to see as a two-dimensional pattern of lines even though that is all it is. Instead, it is seen as the outlines of a three-dimensional cube, and as you look at it you will begin to alternate between seeing one or the other of the vertical lines in the middle of the pattern as being the closest edge of the cube. (b) The lines that form a square appear to be curved inward although they are in fact perfectly straight. This illusion has yet to be explained. (c) An impossible figure. It can exist in two-dimensions, but although it appears three-dimensional, no such three-dimensional object could exist.

between accepting cues about distance or depth and accepting cues about size. If they decide in favor of the accurate cues, there is no illusion; but this special room (known as the Ames room) was purposely designed to persuade people to accept the misleading cues.

Person Perception

The principles of perception apply to all possible objects and stimuli in one's environment—even other people. People build Gestalts of one another—they base their perceptions on a few of a person's characteristics and then fill in the gaps in the person's personality. For example, if you see a woman wearing a riding habit and boots, you may perceive her as a horseback rider. In addition, by the process of perceptual inference, you might assume that the woman is sophisticated, rich, and a snob, on the basis of your past experience.

Relying on perceptual inference in interpersonal relations can be helpful. For instance, it is useful to be able to assume that an auto mechanic will be reliable or that a banker will be trustworthy. But problems arise when people perceive and categorize others on the basis of skin color, ethnic characteristics, or other such broad criteria without regard to individuality. (Such aspects of interpersonal relations are more fully discussed in Chapter 9.)

Person perception then, like all types of perception, is an active process that involves input from the senses that is interpreted in light of one's past experiences and current expectations in order to arrive at a whole picture of a person.

EXTRASENSORY PERCEPTION

It is commonly believed that the only way the brain can receive information about the environment is through one of the senses that has been described. There are a number of scientists, however, who

Figure 2.23
Like the Necker Cube and the reversing figure-ground of Figure 2.15, this figure is ambiguous. It can be seen as an old woman turned slightly toward the viewer or as a young woman turned away from the viewer. In the latter interpretation, the old woman's mouth becomes the young woman's choker. Whichever figure you perceive first depends greatly on your experience, attitudes, and expectations.

now believe that people have a way of being sensitive to the external world that cannot yet be explained physically. This special sensitivity is referred to as *extrasensory perception* (ESP).

ESP is a major branch of *parapsychology,* the study of supernormal powers of the mind. ESP is thought to take three forms: *telepathy,* or mind reading; *precognition,* the ability to see the future; and *clairvoyance,* knowledge of events not detectable by the normal senses.

Scientific investigations into the existence of ESP have been conducted in the United States since the early 1900s. J. B. Rhine is the most famous researcher in this area. He has tried to prove by scientific methods that ESP exists. In tests of telepathy, for example, a "sender" focuses one at a time on each of twenty-five cards in a special deck. The deck consists of five cards each of five symbols. A "receiver" locked in a distant room states which card he thinks has been turned up. With luck alone, the receiver will guess about five cards correctly, sometimes a few more, sometimes a few less. Yet thousands of such tests have shown that some people consistently guess correctly more than five times out of the twenty-five. Scientists have computed that if these people were simply lucky, they would be this lucky only once in a thousand years. It is therefore thought that these people are somehow getting information that is not available to the known senses.

The earliest ESP experiments were sharply criticized. It seemed possible that people were cheating or that the mathematical computations were inaccurate. Recently, however, experiments have been done that seem to be unquestionable, and the mathematics have been carefully checked by trained mathematicians.

In one new study of precognition, subjects must guess which of four colored lamps will light next (the lamps are lit in a totally random sequence, controlled only by a computer). Results of this study have been highly significant: Odds against chance producing these results have been as high as two thousand million to one.

For the most part, American scientists have been highly skeptical of ESP research, although on one of the Apollo missions one of the astronauts acted as a receiver, guessing cards turned by a sender on Earth. In addition, many British, Russian, Czechoslovakian, and other foreign scientists are now heavily involved in trying to prove the existence of ESP and related mental abilities and to determine some of the possible applications. They are working on the premise that ESP can be explained on the basis of natural laws that simply have not yet been discovered. The electrical nature of the nervous system is being considered as a possible source of ESP, while other investigators are exploring subatomic physics for an explanation.

Many advocates of ESP criticize the current approaches to ESP research on the basis that ESP abilities are stifled when placed in a laboratory setting. They say that ESP responses are generated by highly emotional situations or by stimuli relevant to the person's life. Laboratory experiments with cards to guess and buttons to push

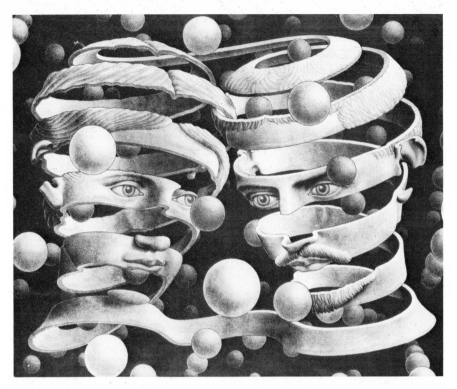

Figure 2.24
M. C. Escher's lithograph, "Bond of Union," suggests that there are ties between people that go beyond everyday physical interactions. ESP may be such a tie.
(Escher Foundation—Haags Gemeentemuseum—The Hague.)

seem particularly boring and irrelevant to most people, so according to this viewpoint ESP would rarely appear in such a setting.

To eliminate the problem, researchers have tried having senders look at paintings while they try to influence the dreams of sleeping receivers, or they have had senders look at pictures and slides about some emotion-arousing news event, such as the assassination of President Kennedy, while they try to influence the thoughts of the receiver. These efforts have been considered successful, but even in these experiments the receiver has obtained only a vague, distorted, uncertain impression of what the sender has concentrated on.

Because ESP experiments have so far shown only that something more than luck is present, and because it has not yet proved possible to repeat a successful ESP experiment at will, the majority of scientists have rejected the possibility that ESP exists. A few, however (some of them noted physicists, astronomers, chemists, and psychologists), have decided that ESP must exist, even though it means that in some basic way the present scientific understanding of the world is faulty. All the other senses can be understood in terms of known scientific principles. ESP cannot.

SUMMARY

1. Man's information about the outside world comes in through his senses. Stimuli in the environment are converted by the sense organs

into chemical-electrical activity that travels to the brain. This process results in sensation.

2. Psychophysics is the study of the relationship between physical stimuli and the sensory experiences they produce. The smallest amount of energy that will produce a sensation is called a threshold. The smallest change in a stimulus that produces a change in sensation is called the just-noticeable difference.

3. The experiencing of a sensation depends more on changes in the stimulus than on the absolute size or amount of the stimulus. Sensory adaptation occurs when a stimulus continues without changing. Motivation can influence whether or not certain stimuli will be detected.

4. The chief stimulus in vision is light. The rods and cones in the retina of the eye convert light energy to impulses, which travel over the optic nerve to the brain. The cones respond to color and work best in daylight. The rods are more sensitive but do not detect color. Color blindness results when cones are absent or malfunctioning. Binocular fusion, the combination of images from both eyes, contributes to depth perception.

5. The stimuli for hearing are sound waves, which are converted to impulses by hair cells in the inner ear. These messages reach the brain via the auditory nerve. The main functions of hearing are detection, identification, and location of sounds.

6. Smell and taste are chemical senses. Receptors in the nose and on the tongue respond to contact with molecules. Most taste sensations involve the sense of smell to some extent.

7. Skin receptors respond to pressure, warmth, cold, and pain. These sensations play an important role in warning the brain of possible external dangers.

8. Internal bodily sensations include balance, kinesthesis, and internal sensitivity to pressure, temperature, pain, and chemicals.

9. Perception is the process of creating meaningful wholes out of information from the senses. Perceptual wholes are called Gestalts. Psychologists study such phenomena as figure-ground relationships, perceptual inference, perceptual development, depth perception, constancy, illusions, and interpersonal relationships to determine how perception works.

10. Extrasensory perception is a field of parapsychology. It includes telepathy, clairvoyance, and precognition. So far most ESP evidence has been based on statistical probability, and most scientists are skeptical about it. If ESP does exist, as some scientists believe, many scientific theories will have to be changed.

ACTIVITIES

1. Hold a pencil about twelve inches in front of your face. Look at it with your left eye closed, then with your right eye closed. Notice how

the pencil seems to jump around. What happens when you look at the pencil with both eyes? What principle does this experiment demonstrate?

2. Fill three bowls with water—hot water in one, cold in another, and lukewarm in the third. Put one hand in the cold water and the other in the hot water and leave them there for thirty seconds. Now put both hands in the lukewarm water at the same time. What do you feel? How does this demonstrate the principle of sensory adaptation?

3. Get a fresh potato and peel it. Do the same with an apple. Now have a friend close his eyes and smell a fresh onion while he takes a bite of each one. Can he tell which food is which without his sense of smell? Try this experiment with various people, using different foods that have similar textures.

4. If sensation consists entirely of electrical signals in the brain that are subject to interpretation by perception, does everyone experience the world differently? Animals have different sensory apparatus than humans—do they live in a different perceptual world?

5. Have a friend stand with his back to you. Touch various parts of his back with one pencil or with two pencils held close together. Each time you touch his back, ask him how many points he felt. Now touch the points to his hand and arm, again asking how many points he feels. What are your results? What accounts for these results?

6. To demonstrate the information shown in Figure 2.11, prepare solutions of salt water (salt), lemon juice (sour), baking soda (bitter), and sugar water (sweet). Dab each solution on various points on your tongue, and see if you can verify which area of the tongue is predominately sensitive to each of these major tastes.

7. Perform the following experiment to test one kind of sensory adaptation. Write a sentence while looking at your writing in a mirror. Do this until it begins to feel natural. Then write the sentence normally. Does normal writing now feel strange?

8. Try the following experiment to demonstrate an illusion of the sense of touch. Stretch a foot-square piece of chicken wire tautly over a frame. Blindfold your subject(s) and ask him to hold the thumb and forefinger of his hand to lightly touch each side of the chicken wire. Slide the wire rapidly back and forth between his fingers. Ask your subject to report the sensation he feels. Most people report feeling a continuous slippery or oily surface. This illusion will probably be stronger if the subject does not know in advance the actual nature of the material he is feeling.

9. Station yourself behind a window or glass door (to eliminate sounds and smells that you might give off) and stare intently at someone who has his back toward you. Pick someone who is within a ten-yard range and who is not engaged in any particular activity at

the moment. Does the person turn around and look at you? If so, how long does it take him to "sense" your presence? How can you explain this phenomenon?

SUGGESTED READINGS

ARNHEIM, RUDOLF. *Art and Visual Perception: A Psychology of the Creative Eye.* Berkeley: University of California Press, 1954 (paper). Using the principles of Gestalt psychology, Arnheim describes the relationship between perception of beauty and the structure of art work.

GREGORY, R. L. *Eye and Brain.* New York: McGraw-Hill, 1966 (paper). Without losing the reader's interest, Gregory deals skillfully with such topics as optics, all aspects of seeing, and perceptual learning.

GREGORY, R. L. *The Intelligent Eye.* New York: McGraw-Hill, 1970 (paper). Gregory stresses his view that perception is a set of simple hypotheses about reality that depend upon sensory experiences. The book is particularly strong on visual illusions.

HANSEL, C. E. M. *ESP: A Scientific Evaluation.* New York: Scribner's, 1966 (paper). Hansel criticizes early ESP experiments on the basis of their poor design and misapplication of the scientific method.

HELD, RICHARD, and WHITMAN RICHARDS (eds.). *Perception: Mechanisms and Models.* San Francisco: Freeman, 1972. This book of readings from *Scientific American* provides accounts of some of the most famous research on perceptual processes in man and animals, including the visual cliff and the active and passive kittens.

KOESTLER, ARTHUR. *The Roots of Coincidence.* New York: Random House, 1972. Koestler writes eloquently and interestingly, asking only that the reader keep an open mind with regard to the possible existence of ESP. He describes ESP research and delves into modern physics for an explanation of ESP phenomena.

MUELLER, C. G., and M. RUDOLPH. *Light and Vision.* New York: Time-Life Books, 1966. This beautifully illustrated book is an excellent introduction to eye function as well as to the nature of light.

STEVENS, S. S., and F. WARSHOVSKY. *Sound and Hearing.* New York: Time-Life Books, 1967. A highly readable and well-illustrated exploration of the nature of sound, the structure of the ear, and the phenomenon of hearing.

3
Memory and Thought

Figure 3.1

In this scene from the film *2001: A Space Odyssey*, an astronaut (Dave, played by Keir Dullea) is removing some of the modules in the memory banks of HAL, his spaceship's giant computer. Dave must disable the computer because it has ceased to obey orders. No computer has yet been built that can act as humanly as HAL, but computers have been built to answer questions, play chess, or draw pictures. By studying how computers remember and think, psychologists have learned a good deal about how humans process information.

Psychology is often defined as "the science of the mind." From this definition, one might assume that psychologists have a good understanding of how the mind works—how human beings think, remember, solve problems, and create ideas. In actuality, however, these important mental processes—called *cognitive* processes by psychologists—are so difficult to study and understand that for many years psychologists practically gave up on them. The situation changed when scientists and engineers learned how to build computers that can do some of the things that humans can do.

Psychologists realized that if a machine could be built to take in information, remember it, analyze it, and put out new information, then it should be possible to understand how humans do the same things. As a result, when psychologists now study such mental activities as memory and thought, they usually treat them as aspects of *information processing*. Information processing involves three steps: input, central processing, and output. *Input* refers to information received from the senses. *Central processing* refers to the storing (in memory) and sorting (by thought) of that information by the brain. *Output* refers to actions that result from the processing.

This sequence occurs continually in humans. For example, someone who translates languages can listen to one language (input), mentally translate it (using thought and memory), and express the ideas in a second language (output). For the skillful translator, the central processing becomes so automatic that he is hardly aware of it.

Psychologists know a great deal about how the senses take in information (see Chapter 2), and about how people behave. But the processing that happens in between the sensory input and the behavioral output has been difficult to study—so far no one has been able to explain exactly what happens when one remembers something or solves a problem or has an idea. Nevertheless, psychologists have been able to come up with some interesting suggestions as to how these mental processes might work. This chapter will present some of the things that psychologists have discovered about information processing.

TAKING INFORMATION IN

Input comes through the senses in many forms—musical sounds, sweet tastes, pungent odors, colorful images, rough textures, painful stings. At any given moment a confusing number of sights, sounds, smells, and other such sensations are vying for your attention. If you accepted all these inputs, you would be unable to act—you would be trying to respond to a thousand things at once. Two processes that help people to narrow down their inputs to the most useful ones are selective attention and feature extraction.

Selective Attention

The ability to pick and choose among the various available inputs is called *selective attention*. This process enables you to "tune out" things that you are not interested in and to "tune in" things that do interest you. If you are at a party where loud music is playing and many conversations are going on simultaneously, you can focus on a friend's voice and ignore all the other sounds. In this way, selective attention is like tuning in a specific television channel.

Unlike television tuning, however, selective attention does not completely block out the other stimuli. You may be listening attentively to you friend's words, but at the same time you are unconsciously monitoring a great deal of information that is coming in over other channels. If your name is mentioned in a nearby conversation, you will notice it and tune in to that input. You may be ignoring the people milling around, but if someone strolls by dressed in a bathing suit, snorkel, and fins, you will notice him. The ability to monitor many channels while attending to one is sometimes called the "cocktail-party phenomenon" because at a noisy party this phenomenon is quite noticeable.

Psychologists investigating how selective attention works tried an experiment with cats. The experimenters made sharp clicking sounds near the cat and recorded the nerve impulses that registered in the hearing area of the cat's brain. (How scientists record such impulses is described in Chapter 5.) When they held a live mouse in front of the cat, the impulses from the clicking sound suddenly became quite small. Similar research showed that brain reactions to a flashing light declined in men when they had a problem to solve or when they were talking to someone.

The conclusion from this type of research is that the brain somehow evaluates the importance of the information that comes in over various channels. Top-priority information is allowed to reach the highest brain centers, whereas unimportant input is suppressed.

What makes an input important? Studies have shown that information that leads to the satisfaction of needs, such as hunger or

Figure 3.2
While staring at this figure, quickly flip the page so that you see the black frame on page 57 for just a moment. What letters and numbers did you see in the third row? The purpose of this experiment will be explained in the text.

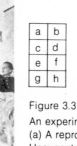

Figure 3.3
An experiment in selective attention.
(a) A reproduction of the painting "An Unexpected Visitor" by the Russian artist I. E. Repin. The blue tracings that appear in the other frames of this figure show the eye movements of a person looking at the painting after being given certain instructions. The instructions were: (b) Examine the picture freely; (c) estimate the material circumstances of the family; (d) give the ages of the people; (e) guess what the family had been doing before the visitor's arrival; (f) remember the clothes worn by the people; (g) remember the positions of the people and objects in the room; (h) estimate how long the visitor has been away. As you can see, the viewer *selectively attended* to different parts of the painting depending on the instructions he was given. In addition, he was *extracting features* relevant to his purpose.

thirst, seems to have top priority. So do inputs that are strange or novel. A third major director of attention is one's interests—when you are interested in something, you are more likely to notice it. For example, if you become interested in chess, you will suddenly begin to notice articles on chess in the newspaper, chess sets for sale in stores, and references to chess moves in everyday speech. All these inputs will have always been there—you have simply never been interested in noticing them before.

Feature Extraction

Selective attention is only the first step in narrowing down input. The second step is to decide which aspects of the selected channel you will focus on. This second process, called *feature extraction,* involves analyzing and identifying specific features of the incoming information. Some features are ignored; others are actually accentuated. Being able to extract the significant features of an input helps to identify it and to compare its similarities and differences with those of other inputs. For example, if you wanted to identify the make of a car, you would look for distinctive features—shape of the fenders, proportion of height to length, and so on. For the most part, you would ignore such features as color, upholstery, and tires, for they might belong to any car.

Feature extraction is an ongoing process. When reading, for example, you look for features that distinguish letters and words from one another and from all other marks that might appear on a piece of paper. Similarly, feature extraction enables you to distinguish faces from one another and yet still be able to notice resemblances between people. You may notice that all the members of a certain family have similar noses, yet you are able to tell them apart on the basis of other features.

Obviously, feature extraction is influenced by experience—you have to know what to look for. Experience is particularly necessary in areas where fine distinctions must be made, such as in wine tasting or in art identification (distinguishing a Da Vinci from a Raphael, or being able to tell a forgery from an original) or in proofreading (being able to notice if a letter is missing from a word in a page of type or if something is set in the wrong typeface). To be a wine taster, an art expert, or a proofreader, one must have training in these areas. And, like selective attention, feature extraction is controlled by an evaluation process. If your interest in cars is purely aesthetic, you will attend only to their design; if your interest is mechanical, you may notice only the intricacies of a car's engineering.

STORING INFORMATION

In order to be used, the inputs that are finally allowed to reach the brain must be held on to in some way—perhaps for just an instant or maybe for a lifetime. The storage of such inputs is called *memory.* Memory storage seems to take three forms, each with a different

Figure 3.4

Can you spot the hidden faces in this picture? To find them, it is necessary for you to extract those features that define a human face from a large amount of irrelevant and misleading information.

purpose and time span: *sensory storage* holds information for only an instant, *short-term memory* keeps it in mind for several seconds, and *long-term memory* stores it indefinitely.

Sensory Storage

The senses seem to be able to hold an input for a fraction of a second before it disappears. For example, when you watch a movie you do not notice the gaps between frames—the actions seem smooth because each frame is held in sensory storage until the next frame arrives.

Psychologists have measured the length of sensory storage by testing subjects with inputs such as that shown in Figure 3.5. This image is flashed on a screen for one-fiftieth of a second, and immediately afterward the subject is signaled to recite one of the lines he has seen. The subject is usually able to report all four items on the required line if the signal is sounded within a quarter of a second after the exposure. It is therefore thought that the subject retains a brief image of the whole picture so that he can still read off the items in the correct row *after* the picture has left the screen.

The information held momentarily by the senses has not yet been narrowed down or analyzed. It is like a short-lived but highly detailed photograph or tape recording. By the time information gets to the next stage (short-term memory), however, it has been analyzed, identified, and simplified so that it can be conveniently stored and handled for a long time.

Short-Term Memory

The things you have in your conscious mind at any one moment are being held in short-term memory. Information may be held in short-term memory even if you are not paying close attention to the input. For example, you have probably had the experience of only partially listening to someone and of having him accuse you of not paying attention. You can usually repeat back to him his last few words because they are still in your short-term memory. Nevertheless, you may not know the meaning or content of those words until you pay attention to them.

Rehearsal A basic property of short-term memory is that information, to be kept there for more than a few seconds, must be *rehearsed.* Rehearsal amounts to repeating the information over and over. When you look up a telephone number, for example, you can remember the seven digits long enough to dial by repeating them to yourself several times. But if you are distracted or make a mistake in dialing, chances are you will have to look up the number again—it has been lost from short-term memory.

Psychologists have measured short-term memory by giving a subject something to remember—such as a three-letter sequence like CPQ—and seeing how long he can remember it without rehearsal. It

Figure 3.5
A pattern of letters and numbers used to investigate information storage. Psychologists use a machine called a tachistoscope to flash such patterns on a screen in front of a subject. The subject is then asked to report what he has seen. By such methods, experimenters can determine how much information a person stores in the fraction of a second after he has seen something.

Figure 3.6
You can discover important aspects of your memory by trying to reproduce here the chessboard presented in Figure 3.10, following the directions in the caption that accompanies it. Your success at this exercise will be influenced not only by your ability to remember but also your interests, motivation, and knowledge of chess. Chess masters, for example, can glance at the arrangement shown in Figure 3.10 and see it as a set of patterns as familiar to them as your handwriting is to you. Their experience with chess enables them to organize and store such information very efficiently.

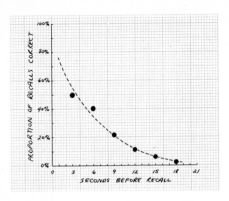

Figure 3.7
This graph shows the results of an experiment on short-term memory. Subjects were shown a group of three letters and were then asked to recall them after a few seconds. During the interval, they performed a confusing counting task that prevented them from rehearsing the letters they had seen. As you can see from the graph, if the subjects had to wait for more than eighteen seconds before recalling, they could rarely recall anything. If they had to wait only three seconds, however, they could recall the letters about half the time. This experiment shows that unless you rehearse information, you lose it from short-term memory very quickly.

is difficult to refrain from rehearsing, so the subject is made to think of something else after he is given the three-letter sequence. For example, he may be asked to immediately start counting backward by threes from 798. If a subject performs this confusing task for only a short time, he can still tell what the letters had been. But if he is kept from rehearsing for more than eighteen seconds, the information is gone forever. Thus, short-term memory seems to last less than twenty seconds without rehearsal.

Chunking   Short-term memory is limited not only in time span but in capacity as well. Psychologists have found that it is impossible to hold more than about seven items in mind at once. Five or six items of information can be handled easily; eight or nine items produce confusion. Seven items is not a large capacity, and twenty seconds is not a long time span. The time limitation can be overcome by rehearsal, but how is the capacity problem solved?

Psychologist George Miller has found that the answer lies in the process of *chunking,* or the packaging of information. One may be able to handle only seven items, but each item may contain large amounts of information. For example, a seven-item shopping list can be remembered almost as easily as a list of seven single-digit numbers, but it contains far more useful information.

To a considerable extent, the ability to think and remember depends on the ability to package large amounts of information into a small number of chunks. That is one reason why a large vocabulary is so useful. The word "euphemism," for example, is a chunk containing the information: "use of a word or phrase that is less expressive or direct but considered less distasteful or less offensive than another." Thus euphemism is a single item that occupies only one-seventh of short-term memory yet contains a good deal of information.

Short-term memory is obviously only a temporary device. It contains information that has been labeled "of possible interest." At

Figure 3.8
Glance quickly at the left figure in this pair, then look away. How many dots did you see? Now do the same with the right figure. You were probably more sure and more accurate in your answer for the right figure because the organization of the dots into a small number of chunks makes it easier to process the information.

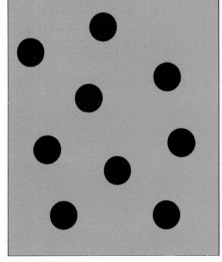
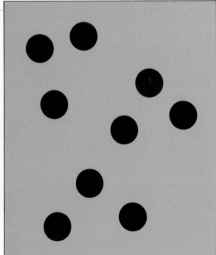

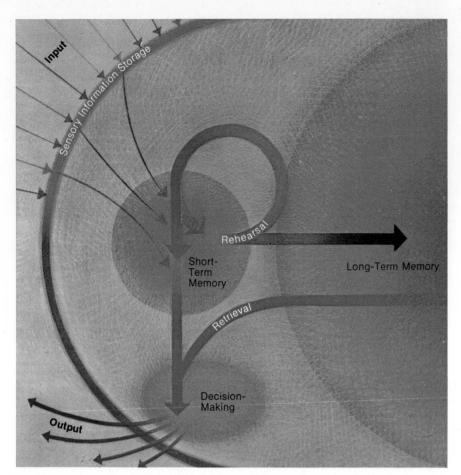

Figure 3.9
The flow of information processing. Input to the senses is stored temporarily, and some of it is passed on into short-term memory. Information may be kept in short-term memory by rehearsal or it may be passed on to long-term memory. Material stored in both short- and long-term memory is used in making decisions. The decision process results in outputs such as talking, writing, or moving. This chapter focuses on those stages that occur in between input and output.

this point an evaluation must be made: Is this information worth holding onto? If so, it should be transferred to long-term memory.

Long-Term Memory

Long-term memory is the process of storing information that may be of use in the future. Long-term memory is often thought of as a storage bin full of words, definitions, dates, names, and so on. But it also contains representations of many experiences and vivid sensations, such as smells and sounds.

Anything that is learned—even the ability to swim or ride a bicycle (see Chapter 6)—is stored in long-term memory. The entire input process may be followed in the example of a person attending a play. As the actors say their lines, the sounds they make flow through sensory storage. Selective attention and feature extraction screen out other sounds and interpret the voice sounds as words. Words accumulate in short-term memory and form phrases and sentences. And along with the words the viewer also remembers the immediate action taking place on the stage. A while later, the playgoer will probably have forgotten the exact words spoken in the scene, but he will have stored in long-term memory the *meaning* of what has been expressed. The next day, he may be able to give a scene-by-scene

Figure 3.10
Study this arrangement for about five seconds and try to memorize it. Now turn back to Figure 3.6 and try to reproduce this arrangement on the empty chessboard. You will be more successful if you can see the pieces in groupings and relationships rather than as many single items. Nevertheless, your ability to do so depends heavily on your experience with the game.

description of the main aspects of the play. What permanently remains in long-term memory, however, may be only a brief outline of the plot and perhaps a few vivid images of particularly impressive moments.

Throughout this process, the least-important information is dropped and only the essentials are kept. To be permanently stored, these essentials are somehow taken apart and are held in the brain in such a way that they can be put back together again when they need to be recalled.

Theories of Memory

What happens in the brain when something is stored in memory? This question is highly controversial; although psychologists agree that some physiological changes must occur in the brain, they are not in complete agreement as to what these changes comprise.

Some researchers think that information is coded in giant molecules in brain cells—in a way similar to that in which genetic information is coded on strands of the molecule DNA. This *molecular theory* has been supported by some controversial experiments on tiny animals called flatworms. The experimenters taught flatworms to respond to a light. Very slowly, the flatworms learned. These flatworms were then ground up and fed to other flatworms that had not been trained. When the experimenters tried to train the second set of flatworms, they had a somewhat easier time. According to the molecular theory, these flatworms had "learned" something by consuming the memory molecules of the first set. Researchers who have tried to re-do this experiment have not always been successful, however.

The molecular theory is doubted by other psychologists, who think that memory is a result of establishing well-worn channels for messages in the brain. Signals travel from cell to cell in the brain, and it is possible for the connections between some cells to become more easily crossed than others. According to this theory, a memory is like the channel cut by a stream. Once a channel has been cut, water will flow in that channel more easily than in any other path. In the brain, the passage of signals through a particular sequence of cells strengthens the connections between those cells so that the next time a signal comes through it is more likely to follow the old pathway.

Whichever of these theories is correct (or if, as usually happens in science, both turn out to contain some element of truth), some explanation is also needed for the fact that individual memories do not appear to be located in particular places in the brain. Memories seem to be distributed over wide areas. No one cell, or group of cells, can be removed to destroy a memory. A famous researcher on this problem, Karl Lashley, discovered that to completely destroy a rat's memory of a problem it had solved, he had to destroy most of the upper part of the rat's brain. As a result, some psychologists believe that a memory is an overall pattern of activity in the brain. A model

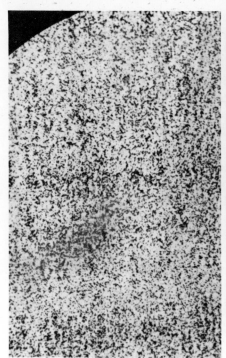

of how such patterns might work is provided by *holography,* a new, three-dimensional photographic process.

In holography, an object is photographed using the light waves of a laser beam. The photograph, or *hologram,* that results does not resemble the original object; instead, it is a pattern of dots and lines. But when this pattern is viewed by the original laser light, an image of the object reappears. Even if the hologram is broken in pieces, viewing one piece with the laser light will provide a complete (although less clear) picture of the object. Perhaps, then, memory is like holography: Memories are broken into patterns and distributed throughout the brain, and when something resembling the original input stimulates the brain, a replica of the original experience is brought into awareness.

All these ideas remain highly speculative at the moment. Many psychologists believe, however, that a better understanding of the processes underlying memory will be reached in the near future.

RETRIEVAL OF INFORMATION

Once information has been stored, it is useless unless it can be retrieved from memory. If you have ever tried to find a lost pen or set of keys in an untidy room, you will have some idea of how difficult retrieval can be. The problem of memory is the problem of storing many, many things in such a way that you can find the one thing you need when you happen to need it. The solution to this problem is *organization.*

Libraries, dictionaries, desk drawers, kitchen cupboards, and bedrooms are all examples of storage places that can be efficiently

Figure 3.11

The hologram, a possible model for human memory. Holography is a method for using laser beams to reconstruct three-dimensional images of photographed objects. The photograph at the far left shows a hologram as it appears on the photographic plate; this diffuse pattern can be compared to the diffusion of memory throughout the cells of the brain. The middle photograph bears an image obtained by illuminating the hologram with a laser light; in human memory, stored information may be said to be illuminated in the light of recall. The image on the far right was obtained by illuminating only a portion of the hologram. Such a hazy image could be compared to the vague or partial memory you might have if you had insufficient reminders to bring the memory completely into focus.

Figure 3.12

Children between the ages of five and seven were shown a bottle half filled with colored water and suspended at an angle, such as is shown in this drawing. After each child had seen this arrangement he was asked to draw it from memory. Some of the results of this experiment are shown in Figure 3.13.

used only if they are well organized. Human memory is extraordinarily efficient; therefore, it must be extremely well organized. Psychologists do not understand its exact organization, but by studying the processes involved in retrieval they are beginning to get some clues.

The two types of retrieval are recognition and recall. In *recognition,* you need only decide whether the object, experience, sound, or word before you is the one you are seeking or are familiar with. *Recall* is far more difficult because you actually have to reconstruct the information in order to be correct. The question, "Do you know the word 'roogle'?" tests recognition. The question, "When was the last time you ate a banana split?" tests recall.

Recognition

The organization of human memory seems to be designed to make recognition quite easy—people can say with great accuracy whether or not something is familiar to them. The ability to recognize often shows that there is much more stored in memory than one might think. For instance, you may think you have forgotten something, but as soon as you are reminded of it by someone, you may say, "Oh, yeah, I remember now."

The process of recognition provides some insight into how information is stored. A person can, for example, recognize the sound of a musical instrument no matter what tune is being played on it; he can also recognize a tune no matter what instrument plays it. This pattern of recognition seems to indicate that a single item of information may be "indexed" under several "headings" so that it can be reached in a number of ways. Thus, "Clarinet playing 'Beer Barrel Polka'" may be indexed under "clarinet," "Beer Barrel Polka," "polka," and possibly other categories as well. The more categories an item is indexed under, the more easily it may be retrieved.

Recall

More remarkable than the ability to recognize information is the ability to instantly recall it. Imagine the amount of recall involved in a simple conversation: One easily uses hundreds of words involving all kinds of information, even though each word and each bit of information must be searched for separately in the vast storehouse of memory.

Recall is actually more than just reproducing a piece of information—it is an active reconstruction of that information. This reconstructive nature of recall was demonstrated in an experiment with children. The experimenter showed a group of children a bottle arranged similarly to that shown in Figure 3.12. Soon after being shown the arrangement, the children were asked to draw from memory what they had seen. Most of their drawings showed marked changes from the original arrangement. Nevertheless, when the same children were asked six months later to draw what they had

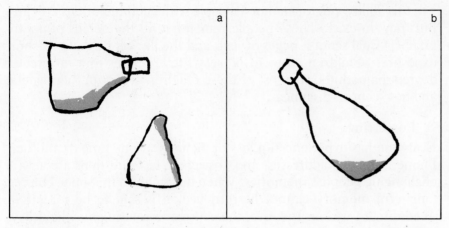

Figure 3.13
Drawings produced by children who had been shown an arrangement like that depicted in Figure 3.12. (a) The five- to seven-year-old children were not too successful in reproducing this arrangement from memory. (b) A drawing done by one of these children six months later. Even though the child had had half a year to forget what he had seen, his reproduction of the arrangement actually improved because he had developed a better idea of what bottles look like and of how water behaves. Such experiments demonstrate that memory for how things *are* depends greatly on one's conception of how things *should be*.

seen, many of them reproduced the arrangement more accurately than before. Apparently they had a better idea of how the bottle arrangement *ought* to look.

Because of this reconstructive process, memories may change over time. They may be simplified, or distorted, or enriched, depending on the experiences and attitudes of the individual. This process may thus give rise to mistakes in memory. One type of mistake is called *confabulation,* in which one "remembers" information that was never stored in memory. Confabulation generally occurs when you remember specific elements of a past situation and then fill in the gaps by making up the rest.

Confabulation can create problems. Suppose a witness is testifying in court about a robbery he witnessed a year before the trial. He may have originally seen the getaway car and the defendant near the bank, but in remembering the event he distorts reality by recalling that the accused person jumped into the getaway car and sped away. His attitudes toward the defendant may have caused him to fill in the gaps incorrectly.

A few people do not need to reconstruct memory because they have what is commonly called photographic memory. Psychologists

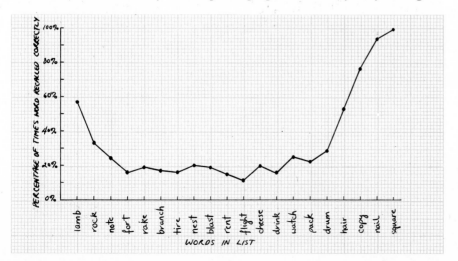

Figure 3.14
When a person is asked to learn a list, to memorize a poem, or to recall a conversation, he invariably finds that it is easier to remember the first and last parts of the material than it is to recall the middle of it. Psychologists call this the *serial-position effect*. This graph shows the average number of times each word in a memorized list was recalled correctly by a group of subjects. The curve clearly shows that words at the beginning and end of the list were remembered better than those in the middle. Psychologists believe that this pattern occurs because there is less confusion and interference from other words at either end of the list. Recall works especially well for words at the end of the list because they have not yet been lost from short-term memory.

call this ability *eidetic* memory. People with such memories are rare, but they do exist. These people remember all the details of photographs, visual scenes, pages of text, and the like on the basis of short exposures. Children seem to possess such abilities to a far greater degree than adults. As most of these children grow up, their eidetic abilities seem to disappear.

Forgetting

Everyone has experienced a loss of memory at one time or another. Phone numbers, addresses, and answers to test questions are always challenging people's memories. When information that once entered long-term memory cannot be retrieved, it is said to be forgotten. According to various theories, the cause of forgetting may be decay, interference, or repression.

Decay is the fading away of a memory over time. Items quickly decay in sensory storage and short-term memory. It is not certain, however, whether long-term memories can ever decay. It is known that a blow to the head or electrical stimulation of certain parts of the brain can cause loss of memory. In these cases, the memories lost are the most recent; older memories seem to remain. The fact that apparently forgotten information can be recovered by such methods as meditation, hypnosis, or brain stimulation has suggested to some psychologists that memories never decay. Instead, they are interfered with or repressed.

The most common form of forgetting is *interference*—the blocking of a memory by previous or subsequent memories. In *proactive interference,* an earlier memory does the blocking; in *retroactive interference,* a later memory is involved. Suppose, for example, that you move to a new place. You now have to remember your new address and phone number. At first, you will have trouble remembering them because the memories of your old address and phone number will interfere (proactively). Later, you will know your new information well, but you will have trouble remembering the old data (retroactive interference).

The old data has not been lost, however; it has only been "misfiled." It is in memory somewhere, if only one can find it. Sometimes this misfiling is no accident—memories may be blocked "intentionally" by a person who does not wish to remember some embarrassing or frightening personal experience. This kind of forgetting is called *repression.* The material still exists in the person's memory, but he has unconsciously decided not to recall the information because the memory would be disturbing. (Repression is discussed further in Chapter 13.)

Improving Memory

There are no magic ways for improving one's memory. Nevertheless, there do seem to be several factors that influence how well something will be remembered. These factors can be manipulated to some

Figure 3.15
The three main theories of how memories come to be forgotten. The interference theory can be compared to the confusion of a cluttered attic: A single piece of information may simply be lost in the jumble of other information. The theory of repression suggests that access to particular memories may be mentally "walled off" to prevent their retrieval. According to the decay theory, some memories may simply fade away, just as neglected objects in an old room may slowly decay and turn to dust. Most psychologists think that forgetting can result from both interference and repression; however, they are not sure whether memories ever actually disappear.

Figure 3.16
The correspondence between letters and numbers on a telephone dial provides a ready-made device for adding meaningfulness to a group of numbers. Although the example shown here is fictitious, businesses do often try to get a phone number that can readily be converted to a word associated with their product or service. If you have trouble remembering your own or a friend's number, you might try creating your own memory device.

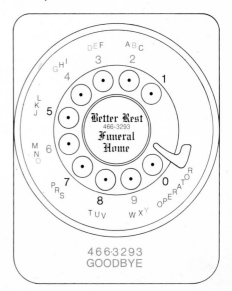

extent in order to remember things better. All these factors are related to the efficient organization of memory and to the principle of chunking information into easily handled packages. The factors include meaningfulness, association, lack of interference, and degree of original learning.

The more *meaningful* something is, the more easily it will be remembered. For example, you would be more likely to remember a series of six letters (such as LHATEH) if they formed a word (HEALTH). Such a meaningful collection of information is easily handled as a single chunk. Similarly, things are remembered more vividly if they are *associated* with a number of other items in memory or if they are associated with a strong emotional experience. As pointed out earlier, the more categories a memory is indexed under, the more accessible it is. If an input is analyzed and indexed under many categories, it will have many associations, each of which can serve as a trigger for the memory. And if it was originally accompanied by distinct sounds, smells, tastes, textures, and so on, a repetition of any of these experiences could quickly trigger the memory. Thus, the more senses used when trying to memorize something, the better it will be stored and retrieved.

For similar reasons, the best way to firmly protect a memory

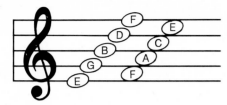

Figure 3.17
Memorization of the locations of musical notes on the staff has long been aided by this popular mnemonic device. The notes that fall in the spaces spell the word "face," and the notes that fall on the lines provide the initial letters for the sentence, "Every good boy does fine."

against interference is to *overlearn* it—to keep on learning it even when you think you know it well. In this way it acquires more associations, and it becomes organized into larger and larger chunks. Information is also more easily remembered if it is not subjected to interference. Thus, when trying to memorize something, it is not a good idea to try to memorize similar information at the same time, for the two will interfere with one another.

One method of improving one's memory is to take advantage of the need for meaning and association in memory by using *mnemonic devices.* All mnemonic devices attempt to relate material to be memorized to some information already in memory. For example, music students are taught the notes that fall in the spaces on a music staff by memorizing the word FACE: the notes that occupy the spaces are F, A, C, and E.

The oldest mnemonic scheme is to imagine that the various items to be learned are located in different physical locations. For example, if you wanted to memorize a poem, you might mentally walk through your house and place each line of the poem in corners, on chairs, and so on. To recall the lines, you would mentally walk through the house again, looking in the corners and on the chairs. This system was so necessary to the ancient Greeks (who frequently made long public speeches) that buildings were designed exclusively for the purpose of placing sections of speeches to be memorized in the corners and against pillars.

CENTRAL PROCESSING OF INFORMATION

If storage and retrieval were the only processes in the handling of information, human beings would be little more than glorified tape recorders or adding machines. But, in fact, human beings are capable of doing things with information that make the most complex computers seem clumsy in comparison. These processes— thinking and problem solving—are most impressive when they show originality or creativity.

Thinking

Thinking may be viewed as the changing and reorganizing of memory in order to create new information. By thinking humans are able to put together any combination of words from memory and come up with sentences that have never before been devised—such as this one.

Units of Thought   The processes of thought depend on several kinds of devices, which might be described as the units of thought. These units include images, symbols, concepts, and rules.

The most primitive unit of thought is the *image,* a sort of pictorial representation of a specific event or object. The representation is not usually a photographic copy but rather shows only the "highlights" of the original. For example, if you try to visualize the home you lived in as a small child, you will recall only a few critical elements—perhaps a very large bed or an unusual window.

A more abstract unit of thought is the *symbol,* or representation of a thing or a quality. The most common symbols in thinking are the words that constitute language; every word is a symbol that stands for something other than itself. An image represents a specific sight or sound, whereas a symbol may have a number of meanings. Because a symbol differs from the thing it represents, it can cause reactions or thoughts without the presence of the thing itself. For example, a

Figure 3.18
An interesting approach to the use of symbols is provided in this painting by the modern surrealist René Magritte. Images of four objects are shown in a window frame and are labeled as though they were on a blackboard. Note, however, that three of the words do not correspond to the pictures with which they are paired. Magritte is pointing out how arbitrary words are as symbols: Why shouldn't the symbol "door" stand for a horse? Magritte is also suggesting associations between these words and objects—might not both a clock and the wind be symbols of the fleeting passage of time? What do the other pairings in this painting suggest to you?

skull and crossbones signals poison, but the poison is not in the picture itself. Numbers, a question mark, and the flag are all familiar symbols of ideas that have no concrete existence.

When a symbol is used as a label for a whole class of objects or events with common attributes, it is called a *concept*. "Animals," "music," "religion," and "trees" are examples of concepts based on the common attributes of many objects in each category. The concept "animal" separates those things that are mobile organisms from things such as automobiles or carrots. It can be the task of a lifetime to identify the common attributes described by such abstract concepts as "justice," "democracy," "love," and "freedom."

The fourth and most complex unit of thinking is the *rule,* a statement of a relation between concepts. "Candy is sweet," "Snakes are dangerous," "The square root of 9 is 3," and "Thou shalt not kill" are examples of such statements of relationships.

Images, symbols, concepts, and rules are the building blocks of mental activity. They provide an economical and efficient way for human beings to represent reality, to manipulate and reorganize it, and to devise a new way of acting on it. One can, for example, think about several possible ways to spend an evening, weigh their pros and cons, and decide on one to follow, without having to try them all.

Kinds of Thinking   There are two different ways in which thought can work. The first way, called *directed thinking,* depends

Figure 3.19
This problem was devised by psychologist Edward De Bono. De Bono believes that conventional directed thinking is insufficient for solving new and unusual problems. He refers to traditional thought processes as "vertical thinking" and says that to solve problems like this one people need to think "laterally." This approach to problem solving requires use of nondirected thinking in order to generate new ways of looking at the problem situation. The answer to this problem is provided in Figure 3.25.

n old money-lender offered to cancel a merchant's debt and keep him from going to prison if the merchant would give the money-lender his lovely daughter. Horrified yet desperate, the merchant and his daughter agreed to let Providence decide. The money-lender said he would put a black pebble and a white pebble in a bag and the girl would draw one. The white pebble would cancel the debt and leave her free. The black one would make her the money-lender's, although the debt would be canceled. If she refused to pick, her father would go to prison. From the pebble-strewn path they were standing on, the money-lender picked two pebbles and quickly put them in the bag, but the girl saw he had picked up two black ones. What would you have done if you were the girl?

heavily on symbols, concepts, and rules and is a systematic and logical attempt to reach a specific goal, such as the solution to a problem. The other type, called *nondirected thinking,* depends more on images and consists of a free flow of thoughts through the mind, with no particular goal or plan.

Nondirected thinking is usually filled with imagery and feeling. Daydreams, fantasies, and reveries are typical examples. People often think in this way when they are relaxing or trying to escape temporarily from boredom or worry. But this kind of thinking may be the source of unexpected insights about one's goals and beliefs. Scientists and artists say that some of their best ideas emerge from drifting thoughts that occur when they have temporarily set aside a problem.

Directed thinking, on the other hand, is not a loose, drifting process. Directed thinking is deliberate and effortful. It is the means by which rules are formulated and followed, goals are worked toward and achieved, and problems are solved.

Problem Solving

One of the main functions of directed thinking is to solve problems—to mentally bridge the gap between a present situation and a desired goal. The gap may be between hunger and food, a column of figures and a total, lack of money and a bill to pay, or cancer and a cure. In all these cases, directed thinking is needed to get from the problem to the solution.

Strategies   Problem solving depends on the use of *strategies,* or specific methods, for approaching problems. One such strategy is to break the problem down into smaller, more easily solvable problems. For example, suppose you want to go to a concert by your favorite singer. You can break it down into three problems: (1) getting the money for the ticket, (2) getting the ticket, and (3) getting transportation to the concert. Working on all three smaller problems at once results in solving the overall problem.

A second strategy used in problem solving is working backward from the solution. Mystery writers often use this method—they decide the ending of their story (who the murderer really is) and work backward from there in devising the story.

A third strategy is to determine the end result desired and then to examine the various ways of getting it. If a businessman wanted to be in London for a conference on July 5, he might look into ships and planes as possible ways of getting there. If he then discovered that no ships were scheduled to arrive in London before July 7, he would contact various airlines to find a flight that would get him to London on the right day.

To determine what strategy to use in a particular situation, one might analyze the situation to see if it resembles some situation one has experienced in the past. A strategy that was successful in the past

Figure 3.20
Given the materials pictured here,
how would you go about mounting the
candle vertically on a wooden wall in such
a way that it can be lit? This problem was
formulated by Carl Dunker to test how well
people are able to overcome functional
fixedness. The solution is
presented in Figure 3.25.

Figure 3.20
Given the materials pictured here, how would you go about mounting the candle vertically on a wooden wall in such a way that it can be lit? This problem was formulated by Carl Dunker to test how well people are able to overcome functional fixedness. The solution is presented in Figure 3.25.

is considered likely to be useful in the present. The more unusual the problem, the more difficult it is to devise a strategy for dealing with it.

Set   There are times when certain useful strategies become cemented into the problem-solving process. When a certain strategy becomes habitual, it is called a *set*—you are "set" to treat problems in a certain way. When a set interferes instead of helps in problem solving, it is called *rigidity*. You probably know the riddle, "What is black, white, and read all over? A newspaper." When you say the riddle, the word "read" sounds like "red," and most people cannot guess the answer. They are set and rigid. Black and white are colors, so "read" must be a color, too. If you asked, "What is read by people everyday and is black and white?" the correct answer would probably come much easier.

One form of set that can interfere with problem solving is called *functional fixedness,* or the inability to imagine new functions for familiar objects. In experiments on functional fixedness, people are asked to solve a problem that requires use of a familiar object in an unfamiliar way. Because they are set to use the object in the familiar way, they tend to pay attention only to the features of the object that relate to its everyday use (see Figure 3.20).

Another type of rigidity occurs when a person makes a wrong assumption about the problem. In Figure 3.21, for example, the problem is to connect the dots with four lines and without lifting your pencil. Many people have trouble with this problem because they falsely assume that they must stay within the area of the dots.

A third type of rigidity is encountered by people trying to solve the problem presented in Figure 3.22. To solve this problem, people must overcome their desire to use the most direct methods because the solution involves going through several intermediate steps before the goal is reached.

Rigidity can be overcome if the problem solver realizes that his strategy is not working and that perhaps he should try to look at the problem in other ways. The more familiar the situation, the more

Figure 3.21
Connect these dots with four straight lines without lifting your pencil. The solution appears in Figure 3.25.

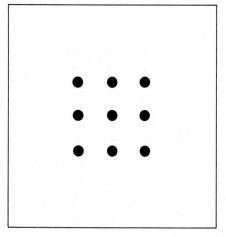

Figure 3.22
How would you go about solving this problem: Eight soldiers need to cross a river, but the only way to cross is in a small boat in which two children are playing. The boat can carry at most two children or one soldier. How do the soldiers get across? You'll find the answer in Figure 3.25.

likely that one will resort to habit. Rigidity is less likely to occur with unusual problems.

Creativity

Creativity is the ability to process information in such a way that the result is somehow new, original, and meaningful. All problem solving requires creativity and originality to some extent, but creative thinking is most apparent in both scientific discovery and artistic production. Psychologists do not know all the reasons why some people are more able to think creatively than others. They have, however, identified a few aspects of thinking that seem to be very much involved in creativity. Among these factors are flexibility, persistence, and the ability to recombine elements to achieve insight.

Flexibility   Flexibility is the ability to overcome rigidity. Psychologists who try to test creativity often use tests designed to assess this aspect of a person's thinking. One such test is shown in Figure 3.23. The individual is asked to name a word that each set of three words has in common. In order to arrive at the correct answer, he must be able to look at the words in all their possible uses. Another test of flexibility is to ask people all the uses they can imagine for a single object, such as a brick or a paper clip. The more uses one can devise, the more flexible one is said to be. Whether such tests *are* good indicators of creativity has not yet been determined. Nevertheless, it is obvious that inflexible, rigid thinking leads only to unoriginal, uncreative solutions, if it leads to any solutions at all.

Persistence   Creativity in problem solving is often the result of persistent use of flexibility, especially with problems that are highly unfamiliar. Such persistent application of varying problem-solving

Figure 3.23
A test devised to measure flexibility in thinking. The task is to name a single word that all three words on a line have in common. For example, the answer to the first item is "foot." (The other answers are given in Figure 3.25.) The ability to come up with meaningful answers on this test is believed to be related to creativity, in that creativity is thought to involve putting things together in unusual, unexpected ways.

1.	stool	powder	ball
2.	blue	cake	cottage
3.	man	wheel	high
4.	motion	poke	down
5.	line	birthday	surprise
6.	wood	liquor	luck
7.	house	village	golf
8.	card	knee	rope
9.	news	doll	tiger
10.	painting	bowl	nail
11.	weight	wave	house
12.	made	cuff	left
13.	key	wall	precious
14.	bull	tired	hot
15.	knife	up	hi
16.	handle	hole	police
17.	plan	show	walker
18.	hop	side	pet
19.	bell	tender	iron
20.	spelling	line	busy

strategies is referred to as the *trial-and-error* approach. Trial and error was studied in a classic experiment with cats conducted by E. L. Thorndike. He presented cats with the problem of finding a way out of cagelike boxes in order to obtain food. The cats seemed to behave randomly until they happened to pull a chain that allowed them to escape. Upon being placed back in the box several times, the cats gradually learned to pull the chain rather than trying other behaviors. From these experiments, Thorndike concluded that trial and error is an important aspect of problem solving.

Recombination   When the elements of a problem are familiar but the required solution is novel, it may be achieved by a mental rearrangement of the elements. This approach also has been shown in animals. Wolfgang Köhler placed chimpanzees in cages where food was out of reach but where material was available that could be useful in getting it. For example, the food was hung from the ceiling and a box was nearby; the animals needed only to stand on the box to reach the food. Köhler noted that the chimps appeared to suddenly realize the solution to their problem. He thus concluded that problem solving involves a mental rearrangement of important elements.

Such *recombination* seems to be particularly vital in creativity. Many creative people have said that no poem, no truly great painting, no original invention has ever been produced by someone who has not spent years of study and discipline in his subject. The creative person is able to take the information that has been compiled by others and himself and to put it together in a totally new way.

A famous example of such recombination is Samuel Taylor Coleridge's unusual poem, "Kubla Khan." Analysis of the poem has shown that almost every word and phrase came from Coleridge's past reading or experience. These words and phrases floated about, combined, and recombined in Coleridge's mind during a period of nondirected thinking—a drug-induced sleep. Coleridge awoke with the entire poem in his mind. As he rapidly wrote the poem down, he was interrupted by a visitor, and the rest of the poem was lost forever.

Insight   The sudden emergence of a solution by recombination of elements is called *insight*. Insight usually occurs with problems that have been particularly resistant to all problem-solving efforts and strategies. The scientist or artist reaches a point of high frustration and temporarily abandons the task. Then, when he is absorbed in some other activity, the answer seems to appear out of nowhere. The recombination process apparently continues to work on the problem unconsciously.

This same sequence has been found to occur in all instances of insight: Intense work on a problem is followed by high frustration, abandoning of the problem, and the sudden arrival of the solution. The achievement of insight seems to be enhanced if the third step

In Xanadu did Kubla Khan
A stately pleasure-dome decree:
Where Alph, the sacred river, ran
Through caverns measureless to man
    Down to a sunless sea.
So twice five miles of fertile ground

Figure 3.24
The poem "Kubla Kahn," according to its author Samuel Taylor Coleridge, was dreamed during an opium-induced sleep. Coleridge estimated that he had two or three hundred lines in mind when he awoke, but he had written no more than fifty-four of them when he was interrupted by a visitor. Coleridge compared the loss of the rest of the poem to the loss of an image on a still pool of water when a rock is thrown into it. As the text points out, this famous poem resulted from a recombination in Coleridge's mind of a number of memories, experiences, and daily events.

(abandonment) involves relaxation, sleeping, daydreaming, or some other form of nondirected thinking that allows the "unconscious" processes to take over.

It has been suggested that the period of high frustration that the creative person must go through to achieve insight is somehow linked to the incidence of "insanity" among artists. The inability to solve a problem or to break down a creative "block" may be so frustrating that the artist cannot handle it. Among the many creative people who suffered from psychological disorder were Jean-Jacques Rousseau, Sir Isaac Newton, Guy de Maupassant, Robert Schumann,

Franz Liszt, Feodor Dostoyevsky, Vincent Van Gogh, and William Blake. The question has been asked, were these men creators because they were neurotic, or were they neurotic because of the frustration of creation?

SUMMARY

1. Information processing involves three steps: input from the senses, central processing (memory, thought), and output in the form of behavior.

2. Two processes that help narrow down inputs are selective attention and feature extraction. Selective attention is the ability to pick and choose among various incoming channels, focusing on some and ignoring others. Channels are chosen when they help satisfy needs, are unusual, or relate to one's interests. Feature extraction is the ability to respond to specific characteristics of a given input and to ignore others.

3. The shortest form of memory is sensory storage, which lasts less than a second. Next is short-term memory, which retains information for half a minute at most. Items stored in short-term memory are quickly forgotten if they are not rehearsed or transferred to long-term memory.

4. Long-term memory contains information that has some significance. There are two theories as to how memories are stored: the theory that specific brain molecules store chemically coded information, and the idea that inputs cause changes in the connections between message-carrying cells in the brain. It is believed that however memories are stored, they are distributed throughout wide areas of the brain.

5. Retrieval is essential if memory is to be useful; consequently, memory must be organized. Retrieval takes two forms: recognition and recall. Recall is an active reconstructive process that may give rise to such errors as confabulation, in which memories are reconstructed incorrectly.

6. Forgetting may possibly be caused by decay, interference, or repression. Decay is the fading away of a memory and, if it occurs at all, is not the main reason for forgetting. Interference occurs when new or old information blocks the memory of a related piece of information. In repression, access to information has been blocked.

7. Information is stored better and is more easily retrieved when (1) it is organized into meaningful chunks; (2) it has many paths, or associations, leading to it; and (3) it has been overlearned.

8. Thinking is the process of reorganizing and rearranging the information in memory to produce new information or ideas. The units of thought are images, symbols, concepts, and rules.

9. Thinking may be directed or nondirected. Directed thinking is deliberate and effortful, as in problem solving and decision making.

Nondirected thinking is more loose and passive, as in daydreaming and reverie.

10. Problem solving is bridging the gap between a present situation and a desired goal by means of specific strategies. When strategies become habitual, they can hamper the problem-solving process. This difficulty is called rigidity.

11. Creativity is the ability to manipulate information to produce something new, original, and meaningful. Flexibility, persistence, and the ability to recombine elements to achieve insight seem to be important aspects of creativity.

ACTIVITIES

1. Mentally determine where the light switches in your home are located and keep track of them in your head. Do you have to use visual images to count the switches? To keep track of the number? If not, could you do it with images if you wanted to?

2. How would you go about memorizing the lyrics to a popular song? State capitals? Edgar Allan Poe's "The Raven"? The parts of the brain and their functions? Would you make up rhymes to fit the material?

Figure 3.25
Solutions to the problems presented in the chapter. Note that in each case the solution requires breaking certain habits of thought. (a) In the De Bono money-lender problem, it is difficult to imagine that control of the situation can be taken out of the hands of the powerful money-lender. (b) Solving the Dunker candle problem requires one to look at the matchbox and candle box as more than containers to be discarded. The presence of the useless piece of string usually serves to confuse problem solvers. (c) As the text points out, the solution to this problem is blocked if the person avoids going beyond the boundaries of the dots. (d) The answers to the test of flexibility require that the individual ignore common associations and look for unusual ones. (e) The first steps in solution of the river problem. Once the solver discovers the first step in the problem's solution, he may become further bogged down if he doesn't realize the lengthy cyclical nature of the process required.

a. hen the girl put her hand into the bag to draw out the fateful pebble, she fumbled and dropped it, where it was immediately lost among the others. "Oh," she said, "well, you can tell which one I picked by looking at the one that's left." The girl's lateral thinking saved her father and herself.

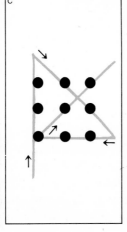

1.	foot	11.	light
2.	cheese	12.	hand
3.	chair	13.	stone
4.	slow	14.	dog
5.	party	15.	jack
6.	hard	16.	man
7.	green	17.	floor
8.	trick	18.	car
9.	paper	19.	bar
10.	finger	20.	bee

Would you assign letters or numbers to parts of the material? Would you make up an easy-to-recall story and include the material in it?

3. Try to remember what you were doing on this day two years ago. As you probe your memory, verbalize the mental steps you are going through. What does this exercise tell you about your thought processes?

4. Suppose you wanted to put together a jigsaw puzzle. What are the problem-solving strategies you might use? Which one do you think would work the best?

5. Solve this problem: A sloppy man has twenty blue socks and twenty brown ones in his drawer. If he reaches for a pair of socks in the middle of the night, how many must he pull out to be sure he has a matched pair? How long did it take you to solve the problem? Can you identify what steps you went through in your mind in order to solve it?

6. In the middle of an ordinary activity, like reading a book, stop for a moment and listen for sounds you normally block out. Jot down the sounds you hear and try to identify them. Why don't you usually hear them? Under what circumstances would you notice them?

7. Ask several friends to take a silent walk with you. When you return, ask everyone to join you in writing down the things you saw on your walk. Compare the writings. Try to find out why each person's notes are different.

8. Relax and engage in nondirected thinking—let your thoughts wander. Things may come into your mind that you thought you had forgotten or that you didn't know you knew. Or, reflect on a recent dream you had—where might the various images have come from? You may begin to see the vast amount of information you have stored in your brain.

9. You and your friends can test the way your memories are organized by playing a popular game called Categories. Make a grid with five columns and five rows, and put a category, such as fruits or furniture, at the top of each column. Now pick five random letters, and assign one to each row. Give yourselves five minutes to think of an item starting with each letter for each category and fill in the boxes in the grid. (Example: If your letters are A, G, P, O, and B, your entries under "fruit" might be apple, grape, peach, orange, and banana.)

10. Try the following game to demonstrate the reconstructive aspects of recall. (You will need at least seven or eight people—the more the better.) Before you gather the group together, write or copy a very short (not more than three or four paragraphs) story containing a fair amount of descriptive details. Memorize, as best you can, the story, and whisper it to one member of the group, making sure the others are out of earshot. Then instruct your listener to whisper the story to another player, and so on until all the players have heard it. When the last person has been told the story, have him repeat it

aloud to the entire group. Then read the original story from your written copy. Chances are good that the two versions are quite a bit different. Discuss among yourselves how, when, and why the story changed.

SUGGESTED READINGS

DE BONO, EDWARD. *The Mechanism of Mind.* New York: Simon & Schuster, 1969. A nonscientific book about how to use your mind effectively. It is particularly instructive about the nature of memory and models.

FABUN, DON. *Communication: The Transfer of Meaning.* Rev. ed. Beverly Hills, Calif: Benziger Bruce & Glencoe, 1968 (paper). A graphic and stimulating analysis of how communication between people is affected by selective attention, use of symbols, different meanings of concepts, and the making of inferences.

GHISELIN, B. (ed.). *The Creative Process.* New York: New American Library, 1952 (paper). An excellent selection of statements by creative people about their own processes of invention.

HALACY, D. S., JR. *Man and Memory.* New York: Harper & Row, 1970. A clearly written, enjoyable presentation of some of the most important research done on memory. Halacy also covers the various theories of memory, the experiments on memory transfer, and the effects of drugs on memory.

HUNTER, I. M. L. *Memory: Facts and Fallacies.* Baltimore: Penguin, 1964 (paper). An interesting introduction to the study of human memory. Hunter surveys a good deal of experimental literature, dating back to the nineteenth century.

HUTCHISON, ELIOT D. *How to Think Creatively.* New York: Abington Press, 1949 (paper). This book is deceptively titled. Actually, it is a fascinating account of the role insight has played in the work of famous creative thinkers.

LURIA, A. R. *The Mind of a Mnemonist.* New York: Basic Books, 1968. This book is about a man Luria met who could remember anything, any amount, for any length of time. Luria, a Russian psychologist, tried to understand the mnemonist's mind.

WATSON, JAMES D. *The Double Helix.* New York: Atheneum, 1968 (paper). An intensely personal account of the process of the discovery of the DNA structure by a leading contemporary scientist.

4
States of Consciousness

What is it like to think, to remember, to plan, to imagine, to decide? What ideas, emotions, and perceptions are roaming through your awareness at this minute? All these mental sensations that you are experiencing right now make up your *consciousness*.

But what exactly is consciousness? If you could answer this question, you would solve a problem philosophers have been working on for centuries. One of the first descriptions of this elusive phenomenon was offered by philosopher John Locke, and it is still useful: "Consciousness is the perception of what passes in a man's own mind." This description implies that consciousness is the ability of the mind to be aware of itself. Consciousness thus enables you to recall information from memory, to daydream, to worry, to examine your emotions, to solve problems, and to muse on your environment as you see it.

Nevertheless, this definition leaves several questions unanswered: Is consciousness a kind of nonphysical substance that permeates the brain and controls the physical body? Or is it a by-product of the physical workings of the brain that would exist in any organism with a complex enough brain?

But even though philosophers and psychologists cannot decide what consciousness is, they do at least agree on a few things about it. They know, for example, that consciousness is limited, that it actively constructs experiences, that it can come apart, and that it can take many forms.

CONSCIOUSNESS IS LIMITED

Consciousness is limited in that people are not aware of much that goes on, inside and outside their bodies. Automatic processes, such as breathing, take care of much of behavior. These processes are very handy—it would be virtually impossible to live if one had to consciously control each breath, each step when walking or running, or

Figure 4.1
Each person experiences the world in a different way, and the same person experiences it differently at different times. As you go through this chapter, you will notice presentations of this scene as recreated through the consciousnesses of seven different artists. These illustrations help to demonstrate the uniqueness of each person's consciousness.

79

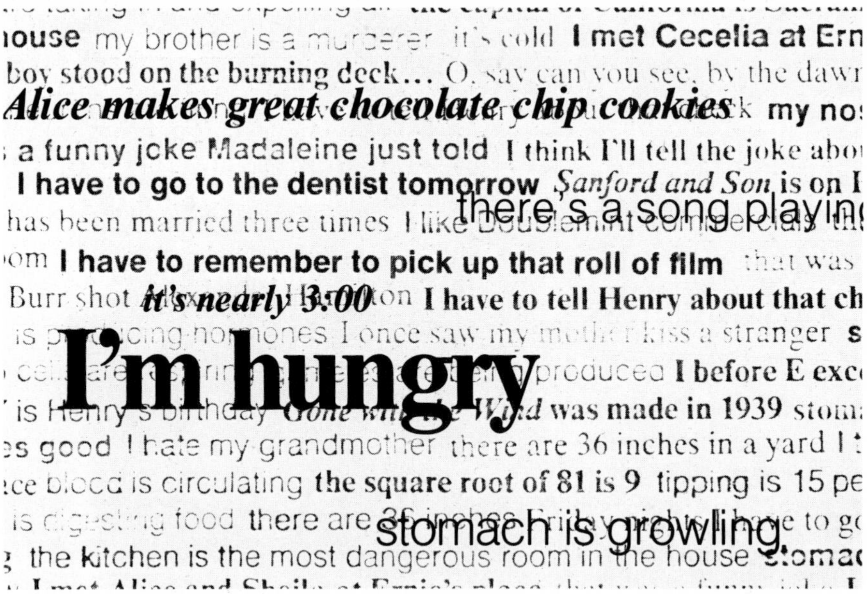

Figure 4.2
Consciousness is not infinite in its range. Some things can never be made conscious. And of the items that are available to consciousness, only a few can be focused on at once. Consciousness has therefore been compared to a searchlight: It illuminates powerfully, but only a small area at a time.

the capital of California is Sacram... ouse my brother is a murderer it's cold **I met Cecelia at Ern** boy stood on the burning deck... O, say can you see, by the dawn *Alice makes great chocolate chip cookies* k my no a funny joke Madaleine just told I think I'll tell the joke abo **I have to go to the dentist tomorrow** *Sanford and Son* is on there's a song playing has been married three times I like Dousle...nt commercials om **I have to remember to pick up that roll of film** that was Burr shot *it's nearly 3:00* ...ton **I have to tell Henry about that ch** is producing hormones I once saw my mother kiss a stranger **s** cel...are ...produced **I before E exc** is Henry's birthday *Gone with the Wind* was made in 1939 stom... good I hate my grandmother there are 36 inches in a yard I ... ce blood is circulating **the square root of 81 is 9** tipping is 15 pe is digesting food there are stomach is growling the kitchen is the most dangerous room in the house stoma

I'm hungry

each movement in tying a shoelace or taking a shower. Even complex behaviors can become automatic, or unconscious: It is possible to play the guitar, sing, and read music simultaneously, even though all three of these behaviors are complex skills that must be learned separately.

Sometimes, however, this kind of unconsciousness is a disadvantage. For example, many people use certain words or phrases repeatedly without knowing it. One person may say "uh" a lot, and another may punctuate his phrases with "you know." If one of your friends has such a habit, stop him and point it out (tactfully), then let the conversation continue. You will probably find that, even though you have made him temporarily aware of what he is doing, it will be extremely difficult for him to stop or even to keep noticing that he is still doing it.

Automatic behaviors such as habits are readily accessible to consciousness—you can notice them if you try. Other automatic processes are not available to awareness—for example, you cannot focus on the functioning of your liver. More importantly, though, many thoughts, feelings, and memories can occur outside of awareness. A person may act on these unconscious feelings and find it hard to explain or understand his behavior. Sigmund Freud believed that most of human behavior is directed by such unconscious desires, feelings, impulses, and needs. (His theory of personality is described in Chapter 12.)

CONSCIOUSNESS IS AN ACTIVE PROCESS

People often assume that consciousness is nothing more than an awareness of objects and events in their environment—a mere passive acceptance of information sent to the brain by the sense organs. Scientists have shown, however, that awareness of the world

Figure 4.3
A demonstration of the constructive nature of consciousness. Hold the book out at arm's length, close your left eye, and focus your right eye on the center of the X. As you slowly pull the book toward you, you should find a position at which the red spot disappears. The image of the red spot is now falling on an area at the back of your eye called, for obvious reasons, the blind spot. The image disappears because there are no light-sensitive cells in this area; the blind spot is the place where nerve fibers from the eye exit to the brain. The fact that no one is normally aware of this "hole" in his vision shows why consciousness can be said to be an active, constructive process.

is not a simple mirror reflection of external reality. Rather, consciousness is an active process that constructs a view of reality from bits and pieces of information provided by the senses. This does not mean that you "make up" reality but rather that there are certain active processes that you use to gain, enhance, and perfect your picture of the world.

The active nature of consciousness can be seen in animals such as porpoises and bats. These animals are able to send out high-frequency sounds and to monitor the echoes from these sounds. By such *echolocation,* these animals actively identify objects and obstacles in their environments. Most animals wait for environmental information to come to them—they wait for the sights, sounds, smells, and so on to reach them, then they interpret the information. But bats and porpoises can readily perceive an object's size, shape, location, movement, and distance without seeing, smelling, or hearing it because they actively "reach out" and find it.

Echolocation can be used to some extent by man—blind people have been using it for ages. When a blind man taps his white cane, he is doing more than just feeling for obstacles. He is sending out sound waves that echo back to him in different ways depending on the nearness and size of objects. Blind people can thus actively try to make up for their missing visual sense.

Sensation, the gathering of information by the eyes, ears, and other sense organs, is only the first process of consciousness. It is followed by *perception,* the organization of information into meaningful wholes. *Thought,* or *cognition,* is the reorganization of information within the brain. (Sensation and perception are described in detail in Chapter 2; cognition is presented in Chapter 3.)

When you look at and touch a table, how do these three processes work? First, the information about the object's shape, size, color, texture, and other such attributes reaches your brain through your senses. Perceptual processes take this information and create a whole picture of the object in your mind. It is something you know—a table. You have automatically sifted through memories and have quickly identified this particular object as a table. Even though you have never seen this individual table before, you still know it is a table because you have been able to build up a concept of what a table is in your mind.

By such cognitive processes you not only construct concepts of objects but concepts of concepts: Tables are put together with other objects to form the concept of furniture. Furniture is only one type

of man-made object, and so on. In this way you are able to contemplate simple objects and to think abstractly about their relationships with other objects in the world.

The range of contemplation can extend infinitely—from "tables and chairs" to "furniture" and "manufactured objects," to "industry," "nature," "society," and "the universe"—there are no limits. In addition, the mind can work in a variety of ways. It may focus intently on a single object outside, or it may drift aimlessly over information already stored in the brain. It may control a car traveling at seventy miles an hour while it simultaneously carries on a conversation. One of the surprising results of this enormous flexibility is that the mind does not always stay in one piece.

CONSCIOUSNESS CAN COME APART

Usually people feel and act as though they are one complete unit. In some cases, however, they may start feeling and acting as though they are split into parts. This phenomenon is called *dissociation.* Dissociation occurs when a person seems to have more than one consciousness operating simultaneously. Extreme examples of dissociation can be seen in people with split brains or with multiple personalities.

The Split Brain

The brain physically consists of two halves (see Chapter 5). Each side, or hemisphere, dominates one-half of the body: The left hemisphere receives and sends messages to the right side, and the right hemisphere does the same for the left side. Although many of the functions of both sides are similar, studies on hundreds of brain-damaged patients have shown that each hemisphere seems to have certain specialized responsibilities. Thus, in most people the left hemisphere is responsible for logical thinking and speech, whereas

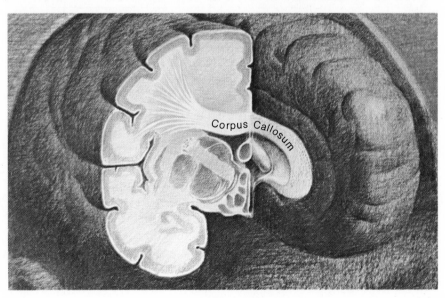

Figure 4.4
The corpus callosum, the band of nerve fibers that connects the two halves of the upper part of the human brain. Information received by one side of the brain becomes available to the other side by crossing the corpus callosum. Cutting this tract, as is sometimes done to prevent epileptic seizures from spreading over the whole brain, essentially produces two consciousnesses in one body.

the right hemisphere is more involved in spatial orientation, artistic talents, recognition of faces, and intuition.

Normally, these consciousnesses work together as one. But when the nerve fibers that connect the two sides of the brain are cut, as they are in certain operations for epilepsy, two distinct consciousnesses emerge. Because of the specialization of functions, only the consciousness on the left side is able to speak, although the right-side consciousness can communicate by using the left hand.

The two consciousnesses tend to go to sleep and wake up at about the same time, but they have largely independent memories and do not seem to have access to each other's awareness. If the right-half consciousness is shown an erotic picture, the person's body will react—perhaps by blushing. If the left-hand consciousness is then asked why the blushing occurred, the person becomes confused and cannot readily explain why he blushed.

In general, the person who undergoes the operation is able to function quite well in everyday situations because the two hemispheres are both able to receive the same information about the

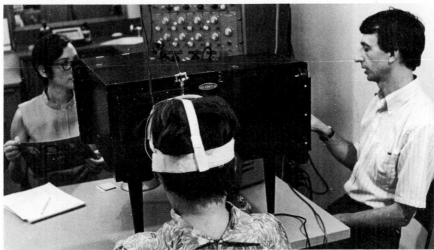

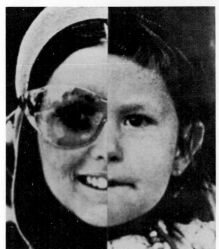

Figure 4.5
This apparatus is used to study the functioning of people who have undergone split-brain surgery. Here, a housewife who underwent the operation is being shown a series of faces to identify. The apparatus is designed to direct the right side of the picture to the left half of the brain and the left side of the picture to the right half of the brain. When the housewife is shown a picture made up of two split faces, a woman's on the left and a child's on the right, she says she has seen only the woman's face. Why? Because the right side of the brain controls speech, she reports what is in the left visual field. When, however, she is asked to use her right hand to indicate which picture she saw, she points to the child's face. This is because the left side of the brain, which saw only the child, controls the right hand.

environment. It is only in the experimental setting that researchers are able to discover the differences in functioning between the two.

Multiple Personalities

There are several well-documented cases of multiple consciousnesses in people who have not had split-brain surgery and are not suffering from any known brain damage. One of the most striking instances is the occurrence of *multiple personality,* a rare condition in which one person shows two or more separate consciousnesses with distinct personalities. Unlike the individuals with a split brain, these people do not have consciousnesses corresponding to specific brain areas.

A famous case of multiple personality was described in the book *The Three Faces of Eve.* A twenty-five-year-old woman came to a psychiatrist for therapy, complaining of emotional problems and "severe and blinding headaches" followed by blackouts. The woman, whom the authors called Eve White, was an extremely self-controlled, shy, and conscientious person. During one of her therapy sessions, a strange expression suddenly came over her face, and she quickly put both hands to her head. After a moment, her hands

Figure 4.6
Scenes from a film version of *The Three Faces of Eve.* (a) Eve White, the shy, demure personality that decided to go to a therapist because of frequent headaches and blackouts. (b) Eve Black, the outgoing, fun-loving personality. (c) Jane, the personality that emerged after a long period of therapy.

dropped, she smiled brightly, and in a sparkling voice she said, "Hi there, Doc!" A second consciousness, whom the authors later called Eve Black, had appeared.

Eve Black's personality, speaking style, and even her walk were quite different from those of Eve White. She was childlike, fun-loving, and irresponsible. She reported that she was conscious at all times and could follow the thoughts, actions, and feelings of Eve White, but she could not participate in them and did not call them her own.

Eve White, on the other hand, became unconscious when Eve Black was in control; that was why Eve White reported periodic blackouts. Eve Black seemed to have had an independent conscious life since early childhood, when she would periodically "come out" and do mischievous deeds. But most of the time, Eve White was in control, and Eve Black could not gain control or come out at will.

After about a year of psychiatric treatment, a third consciousness emerged. This personality, who called herself Jane, was more mature, self-confident, and capable than either Eve. She did not exist before therapy and somehow seemed to grow out of the therapy process. Although she had access to the consciousnesses of both Eves, she did not have complete use of their knowledge and memories preceding her emergence. The therapist tried to use Jane's strengths to resolve the problems encountered by the two Eves.

Although there are several well-documented cases of multiple personality besides the case of Eve, the condition is rare. Several other, more common, psychiatric conditions also show dissociation. These conditions include some forms of schizophrenia, a severe mental disorder; amnesia, a temporary loss of the sense of self; and hysteria, loss of control over a limb or some part of the body, even though there is nothing physically wrong. Dissociation also occurs in normal people, during dreaming and hypnosis, for example.

ALTERED STATES OF CONSCIOUSNESS

It is usually assumed that everyone experiences things much in the same way. When someone acts as though his experience is different from that of other people, he may even be considered "crazy." But psychologists are discovering whole new realms of consciousness, in which perfectly normal people experience things in unusual ways. By examining these little-known states of consciousness, psychologists hope to understand how it can be useful for people to experience things differently if they choose to.

Sleep and Dreaming

Sleeping is one of man's most mysterious behaviors. Although people spend one-third of their lives asleep, no one really knows what sleep is or what purpose it serves. Most people think of sleep as a time when they are "unconscious" except for a few brief periods of dreaming. In the past twenty years, however, research has shown

that sleep is actually a different level of consciousness than waking experience. Everyone is mentally active during sleep, and everyone dreams, but most people remember little or nothing when awakened.

Psychologists have learned a great deal about sleep and dreaming by conducting sleep laboratories. In such laboratories, ordinary people report each night and are escorted to comfortable rooms where they will sleep. Electrodes from an electroencephalograph (EEG) machine are attached to the subjects so that their brain waves can be recorded.

From thousands of such studies researchers have shown that a person's EEG pattern changes consistently during the night as he goes from wakefulness to light sleep to deep sleep (see Figure 4.7). His brain waves show a regular cyclical pattern that occurs about every ninety minutes. First the brain waves indicate that he is falling into deeper and deeper sleep, then they return to the original pattern and start the cycle all over again.

REM Sleep   One group of sleep researchers discovered that during one stage of sleep a person's closed eyes usually begin to move rapidly back and forth. Because of these *rapid eye movements,* they called this stage *REM sleep.* In some ways this stage of sleep seems similar to being awake, but in other ways it seems to be a very deep sleep. The EEG pattern of REM sleep is similar to the pattern of people who are awake; on the other hand, people in REM sleep are often as

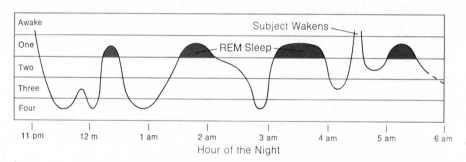

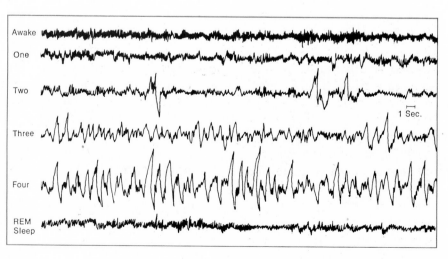

Figure 4.7

(*top*) A diagram showing the passage of a sleeper through the various stages of sleep over a seven-hour period. Note that after first falling asleep and after each REM period, the sleeper rapidly descends into the deepest stage of sleep and then gradually rises out of it. (*bottom*) The patterns of electrical activity (EEGs) in the brain that correspond to the various stages of sleep. The EEG pattern shown for being awake is one that occurs when the person is resting quietly with his eyes closed. It is referred to as the "alpha" pattern.

difficult to wake up as they are in the deepest stage of sleep. Because of these contradictory patterns, REM sleep has been called "paradoxical sleep"; the person seems to be almost awake and yet deeply asleep at the same time.

When researchers wakened sleepers during the REM periods and other stages of sleep, they found that it was during the REM periods that dreams with vivid visual imagery usually occurred. Subjects wakened during non-REM periods reported mental activity that was much less vivid—like drifting thoughts rather than dreams. It is believed that the rapid eye movements correspond to the movements the eyes make during the events of dreams.

Evidence also indicates that REM sleep is necessary for health. If people are awakened every time they begin REM sleep but are allowed to sleep as much as they want otherwise, they tend to make up those lost periods as soon as they have the chance. If they do not get the chance, they begin to show abnormal behavior when they are awake. They become anxious and irritable, have difficulty in concentrating, and in some cases have hallucinations and ravenous appetites. These negative behavioral changes disappear once the sleepers are allowed to regain their REM periods.

Dreams   It is believed by most psychologists that when a person dreams he becomes aware of unconscious thoughts and desires for a short time. It is as if people can experience the brain talking to itself in its own language. This language is the language of dreams, and it can reveal things the mind considers important.

The dreams a person is able to recall represent only a few of those that actually occur. Sleep researchers sometimes make a point of waking up their subjects near the end of each REM period to ask them what they were dreaming. Such research has shown that the first few dream periods are the hardest to recall in the morning and are concerned primarily with vague thoughts left over from the day's activities ("I was watching TV"). As the night wears on, dreams become more vivid and dramatic. It is the last type that occur closest to morning and that are most likely to be remembered.

Researchers who have recorded the contents of thousands of dreams have found that for the most part dreams occur in commonplace settings—living rooms, cars, streets, classrooms. Most dreams involve strenuous recreational activities or quiet, passive behaviors (sitting, watching) rather than work, study, or business. A large percentage of the emotions experienced in dreams are negative or unpleasant—apprehension, anger, sadness, and so on. Contrary to popular belief, dreams do not occur in a "split second" but rather correspond to the same time scale as they would in reality.

Dream Interpretation   Dreams often symbolically report about significant emotions, problems, and disturbances that are a part of a person's daily experience. By studying the dreams and the lives of

Figure 4.8

The paintings of Marc Chagall—this one is titled "I and the Village"—often have a dreamlike quality. Images are intermingled, and space, time, and color are rearranged in ways that are rarely experienced in a waking state but that seem natural in the dream state.

(Marc Chagall, *I and the Village*, 1911. Oil on canvas, 75 5/8" x 59 5/8". Collection, The Museum of Modern Art, New York. Mrs. Simon Guggenheim Fund.)

patients, psychiatrists have been able to translate the symbolic language each patient uses in his dreams.

The individual who has had the greatest influence on interpretation of dreams is Sigmund Freud, who felt that dreams had important hidden meanings, no matter how simple or mundane they appeared. He viewed dreams as expressions of unfulfilled wishes or frustrated yearnings. Through his method of interpretation he tried to break through the disguise of dream imagery and discover the true wishes and desires of the dreamer.

Freud's approach to dream interpretation was very much a part of his theory of personality. He felt that dreams were the language of the unconscious mind trying to express the dreamer's repressed sexual and aggressive desires.

Freud's interpretations of dream symbols were thus primarily sexual and were made in light of his theory of child sexuality

(described in Chapter 7). He interpreted most elongated pointed objects (such as pencils, sticks, knives, and pillars) as representing the penis, and he saw containers such as caves, boxes, and houses as symbols of the vagina. Symbols that were not sexual he saw as being related to childhood—as symbols of parents, for example.

Since Freud, many psychologists have come up with more extensive theories about the meaning of dreams. In general, they are dissatisfied with Freud's exclusive focus on childhood and sex. Carl Jung, for example, did not always look for hidden meanings but, rather, felt that dreams could be taken at their face value. Thus, if you dream that you are fighting with your best friend, it may indicate that you have an unresolved conflict with that friend that needs to be worked out. Similarly, a dream might represent what you *hope* may happen, or it may show what you are *afraid* might happen.

Calvin Hall, a contemporary psychologist, sees dreams as abstract thoughts converted in concrete and visible images. Thus, when someone tells his dreams to another person, he is actually communicating his thoughts. Hall points out that the purpose of dream interpretation is to translate the pictures back into ideas, thus providing a view of the dreamer's self-concept and of his attitude toward life. In this way dreams reveal the individual's most personal and intimate conceptions.

A person can learn to interpret his own dreams if he recognizes that they represent what his mind feels to be important. For example, many people dream of appearing in public wearing nothing but their underwear. To understand this dream, one need not take it literally. Instead, the dreamer might interpret it as meaning that he fears he is inadequate or unprepared for life. His unclothed state is a symbol representing the fear of being "naked" in a different sense—of having his private self exposed publicly.

In interpreting dreams it is important to remember that dream symbols vary from person to person—one symbol may signify innocence to one person, motherhood to another, and so on. The

Figure 4.9

Dream sequences designed by Salvador Dali for Alfred Hitchcock's film *Spellbound*. The strange dreams belong to "J. B.," a mysterious man with amnesia who also has a fear of creases in white surfaces (such as tablecloths). In analyzing J. B.'s dreams, a psychiatrist discovers that he has repressed memories of having witnessed two deaths: his brother's accidental death in childhood, and the recent murder of a man on a ski slope. The psychiatrist is able to connect the symbols in the dreams and in J. B.'s fears (creases in white resemble ski tracks) to cure his amnesia and to solve the mystery.

symbolism of dreams is a private language that each individual has invented for himself. The attempt to understand this language can teach a person quite a bit about himself.

Hypnosis

Hypnosis seems to be a form of altered consciousness in which a person gives some of the control of his thoughts and perceptions to another individual. By allowing the hypnotist to guide and direct one aspect of his consciousness, a person can be made conscious of things he is usually unaware of and unconscious of things he usually notices.

Hypnosis is popularly thought to put a subject to sleep, but actually the hypnotic trance is much different from sleep. In fact, the subject becomes highly receptive and responsive to certain internal and external stimuli. He is able to focus his attention on one tiny aspect of reality and to totally ignore all other inputs.

Psychologists who use hypnotism stress that the relationship between hypnotist and subject involves cooperation, not domination. The subject is not under the hypnotist's "power" and therefore cannot be forced to do things against his will. Rather, he is simply cooperating with the hypnotist by becoming particularly responsive to the hypnotist's suggestions. Together they try to solve a problem or to learn more about the workings of the subject's mind.

The hypnotist induces a trance by slowly persuading the subject to relax and to lose interest in external distractions. Trance induction may take only a few minutes or may involve months of interaction, depending on the purpose of the hypnosis.

Ever since hypnosis became widely known, many people have been skeptical about its reality. It is common for disbelievers to assert

Figure 4.10
Hypnosis, as depicted in a woodcut and an engraving from the late eighteenth and early nineteenth centuries. Hypnosis was originally called Mesmerism, after Anton Mesmer, its first proponent. Mesmer believed hypnosis to be some kind of psychic magnetic force. Later, it was thought of as artificially controlled sleep-walking. This form of consciousness is still not fully understood; in fact, some psychologists consider it to be nothing more than deliberate self-deception.

that hypnotized people are simply faking. However, one line of research has provided some convincing evidence that hypnosis is a real phenomenon.

In this research, a hypnotist was asked to put several people in a trance. Some of these people had been told to fake the trance, although the hypnotist did not know this. It was found that the subjects who had been told to fake acted differently from the rest after they were "hypnotized." The hypnotist told each subject that he would see a third person sitting in a chair that was actually empty. This third person was in fact standing *behind* the subject. When the faking subjects turned around and saw the third person, they said either that they saw no one or that they did not recognize the person they saw. The other subjects had a different reaction. When they saw the third person, they acted surprised and reported seeing two images of the same person. Such a reaction is referred to as *trance logic*. With trance logic a person readily perceives hallucinations suggested to him by the hypnotist and mixes them freely with perceptions based on real objects and events, without attempting to be logical. The fakers were exposed by their own efforts to respond in a conventionally logical way.

Hypnotists can also suggest things for their subjects to remember when the trance is over. These *post-hypnotic suggestions* can lead to particular behavior after the trance. For example, the hypnotist might suggest that after the person is awakened he will be unable to hear the word "psychology." When he comes out of the trance, the subject may report that some people around him are speaking strangely. They seem to leave out some words occasionally, especially when they are talking about topics involving the taboo word "psychology." The subject is not aware that part of his consciousness has been instructed to block out that word. Post-hypnotic suggestion has been found to be particularly helpful in changing unwanted behaviors, such as breaking bad habits.

A form of hypnosis may occur in everyday life when one becomes so entranced by another person—an orator, for example—that the rest of reality seems to slip away and all that exists is the speaker's words. At the other extreme, particularly boring stimuli can cause a trancelike state, as any long-distance truck driver knows.

About one person in twenty is particularly susceptible to hypnosis and can easily be put into a trance. Nevertheless, anyone can resist hypnosis by simply choosing not to open his consciousness to the hypnotist. It is also the case that a hypnotized person cannot be induced to directly do anything he would not or could not normally do when awake—he would not follow a command to jump off a building, for example, and he would not be able to play the piano if he had never learned how.

Many stage performers have used hypnosis to make themselves appear to have mystical abilities. Because people can lose awareness of some of their usual inhibitions while in a trance, stage hypnotists

have induced subjects to perform a wide variety of acts, from singing to barking to standing on their heads. Nevertheless, people will not behave in this manner unless they want to.

Meditation

When you hear the word meditation, you probably think of religion. It is true that the followers of certain Eastern religions practice meditation as a form of achieving a "higher consciousness." Many meditators report that they can separate their minds from their senses at will and that meditation can produce kinds of awareness that are free from worry. They say that they can experience something for the thousandth time as freshly as they did the first.

Perhaps the most dramatic display of meditative consciousness occurs in the Oriental martial arts, which include the swordsmanship of the samurai, aikido, and karate (a form of weaponless fighting). The secret of these disciplines seems to lie in perfect concentration. One aikido instructor tells his students to learn to maintain bodily, emotional, and physical calm by concentrating on a single spot in the lower abdomen. Using such concentration, his students are able, for example, to pass amazing tests of self-control. They are required to

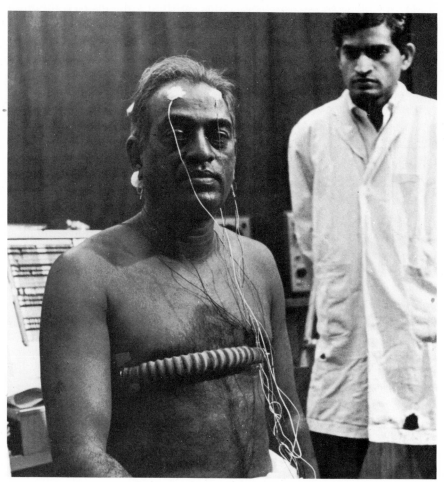

Figure 4.11
The measurement of bodily functions during meditation. It has been found that practiced meditators, such as this Indian yogi, are capable of producing physiological changes in themselves that are usually thought to be outside conscious control. Measurement, using the devices shown, has indicated that heart rate and oxygen consumption decrease during meditation and that alpha waves (see Figure 4.7) constitute the characteristic brain wave pattern. These alpha waves appear even when the meditator's eyes are open, although people normally exhibit alpha waves only when their eyes are closed. The conscious control of such internal functioning can be trained with the use of biofeedback, which is discussed in Chapter 6.

immerse themselves in an icy mountain stream in mid-winter and are able to do so without so much as trembling as long as they can maintain concentration on this central spot.

In studies of meditative concentration, people who have not meditated before have learned to meditate on a certain object. In one case subjects were taught to meditate on a blue vase. The participants soon reported that the color of the vase became very vivid and that time passed quickly. The people could not be distracted as easily as they normally might. Some people felt themselves merging with the vase. Others reported that their surroundings became unusually beautiful, filled with light and movement. All the meditators found the experience pleasant. After twelve sessions they all felt a strong attachment to the vase and missed it when it was not present during the next session.

Evidence that meditation is a different state than ordinary consciousness has come from studies on the bodily functions of yogis and Zen monks. Researchers found that during meditation distinct EEG patterns appeared and that the meditators were highly relaxed but awake. There were also indications that meditation reduced anxiety and other signs of stress. Some psychologists have suggested that meditation might thus prove to be an important technique for the maintenance of health, especially in the bustle of industrial society.

Hallucinations

Hallucinations are sensations or perceptions that have no direct external cause—they occur when your brain performs perceptual operations without any input from the outside.

When people are not permitted to see, hear, or touch for extended periods of time, they begin to see and hear things that are not present in the external environment. Because they are deprived

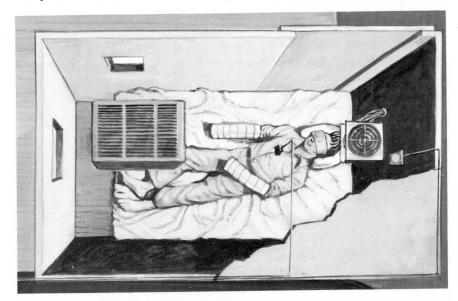

Figure 4.12

A classic series of experiments on boredom was conducted at McGill University in the 1950s. Subjects were paid $20.00 a day to live with as little sensory input as the experimenters could arrange. Gloves and cotton cuffs prevented input to the hands and fingers; a plastic visor diffused the light coming into the eyes; a foam pillow and the continuous hum of the air conditioner and fan made input to the ears low and monotonous. Except for eating and using the bathroom, the subjects did nothing but lie on the bed. After a day or so of this routine, subjects began to report hallucinations: geometrical shapes, abstract patterns repeated like a wallpaper design, feelings that another body overlapping with their own was lying beside them, cartoon sequences, or sometimes voices or music. Similar experiences are common in certain drug states.

(After "The Pathology of Boredom," by Woodburn Heron. © 1957 by Scientific American, Inc. All rights reserved.)

of sensory stimulation, they begin to have sensory experiences without any assistance from outside reality.

Hallucinations occur as a normal part of dreaming, hypnosis, deprivation of REM sleep, meditation, and the "trips" stimulated by certain drugs. They also often accompany periods of high emotion, concentration, or fatigue. In addition, hallucinations may occur as symptoms of certain physiological and psychological problems: drug withdrawal (the "DTs") and severe mental disorder, for example.

Most people are capable of hallucinations of some kind, even when they are awake. For instance, truck drivers on long hauls have been known to swerve to avoid stalled cars that did not really exist. Even daydreams often involve mild hallucinations.

Drug States

Many drugs are consumed because of their psychological effects. Some, such as tranquilizers, cause reduction of anxiety; others, such as stimulants, produce increased alertness. Of particular interest here, however, are those drugs classed as *hallucinogens,* or *psychedelics.* Such drugs are often used to alter awareness or to produce unusual states of consciousness.

Marijuana is a mild hallucinogen that has been used as an intoxicant among Eastern cultures for many centuries. Marijuana smokers often report that when they get "high" most of their perceptions are greatly enhanced—colors are brighter, smells are richer, foods taste better. Users often experience feelings of serenity, may become happy and talk or laugh a great deal, and may discover that even the most ordinary events and objects are suddenly more meaningful.

Marijuana can intensify unpleasant as well as pleasant experiences. If a person is frightened or unhappy when he takes the drug, these feelings may be increased enough to make his world, temporarily at least, very upsetting. Nervousness and irrational fears are commonly experienced.

Few reliable studies have been done on marijuana's effects. In the most famous study, seventeen college students were given marijuana for the first time. Only one student said he actually got high, but all performed less well than usual on tests of both intellectual ability and physical skills. Experienced users, on the other hand, showed no impairment of either intellectual abilities or of physical skills when they smoked marijuana.

LSD is the most potent of the hallucinogens and the one most studied in recent years. Its effects, although far more profound than those of marijuana, also seem to depend heavily on the people around the user, on where and when he takes the drug, on his previous experience, and on what he expects to happen. LSD usually produces a pronounced alteration in awareness, called a *trip,* which lasts for several hours. A trip often includes intense hallucinations and emotions that can range anywhere from intense happiness to

Figure 4.13
Drawings done by a man on an LSD trip. (a) 20 minutes after taking the drug: no effect yet. (b) 85 minutes after first taking the drug and 20 minutes after taking a second dose: The subject sees the model clearly but has some difficulty controlling the wide sweeping movements of his hand. (c) One hour later: The subject sees the model very vividly, with changed colors. He says, "I feel as if my consciousness is situated in the part of my body that is now active." (d) A few minutes later: "The outlines of the model are normal but those of my drawing are not. I pull myself together and try again: it's no good. I give up trying and let myself go at the third attempt." (e) Shortly after the fourth drawing: "I try again and produce this drawing with one flourish." (f) Two and three-quarter hours after first taking the drug: "The perspective of the room has changed, everything is moving . . . everything is interwoven in a network of color . . . The model's face is distorted to a diabolic mask." (g) Four and one-quarter hours: The subject is in a very happy state. As he attempts yet another portrait he says, "If I am not careful, I lose control of my movements." (h) Five and three-quarters hours: "It is probably because my movements are still too unsteady that I am unable to draw as I normally do . . . The intoxication is wearing off, but I can both feel and see it ebbing and flowing about me (now it only reaches to my knees); finally, only an eddying motion remains." (i) Eight hours: The effects of the drug have now worn off except for a few small waves (for example, sudden distortions of faces from time to time). The subject feels bewildered and tired. "I have nothing to say about the last drawing, it is bad and uninteresting."

extreme panic. Thoughts become vivid and generally seem to be beyond the individual's control—somewhat as in a dream.

While "tripping," a person may focus on a single object for hours as if seeing it and understanding it for the first time. For example, one person reported that he finally understood the meaning of an empty cola bottle and its relationship to the universe. These discoveries often lose their importance once the user "comes down" from his trip, but sometimes people find that their religious feelings have been increased or that their understanding of themselves has changed.

Research with hallucinogenic drugs is extremely limited because these substances are illegal and difficult to obtain for experimental purposes. Thus, it may be many years before their full benefits and dangers are known.

SUMMARY

1. Consciousness is difficult to define, but in general, it is the ability of the mind to be aware of itself and of external events.

2. Consciousness is limited, in that people are not conscious of much that goes on, inside and outside their bodies. It is, however, an active process, in which one's experience of reality is constructed rather than passively received.

3. Consciousness can be dissociated—split into parts. Dissociation occurs for people who have undergone split-brain operations or who have multiple personalities. It also occurs during dreaming and hypnosis.

4. The most common altered state of consciousness is dreaming. The stage of sleep in which vivid dreams occur is called REM sleep. Dreams often symbolically report about significant emotional problems and disturbances that are part of a person's daily experiences.

5. Hypnosis is an altered state of consciousness in which a subject becomes highly receptive to the suggestions of another person. He does so willingly and cannot be made to do anything he would not normally do while awake. Hypnosis was proved to be a real phenomenon by the discovery of trance logic.

6. Meditation is a state of consciousness involving high levels of concentration. Experienced meditators are able to achieve a high state of relaxation with greatly reduced anxiety.

7. Hallucinations often accompany altered states of awareness. They

are sensations or perceptions that have no direct external cause.

8. Among the drugs that alter awareness are hallucinogens, or psychedelics. Marijuana and LSD are the two most common of these drugs.

ACTIVITIES

1. What behaviors do you perform automatically? The chapter mentions breathing, walking, running, tying shoelaces, taking a shower, and using speech mannerisms. What are some others? Pick one of your automatic behaviors and pay close attention to how you perform it. What are the individual parts that make up the behavior? How does consciously thinking about the behavior affect your performance of it?

2. Keep track of your dreams for at least a week. Dreams are difficult to remember, so keep a paper and pencil by your bed. When you wake up after a dream, keep your eyes closed and try to remember it in your mind. Then write it down, including as much detail as you can. Also write down any ideas you may have about what the dream means and any feelings you may have about the dream. After you have kept track of your dreams for several days, ask yourself: Am I able to consciously control my dreams in any way? Am I better able to understand myself by examining my dreams?

3. Practice meditation for a half an hour to an hour every day for a week. Choose an object or monotonous sound and concentrate all your attention on it while sitting very still in a chair with both feet flat on the floor. You should be as relaxed as possible. What do you experience? Are you easily distracted? Do you feel any "dissociation"?

4. Ask a friend to balance a wooden rod on the index finger of each hand, one hand at a time. Generally, right-handed persons do better with the right hand, and left-handed persons with the left. Ask your friend to speak while balancing the rod and measure the time she or he is able to keep the rod balanced. How does talking affect balancing time for each hand? Why do you suppose you got these results?

5. Have you ever experienced a moment of dissociation, of feeling split into different parts or of "getting outside yourself" and observing your behavior? What were the circumstances of this experience? (Remember that dissociation is a normal aspect of certain states of consciousness.)

6. Have you ever hallucinated a sight or sound—perhaps when you were very tired or upset? What did you experience? Why do you suppose you created this particular hallucination?

7. Make a list of as many fairly common dream symbols as you can think of. Next to each symbol give an interpretation of what you think that symbol represents. Compare your interpretations with

those of other students in the class. Do you find any patterns of interpretations? Are interpretations by females different from interpretations by males?

8. As suggested in the chapter, hypnotized people will readily accept suggestions as long as they are not contrary to their beliefs or harmful. You can test this idea of suggestibility without knowing anything about hypnosis. Make a pendulum from a foot-long piece of string tied to a small rock or other weight. Suggest to your subject that the pendulum will, of its own accord, swing in a circle over the hand of a female and in a straight line over the hand of a male. You will probably notice that very young subjects will tend to make an obvious attempt to control the direction of the pendulum but that in older subjects attempts at conscious control of the action are missing or are well hidden. Write a report telling how successful you were in directing your subjects' actions. You might find that by being more mysterious—by telling your subjects that this is an experiment in ESP or the occult—you will be more effective in putting over this experiment.

9. Here is another simple experiment you can try to test suggestibility. Think of a lemon. Picture its shape and its yellowness. Smell the aroma. Now imagine a person starting to slice it in half. Visualize the knife slicing the skin and separating the two halves. Smell the increased aroma. How do the insides of your cheeks feel? Repeat the above sentences to a friend and see what kind of reaction you get. What is the difference between reading this description and hearing it? How willing were you to accept these suggestions? How willing were your subject(s)?

10. Many people argue in favor of repealing all drug laws. They maintain that an adult individual should have the right to decide for himself, without fear of punishment, what to do with, and to, his own body. Do you feel that most people would behave responsibly if all drugs, including narcotics, were available for sale? What does it mean to "behave responsibly"? Debate this issue with a friend, then reverse positions and continue the debate. How does this argument apply to such other issues as suicide and abortion?

SUGGESTED READINGS

CASTANEDA, CARLOS. *A Separate Reality*. New York: Simon & Schuster, 1971 (paper). In this sequel to his first book, *The Teachings of Don Juan: A Yaqui Way of Knowledge*, Castaneda describes his continuing efforts to learn to think in a new way, to move outside old patterns of thought learned in his own culture.

FARADAY, ANN. *Dream Power*. New York: Coward, McCann & Geoghegan, 1972. As an alternative to classical Freudian dream analysis, Farady explains the kinds of messages that dreams convey and gives the best procedures for decoding them into useful self-knowledge.

LUCE, GAY GAER, and JULIUS SEGAL. *Sleep.* New York: Coward, McCann & Geoghegan, 1966 (Lancer paperback). An enlightening sojourn into existing knowledge on the nature of sleep and dreams.

NARAJANO, C., and R. ORNSTEIN. *On The Psychology of Meditation.* New York: Viking, 1971. A comparative discussion on the wide range of meditative techniques and their relations to the control of internal body and brain states.

ORNSTEIN, ROBERT. *The Psychology of Consciousness.* New York: Viking, 1972. Ornstein explores the idea that man has two modes of consciousness, one in each brain hemisphere. Among the phenomena he discusses are meditation and biofeedback.

TART, C. T. (ed.). *Altered States of Consciousness.* New York: Wiley, 1969. A collection of fascinating readings on a wide range of topics, including dreaming, hypnosis, drugs, and meditation. Also included is a "fact sheet" on marijuana and many useful papers that are difficult to obtain elsewhere.

THIGPEN, C. H., and H. CLECKLEY. *The Three Faces of Eve.* New York: McGraw-Hill, 1957. An intriguing psychiatric account of a case of multiple personality. This book reads like a novel, and was, in fact, made into a movie.

THOMPSON, RICHARD F. (ed.). *Physiological Psychology.* San Francisco: Freeman, 1971. A collection of articles from *Scientific American* covering studies on split-brain patients, dreaming, drugs, the senses, brain functioning, memory, thought and language.

WEIL, ANDREW. *The Natural Mind.* Boston: Houghton Mifflin, 1972. Weil examines alternatives to ordinary consciousness. He is particularly interested in what he calls "stoned thinking," a non-drug-induced state.

Figure 4.14
With this, the last of the seven transformations of the street scene that opened this chapter, you are left to construct your own experience. How do *you* experience the scene?

*. . . the human brain
is probably too large already to use
in an efficient manner . . .*

Norbert Weiner (1948)

Unit II

The Behaving Organism

When a system or mechanism becomes too big or too complex, it can easily go wrong. This fact has become obvious to people who manage corporations, design automobiles, run governments, or build computers. They know that giant machines and organizations often work imperfectly. Few people realize, however, that this same principle applies to themselves.

The human body is an enormously complex system that works remarkably well despite its complexity. It is composed of many subsystems, each an incredibly intricate mechanism in itself. And of all these components that make up the body, none are more complex than the brain and nervous system.

The workings of the human system, and particularly of the brain, are explored in this unit. In Chapter 5, it becomes clear that there are certain ways that the human system must function in order to maintain itself. People *have* to get hungry when they run out of food; they *have* to feel stimulated when caffeine is released into their bloodstreams; they *have* to pay attention when they hear a baby crying—that is how the system is built. Yet, as Chapter 6 explains, the human system has a remarkable capacity to modify these built-in reactions—the capacity to learn.

This interaction of built-in structures and learned modifications helps explain several aspects of behavior. Psychologists have discovered, for example, that when the body goes wrong, it often does so because the organism has learned behaviors that are not good for it. Conversely, when an organism has difficulty learning something, it may be that too little attention has been paid to the workings and needs of the body. Whether a perfect balance can be achieved between these two factors remains to be seen. Perhaps the brain *is* too big; but it is more likely that people simply have not yet learned to use it well.

5
Body and Behavior

THE NERVOUS SYSTEM
HOW SCIENTISTS STUDY THE BRAIN
EMOTIONAL REACTIONS:
Stress / Emotions and the body / Emotions and the mind
BASIC DRIVES AND NEEDS:
Hunger and thirst / Sex / Fear and anger / Curiosity
PSYCHOLOGICAL STUDY OF ANIMALS:
Evolution of behavior / Ethology
HEREDITY AND ENVIRONMENT

There are 13 billion nerve cells inside your brain. At this moment, some of them are extremely active in handling the information coming in through your eyes. Now, if you take a deep breath and hold it, many more brain cells will become active, and they will get busier as you read along. Your body will start telling the lower part of your brain, with increasing urgency, that too much carbon dioxide is accumulating and that your body's cells are not getting sufficient oxygen. But as long as you consciously hold your breath, the upper part of your brain is telling the lower part not to respond. Nevertheless, the lower part will eventually get its way, and you will be forced to breathe.

This simple experiment effectively demonstrates that you are, among other things, a biological organism built to work in certain ways. By studying the biological nature of man, psychologists have learned a great deal about human behavior that they would not have otherwise discovered.

This chapter will explore those aspects of man's biological nature that have the greatest effect on the way he acts. It will describe how your nervous system creates and directs your behavior, what happens in your body when you feel an emotion, and what biological drives control a part of your life. It will also show how scientists have probed the brain to discover its role in behavior and how other researchers have studied behavior in lower animals in hopes of shedding light on why humans behave as they do.

Figure 5.1
The human body is an incredibly complex biological mechanism that psychologists must understand if they are to understand the experience and behavior of human beings. It is also an object to which humans have strong reactions: The body may appear very beautiful or very ugly to its owner and to others. Finally, it is through the body that the similarities between humans and other animals are seen most clearly.

THE NERVOUS SYSTEM

Imagine a city struck by an earthquake. Scores of buildings are ablaze, and electric lines are down, causing a major power failure. Immediately the fire, police, and other emergency departments

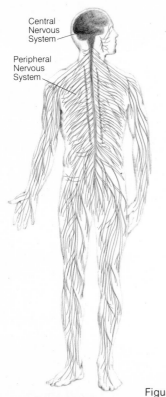

Central
Nervous
System

Peripheral
Nervous
System

Figure 5.2
The human body depends on the
nervous system for communication
and organization. The central nervous
system (colored black) is constantly active,
sending coded messages to, and receiving
them from, all parts of the body. The same
fibers contain pathways that carry
messages out to the effectors (red lines)
and pathways that bring messages in from
the receptors (blue lines). This whole
network of fibers is called the peripheral
nervous system, and like the central
nervous system, it is made up of billions of
tiny nerve cells, each capable of
transmitting signals.

spring into action to handle the crisis. Newsmen and photographers rush to the scene of the disaster to keep the city's inhabitants informed of the danger. Charities provide food and shelter for homeless victims, while ambulances carry the injured people to waiting hospitals. Despite the chaos, groups of people are solving the problems that the earthquake has created.

To be able to mobilize against such emergencies, and to function smoothly the rest of the time, communities must have a central organization, such as a city government, that can tie together all the separate parts of the community and see to it that all segments function well together.

The human body also relies on such organization. Like a city, the body is sensitive to inputs from its environment and is able to quickly respond. The brain is the body's "city hall," and the nervous system is its communications network for receiving information from and giving messages to billions of individuals—the body's cells.

The brain monitors what is happening inside and outside the body by receiving messages from *receptors*—cells whose function is to gather information. The brain sifts through these messages, combines them, and sends out orders to the *effectors*—cells that work the muscles and internal glands and organs. For example, receptors in your eye may send a message to the brain such as: "Round object. Size increasing. Distance decreasing rapidly." Your brain instantly connects this image with information from memory to identify this object as a baseball. Almost simultaneously your brain orders the effectors in your arms to prepare them for catching the ball.

How the Nervous System Works

Messages to and from the brain travel along *nerves,* which are strings of long, thin cells called *neurons* (see Figure 5.3). Chemical-electrical signals travel down the length of the neurons, much as a flame travels along a firecracker fuse—only in the neuron the fuse can burn over and over again hundreds of times a minute. When a neuron does so, it is said to be *firing.* Neurons can make other neurons fire faster or slower by releasing chemicals, called *transmitter substances,* across the gaps, or *synapses,* that occur between all neurons. It is by this method that messages travel through the body.

The nerves of the body run in and out of a huge mass of neurons clumped together to form the *central nervous system* (CNS): the brain and spinal cord (see Figure 5.2). The *spinal cord* is a bundle of nerves running down the length of your back, much like a telephone cable. Branching out from this cable is the *peripheral nervous system,* a network of nerves through which the spinal cord can send and receive messages.

The spinal cord, which is about as thick as a pencil, is well protected by the backbone, just as the brain is protected by the skull. This protection prevents any interference with the line of communication between the brain and the rest of the body. Without the spinal

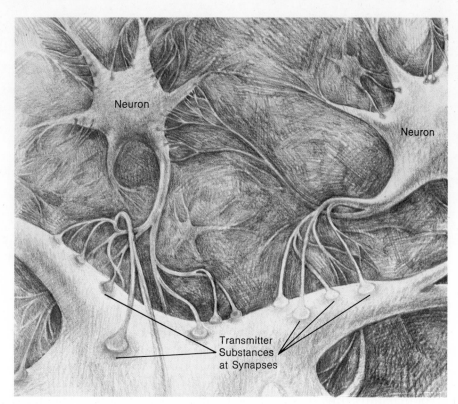

Figure 5.3

A representation of a few of the billions of neurons in the human body. These neurons are shown tens of thousands of times bigger than they really are, and just a few of the hundreds of connections between them are shown. One of these neurons (colored blue to distinguish it) has the effect of slowing the firing of the others. The other two have the effect of increasing the firing of any neurons to which they are connected. The connections take place at the synapses, where small amounts of transmitter substances cross the gap from one nerve cell to the other.

cord, messages from your brain would never reach any of your muscles except those in your face. You would be paralyzed from the neck down.

The Brain

Signals from receptors in the peripheral nervous system travel up the spinal cord and enter the brain. The first part of the brain reached by incoming signals is a section often referred to as the "old brain," so named because of its similarity to the brains of primitive creatures, such as fish and frogs. Fish can do little else but eat, sleep, and try to escape danger. Their tiny brains are responsive only to basic needs, and their behavior is, for the most part, rigidly and automatically controlled. The portion of the human brain comparable to the fish's primitive brain carries out similar functions.

Together with the spinal cord, for example, your old brain handles the hundreds of reflex actions that are a normal part of your daily life—pulling your hand back when you touch a hot object, coughing when food gets into your windpipe, tearing when dust gets in your eye, and so on.

Unlike fish and frogs, men are able to learn to behave in entirely new ways, to think, and to imagine. These powers come from a section of the brain that is miniscule in fish, larger in mammals such as cats and dogs, and huge in humans. This "new brain," the *cerebral cortex*, surrounds the old brain in humans like a halved peach surrounds the pit. Your old brain guides your biological needs and

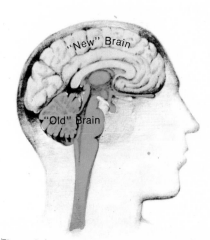

Figure 5.4

A cross-section of the human brain, showing the "old," or lower, part of the brain that humans have in common with most animals and the "new," upper part of the brain, which humans have in common only with higher animals.

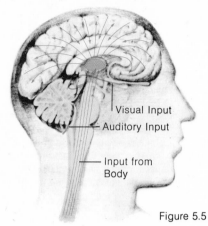

Figure 5.5

The activity of the reticular formation. Messages coming from the spinal cord or directly from the head senses travel through the reticular formation and cause it to send generalized messages to the rest of the brain, arousing and activating it. During sleep, the reticular formation blocks out much of this input, keeping the brain at a low activity level.

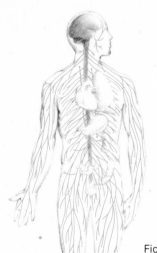

Figure 5.6

The autonomic nervous system. It sends and receives messages through two chains of nerves that run up and down either side of the spinal cord. These messages regulate the working of most of the internal organs. In general, the autonomic nervous system has two opposing functions: (1) to stimulate energy usage (by increasing blood sugar level and heart rate, for example), and (2) to conserve energy (by slowing heart rate during digestive activity, for example).

"animal instincts." Your new brain enables you, among other things, to read, to solve problems, to play musical instruments, and to participate in sports.

The Old Brain   The portion of the old brain that first receives signals is the *reticular formation* (see Figure 5.5), which controls an activating network of nerves that runs through the whole brain. This network, the *reticular activating system,* is the brain's waking and attention system. It screens incoming messages, blocking out some signals and letting others pass. During sleep it blocks most inputs, but in response to a loud or unusual sound it sends messages to the rest of the brain, alerting it and raising its activity level to a state of wakefulness.

In the center of the brain is the *thalamus,* the brain's great relaying center. It sorts incoming impulses and directs them to various parts of the brain, and it relays messages from one part of the brain to another.

At the base of the brain, below and to the front of the thalamus, is the *hypothalamus,* a small, closely packed cluster of neurons (see Figure 5.7) that is one of the most important parts of the brain. This structure regulates the *autonomic nervous system,* a system of peripheral nerves that controls internal bodily functioning. The hypothalamus thus regulates such biological functions as digestion, heart rate, and hormone secretion. By sensing the levels of water and sugar in your blood, your hypothalamus can tell when you need food or water and can then cause you to feel hungry or thirsty.

Among its other duties, this portion of the brain regulates body temperature through monitoring the temperature of the blood. If your body is too cold, it causes tiny vibrations in your muscles (shivering) that bring the temperature up to normal. If your body is too hot, the hypothalamus signals your sweat glands to perspire. The hypothalamus also plays an important role in determining emotional responses because it regulates the endocrine system, which will be discussed later in this chapter.

The New Brain   Wrapped around the old brain is the cerebral cortex, or new brain. It is a great gray mass of ripples and valleys, folded so its huge surface area, on which most of the higher brain functions take place, can fit inside the skull. The cortex is divided into several regions called *lobes* (see Figure 5.7). Some lobes receive specific kinds of sensory messages. Visual information goes mostly to the *occipital lobe* at the back of the brain, whereas auditory sensations go primarily to the *temporal lobes* on each side of the brain. At approximately the middle of the brain surface are the *parietal lobes,* which include the *somatosensory cortex,* where information from the skin, muscles, and joints is received.

Just in front of the somatosensory cortex, across a deep fold, is the *motor cortex,* which is part of the *frontal lobes.* The motor cortex controls bodily movement. Areas of the body that are involved in complex tasks receive the greatest representation on the motor cortex. Areas with the greatest sensory input receive the greatest representation in the somatosensory cortex (see Figure 5.8). For example, the hands are highly represented in both these areas of the cortex, which is reflected in the great ability of humans to make skillful movements with their hands.

The cortex is made up of two hemispheres connected by a band of nerves, called the *corpus callosum,* that carries messages back and

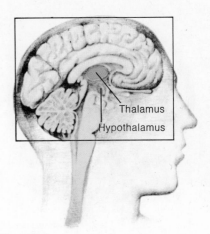

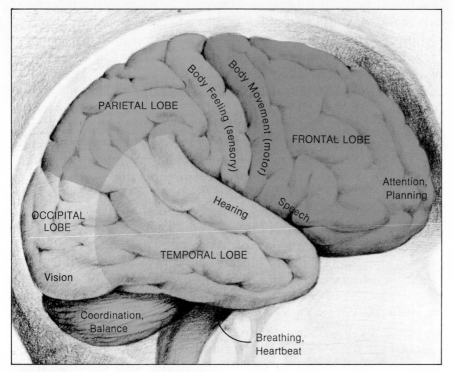

Figure 5.7
The exterior surface of the brain, showing the lobes of the cerebral cortex. The cortex surrounds and conceals from view almost all the "old" brain, whose parts are shown in cross-section in the insert. The main functions of various parts of the brain are indicated. The insert also indicates the locations of the thalamus and hypothalamus. Every message received by the cortex must go through the thalamus, which serves as a "switchboard" for the brain. The hypothalamus has many important functions, including regulation of the pituitary gland, located just below it. The pituitary controls the secretions of all the other endocrine glands.

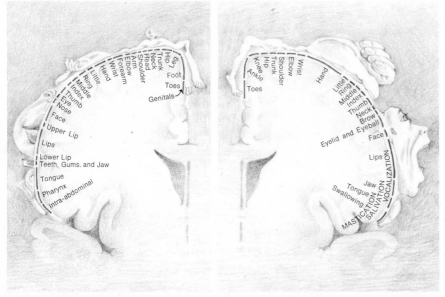

Figure 5.8
How the body might appear if the parts were proportional to their representation in the sensory and motor areas of the cortex. (*left*) The various regions of the body in the order that they are represented in the area of the brain responsible for bodily sensation. (*right*) A similar orderly arrangement of body regions in the area of the brain that controls muscular movements.

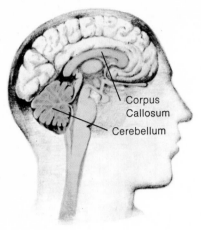

Figure 5.9
A cross-section of the brain, showing the corpus callosum and the cerebellum.

forth. Each half is connected to half of the body, but connections are criss-crossed: The left half of the brain controls the right half of the body and vice versa. The two sides of the brain are almost identical, but there are certain important differences. For example, only one hemisphere controls speech. Right-handers, whose left hemispheres are said to be dominant, have their speech center in the right hemisphere. Left-handers have it in the left.

The very front of the brain, the furthest forward part of the frontal lobes, seems to have nothing to do with the regulation of any bodily functions. It is believed to have more to do with intellect and personality. It is this part of the brain that enables people to be witty, sensitive, or easygoing. Damage to the frontal lobe can result in major personality changes. For example, in the mid-1800s a railroad-man named Phineas Gage was injured in an explosion. The force of the blast drove an iron stake into Gage's brain, striking the frontal lobe. Gage survived the accident, but he changed dramatically. His friends no longer "knew" him. He was childish, fitful, irreverent, impatient, and capricious, where once he had been trustworthy and dependable. Yet the damage did not affect his memory, his powers of thought, or such basic functions as seeing, moving, or talking.

At the very back and bottom of the brain is the *cerebellum,* the brain's "executive secretary." It is concerned with regulating the details of major commands from the cortex. Among other things, it controls your posture and balance as you move about so that you do not fall over or bump into objects. Without your cerebellum, you might hit a friend in the stomach as you reach to shake his hand.

HOW SCIENTISTS STUDY THE BRAIN

Mapping the brain's mountains, canyons, and inner recesses has supplied scientists with fascinating information about the role of the brain in behavior. Psychologists who do this kind of research are called *physiological psychologists.* They use three methods for exploring the brain: recording, stimulation, and lesioning.

Recording

Scientists are able to detect the minute electrical changes that occur when neurons fire, by inserting wires (called *electrodes*) into the brain. These wires are connected to electronic equipment that amplifies the tiny voltages the firings produce. Even single neurons can be monitored. For example, when tiny probes were sunk into the hearing part of a bat's brain, researchers found that only certain brain neurons respond to certain stimuli. For instance, one type of neuron will fire rapidly only when a particular sound is heard by the bat. If a wavering sound changes to a steady sound, some neurons will stop firing and others will start.

Scientists can also record the electrical activity of whole areas of the brain, using the *electroencephalograph* (EEG). Wires from the EEG machine are attached to the scalp so that millions upon millions of

Figure 5.10
This drawing was adapted from one of the sketches made by the doctor who attended Phineas Gage. It shows the path taken by the railroad tamping iron that was propelled through Gage's skull. Gage's intellect did not seem affected by the accident, but aspects of his personality definitely changed, as is described in the text.

neurons can be monitored at the same time. Psychologists have observed that the overall electrical activity of the brain rises and falls rhythmically and that the pattern of the rhythm depends upon whether a person is awake, drowsy, or asleep (as illustrated in Chapter 4). These rhythms, or brain waves, occur because the neurons in the brain tend to increase or decrease their amount of activity in unison.

Closely related to the brain's rhythmical activity is the brain disorder of *epilepsy*. During severe epileptic seizures, brain rhythm goes out of control. Beginning in a small piece of abnormal brain tissue, intense surges of activity spread to neighboring areas, until the whole brain is surging wildly. The victim suffers violent spasms and sometimes sees blinding flashes before blacking out.

Stimulation

Electrodes may be used to set off the firing of neurons as well as to record it. Brain surgeon Wilder Penfield is famous for stimulating the brains of his patients to determine what functions the various parts of the brain perform. When Penfield applied a tiny electric current to points on the temporal lobe of the brain, he could trigger whole memory sequences. During surgery, one woman heard a familiar song so clearly that she thought a record was being played in the operating room.

Stimulation deeper inside the brain has produced other surprising effects. Researchers have placed electrodes deep in the brain of a chicken, for example. Stimulation of some areas in the chicken's brain produced such behavior patterns as grooming, eating, attacking, or courtship rituals. When the experimenters stimulated areas that performed the two opposing functions of attack and retreat, the chicken was overtaken with confusion and ran excitedly back and forth, crying loudly and shrilly.

Using the stimulation technique, other researchers have shown that there are "pleasure" and "punishment" centers in the brain. One researcher implanted electrodes in certain areas of the old brain of a rat, then placed the rat in a box equipped with a lever that the rat

Figure 5.11
This animal has an electrode implanted in an area of its "old" brain. Each time the rat presses the lever, a tiny pulse is delivered to its brain. The extremely high rates of lever pressing performed by animals with such implants indicate that a "pleasure center" is probably being stimulated by the electricity.

Figure 5.12
José Delgado made the front page of *The New York Times* when he dramatically demonstrated ESB (electrical stimulation of the brain) in the bullring. Delgado is one of many psychologists who believe that similar techniques should be used with humans who have certain severe psychological disturbances. These psychologists have been sharply criticized by people who fear that giving doctors permission to perform psychosurgery, as it is called, would violate the rights of mental patients.

could press. Each time the rat pressed the lever, a mild electrical current was delivered to its brain. When the electrode was placed in the rat's "pleasure" center, it would push the lever several thousand times per hour until it dropped from exhaustion.

Another experimenter, José Delgado, found that he could control the rage-fear portion of the brains of various animals. He proved his point dramatically by entering a bullring occupied by an angry bull whose brain contained electrodes Delgado had placed there. Delgado carried a small transmitter that could send an electric current through those electrodes. The bull charged, but just before Delgado would have been gored, he pushed the transmitter button, bringing the bull to a skidding halt.

Scientists have used *chemicals* as well as electricity to stimulate the brain. In this method, a small tube is implanted in an animal's brain so that the end touches the area to be stimulated. Chemicals can then be delivered through the tube to the area of the brain being studied. Such experiments have shown that different chemicals in the hypothalamus can affect hunger and thirst in an animal.

Stimulation techniques have aroused great medical interest. They are now used with terminal cancer patients to relieve them of intolerable pain without using drugs. A current delivered through

Figure 5.13
The technique for stimulating the inside of a rat's brain with chemicals. (a) The rat is prepared for brain surgery. (b) A small funnel at the top of a tiny tube is permanently implanted in the rat's skull. The other end of the tube is deep inside the brain. (c) A small amount of some chemical that affects the nervous system is passed into the tube in a solution of water. The effects of the chemical stimulation of this area of the brain can then be observed.

a

b

c

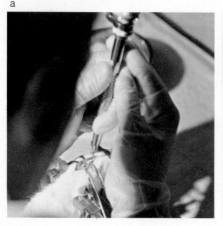
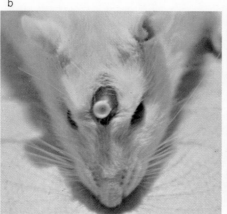
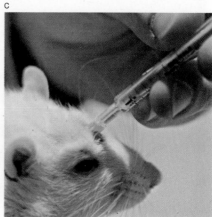

electrodes implanted in certain areas of the brain seems to provide a sudden temporary relief of such pain. Furthermore, some psychiatrists use similar methods to control violent emotional behavior in otherwise uncontrollable patients. In these ways, the science-fiction image of people controlling one another's minds has to some extent become a reality.

Lesions

Scientists often cut out or destroy a part of an animal's brain in order to see what function that part performs. This destruction is called a *lesion.* One kind of lesion of the hypothalamus can cause a rat to eat so much that he dies, because without this part of his brain the animal cannot judge when he has eaten enough.

Lesions in human beings usually occur as the result of accidents, as in the case of Phineas Gage. Occasionally, however, brain-lesion operations are performed on people. One such operation, called a *prefrontal lobotomy,* was once performed quite frequently on extremely violent mental patients. Today this type of surgery is severely criticized because it tends to leave the patients dull and docile, with no possibility of return to normal brain functioning.

PHYSIOLOGICAL BASES OF EMOTIONS

Everyone has experienced bodily sensations that accompany emotions—a racing heart, cold or clammy hands, profuse sweating, blushing, tensed muscles, and so on. These are the reactions that can be compared to the emergency measures taken by a city in response to a disaster such as an earthquake. In the human body these reactions are highly related to the functioning of the *endocrine system.* The glands of this system secrete *hormones* into the bloodstream. Hormones carry chemical messages to the major organs of the body and can change the way these organs function.

The *pituitary gland,* situated just underneath the brain, is the "master gland" whose secretions control the nine other endocrine glands. The pituitary, in turn, is controlled by the hypothalamus in the old brain. Of particular importance in behavior are the *adrenal glands* (located on top of the kidneys) and the *gonads* (the ovaries and testes). As will be discussed later in the chapter, the adrenals secrete adrenalin to mobilize the body for intense action, such as fleeing from danger or fighting for one's life. The gonads produce hormones (androgens and estrogens) that regulate sex drive and the physiological changes that accompany maturity (see Chapter 8).

The bodily changes that occur with emotions can be observed directly and can also be measured with scientific instruments. One such measuring device is the *lie detector,* or *polygraph.* Most lie detectors record four kinds of bodily change: pulse, blood pressure, respiration, and skin moisture.

When using a lie detector to question a suspect, police will often ask him a series of neutral questions in order to determine his normal

Figure 5.14
This rat weighs more than 1,000 grams (about two pounds). Following the destruction of a small part of his hypothalamus, he has overeaten until he is three or four times his normal weight. Interestingly, a rat with this type of lesion will not work to get extra food, even though he will eat enormous amounts of food if it is tasty and easily available.

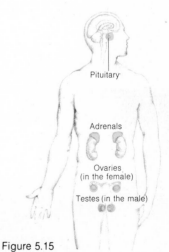

Figure 5.15
The endocrine system, showing the major glands involved in the regulation of behavior.

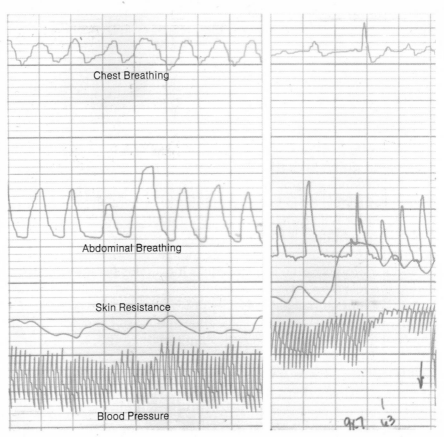

Chest Breathing

Abdominal Breathing

Skin Resistance

Blood Pressure

Figure 5.16

A polygraph (lie detector) examination. Note that the surroundings are calm and unthreatening. They have to be if the subject's responses to significant questions are to be measured against a stable baseline. Such a baseline is shown in the left half of the graph. Breathing, the tendency of the skin to conduct electricity (related to sweating), and changes in blood pressure (the jaggedness is due to the beating of the heart) are all showing regular patterns. In the right half of the graph, the subject's response to a question he did not expect ("What is seven times nine?") is reflected in sudden irregularities in breathing, a large swing in skin resistance, and a sudden jump in blood pressure. The arrow on the record indicates that the examiner reset the pen on the polygraph to keep the blood pressure marker on the scale.

polygraph readings. They will then quiz the suspect on topics more closely related to the crime. If he is guilty, his internal reactions to the questions may expose him. His adrenal glands will pour out adrenalin, making his heart and lungs work faster. His palms will become sweaty. The machine will indicate these changes in body activity, pointing to the suspect's guilt.

Nevertheless, the lie detector is not foolproof. The intimidation a person may feel when finding himself connected to a machine may very well lead him to react guiltily, even if he is innocent. Also, the lie detector can be fooled because people are able to exercise a certain amount of conscious control over their emotions. If the suspect can either "forget" his guilt or, at the other extreme, think only about his guilt no matter what the interrogator asks, the lie detector will be unable to measure any change in body activities. Some people can exert enough deliberate control over their organs that the machine fails to register anything at all.

Stress

The internal changes monitored by a lie detector are those that accompany fear in any situation. If an animal is threatened or if a person becomes angry or scared (feels threatened), a number of processes begin in the body to prepare it for fast action, be it fight or flight. Heart rate and breathing speed up to provide more oxygen;

blood rushes into those organs that will be most needed (muscles, heart, and brain); digestion virtually stops; fuel such as sugar is released from storage; muscles tighten; senses quicken.

But what happens when the organism cannot fight the danger or run away from it? What happens under *chronic stress,* when the strain never stops? In modern society, where most threats are no longer ones that can be dealt with by fight or flight, such stress has become a major problem.

Hans Selye theorizes that a person undergoing such stress passes through a three-stage *general adaptation syndrome.* The first stage occurs when an organism is exposed to a stressful situation. For example, when a laboratory animal is confined to a small cage or is subjected to near-freezing temperatures, its adrenal glands swell and its hormone levels go out of balance. These changes characterize a stage of alarm.

As the stress continues, the animal enters a stage of resistance. Its adrenals and other internal reactions appear to return to normal, but it takes all of the animal's energy to maintain this normality. If the stress continues long enough, the animal's resistance breaks down and the signs of the first stage reappear. At this point, a stage of exhaustion, even a small amount of additional stress may cause a breakdown. If the stress is prolonged, the animal may die.

Stress is thought to be involved in many *psychosomatic disorders*—illnesses that seem to have no physical basis. For example, people who are prone to backaches, migraine headaches, asthma, high blood pressure, or stomach ulcers may be reacting to psychological stress. Stomach ulcers are an interesting type of psychosomatic disorder. Fear, tension, and long periods of frustration and unexpressed anger increase stomach acids, which literally start digesting part of the stomach wall.

The Power of Emotion

Emotions can also affect the body by changing people's appearance, particularly their postures. Imagine a child who is habitually oppressed by his parents. Every time he opens his mouth or asks a question, he is greeted with silence or a slap. He is forced to live as though this situation is normal, and he begins to walk as if he is constantly defending himself. His shoulders grow round, his back muscles collapse, and he always looks as if he is hiding his face behind his distorted body. His whole personality and posture are that of someone who never stops dodging assaults. Such extreme cases are rare, but many psychologists believe that a sunken chest, a withdrawn chin, rounded shoulders, or a permanent frown indicates the presence of an emotional problem.

The most extreme expression of emotion exercising power over the body can be found in voodoo. Voodoo is a primitive religious practice involving faith in the power of witchcraft and curses. A voodoo curse can be as deadly as a bullet. In one tribe, for example,

Figure 5.17
Faith-healing is a little-understood phenomenon that seems to be related to the influence the emotions have on the body. As the text points out, a person's feelings can cause dramatic changes in his physiological functioning. In some cases of faith-healing, the sick person's strong faith in the power of a healer may actually bring about the desired physical changes. In the case shown here, the effect is more indirect: The mother's faith that her child will get well may cause her to unconsciously act in ways that will help cure the child. Such explanations of faith-healing are still hypothetical, however.

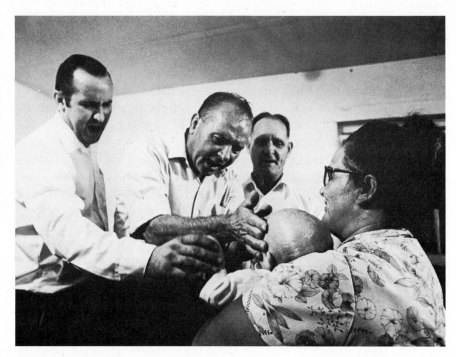

the witch doctor can put the final curse on someone by shaking a bone at him. Believing in the curse, the victim fears that he will die in a few hours or days unless the witch doctor removes the deadly charm. The cases of sudden death that occur in such situations are apparently caused by emotional reactions so severe that the victim's body cannot adjust.

This sudden-death phenomenon is not always so primitive. A Baltimore city coroner has reported that many people die each year from minor injuries and nonlethal doses of poison, perhaps from the shock of the psychological stress. During battles, for example, many deaths are reported among men who are in good health and have no combat injuries. At autopsy, no death-causing illness can be observed. Authorities have therefore surmised that the soldiers were literally scared to death.

Emotions and the Mind

Psychologists are in disagreement as to what occurs when a person experiences an emotion. The chief argument centers around whether thinking or internal bodily reaction is the most important factor in an emotion.

An experiment that separated these two aspects showed that they have to act together if an emotion is to be experienced. Stanley Schachter and Jerome Singer tested subjects by using adrenalin, the hormone that activates the internal organs. If only bodily changes are involved in emotion, injection of this substance should cause people to feel some emotion. Two experimental groups were injected with adrenalin. One group of subjects was told the truth, that the drug would make their bodies tremble and their hearts race. The

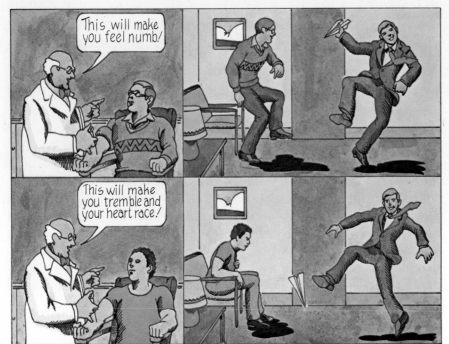

Figure 5.18
These cartoons depict the subjects' reactions in Schachter and Singer's experiment on emotion. (*top*) A subject is being misled about the effects of the adrenalin injection he is receiving. Placed with a jovial companion, he attributes his inner sensations to a similar mood in himself, so he joins in. (*bottom*) A subject is told exactly what to expect from the injection, and he does not find himself moved to join the actor in his fun.

other subjects were misinformed about the drug's effects—they were told the injection would make them feel numb. A third group of subjects was given a neutral solution (of slightly salty water), and they were not told what to expect.

Each subject was then put in a waiting room with another subject who was really a confederate of the experimenters. This "stooge" deliberately behaved angrily with some of the subjects and jumped around happily with others. The misinformed subjects joined in with the stooge, but the subjects who knew that the injection had caused their reaction actively resisted his mood. The neutral group was only mildly affected by the stooge.

What does this experiment demonstrate? For one thing, it shows that internal sensations (such as those caused by an injection of adrenalin) affect each person differently, depending on his mental interpretation and the social situation. It also shows, however, that internal cues are important—otherwise the misinformed group and the neutral group would have acted the same. Thus, *both* mental and internal bodily components are involved in emotions.

At what point does the thinking part of an emotion come in? According to the James-Lange theory, emotional experiences come *after* an awareness of internal bodily changes. In other words, if you see a rattlesnake, your stomach knots, you feel a lump in your throat, and your heart beats faster, so you decide that you are afraid. Or in William James' words, "We are afraid because we run; we do not run because we are afraid."

Psychologists such as Magda Arnold believe, however, that mental appraisal comes *before* the internal response in an emotion.

Figure 5.19
Why do some people eat too much? Stanley Schachter investigated eating patterns of fat and nonfat people and found that nonfat people eat only when they are hungry, whereas fat people eat whenever they are reminded of food, whether they are hungry or not. Schachter concluded that people who eat a reasonable amount respond primarily to their internal hunger drives and ignore external cues, whereas fat people are controlled largely by external cues to eating.

For example, if you think something is going to hurt you, you will fear it. If you think someone is taking your place in your best friend's affections, you will feel jealous. You run because you are afraid.

BASIC DRIVES AND NEEDS

In addition to studying the biological basis of emotions, psychologists are also interested in the physiological sources of *drives* and *needs.* Again, it is possible to compare these conditions to those that might exist in a city. Consider the response of a city to pollution in its water supply, a shortage of food, or a newspaper strike. The city would immediately seek ways to restore clean water, obtain food, and find a source of outside information. In an organism, the individual's requirements for survival—water, food, air—are called needs. Drives are the forces that cause the individual to try to satisfy those needs. Hunger is the drive to satisfy the body's need for food. Thirst is the drive to satisfy its need for water. A drive is activated when the body is deprived of something it needs, and it is not turned off until that need is satisfied. And although hunger and thirst are experienced in the stomach and mouth, it has been shown that all such drives originate in the brain.

Hunger

Lack of food affects the body in many ways: It causes stomach contractions and changes in blood sugar level, in taste sensitivity, in endocrine conditions, and in neural control. All these mechanisms tell the body one thing: Eat!

Not only does the hunger drive tell you *when* to eat, it sometimes tells you *what* to eat. Scientists have found that when a body develops a specific nutritional demand, food that satisfies this need seems to taste better. This function was tragically illustrated in the case of a three-year-old boy who died after spending a week in a hospital, where he was put because of irregular physical development. An autopsy showed that salt was passing through his body without being utilized. The boy had survived at home by replacing the salt as fast as he could. He had craved salt and had consumed large extra amounts of it, gulping down a tablespoonful at a time or eating it directly from a salt shaker. He was unable to continue this behavior in the hospital, and no one knew he needed extra salt until it was too late.

To study the complex mechanism of hunger, Vincent Dethier experimented with a simple insect, the blowfly. The blowfly, like many other insects, has taste receptors in its legs. When a group of these receptors is stimulated by sugar, the fly places its "nose" down into the sugar source. Once its nose is stimulated by sugar, the fly begins sucking the sugar into its esophagus and gut. After a minute or two, its receptors lose their sensitivity to sugar, and it stops feeding.

The state in which an animal's hunger is fulfilled is called *satiation.* Why does an animal continue eating, and what tells it to stop? Dethier found two nerves that, if cut, affected the blowfly's eating behavior. Cutting one nerve caused the blowfly to eat somewhat more than usual. Cutting the other nerve caused the fly to eat so much that it actually exploded!

The body's ability to maintain a balance is called *homeostasis.* Like the blowfly, people are built to perform in such a way as to eliminate any deficits or excesses. Try holding your breath for ninety seconds. You will create a terrific drive to breathe. In fact, it is impossible for you to suffocate yourself in this manner because the excess of carbon dioxide in your bloodstream will alert your hypothalamus, which will force you to breathe. Homeostasis can also be seen in your response to weather changes. When it is too hot, you try to cool yourself; when you are too cold, you warm yourself. In both cases you are trying to bring your body into balance. Nevertheless, human beings are able to willfully disobey their bodies' drives toward homeostasis as can be seen in people who are able to go on hunger strikes or who can eat well past the point of satiation.

Sex

Unlike the hunger and thirst drives, which are geared toward survival of the individual organism, the sex drive reflects a physiological need for survival of the species.

In lower animals, sexual behavior seems to be rigidly controlled by sex hormones and by the lower centers of the brain. For example, a female dog is receptive to males only when she is in heat. At other times, the female is not receptive and the male is not attracted.

The importance of hormones in rats was demonstrated by scientists who injected male hormone into female rats during a certain critical period in infancy. The hormone injections caused "masculinization" in the rats—they did not behave like females upon reaching adulthood. Similarly, male rats castrated in infancy showed more female behavior, even when given hormone replacements in adulthood.

In higher mammals, the glands play a less important role, and the higher centers of the brain, where learning takes place, have more influence. There is no biologically determined period of receptivity in women, so humans may mate at any time. Sexual behavior in human beings is more closely related to psychological factors than to physiological ones. (Human sexuality is further discussed in Chapter 8.)

Fear and Anger

Fear is preparation for flight from danger, whereas anger prepares one to fight it. Both reactions bring the body to a high state of arousal, as described earlier in this chapter. Because both fear and anger are responses to threat, they may occur together and it may be difficult to predict which action will predominate.

Some psychologists classify fear and aggression as basic physiological drives, built in for protection, but these responses also play an

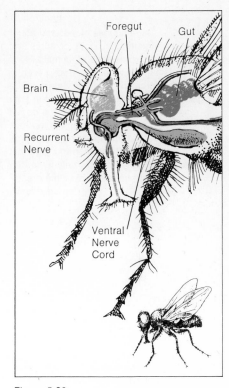

Figure 5.20

The internal organs of the blowfly. The recurrent nerve informs the brain about whether the foregut (the first chamber in the fly's digestive system) is being overinflated. The ventral nerve tells the brain about whether the fly's body walls are being stretched. The effects of cutting these nerves are described in the text.

Figure 5.21
The emotions of fear and anger produce characteristic bodily postures and facial expressions in animals. Such automatic responses are also seen in humans. Increasing aggressiveness in the dog's face is shown from left to right in both rows. In the bottom row, the dog is experiencing more fear than in the top row. The face at the lower right corner is expressing extreme fear and rage that would be likely to occur only if the dog were cornered by some greatly feared enemy.

important role in maintaining social stability. The "pecking orders," or status hierarchies, found in both human and animal groups, are maintained by mild fear and anger. People or animals will flee from those above them in the order and will attack those below them whenever a conflict occurs.

Fear (and less often, anger) is easily produced in human beings by such stimuli as the kinds of distortions of the human body that are seen in horror movies. There is evidence that these fear reactions are instinctive and occur naturally in all highly intelligent species, especially in the older children of a species. Half-grown chimpanzees, for example, are terrified by a model of a chimpanzee head without a body. It seems that fear of snakes also occurs instinctively in chimps. Such irrational fears are regularly overcome by humans; they learn not to dread strange but harmless objects.

Curiosity

Many other human activities that do not seem to involve physiological needs have been classified as drives. The expression of curiosity as a basic drive has been demonstrated in experiments with monkeys. It is known that monkeys spend much of their time watching what goes on around them. One experimenter was testing a monkey that was situated behind a screen, hidden from the experimenter. Because the experimenter was unable to see the monkey, he became curious as to what the monkey was doing. The experimenter made a small peephole in the screen, but the curious monkey quickly discovered it and began to observe the experimenter.

In survival terms, exploration and curiosity seem to be drives that help an animal to prepare for unpredictable situations. Some psychologists have theorized that, because people are able to learn, they are motivated to learn as much as they can about themselves and the world. Through the basic drives of curiosity and exploration, human beings gain *competence*. It is these drives that make children want to

Figure 5.22
Monkeys will eagerly press levers in order to obtain brief opportunities to watch an electric train running around a track. They will also work to see another monkey, to see a human being, or to be given a puzzle to solve. At one time psychologists doubted that mere curiosity motivated any organism. It now seems that anything an organism (including a human being) *can* do is something that it will *want* to do.

learn to walk, to talk, to play with toys, and, in general, to try everything they possibly can.

THE RELATIONSHIP BETWEEN HUMANS AND ANIMALS

The research that has been described in this chapter has been done primarily with animals—with bulls, monkeys, chickens, rats, cats, and flies—even though the people doing the research have been interested in humans. The reason for this recourse to animals is simply that researchers cannot perform a risky operation on a human being without a better reason than scientific inquiry. The research that has been done on humans has either been done as a part of some necessary medical operation or with humans who have suffered some injury by accident.

It is now commonly accepted that the study of animals can help in the study of human beings, even though direct experiments on humans would be even more useful if they could be done. Animal studies are especially valuable in medicine and physiology. Drugs, vaccines, and new forms of surgery are regularly tested on animal subjects. The reason that such research is considered useful is that human beings are believed to have evolved from more primitive animal origins and that their bodies are therefore in many respects similar to the bodies of other animals.

The Evolution of Behavior

What many people do not often realize is that *evolution* applies not only to anatomy and physiology but also to behavior. Charles Darwin, the biologist who first presented the theory of evolution to the world, believed that all the species of animals (and plants) are related to one another. Consequently, the configurations of their bodies and the patterns of their behavior can be distinguished and compared just as one may compare a child's nose or his temper to those of his father. Just as the bones in a bird's wing are different but comparable to the bones in a human arm, so the way birds flock together can be compared to the way humans gather in groups. And just as the parts of a chimpanzee's brain can be compared to those of a human one, so can a chimpanzee's ability to solve problems be compared to human thinking ability.

Darwin's theory does not mean that the unique qualities of human beings are to be discarded, but it does make it possible to think of man as a particularly complex, interesting kind of animal instead of as a totally different kind of creature.

Ethology: The Biology of Behavior

One of the major outgrowths of Darwin's theory of evolution is *ethology,* the study of human and animal behavior from a biological point of view. Ethologists are interested in studying the natural behavior patterns of all species of animals. They are interested in seeing how these patterns have changed and developed in evolution and how they are expressed in man, the most highly evolved species.

Figure 5.23 (*opposite*)
The coordinated movements of a horse's legs fall naturally into three gaits, which are fixed action patterns in the horse species. The photos shown here are from a famous series of motion studies by Eadweard Muybridge. These studies proved conclusively that a galloping horse has all four feet off the ground at the same time at one point in its stride.

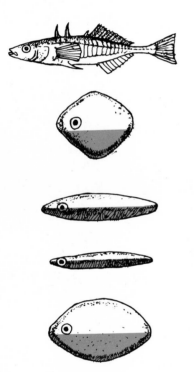

Figure 5.24
In the spring the male stickleback develops a bright red belly. This coloration is a sign stimulus for attack from other sticklebacks. They will attack red-bellied models like the ones above before they will respond to a realistic model of a stickleback that does not have a red belly. (*right*) The male's red belly is also a sign stimulus to the female stickleback. Her response to it is to swim toward him. He responds by leading her to the nest he has built, where the female deposits her eggs and the male fertilizes them. It is the male who later broods the eggs and cares for the young.

Ethologists call these natural behavior patterns *species-specific behavior:* behavior that is characteristic of a particular species of animal. Ethologists study how animals behave in their natural environment, because it is there that these animals evolved.

Ethologists have found that the behavior and experience of more primitive animals (such as insects or fish) are less flexible, or more *stereotyped,* than the behavior of higher animals, such as apes or humans. Stereotyped behaviors consist of patterns of responses that cannot change readily in response to changes in the environment. They work well only if the environment stays as it was when the behavior pattern evolved.

For example, when a horse is confronted with danger and requires a quiet escape, it is impossible for it to tiptoe away. Its escape behavior consists of only three behavior patterns: walking, trotting, and galloping (see Figure 5.23). Each pattern is a distinct series of movements that vary little from one horse to another, and all normal horses display these patterns. Such patterns are called *fixed action patterns* because they are inflexible—an animal can react to certain situations only in these ways.

Fixed action patterns are one kind of *instinct*—a behavior pattern that is inborn rather than learned. People often misuse the word "instinct" to refer to behaviors that become automatic after long practice. A professional baseball player may be described as "instinctively" making the right play, for example. But ethologists use the term "instinct" to refer only to those abilities that seem to be present from birth.

Ethologists have found that animals are born with special sensitivities to certain cues in the environment (as well as with special ways of behaving). These cues are called *sign stimuli.* For example, Niko Tinbergen showed that the male stickleback, a small fish, will attack a model of another stickleback if it has a red belly. Even if the model is distorted, as in Figure 5.24, the male will still attack. Yet if it

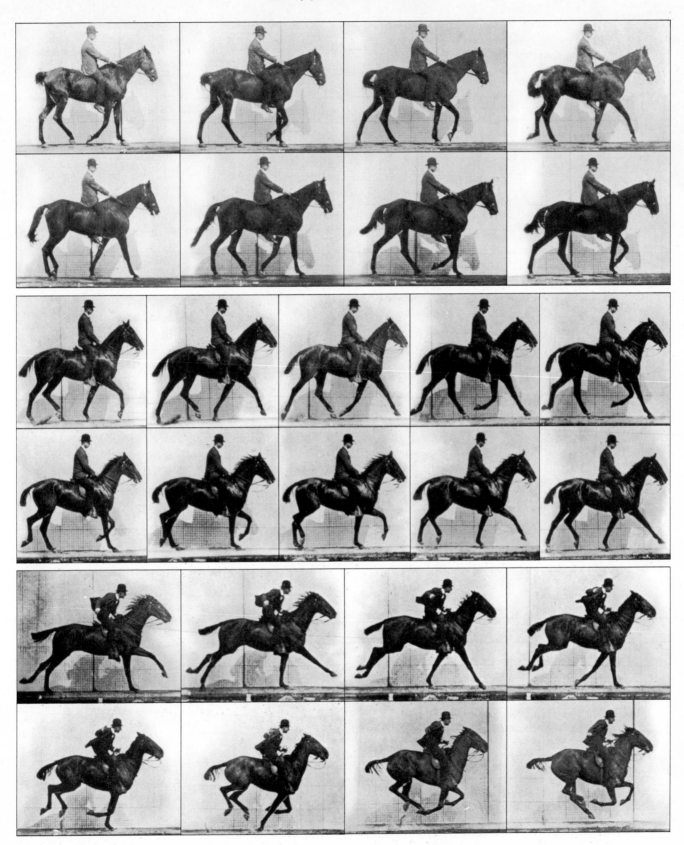

Figure 5.25
The oystercatcher, a European coastal bird, responds to the sight of its eggs with a pattern of nesting and brooding behavior. The significant aspect of the stimulus seems to be size: If the bird is offered a huge dummy egg, a "supernormal" sign stimulus, it will try to brood it rather than its real, regular-sized eggs.

sees a very lifelike model of a stickleback without a red belly, the male will leave it alone. In this case, the sign stimulus that triggers attack is the color red. In other species other sign stimuli can trigger certain behaviors, as shown in Figure 5.25.

Do sign stimuli occur in humans? Although instincts are less common and less powerful in human behavior, there is evidence that some stereotyped behaviors exist. For example, Konrad Lorenz found that a "parental instinct" seems to be aroused by the appearance of the human baby. When he compared human infants to other young animals, he noticed that they all seem to display a similar set of sign stimuli, which appear to stir up parental feelings. Short faces, prominent foreheads, round eyes, and plump cheeks all

Figure 5.26
Certain stimulus patterns seem to trigger predictable sets of responses even in human beings. The profiles on the right of each pair all share certain features that trigger the kind of feeling in humans that makes people smile and say, "Isn't he cute?" The adult profiles elicit no such response. In this sense, then, humans can be said to have certain instinctive reactions in common with animals.

seem to arouse the parental response (see Figure 5.26). Generally, though, automatic inborn reactions seem to play a fairly minor role at the human level of evolutionary development.

HEREDITY AND ENVIRONMENT

People often argue whether behavior is instinctive (due to heredity) or learned (due to environment). Do people learn to be good athletes, .or are they born that way? Do people learn to do well in school, or are they born good at it? Do people learn to be homosexual, or are they born that way? The reason for the intensity of the argument is that something learned can probably be changed, whereas something inborn will be difficult or impossible to change. But whenever psychologists investigate a particular case they find that the issue is not that simple. In every case inherited factors and environmental conditions act together in complicated ways. Asking whether heredity or environment is responsible for something always turns out to be like asking, "What makes a cake rise, baking powder or heat?" Obviously, an interaction of the two is responsible.

In some cases the relationship between heredity and environment is obvious. If a person inherits his tallness from his parents, there is a greater likelihood that he can become an outstanding basketball star—but he has to learn to play basketball first. Other cases are much more complex.

Ethologists have studied the dynamic relationship between heredity and environment by asking, what makes a bird able to sing its own song? A chaffinch is born able to produce all the parts of the chaffinch song even if it has never heard another chaffinch. The ability of the bird to sing is hereditary, or inherited. However, the isolated bird does not put the parts together properly unless it hears other chaffinches. If it listens to tape recordings of backward songs, it begins to sing its own song backward. In this case, the bird couples instinct with learning to produce unusual songs.

These findings are readily applicable to the human situation, keeping in mind that human beings are more flexible and capable of learning than any other species. Environmental influences play such

Figure 5.27

The interaction of heredity and environment can be seen in the behaviors of this domesticated wolf. Although this wolf has never heard or seen another of its species since birth, it does not have to be taught to howl. Certain stimuli, in this case the sound of a clarinet, will bring out this inherited behavior. An innate ability might be best thought of as something that is very easily learned. Other abilities may be less easily learned depending on the inheritance of the organism. Wolves, for example, find it fairly easy to learn to shake hands because they have some innate tendencies to use their paws in this way. It is much more difficult to teach a wolf to sit because sitting is not something wolves naturally do.

a large part in human life that the hereditary influences may be hard to see. Even more than chaffinches, humans may develop differently depending on the experiences they have. There has been particularly intense discussion of this matter with regard to sex roles (see Chapter 8) and intelligence (see Chapter 15).

But it should not be concluded, on the other hand, that human beings are infinitely flexible. This chapter has shown that the human body, like the bodies of animals, is built to work in a certain way. The huge cortex of the human brain enables man to change himself and his environment more than can any other animal, but it does not enable him to become nonhuman. He must live with hunger and thirst, fear and desire, anger and pain. These he cannot escape even if he wants to.

Figure 5.28
In a newborn baby lie the seeds of an adult human being, the factors of inheritance. How these seeds grow depends on the child's experiences. Learned patterns and innate ones are woven together and built on one another in the process of development.

SUMMARY

1. The human body is highly organized, served by its communications network, the nervous system. Receptors receive messages, which are sent to the central nervous system (the brain and spinal cord), which in turn sends messages out to the effectors that control the muscles.

2. Messages travel through the nervous system in the form of chemical-electrical firings of individual nerve cells, or neurons. Signals from the peripheral nervous system travel to and from the brain through the spinal cord.

3. The "old brain" is that portion of the brain responsible for one's more biological needs and "animal instincts." It includes the reticular formation, which controls the reticular activating system; the hypothalamus, which regulates the autonomic nervous system; and the thalamus, which is the brain's relay center.

4. The "new brain," the cerebral cortex, enables one to do such things as think and learn complex skills.

5. The two halves of the cerebral cortex, the cerebral hemispheres, are connected by the corpus callosum. The cerebral cortex is further divided into several lobes. Each lobe receives specific kinds of sensory messages. One of the regions, the frontal lobe, is thought to control personality. At the back and bottom of the brain is the cerebellum, the brain's executive secretary.

6. Three methods that scientists use to study the brain's functioning are recording, stimulation, and lesioning. The brain's electrical activity may be recorded by the use of electrodes inserted into the brain or by the use of the EEG machine. Stimulation and lesioning techniques have been useful for determining the functions of certain areas of the brain.

7. Emotions are related to the functioning of the endocrine system, and they affect the body in many ways. One way to detect bodily

responses that accompany an emotion is by use of the polygraph, or lie detector. Chronic emotional stress may result in psychosomatic disorders or distorted postures. Severe emotional reactions to a particular situation may even result in death.

8. Experiments have shown that both thinking and an internal bodily reaction must occur together in order for an emotion to be experienced.

9. Drives are psychological representations of biological necessities. Hunger, thirst, and the need for air are drives that must be satisfied for the organism to survive. Sex, fear, anger, and curiosity, although not as closely related to biological needs, are drives that nevertheless play a vital role in maintaining social development and stability.

10. Ethology is the study of human and animal behavior from a biological point of view. Fixed action patterns and sign stimuli are forms of species-specific behavior. Such behavior is commonly described as instinctive.

11. Scientists frequently argue about the roles of heredity and environment in determining an organism's characteristics. Both factors are involved to some extent in any given characteristic. In each case, heredity and environment interact in a unique way to produce a unique result.

ACTIVITIES

1. Try eliminating salts or sweets from your diet for a few days, and observe the changes in your desire for those substances. Describe the changes in their taste and smell as a result of deprivation.

2. Can you observe species-specific behaviors in cats, dogs, or any other animals you see regularly? If you have an animal that you can observe carefully, try to identify fixed action patterns that are common to the animal's species. Do they exist in any form in yourself?

3. Advertisements, especially in the cosmetic and fashion industries, are said to have taken advantage of human use of sign stimuli. Look through some current and old popular magazines for comparison. True sign stimuli should remain the same whatever the age of the publication.

4. Much of what scientists know about the biological sources of behavior has come from studies on animals. Do you think it is valid to relate the results of animal studies to humans? Why or why not?

5. What aspects of your personality, your way of acting, and your appearance are most obviously the result of heredity? Which seem to be more related to your environmental upbringing? What factors make it difficult to decide whether hereditary or environmental factors are of greatest influence?

6. To gain a clearer understanding of the range of emotional reactions you experience, keep an "emotion diary" for one day. Try

to jot down what you felt, how you interpreted your feelings, and what brought on your reaction. At the end of the day, analyze your diary to determine the differences in physiological reactions that you experienced in response to each situation. What conclusions can you draw about your emotional responses on that day?

7. Many animals establish territorial boundaries that they defend against intruders. What determines these boundaries and what purposes do they serve? Watch the behaviors of dogs in a local neighborhood. Determine what each dog considers to be the boundary of his territory. Observe other animals to see if each one stakes out a territory that he defends against others of his own kind. Does he defend this territory against other species?

8. Explore the existence of the territorial imperative in human beings: Walk up to a secretary you do not know, open one of her desk drawers, and take a piece of paper. Ask a physician how he reacts when a patient makes a self-diagnosis and demands a specific medicine. Find a man sitting in his parked car and sit down on the fender of the car. Walk up to a woman and drop a paper clip into her purse. Do you think territorial behavior is learned or instinctive? What are your reasons?

9. Spend a day at the zoo observing the behavior of various animals, trying to identify species-specific behaviors. Which behavior patterns are common to all species? Which patterns are different? (You will need to spend a minimum of two hours with each species to develop an adequate picture of even a few species-specific behaviors.)

SUGGESTED READINGS

ASIMOV, ISAAC. *The Human Brain: Its Capacities and Functions.* Boston: Houghton Mifflin, 1963. An easy-to-read book about the human brain by one of America's most versatile and prolific writers.

CALDER, NIGEL. *The Mind of Man.* New York: Viking, 1970. A profusely illustrated, interesting presentation of current research on the brain and nervous system.

CRICHTON, MICHAEL. *The Terminal Man.* New York: Knopf, 1972. An engrossing novel about a man who is turned into a machine, with forty microscopic wires buried in his head. At the end of the novel is a five-page annotated scientific appendix on mind control.

LAWICK-GOODALL, JANE VAN. *In the Shadow of Man.* Boston: Houghton Mifflin, 1971. For ten years Jane Goodall lived in the midst of wild chimpanzees, and in this book she writes about their social structure, their behavior, and their personalities somewhat as if they comprised an interesting and intimate circle of friends. The narrative style of the book reads much like a good novel—it is difficult to put down.

LORENZ, KONRAD Z. *King Solomon's Ring.* New York: Crowell, 1952. A classic study of nature by one of the world's outstanding scientists. An absorbing and beautiful book of essays; light and easy to read.

LORENZ, KONRAD Z. *On Aggression.* New York: Harcourt, Brace & World, 1966 (paper). In Lorenz's words, aggression is the fighting instinct in beast and man that is directed against members of the same species. Lorenz describes man as having few inhibitions against aggression and as being easily able to remove those he has.

McGAUGH, J., N. M. WEINBERGER, and R. L. WHALEN (eds.). *Psychobiology.* San Francisco: Freeman, 1967. A volume of readings from *Scientific American* on the biological basis of behavior. Research in numerous disciplines is included in this comprehensive book.

MORRIS, DESMOND. *The Naked Ape.* New York: Dell, 1967 (paper). Although critics have shown that many of Morris' conclusions are unsound, this book has helped arouse enough interest to provoke more careful biological examinations of the behavior of *Homo sapiens.* Man *is* an animal.

WOOLDRIDGE, D. E. *Machinery of the Brain.* New York: McGraw-Hill, 1963. A fascinating and highly readable survey of man's basic knowledge of the brain and how it works.

6
Learning

PATTERNS OF LEARNING
HABITUATION
CLASSICAL CONDITIONING
OPERANT CONDITIONING:
Reinforcement / Biofeedback / Aversive control
LEARNING COMPLICATED SKILLS:
Imitation and shaping / Combining responses
FACTORS THAT AFFECT LEARNING
LEARNING OF STRATEGIES
Learning to learn / Helplessness and laziness

One of the most striking characteristics of human beings is their adaptability. Consider the differences between the life of a sailor on a seventeenth-century warship and the life of an assembly-line worker in a twentieth-century factory. Or consider the differences between the life of a peasant woman in fields of seventeenth-century France and the life of a typist in twentieth-century New York. These social and physical environments vary greatly, yet the same men and women could live these widely differing lives. The ability of human beings to change themselves so radically is the ability to *learn.*

This chapter will describe the basic ways in which learning occurs, how psychologists study learning, and what factors help or hinder learning. It will also explain how skills and strategies of dealing with the world can be learned.

PATTERNS OF LEARNING

Learning is usually defined as a lasting change in behavior that results from experience. The ability to swim, for example, results from the experience of interacting with water in certain ways. In any learning situation—and virtually every situation in life is one in which learning can take place—it is possible to identify *stimuli* and *responses.* Stimuli are units of the environment that one can respond to—such as the properties of water, in the case of swimming. Responses are units of behavior, or actions—such as movements of the arms and legs in swimming.

An uneducated swimmer's responses might be disorganized and useless. He might splash randomly and keep trying to stand up. After

Figure 6.1
The mastery of complex skills, such as gymnastics, is one type of learning that is of interest to psychologists. They try to distinguish the elements that can be found in all types of learning, from a rat's learning to press a lever to this young gymnast's learning of a difficult routine to a surgeon's learning how to perform a difficult operation. Learning psychologists view rats and people as organisms that are sensitive to certain stimuli, capable of certain responses, and hence, able to learn.

much practice, however, the relationship between his behavior and the environment changes. He responds to the stimulus of water by lying flat, kicking with his legs, and pulling with his arms. He has learned to swim.

Learning to swim, make speeches, shuck corn, or read books is a complex achievement that will be discussed toward the end of the chapter. Each of these skills, however, is made of many small stimulus-response relationships. Each of these relationships is the result of stimuli and responses being repeatedly arranged in certain patterns.

HABITUATION

One of the most fundamental patterns in which an organism adapts to its world is by ceasing to respond to most stimuli and instead responding only to what is important or new. A newborn baby may be startled, frightened, or fascinated by almost every sound and sight he experiences. In time, however, many of the sights and sounds become familiar, and the baby learns to ignore them. This process of learning *not* to respond to familiar stimuli is called *habituation*.

Habituation is a form of learning so simple that it can be observed in the brainless sea slug. The sea slug has only a primitive nervous system, and although it cannot think, it can learn. When a sea slug is first poked with a stick, it automatically withdraws the affected part of its body. If the same part of its body is repeatedly stimulated, the sea slug stops responding—the response has become habituated.

Habituation regularly occurs in people who live near a train track. Such people have learned not to respond to the vibrations, screeching, and clanking of the trains going by. Yet if for some reason a train

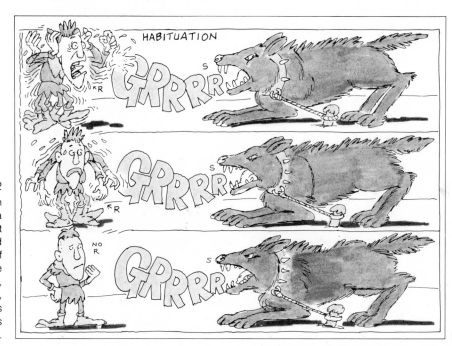

Figure 6.2

The process of habituation is shown in this sequence of illustrations featuring a hypothetical medieval character, Emmett Cerf. At first Emmett is frightened (response) by the growling and barking of an angry watchdog (the stimulus). As the stimulus continues to be presented, Emmett's fear responses (sweating, trembling) gradually die out. Emmett is featured in several other learning situations in the following pages.

130

fails to go by at the usual time, these normally sound sleepers have been known to waken, feeling as though something is wrong.

CLASSICAL CONDITIONING: LEARNING BY ASSOCIATION

The ability of organisms to learn not to respond to a regular, uninteresting stimulus is obviously a useful adaptation. A second type of learning has an even more useful function. It enables the organism to take advantage of the fact that an interesting stimulus is usually preceded or accompanied by uninteresting stimuli. It can be useful for the organism to learn to respond to the uninteresting stimulus in the same way it does to the interesting one. For example, if you were not able to learn to respond to the *sight* of a hot flame in the same way you do to its *touch,* you might not be here to read this.

The importance of this learning of reactions to uninteresting stimuli was first noticed by the Russian physiologist Ivan Pavlov. His work became the foundation for an entire field of psychology.

Like many great discoveries, Pavlov's was accidental. He was studying the digestive tract in dogs, focusing on the secretion of juices into the mouth. By attaching a tube directly to a dog's salivary gland, Pavlov could measure the flow of saliva from the dog's mouth. At first, the dog salivated after a meat powder had been put into its mouth. Later, it began to salivate as soon as the food was placed in its dish. Pavlov's assistants then noticed a strange phenomenon. Because the dog now anticipated the arrival of the food, it began to salivate at the first sight of the meat powder or even at the sound of an experimenter entering the room. Eventually, the dog began to salivate as soon as it was placed in the testing apparatus.

Pavlov began to wonder why these seemingly unconnected stimuli caused the salivating response. Could any stimulus, if paired

Figure 6.3
The apparatus used by Ivan Pavlov to study conditioned salivation in dogs. The harness held the dog steady, while the tube leading from the dog's mouth desposited saliva on an arm connected to the recorder on the left. Drops of saliva moved the pen, making a permanent record of the dog's salivation response to such stimuli as food and sights or sounds that had been associated with food.

with food, bring about this response? He set out to explore this phenomenon, abandoning his original work.

Pavlov's Experiment

Pavlov began his new experiments by ringing a tuning fork and then immediately placing some meat powder on a dog's tongue. After only a few times the dog started salivating as soon as it heard the sound, even if food was not placed in its mouth. Pavlov had discovered that any *neutral stimulus* (one that is uninteresting in the sense that it is unrelated to the response in question) can come to *elicit* that response (cause it to happen) if presented regularly just before the stimulus that normally makes the response happen.

Using Pavlov's terms, food is an *unconditioned stimulus* (UCS): a stimulus that elicits a certain response without previous training. Food normally elicits the *unconditioned response* (UCR) of salivation. The term "unconditioned" usually refers to natural, automatic behaviors—startles, blushes, and shivers, for example. A neutral stimulus, such as the sounding of a tuning fork, that comes to elicit a response such as salivation is called the *conditioned stimulus* (CS); the salivation that it causes is called the *conditioned response* (CR). This process is diagrammed in Figure 6.4. A conditioned response is learned. Any of a large variety of stimuli can serve as a conditioned stimulus for salivation: the sight of food, the sound of a tone, the flash of a light. The process of controlling an animal's reactions in this way is called *classical conditioning.*

In this same set of experiments, Pavlov also explored the phenomena of generalization and discrimination. *Generalization* happens when a conditioned response is elicited by a range of stimuli similar to the original conditioned stimulus. When Pavlov conditioned a dog to salivate at the sight of a circle (the CS), he found that the dog would salivate when it saw an oval shape as well. The dog had generalized its response to a similar stimulus. Pavlov was able to teach the dog to respond only to the circle by always pairing meat powder with the circle and never with the oval. He thus taught the dog *discrimination:* the ability to respond differently to similar but distinct stimuli.

Classical Conditioning in Children

Some years after Pavlov's experiments, John B. Watson showed how conditioning could work on a human infant. Watson experimented on a happy eleven-month-old child named Albert. He presented Albert with many objects, including a white rat, a rabbit, blocks, a fur coat, and a hairy Santa Claus mask. Albert showed no fear of any of these objects—they were all neutral stimuli for the fear response.

Watson decided that he would attempt to condition Albert to fear rats. He began by placing a rat in front of Albert. Because Albert found the rat delightful, he would reach out to play with it. Each time he did, one of Watson's assistants would strike a metal bar with a

Figure 6.4 (*opposite*)
Classical conditioning. Emmett Cerf comes to associate the bird's song, a neutral stimulus (NS), with the unconditioned stimulus (UCS) of food because while he eats, the bird sings. Eventually, the unconditioned response (UCR) of salivation is elicited simply by the bird's song. At this point the bird's song has become a conditioned stimulus (CS), and salivation has become a conditioned response (CR). Generalization: Emmett salivates when he hears another neutral stimulus similar to the bird's song. Discrimination: he does not respond to a neutral stimulus that is different from the bird's song. (Note: Emmett could have been conditioned to discriminate between the bird's song and the instrument's notes if he had originally heard the instrument playing at times when he was not eating.) In extinction, the bird's song gradually loses its power to elicit salivation because it is no longer paired with food.

hammer right behind Albert's head. The first time the metal bar was struck, Albert fell forward and buried his head in a pillow. The next time that he reached for the rat and the bar was struck, Albert began to whimper. The noise, the unconditioned stimulus (UCS), brought about a natural, unconditioned response (UCR), fear.

Each time the original neutral stimulus, the rat, was presented to Albert, he began to cry and cringe in fear. The rat was now a conditioned stimulus that elicited a conditioned response, crying and cringing.

After Watson conditioned Albert to fear rats, he presented him with a furry white rabbit. Albert now reacted fearfully to the rabbit. Watson found that the degree of fear Albert felt toward other neutral stimuli depended upon how much they resembled the furry white rat. His conditioned fear response had generalized to the sight of the rabbit. Other furry white objects, such as a fur coat and a Santa Claus mask, also caused Albert to cry and try to escape whenever Watson presented them.

Extinction

Albert learned to respond emotionally to the sight of the rat in the same way that Pavlov's dogs learned to respond with their salivary glands to the sound of a tone. Pavlov discovered, though, that if he stopped presenting food after the sound of the tuning fork, the sound gradually lost its effect on the dogs. After repeatedly striking the tuning fork without giving food, Pavlov found that a previously conditioned dog no longer associated the sound with the arrival of food—the tuning fork lost its power to elicit the salivation response. Pavlov called this effect *extinction* because the conditioned response had gradually died out. Similarly, Watson could have extinguished fear of rats in Albert by presenting the rats without the jarring sound. Unfortunately, Albert's mother took her son away before such extinction could be accomplished.

Practical Applications

Many psychologists believe that if fears can be learned, as they were by Albert, they can also be unlearned. Behavior therapy (described in Chapter 14) uses this principle to cure people of irrational fears by associating the feared objects (snakes, dogs, or crowds, for example) with situations that elicit relaxation and feelings of calm.

The same principles can be applied by any individual. Many people, for example, experience boredom at times when they are trying to do some difficult or tedious work. Students almost always have this problem. After an hour or two of work a student begins to respond to the situation by daydreaming and feeling bored. If he keeps on trying to study, he is pairing the stimuli of his textbook and study area with stimulus conditions that elicit daydreaming and boredom. If this pairing happens often enough, even the thought of studying will eventually elicit these responses. By trying to study when he is bored, the student actually learns not to be able to study.

To change this association he would have to make studying a nonboring experience. One method would be for him to study for only five minutes at a time, throwing himself into each study period with all the enthusiasm he can muster. In between these study sessions, he might do something different from studying—listen to a record, have a bite to eat, talk to a friend. Gradually he might build up his studying sessions to ten minutes, fifteen minutes, and so on, with brief rest periods in between. But whenever he begins to daydream or feel bored, he leaves his study area. In this way he can extinguish his boredom response and begin to associate his books and desk with stimuli that elicit more appropriate responses.

The pairing of stimuli through classical conditioning usually occurs unconsciously and is often the source of bad habits. To extinguish such responses one must examine them closely to determine how they were originally learned.

OPERANT CONDITIONING: LEARNING FROM CONSEQUENCES

In classical conditioning the responses that are conditioned are *involuntary*. One has little or no control over such things as fear, salivation, and boredom. They are usually described as reflexes or instinctive behaviors. These responses can be elicited or forced out of you by the appropriate stimuli. The third form of learning has to do with the conditioning of responses that are not reflexes or instinctive.

Much of an organism's behavior is *voluntary;* it picks and chooses its responses. A dog, for example, does not shake hands because of instinct or reflexes. Shaking hands is voluntary and represents only one response among thousands of possibilities. Such spontaneous action is called *operant behavior* because the organism *operates* on its environment without being forced to respond to some stimulus.

When you enter a darkened room and begin to search for the light switch, your behavior is spontaneous. You reach up and down. If you fail to locate the switch, you reach left, and then right. Finally, you find the switch and turn on the light. During this procedure you are spontaneously operating on your environment until you find the switch. There is no stimulus that forces you to reach in some particular direction. When you return to the room again, however, you do reach in approximately the correct direction and quickly find the light switch. What factor makes you eliminate all the possible wrong movements this time and settle on the right one? Psychologists have shown that the environmental *consequences* of your actions determine what you will and will not do.

Reinforcement

B. F. Skinner is the name most closely associated with operant conditioning. He and his colleagues have shown that most behavior is controlled by the *rewards* and *punishments* it has produced in the

Figure 6.5

Rats are used a great deal in psychological research because they are small, cheap, and sturdy. In addition, learning can be studied more simply and objectively in rats than in humans. This particular rat is pressing a bar in an apparatus commonly called a Skinner box, named for its designer, B. F. Skinner. The Skinner box is an artificial environment in which lights, sounds, rewards (food or water), and punishments (electric shock) can be delivered and controlled and in which some of the animal's behaviors (such as bar pressing) can be recorded by automatic switches.

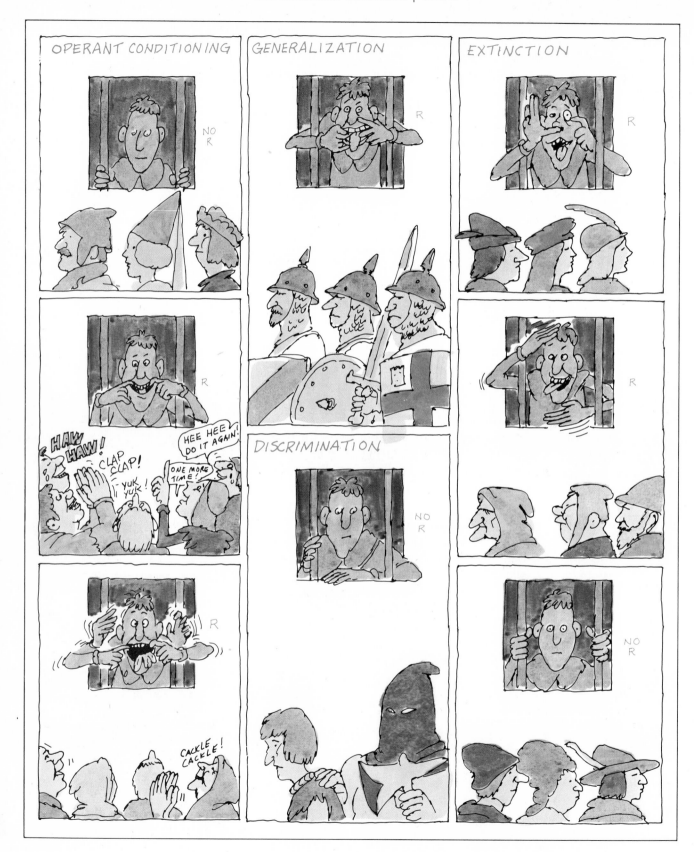

past. To get a dog to shake hands, a trainer will give him a biscuit or pat on the head whenever he moves his paw in the appropriate directions. The biscuit or pat is called a *positive reinforcement.* Reinforcement strengthens the desired response. When you find the location of a light switch, you are rewarded by being able to see, so your finding of the switch is reinforced. Learning from reward is one kind of *operant conditioning:* Reinforcement makes the operant behavior more likely to occur again.

On the other hand, if a dog is beaten whenever he tries to shake hands, he will soon stop shaking hands. Similarly, if you finally locate the light switch but get an alarming shock when you touch it, you will probably avoid grabbing for it in the future. In these examples, the consequences of a behavior result in a decrease in the likelihood of such behavior. This kind of consequence is called *punishment.*

Thus, the nature of a consequence influences the organism's tendency to engage in the same behavior in the future. Behavior that is reinforced tends to be repeated; behavior that is not reinforced or that is punished tends not to be repeated.

Suppose that a dog has learned to shake hands effectively but no longer receives a reward after each shake. In other words, its reinforcement is withdrawn. Its hand-shaking behavior will gradually disappear. Behavior that is no longer reinforced eventually dies out. This discontinuation of behavior is called *extinction,* similar to the extinction of a conditioned response in classical conditioning.

Extinction in operant conditioning, however, does not occur smoothly. Even though hand shaking is not reinforced, the dog still anticipates a reward for its behavior. In fact, when there is no reward the dog becomes impatient and its behavior becomes more forceful than before. The dog may begin to bark or pace back and forth, occasionally lifting its paw.

Extinction effects can also be observed in humans. Suppose you put a dime in a vending machine expecting to be reinforced with a

Figure 6.6 (*opposite*)

Operant conditioning. Emmett Cerf, in prison for poaching, occasionally passes the time by making faces from the window. On one occasion this spontaneous behavior is reinforced by the attention of people passing by. As a result, Emmett emits more of the behavior and does so more vigorously. Because he is rewarded only when people pass by, the stimulus "people" becomes a signal for him to respond. (Signals are discussed on page 138.) Emmett generalizes from this stimulus to many kinds of people, but he discriminates between regular passersby and the executioner with a prisoner. The face-making response gradually extinguishes when passersby become bored with him and stop reinforcing the behavior.

Figure 6.7

Pigeons are another species commonly used in learning research. This pigeon is showing signs of emotional upset common in extinction of an operantly conditioned response. The bird was trained to obtain food from the square hole by pecking at the key in the round hole. When the experimenter switched off the circuit that made this arrangement work, the bird pecked the key for a while and then, finding no food, began to jump around and flap its wings.

soft drink but instead the dime falls through and you do not get the drink. You will probably reinsert the dime a few times, hoping that it will eventually work. You may then jiggle the machine or kick it angrily, trying to get it to accept your money. If all these methods are unsuccessful, you will eventually stop trying to get the soft drink from the machine. Your responding will have been extinguished.

Control of Involuntary Behavior

Such classically conditionable responses as salivation, blushing, and fear are involuntary—they occur without the deliberate efforts of an organism. In contrast, operant responses include such voluntary activities as walking, talking, and driving a car. Recently, however, psychologists have discovered that operant conditioning can be used to control involuntary behavior.

Normally, involuntary behaviors such as breathing and heartbeat rates are controlled automatically by the nervous system, and psychologists have thought it impossible for people to deliberately modify this behavior. Recent findings indicate, however, that if a person is provided with information about his bodily functioning, he can learn to exercise some control over it. The method devised for monitoring internal physiological processes is called *biofeedback.*

In one experiment, subjects listened to the amplified sounds of their own heartbeats and learned to avoid a mild electric shock by increasing their heartbeats to a certain rate at specific times during the experiment. In other studies, subjects have been able to lower their blood pressures and change their brain waves by receiving some sort of feedback on how well they are doing. Using the operant technique of biofeedback, doctors may be able to teach patients how to alter their internal functioning in order to control heart conditions and other such medical problems.

Signals

In operant conditioning, stimuli that are associated with getting rewards or punishment become signals for particular behaviors. For example, everyone learns to cross a street only when the green light signals safety or to answer the phone only when it rings. These signals simply indicate that if one crosses the street or answers the phone, reinforcement is likely to follow, in the form of safe arrival on the other side of the street or a voice on the phone.

Just as organisms generalize from and discriminate between conditioned stimuli in classical conditioning, they also generalize and discriminate stimuli that serve as signals in operant conditioning. For example, a child who has been rewarded for saying "doggie" every time he sees the family's basset hound may also generalize and say "doggie" when he sees a sheep, a cow, or a horse. These animals are similar enough to the hound for them to become signals that "doggie" will produce a reward. Discrimination results when "doggie" fails to produce a reward in these other cases. The child learns to

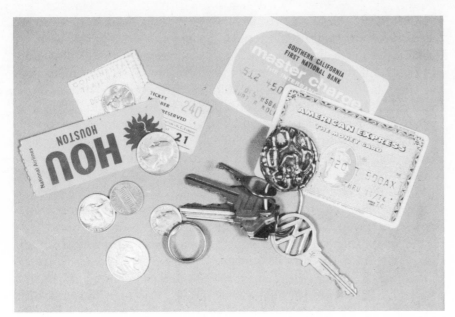

Figure 6.8
Many ordinary objects have significance because they function as conditioned reinforcers and discriminative stimuli. Because they signal rewards and punishments to come, they have rewarding or punishing values themselves.

confine the use of "doggie" to the hound and to other dogs and to respond differently when horses, cattle, or sheep are the stimuli.

Because signals are guides to future rewards and punishments, they often become rewards or punishments themselves. In this case, the signal is called a *conditioned reinforcer*—without the conditioning process, it would have no reward or punishment value to a person. In this way, almost any stimulus can acquire almost any value: The Christian cross, which originally represented torture and execution, has come to represent comfort and security.

Did you ever walk into the wrong bathroom? The ability to respond differently to the signs MEN and WOMEN provides a good example of discrimination between signals and of the fact that signals can become reinforcers. Even before he can read, a child is guided and directed into the appropriate bathroom door. At first he does not discriminate between the MEN and WOMEN signs, but he is trained to enter the appropriate door: When he enters the correct door, he is given approval; if he goes toward the wrong door, he is greeted by panic and disapproval.

In this case, the approval is the *primary,* or natural, reinforcer for the correct response. The incorrect response is met by punishment (the parents' panic and disapproval). The child learns to discriminate between the MEN sign and the WOMEN sign, and if he needs to go to the bathroom, one of these signs will be rewarding to him and the other punishing. Most human behavior is reinforced in this way—by conditioned reinforcers (such as money) rather than by primary reinforcers (such as food).

Schedules of Reinforcement

One might suppose that behavior would best be maintained by reinforcing every response. However, it has long been known that when reinforcement occurs only some of the time, responding is more stable and more persistent. Consider, for example, a man who has two cigarette lighters; one lights immediately every time (continuous reinforcement), whereas the other must be flicked four or five times before it lights (intermittent reinforcement). Next, suppose that both lighters stop lighting completely. Which lighter will he give up on first? Most likely, he will discard the first one immediately because it is now functioning differently from his expectations for it. But he will probably not consider it at all unusual for the first five or six attempts to fail with the second lighter.

Although reinforcement may be arranged in a number of ways, four basic methods, or schedules, have been studied in the laboratory (see Figure 6.9). Schedules may be based either on the number of correct responses that the organism makes between reinforcements (*ratio* schedules) or on the amount of time that elapses (*interval* schedules). In either case, reinforcement may appear on a regular, or *fixed,* schedule or an irregular, or *variable,* schedule. The four basic schedules result from the combination of these four kinds of possibilities.

On *fixed-ratio schedules,* reinforcement comes after the completion of a fixed number of responses: The number of required responses never changes. A person is reinforced in this manner when he gets paid every time he types a certain number of pages or drives a certain number of miles. On *variable-ratio schedules,* the number of required responses varies from reinforcement to reinforcement. A door-to-door salesman may make a sale at the fourth house, the tenth house, and then not again until the twentieth house.

On a *fixed-interval schedule,* reinforcement comes at a fixed amount of time after the previous reinforcement. For example, employees who are paid by the week or by the month are operating on a fixed-interval schedule. On a *variable-interval schedule,* the interval varies from reinforcement to reinforcement. This type of schedule is used by teachers who give surprise tests periodically throughout the semester.

People behave differently depending on the schedule on which their responses are reinforced. If they are rewarded for every ten items they produce (fixed ratio), they will work at a high rate, pausing briefly after receiving each reward. But if the reward comes sometimes after one item and sometimes after twenty (variable ratio), they will work steadily at an even higher rate. Gamblers at a slot machine are on such a schedule. The faster they put money in the machine, the closer they are to a payoff—but they never know when the payoff will come.

People are probably least efficient when they are rewarded on interval schedules because they know that no matter how much they produce they cannot increase the frequency of their rewards. On fixed-interval schedules they tend to respond slowly until just before the reinforcement time, when rates suddenly increase—as when

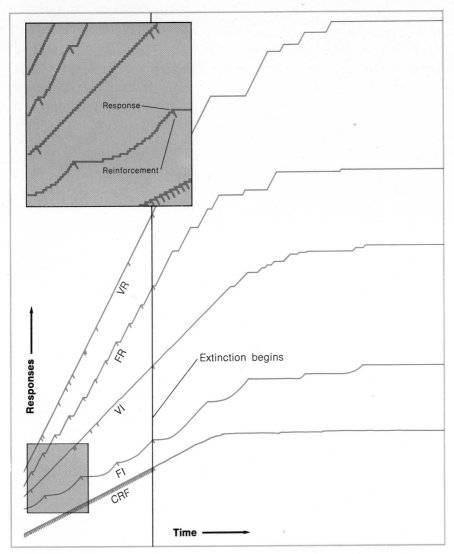

Figure 6.9
Laboratory recordings of behavior on schedules of reinforcement. Each time the organism under study makes a response, a pen moves one step upward on a slowly moving sheet of paper. (The insert shows these markings in detail.) A steep upward line therefore indicates rapid responding; a horizontal line indicates no responding at all. The angled "blips" occur wherever a response has been reinforced. Note that a distinctly different pattern of responding occurs with each schedule of reinforcement: The "scallop" shape is characteristic of the fixed-interval (FI) schedule, whereas the "pause-and-run" pattern occurs with the fixed-ratio (FR) schedule. Responses occur at a moderate, steady rate on variable-interval (VI) schedules, whereas the pace is constant and rapid on the variable-ratio (VR) schedule. As the illustration shows, these patterns are maintained during the extinction process, which is slower for all intermittent schedules than for continuous reinforcement (CRF).

students cram on the nights before exams. On variable-interval schedules, responding occurs at a more steady rate because reinforcement may occur at any time.

In general, responses are learned better and are more resistant to extinction when reinforced on variable-ratio and variable-interval schedules because although the person knows that the reward should come at some time, he never knows whether it will be on the next response or far in the future.

Aversive Control: The Effects of Pain

Pleasant consequences are one way of influencing behavior. But unpleasant consequences can also be used. There are three common ways in which unpleasant events, or *aversive stimuli,* can be used to affect behavior: punishment, avoidance, and escape.

As pointed out earlier, *punishment* works in much the same way as reward, but instead of increasing the frequency of the response

Figure 6.10
A rat in a Skinner box jumps clear of the grid through which it is receiving electric shock, an aversive stimulus. Psychologists perform experiments such as this one to find out how rewards and punishments control behavior. They have found that behavior can be changed more effectively by reinforcing what is desirable than by punishing what is undesirable.

that it follows, it decreases that response. If you are punished for doing something, you are less likely to try it again.

Avoidance is used to postpone or prevent unpleasant events, whereas *escape* is used to shut off something unpleasant. These responses can easily be demonstrated in laboratory rats put into a cage with a grid floor. If a brief shock is delivered through the grid every ten seconds, the rats will first learn to escape it by jumping when the shock is delivered. Before long, however, they will learn to avoid the shock completely by jumping before the shock arrives.

Anything that brings pain can serve as punishment, whether inflicted physically (shocks or blows) or psychologically (isolation or disapproval). If your mother frowns or glares when you hum at the dinner table, you are less likely to do so again.

Escape is also called *negative reinforcement* because in this case a response becomes stronger (is reinforced) by the removal of a stimulus (instead of the appearance of one). People often try to escape painful situations by making responses that excuse them or shut the situation out of their minds. For example, in a dentist's chair you may learn to think distracting thoughts to shut off the pain of drilling. If you happen to "forget" the dental appointment altogether, however, you are using avoidance. Procrastinating is usually an avoidance response, and many of the routines of everyday life are avoidance responses—you brush your teeth to prevent cavities, and you drive safely to avoid accidents and traffic tickets.

Psychologists have found that there are several disadvantages to using aversive stimuli to change behavior. For one thing, aversive

Figure 6.11

Types of aversive control. In escape, Emmett Cerf finds that begging ends the guard's lashing (the aversive stimulus). Begging has been negatively reinforced and is likely to occur more frequently in the future. In avoidance, Emmett learns that begging now prevents the guard from giving him a lashing. However, Emmett's begging behavior now occurs so often that it annoys the guard, who punishes Emmett's begging. The punishment should cause a dramatic drop in the frequency of Emmett's begging behavior.

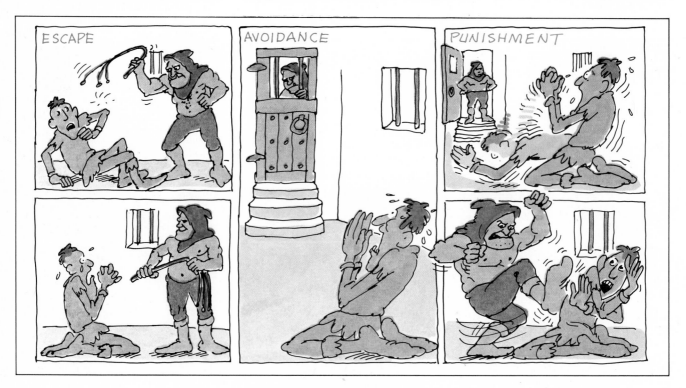

stimuli can produce side effects such as rage, aggression, and fear. For another, the whole situation may become a *conditioned aversive stimulus,* in the same way that signals for reward situations become conditioned reinforcers. For example, if a parent tries to control a child by punishing him, the child may try to escape and avoid the whole family situation.

Punishment may often achieve the opposite effect of what is desired—the person who is punished may actually increase the punished behavior. This situation occurs when what one person thinks is punishment is actually a reinforcement for the person receiving it. For example, teachers may find that the more they reprimand a disruptive child, the more he will misbehave. What such children really want is some sort of attention, and even punishment will provide this type of reward.

Psychologists thus recommend to parents and teachers that they ignore—not reinforce—a child's misbehavior and that they instead concentrate on rewarding more desirable behaviors.

Implications of Conditioning

The simple principles of operant conditioning and aversive control have been found useful for training animals and for influencing human behavior. For example, conditioning methods are used for helping mentally retarded children to learn to dress themselves, to brush their teeth, and to otherwise take care of themselves. Mentally ill patients who have refused to talk or eat have been coaxed into these behaviors through the use of reinforcement. (Such applications of conditioning techniques are described in Chapter 14.)

Behaviorists—psychologists who explain human behavior in terms of conditioning—have even suggested that entire countries be run on the basis of sophisticated operant techniques. Other experts reject this idea, however, saying that there is more to life than manipulation by reinforcement. Most acknowledge, nevertheless, that rewards and punishment do play a major role in how and what people learn.

LEARNING COMPLICATED SKILLS

When you acquire a skill such as knitting, photography, shooting a basketball, or talking persuasively, you learn more than just a single new stimulus-response relationship. You learn a large number of them, and you learn how to put them together into a large, smooth-flowing unit. Psychologists have devoted considerable attention to how new responses are acquired and to how they are put together in complex skills.

Imitation and Shaping

Two important processes that help in learning skills are imitation and shaping. *Imitation* occurs when one organism watches another to get an idea of how to perform a skill. For example, imagine how

Figure 6.12

The principles of reinforcement have long been used by animal trainers, even though they may never have heard of the term "operant conditioning." Conditioning principles were consciously applied, however, to train this killer whale to perform a variety of behaviors, including "kissing" her trainer, as part of an act for Sea World in San Diego, California. The whale's responses are reinforced with fish.

difficult it would be to swing a baseball bat if you had to rely on trial-and-error responses to determine which end you should grasp when swinging it. By simply watching one game, a stranger to baseball can obtain a rough "learning" through the imitation process. Although the beginner may never hit the ball, he can at least take the first step toward learning.

Shaping is a process in which reinforcement is used to sculpture new responses out of old. An experimenter can use this method to teach a rat to do something it has never done before and would never do if left to itself. He can shape it, for example, to raise a miniature flag. The rat is physically capable of standing on its hind legs and using its mouth to pull a miniature flag-raising cord, but at present it does not do so. The rat will probably not perform this unusual action by accident, so the experimenter begins by rewarding the rat for any action close to the wanted response.

Imagine the rat roaming around on a table with the flag apparatus in the middle. The rat inspects everything and finally sniffs at the flagpole. The experimenter immediately reinforces this response by giving the rat a food pellet. Now the rat frequently sniffs the flagpole, hoping to get another pellet, but the experimenter waits until the rat lifts a paw before he gives it another reward. This process continues, with the experimenter reinforcing close responses and then waiting for even closer ones. Eventually, he has the rat on its hind legs nibbling at the cord. Suddenly the rat seizes the cord in its teeth and

Figure 6.13
When a skilled carpenter engages in a task such as shingling a roof, he is actually combining a number of simultaneous response chains into a single coordinated movement pattern. Each response chain is composed of smaller response units, which originally had to be shaped by themselves. To perform this roofing task, the carpenter first had to learn to balance himself on sloping surfaces, to hold objects with his toes, his hands, and his mouth, and to coordinate his hands and eyes.

yanks it. Immediately the rat is rewarded, and it begins pulling rapidly on the cord; a new response has been shaped.

Shaping has been used to teach language skills to impaired children. Psychologists at first reward the children for simple sounds, such as "bah." Later the children are only rewarded for complete words, such as "beans," and later for complete sentences such as "Beans, please." Many such children have successfully learned to use language by this method.

Combining of Responses

In order to learn a skill, a person must be able to put various new responses together. Responses that follow one another in a sequence are put together in *chains*. Each response produces the signal for the next one. For example, to hammer in a nail, one would have to put together the following chain of responses: pick up hammer, pick up nail, position nail, swing hammer, hit nail, swing hammer, hit nail, and so on until the nail is completely sunk in. Each hit of the nail signals that one is striking it correctly, and the nail's being flush with the board's surface signals that no further responses are required.

In learning, chains of responses are organized into larger *response patterns*. For example, the complex skill of swimming has three major chains that are combined to make up the whole swimming pattern: an arm-stroke chain, a breathing chain, and a leg-kicking chain. Furthermore, simple response patterns may be combined to make up more complex response patterns: Building a house is made up of such smaller response patterns as hammering, measuring, and sawing wood.

It is necessary to learn simpler responses first before mastering the complex pattern. If you cannot hit a nail with a hammer, you certainly cannot build a house. Therefore, before a person can learn to perform a particular skill he must learn all the subordinate skills that make the larger skill possible.

The learning of complicated skills thus involves not only mastering individual responses but being able to put them together into chains, simple patterns, and complex patterns. Imitation and shaping are two ways in which responses can be acquired and put together.

FACTORS THAT AFFECT LEARNING

Several factors can help or hinder the learning process. Among them are attention, feedback, transfer, and practice.

Attention

In order for a learner to be able to establish a relationship between his responses and certain stimuli, he must first be able to detect the stimulus and to discriminate it from other stimuli. Many people have trouble learning simply because they do not give *attention* to the right thing—they do not focus their mind on the object or idea that they want to learn about. Instead they are distracted—they pay attention to something other than the stimuli that matter. In tennis, for example, attending to the other player rather than to the ball is a common problem.

In studying, students are often distracted by noises, minor interruptions, and their own roving thoughts. It is possible to learn not to be distracted by analyzing the situations in which concentration is difficult. Outside distractions can usually be ignored if the student recognizes that they have nothing to do with him. It is tempting for most people struggling with a difficult problem to respond to other people's voices by saying to himself, "Why can't they be quiet? Don't they know I'm trying to study?"

If the student realizes that people are not purposely making these noises and that his own feelings of irritation are the true distractors, he can modify or eliminate his reactions to external stimuli and persevere in his work. Sometimes it helps to jot down distracting thoughts so they can be focused on after the study period. They may be well worth pursuing when he can give full attention to them.

Feedback

When learning a new skill, people constantly want to know how well they are doing. They want to know how their performance can be corrected and improved. The dancer wants to know how he looked, the student wants to know the results of her tests, and the marksman wants to know where his bullets hit. Finding out the results of an

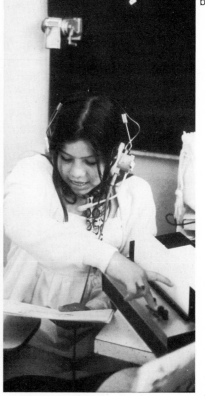

Figure 6.14
Examples of feedback in learning. (a) This device, called a pursuit rotor, is commonly used to study skill learning. The problem is to keep the tip of the stylus in contact with the small metal disk as the turntable rotates. Mastery of this skill depends on establishing a rhythmic motion of the arm, which can only be accomplished through the use of internal feedback. The task is extremely difficult for those who rely only on external feedback (such as the sight of the stylus tip on the disk). (b) Teaching machines, which provide instant feedback about the correctness of one's answers, are highly effective for certain kinds of instruction. (c) Social skills also depend on feedback. Each person must pay attention to external feedback (the reactions of the other person) and to internal feedback (his own feelings about his behavior).

action or performance is called *feedback*. Without feedback, you might repeat the same mistakes so many times that you develop a skill incorrectly—you would never learn what you were doing wrong. Even if you were performing correctly, you would not be receiving reinforcement for continuing.

Often feedback comes from one's own body. If a dart player is blindfolded and his only source of outside information is a friend telling him where each dart hits, he can still learn to hit the bull's-eye. He must rely almost entirely on his kinesthetic (movement) sensations, which report almost immediately on the results of his movements. Learning to use this source of feedback is a big step toward mastering a difficult motor task.

Mastery of a skill requires sensitivity to both internal and external feedback. A swimmer, a mathematician, and a salesman all pay attention to information from within and from outside themselves to perfect their performances.

Transfer

Often a skill that you have already learned can help you to learn a new skill. If you have learned to play the saxophone well, it will be much easier for you to learn to play the clarinet. You can transfer much of your saxophone-playing skill to clarinet playing. If you had no previous musical training, learning the clarinet would be far more difficult. But if you have mastered the saxophone, you have already developed certain skills, such as reading notes and converting them into responses in your lips, tongue, and fingers. When previously learned responses help you to learn a new task, it is called *positive transfer*.

When a previously learned task hinders learning, *negative transfer* has occurred. An American may find driving in England to be more difficult than it is for an Englishman who is learning to drive for the first time. In England, the steering wheel is on the opposite side of the car, and people drive on the opposite side of the road. The learned skill of driving American-style makes it difficult to perform the necessary new mental and motor tasks. An American's responses are often the exact opposite of what is needed.

The degree to which a skill is transferable usually depends on how well it has been learned. The ability to drive a car would certainly aid in learning to drive a truck. But if a person has been driving a car for only two weeks and still isn't sure of himself, taking up the new task of learning to drive a truck will slow down the mastery of both tasks. If, on the other hand, a person learns two dissimilar skills, such as car driving and horseback riding, there will be no interference, whether the skills are well learned or not.

Practice

It is obvious that in order to learn a complex skill you must practice, practice, practice. Practice, the repetition of a task, is the only way to bind responses together. It is the key element that makes for smooth and fluent movement from response to response.

Because practice takes time, psychologists have been interested in determining how to use that time most efficiently. They have found that whatever type of skill a person is learning, it is better to space out practice rather than do it all at once. Obviously, learning a motor skill such as high jumping or even typing requires frequent rest periods because the muscles become fatigued quickly. Learning a mental skill also requires rest periods. The mind can absorb only so much new information in one session before it, too, becomes fatigued.

It has been found possible to practice by imagining oneself performing a skill. Athletes imagine themselves making golf swings over and over again or mentally shooting free throws in basketball to improve their performance. Psychologists call such effort *mental practice.* Although it is not as effective as the real thing, it is better than nothing at all.

LEARNING OF STRATEGIES

It would be difficult to solve problems if people had to relearn the solution process each time a problem occurred. Fortunately, when you learn to solve one problem, some of the problem-solving experience may transfer to other, similar problems. Once you learn certain *strategies* for solving problems and learning tasks, you can be assured of an easier time on your next attempts. (Such problem-solving strategies are also discussed in Chapter 3.) Many learned principles for dealing with life are valuable; others may actually be handicaps.

Learning to Learn

Harry Harlow has shown that animals can learn to learn: They can learn to use strategies for solving similar problems and tasks. He gave monkeys the problem of finding a raisin under one of two wooden lids, one red and one green. The raisin was always hidden under the green lid, but because the experimenter kept changing the position of the lids the monkey took a while to realize that color was important, not location.

When the monkey had learned to always pick the green lid, the experimenter changed the problem. Now the monkey had to choose between triangular and circular lids. The raisin was always placed under the circular lid, and the experimenter again changed the location of the lids on each trial. As before, it took several tries for the monkey to realize that the shape of the lid, not its location, indicated where the raisin would be. After doing hundreds of problems like these, the monkey began to learn that the difference between the two lids always contained the key to the problem. Eventually the monkey could solve any similar two-choice problem with, at most, one error.

The learning of strategies and principles is extremely important in

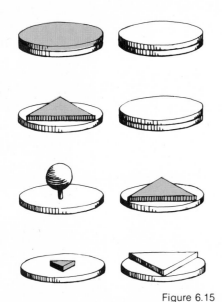

Figure 6.15

Harry Harlow presented monkeys with pairs of lids like those shown here and required them to learn strategies for determining which lid in each pair covered a morsel of food. After being presented with a few hundred such problems, the monkeys learned to use the same strategy for dealing with each new pair.

human behavior. In school you get practice in such skills as reading books, writing essays, and taking tests. In many cases the particular things you have learned will be less important in the long run than what you have learned about learning generally. Learning to extract information from a book, for example, will be helpful whether the book is about physics, grammar, or cooking. Just as Harlow's monkey acquired a general method for quickly solving particular problems, you are acquiring a general strategy for learning particular pieces of information.

Helplessness and Laziness

Psychologists have shown that general learning strategies can affect a person's whole relationship to his environment. For example, if a person has prolonged experiences of situations in which his actions have no effect on his world, he may learn a general strategy of helplessness or laziness. These strategies are peculiar and not very useful, but they are adopted for the same reasons as other strategies—they have seemed appropriate to the situation.

Learned helplessness was demonstrated in an experiment with dogs. The dogs were strapped into a harness from which they could not escape and were then given electric shocks at unexpected intervals. After days of shock treatment, the dogs were unharnessed. Now they could escape the shocks or avoid them entirely simply by jumping over a hurdle into a safe compartment. But more than half the dogs failed to learn to jump. When several dogs that had not had the experience of being shocked were also tested, almost all of them quickly learned to jump to safety. Apparently, many of the dogs in the first group had learned to stand and endure the shocks, resigned to the fact that any effort to escape would be useless.

In another experiment, pigeons that had been receiving food for free were compared with pigeons that had to push levers with their

Figure 6.16
People who live for prolonged periods in conditions such as these are likely to feel depressed and helpless. They are unable to make changes through their own actions and may eventually stop trying to obtain any rewards at all.

Figure 6.17
For many people, the environment of a communal farm provides satisfying rewards that result from their actions. This photograph was taken at Twin Oaks, a community designed according to the principles of learning developed by B. F. Skinner, who described such a community in his novel *Walden Two.*

feet in order to get food. Both groups were required to learn to peck a disk on the wall to get food. The group that was used to getting food free learned slowly. The group that already had work experience learned quickly. The first group had to overcome *learned laziness.*

It is not hard to see how these results can apply to human situations. People who experience prolonged pain and suffering and are unable to do anything about them may learn a helpless attitude and find it difficult to struggle, even when it might do some good. Similarly, people who experience an easy life and are able to let other people do everything for them may learn to be lazy. They may find it difficult to make the necessary effort to solve problems that they cannot avoid.

In order to be able to try hard and to be full of energy, people must learn that their actions *do* make a difference. If rewards come without effort, a person never learns to work. If pain comes no matter how hard one tries, a person gives up.

Many more aspects of daily life and ways of handling it are learned, consciously or unconsciously. The more that is understood about the learning process, the better able people will be to learn what they want to and to "unlearn" their undesirable ways of behaving.

SUMMARY

1. Learning refers to changes in the relationships between stimuli (pieces of the environment) and responses (pieces of behavior) as a result of experience.

2. One simple form of learning is habituation, in which a response to a stimulus disappears with repetition. Another form of learning, classical conditioning, was discovered by Ivan Pavlov. In this process, a previously neutral stimulus comes to elicit a response because it has been paired with a stimulus that already elicited that response. Extinction of a classically conditioned response occurs when it is no longer associated with the neutral stimulus.

3. Operant conditioning occurs when an organism's spontaneous activities are either reinforced or punished. Any consequence that increases the likelihood of a response is called a reinforcement. Extinction of a response occurs when it is no longer reinforced.

4. It is possible to learn to control certain involuntary behaviors by the use of biofeedback and operant conditioning techniques.

5. Signals are stimuli that come to be associated with getting rewards or punishments. Organisms have the ability to generalize from and discriminate between signals. A signal becomes a conditioned reinforcer when the signal itself serves as a reward or punishment.

6. Different schedules of reinforcement produce different patterns of behavior. When reinforcement depends on number of responses (ratio schedules), the organism tends to respond faster than it does if

reinforcement is dependent on time (interval schedules). When reinforcement comes on a highly regular basis (fixed schedules), the organism will tend to pause after a reward. If reinforcement appears irregularly (variable schedules), the organism will keep going at a steady rate.

7. Aversive control means using unpleasant influences on behavior. In punishment, the unpleasant event comes as a consequence of a response; in avoidance and escape conditioning, the response has the effect of removing the unpleasant event.

8. To learn a complicated skill, a person must acquire and coordinate a number of new responses. Skills require continuous coordination of stimulus-response relationships in order to produce a smooth, flowing action. Learning of skills may be facilitated by imitation and shaping. Skill learning requires putting new responses together in chains, which are then organized into response patterns.

9. Factors that influence learning include attention, feedback, transfer, and practice.

10. Organisms can learn to learn by discovering certain strategies. A strategy for solving problems or learning tasks can be applied to subsequent, similar situations. Organisms learn strategies of laziness or helplessness if they experience situations in which their behavior has no consequences.

ACTIVITIES

1. Here's a simple experiment to show habituation. Locate a friend or family member who is willing to be your subject. Puff gently through a straw at his (her) eye causing it to blink. Keep puffing. If the eye blink eventually ceases, habituation has occurred.

2. You can also use the eye-blink response to demonstrate classical conditioning. Puff air at your subject's eye, but about a half-second *before* each puff make a distinctive noise—thump a pot or sound a buzzer, for example. After twenty or thirty such pairings, stop puffing but continue making the sound. If conditioning has occurred, the sound alone will bring the eye blink. Keep making the sound; at a certain point it should no longer elicit the eye blink. The response is extinguished.

3. Businesses often make use of conditioning techniques in their commercials. They associate the name of their product with pleasant tunes or exciting scenes, so that the name alone will elicit conditioned relaxation or excitement. Think of specific ads that use these techniques. Can you think of selling methods that use operant conditioning?

4. Using the principles outlined in the skill-learning section of the chapter, how would you go about learning to do a simple dance step; to make an omelet; to drive a car; to pitch a baseball?

5. Which of the schedules of reinforcement do your instructors

generally use in conducting their classes? How would your classes be different if they used the other schedules? Give examples for your answers and justify your reasoning.

6. Children learn by receiving signals from their parents. Often these signals represent positive and negative values of the parents, which they desire to impart to their children. (Positive values are what your parents want you to do; negative values are what they don't want you to do.) You can gain an insight into yourself by becoming aware of those values that you have been "taught" by your parents. Make a four-column chart with the following headings: (1) positive values of parents; (2) how parents enforce these values; (3) negative values of parents; (4) how parents enforce these values. Write as many examples as you can think of in columns (1) and (3), then fill in columns (2) and (4). Which of these enforcements are examples of operant conditioning? Which values do your parents emphasize most, the positive or the negative? If you were your own parent, how would you change your behavior to get the results you want?

7. If you have a dog or a cat, or have access to one, try a simple conditioning experiment on it. Using Pavlov's techniques of classical conditioning as discussed in the chapter, teach the animal to like a neutral stimulus by pairing it with a pleasing stimulus. After the animal is sufficiently conditioned, apply extinction techniques.

8. If you take a moment to sit in a room, listening for sounds and concentrating on looking around, you will undoubtedly hear and see things that you usually ignore. Why? Give five examples of habituation that occur in your everyday experiences.

9. Using a dartboard, darts, and blindfold, set up your own research project on the effects of feedback. Ask several subjects to participate. Divide them into three groups: correct feedback; incorrect feedback; and no feedback. Blindfold each subject, stand him at the boundary line facing the dartboard, give him twelve darts, and proceed to record his progress under the heading you have chosen for him. At the end of your research, compare the results of each group. What conclusions can you draw from your research? What does this research tell you about the effects of feedback?

10. In the experiment on learned helplessness, the animals who were unable to change their situation for long periods of time seemed unable or unwilling to change when the possibility was opened to them. What implications do such experiments have for humans? Can you think of situations in your life that have had the effect of learned helplessness?

11. Take a real-life situation, such as waiting for an elevator, eating a sandwich, or climbing a tree, and analyze the stimuli, responses, rewards, punishments, and signals in the situation.

12. Select some particular subject of study that you find difficult or

unpleasant. Whenever you sit down to study this subject, play one of your favorite records or tapes as you study. In time, the favorable feelings toward this music may become associated with the subject of study, making it easier to learn and remember.

SUGGESTED READINGS

BARBER, T. X. (ed.). *Biofeedback and Self-Control.* Chicago: Aldine-Atherton, 1970. An excellent collection of papers on biofeedback. The readings cover experiments on meditation, hypnosis, drug states, EEG feedback, and other such topics.

BURGESS, ANTHONY. *A Clockwork Orange.* New York: Ballantine, 1962 (paper). A violent and powerful novel about a sadistic anti-hero who is "treated" by an extreme form of classical conditioning technique.

MORGAN, C. T., and J. DEESE. *How to Study.* New York: McGraw-Hill, 1957 (paper). This booklet describes a variety of techniques for learning how to study effectively.

McINTIRE, ROGER. *For Love of Children: Behavioral Psychology for Parents.* Del Mar, Calif.: CRM Books, 1970. As the title suggests, this book is a guide to child rearing based on the principles of operant conditioning. The author's premise is that children (and everyone) behave in ways that have been reinforced. Parents can therefore control their child's behavior by making themselves aware of why behavior is occurring and by shaping desired behavior in accordance with conditioning principles.

SKINNER, B. F. *Science and Human Behavior.* New York: Free Press, 1953 (paper). This widely read book discusses the relationship between a science of behavior and everyday ways of talking about personality, self, and culture. Skinner begins with an explanation of the scientific principles of behavior and then goes on to explain his analysis of "self-control," thinking, social interaction, psychotherapy, economics, and religion.

SKINNER, B. F. *Walden Two.* New York: Macmillan, 1948. Skinner's best-known work is a novel of an ideal, behaviorally engineered community. It is readable, interesting, and instructive.

WHALEY, D. *Contingency Management.* Behaviordelia, P. O. Box 1044, Kalamazoo, Michigan 49001. A 250-page comic book created by Whaley and some of his graduate students. A painless and humorous introduction to the conditioning approach to learning.

WHALEY, D., and R. MALGOTT. *Elementary Principles of Behavior.* New York: Appleton-Century-Crofts, 1971. One of the most readable introductory texts on Skinnerian behaviorism and the principles of behavior modification. It puts behavioral techniques to practice by pacing and rewarding the reader throughout the text.

Whirl round
And round.
This yearning
Has no ending.

Charles Angoff (1966)

Unit *III*
Psychological Growth

For those who take the most from life and give the most to it, existence has a cyclical quality. For them, the joys and pains of childhood are never lost because they are continually recreated in new experiences. During the cycle of life, they are always making fresh starts, facing new difficulties, encountering new ideas. For them, growth and change never stop, their yearning for new experience has no end.

Continuing growth and change are of particular interest to developmental psychologists, who study the general principles that govern human development. They have discovered that some processes are the same for all individuals, regardless of parentage, social class, race, or cultural background. For example, all people progress through the same stages, which they encounter at about the same age and handle in much the same way.

This unit presents some of the basic principles psychologists have discovered about human growth and development. Chapter 7 concentrates on the earliest years of life, during which the most basic skills and capacities are developed. Chapter 8 traces the path toward adulthood, showing how these basic skills and capacities are utilized and modified to fit the individual's particular world.

The study of development has at least three important functions. First, it provides insights into why a particular individual thinks and behaves as he does at a particular point in his life. Second, the wisdom gained from examining past development can guide one in proceeding further. Third, knowledge of how people grow and develop can give one a better understanding of children and how best to rear them, teach them, discipline them, love them, and give them the freedom to discover the never-ending joys and pains that are a part of being an ever-growing human being.

7

The First Five Years

Some of the most decisive experiences of your life occurred when you were so young that you cannot remember them. Can you recall your first toy or the first time you stood on two legs? Do you have any memory of first being lifted into your father's arms or of realizing what the word "no" means? You probably remember few if any of these events, yet you changed faster and learned more in your early years than you ever will again.

Psychologists who study human development are interested in the changes that take place in an individual from before birth until death. They try first to describe the changes and then to understand why they occur. These psychologists are interested in studying the roots of behavior common to all human beings and also how human beings come to differ from one another—how they become unique beings. The purpose of this chapter is to present some of the major mechanisms involved in development and to describe the major changes that occur in the first five years of life. Chapter 8 is devoted to the later years of development, particularly childhood and adolescence.

THE BEGINNING OF LIFE

Life begins psychologically as well as physically long before the infant emerges from his mother's womb. Any mother can tell you about the strong kicking and sometimes bothersome hiccupping that occur inside her in the later stages of pregnancy, and it is common for a fetus (the unborn child) to suck its thumb long before it tastes a bottle or its mother's breast.

If an unborn baby is able to act while still in the womb, is it possible for it to learn things, as well? By placing vibrators on the

Figure 7.1

Psychologists used to think of the human baby as practically helpless. Although an infant is certainly highly dependent on others for his survival in his early years, psychologists are beginning to see him as active, capable, and possessed of a distinctive personality right from birth.

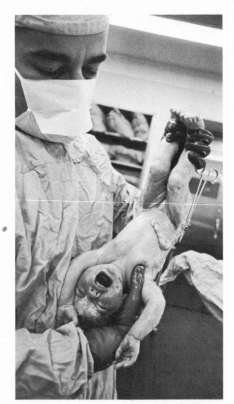

Figure 7.2
Birth must be an overwhelming experience for the baby as well as for the mother. Unfortunately, no one really knows what the newborn infant feels. Nevertheless, some people have reported re-experiencing this struggle from the womb into the open air of the world during drug experiences or while in intensive psychotherapy.

bellies of pregnant women, one psychologist discovered that he could teach a fetus to prepare itself for a loud, startling noise. He would buzz the vibrator just before he made a loud clap, and after he had done so several times, the fetus would jump as soon as the buzzing began. It seems possible then, that a baby starts learning something about the world before he has even entered it.

The birth of a child puts staggering new demands on his capacity to adapt and survive. He goes from an environment in which he is almost totally protected from the world to one in which he is assaulted by lights, sounds, touches, and extremes of temperature.

But the infant is far from the helpless, passive organism some people imagine. He pulses with the rhythms of life—heartbeat, brain waves, breathing. He sleeps and feeds in rhythmic cycles, too, as his mother learns when roused in the night to answer a hungry cry.

At birth the baby is capable of certain coordinated movement patterns that can be triggered by the right stimulus. The *grasping reflex,* for example, is a response to a touch on the palm of the hand. Newborn babies can grasp an object, such as a finger, so strongly that they can be lifted into the air. Earlier in human evolution, when parents were hairier and life was more precarious, babies may have needed this reflex to cling to their mother's chest while she was climbing or looking for food.

Another vital reflex is the *rooting reflex.* If an alert newborn is touched anywhere around the mouth, he will move his head and mouth toward the source of the touch. In this way the touch of his mother's breast on his cheek guides the baby's mouth toward her nipple. The sucking that follows contact with the nipple is one of the baby's most complex reflexes. The baby is able to suck, breathe air, and swallow milk twice a second without getting confused.

Besides grasping and sucking, the newborn baby spends a lot of

Figure 7.3
Reflexes in infants. (a) The strength of the grasping reflex is demonstrated in a baby who is only a few days old. (b) This infant is responding to a touch on the cheek by opening his mouth and turning his head. This response is referred to as the rooting reflex. The baby has been placed in the apparatus by an experimenter so that his head movements can be recorded.

a
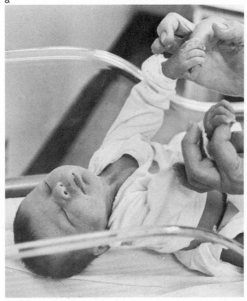

b
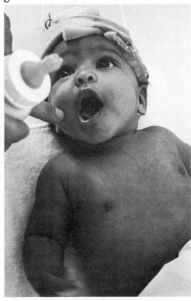

Figure 7.4
The child's interaction with his mother is the first and, as will be seen later in the chapter, probably the most important relationship with another human being in his life. Some psychologists believe that the child learns at the breast and in his mother's arms whether to believe that life is basically good and rewarding or basically painful and uncertain.

time just looking. From birth, unless he is sleeping, feeding, or crying, the baby is watching with curiosity, directing his gaze toward bright patterns and tracing the outlines of those patterns—when he finds them—with his eyes.

HOW DOES DEVELOPMENT HAPPEN?

In the short period of two years, a baby becomes a child who can walk, talk, and feed himself. *Developmental* psychologists are interested in studying this process of growing up and in understanding what kind of a process it is.

Maturation

Some psychologists have thought of the child as being like a tiny plant that shoots up and unfolds according to a plan contained inside him. From this point of view, the process of growth is a process of *maturation.* Child psychologist Arnold Gesell believed that maturation is the most important principle of development, and in his writings he assured parents that the developing child is able to follow his own course unless his environment is extremely adverse.

Other psychologists have found this theory to contain a good deal of truth, for only if a child is persistently underfed, severely restricted in his movements, or deprived of stimulation will he be slow to start talking and walking and appear to be "stupid." And, conversely, it does not appear to be possible to greatly speed up a child's development by giving him enormous numbers of toys or by hanging crowds of mobiles over his crib.

The importance of maturation, or internally programed growth, can be seen most easily in the development of bodily movement. The

159

ability to walk, for example, could not develop without certain changes in the body. In the first few months of life nerves are growing and their connections with muscles are becoming more complicated. Muscles are growing stronger and bones are becoming harder. That is why children walk when they are physically ready—no sooner and no later. Practicing movements ahead of time does not seem to help, and lack of practice does not seem to hurt.

The same sort of process seems to be true to some extent in learning to talk, in learning to understand the physical world, and in learning to love and respect other people, as will be seen later in the chapter, but just how large a part maturation plays in the development of these capabilities is not yet clear.

One of the most important implications of the principle of maturation is that the child is, from the earliest moment of his life, an individual personality. The plan inside him is unique to him in some respects, although it does have much in common with the plans of other babies. On the average, for example, babies start walking at thirteen months. Some, however, are ready at nine months, and others delay walking until they are one and a half.

Each baby has his own *temperament*. Some infants are more active than others; some are less willing to suck; some are cuddly to hold while others seem wiry. Some cry a great deal; others cry little. All these differences are expressions of the child's inner plans and programs. It is important, therefore, that parents recognize each child as an individual whose desires, preferences, and personal styles are distinctive and needful of respect.

Learning

Maturation is only part of the process of growing up. Some psychologists, in fact, think that it is a very small part. They see an infant more as a piece of clay in the hands of many sculptors. Each specific experience changes the child, teaches him something, or pushes him in some direction. Because of his experiences, the child learns to associate certain things and to expect certain events—such as mother and food—to come together. He also learns to do things that produce rewards and to avoid doing things that produce punishments. Finally, he learns by *imitating* others—his parents, his brothers and sisters, and his friends. (The importance of learning by imitation will be seen later in this chapter.)

Just how changeable and trainable human beings are remains open to question, but there is no doubt that the process of growing up is one of exploration, experimentation, and learning—as you can see by watching any healthy baby's bright-eyed wonderment at the world. One psychologist has shown experimentally that six-month-old babies will learn to solve puzzles just for the fun of it. He found that he could teach them to make complex sequences of head turns in order to switch on a white light. It was not the light itself that interested the babies. Once they had succeeded in making it go on a

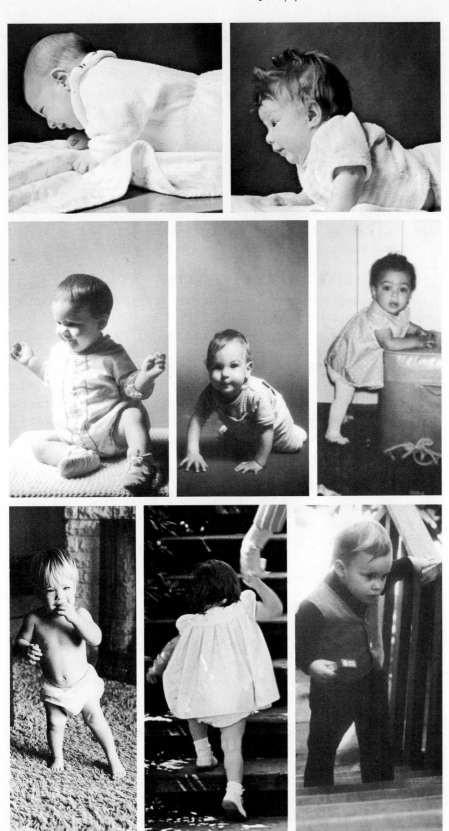

Figure 7.5
Maturation is the principal factor
that determines when a child begins
to walk. As the child's nerves and muscles
develop, he is able first to lift his head (at
about twelve weeks), then to sit (at about
six months), then to crawl (at ten months),
then to walk with one hand held (at about
one year). Running and climbing stairs are
not mastered until about the age of two.
Although maturation controls this
development, learning is very much
involved. The mastery of every new ability
is an exciting adventure full of risks,
mistakes, and triumphs.

few times—by turning their heads twice to the right, three times to the left, and once to the right again, for example—they would lose interest until the experimenter changed the problem.

These problem-solving experiments with infants show that, although the infant may learn most of what he knows from the world around him, he is not necessarily being pushed around by it. He may be actively seeking understanding and knowledge according to some plan. Conversely, the fact that the child follows a plan in development does not mean that he is immune to the forces of the outside world. Even plants grow quite differently depending on the light they receive, the soil they are rooted in, and the nature of other plants around them. The way in which inner plans and outside influences work together as a child grows up will become clearer as the development of intellect, speech, love, and morality are described.

THE DEVELOPMENT OF INTELLECT

The leading psychologist in the study of how children develop an understanding of the world in which they find themselves is Jean Piaget. Piaget is a Swiss psychologist who has been watching children and talking to them for more than fifty years. Piaget's original goal was to define intelligence. He knew that it is something that has to develop—younger children cannot understand things that older children can. His first clue about the nature of intelligence was his discovery that young children are not "dumber" than older children but that, in fact, younger children think in a different *way* than older children.

Piaget found by talking to children of various ages that there are certain things that the sharpest, most inquisitive four-year-old can never understand even though the same idea is easily understood by any seven-year-old. Piaget concluded that intelligence, or the ability to understand, must grow in *stages* according to a plan that is the same for all children. The plan can be carried out in only one way because each stage is built on the stages that have come before it.

The Process of Knowing

The construction of an understanding of the world is the construction of *schemes,* or plans for knowing. Every human being is his own architect and engineer in this respect, constructing schemes, applying them, and changing them as necessary. Two schemes that a baby begins with, for example, are a grasping scheme and a sucking scheme. In other words, the baby understands things in terms of grasping them or sucking them—whether they be breasts, fingers, wooden blocks, or rattles.

When a person puts a scheme into action he is trying to know or understand something. In this process, he *assimilates*—he tries to fit the world into his scheme. He also *accommodates*—he changes his scheme to fit the characteristics of the world. Consider what happens when a baby grasps a block. The baby assimilates objects, such as

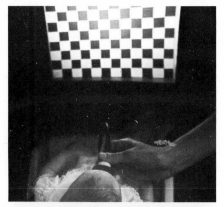

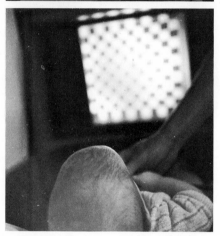

Figure 7.6
Psychologists have tried to devise experiments to determine how infants think and learn. In this experiment, a four-month-old infant is shown a pattern on a screen. He can keep the pattern in focus by sucking on a pacifier hooked up to the projector. For a while the infant will suck with great energy and interest to obtain the reward of the picture. He eventually gets somewhat bored, however, so he does not suck as hard, and the picture fades. When a different picture is made available, the energy he puts into sucking once again increases.

162

blocks, with the grasping scheme, but cannot do so without also accommodating—fitting his grasp to the particular block.

Another example of assimilation and accommodation is given in the series of photographs beginning with Figure 7.8. Look at each one and try to determine what it shows before turning to the next, more focused version. You automatically use the processes of assimilation and accommodation to eventually determine the content of the photograph.

How Knowing Changes

A baby, obviously, has a rather simple kind of understanding. An adult has a more complex set of schemes. Piaget believes that growth to a new kind of understanding happens when old schemes cannot be accommodated enough to assimilate the world. New, grander schemes have to be created. The change in a baby's conception of objects provides an excellent example.

For a six-month-old baby, the sight of an object, its movement between his fingers, and its sensation in his mouth constitute his understanding of it. This understanding lies totally in the here and now. If an infant's toy is hidden from him, he acts as if it has ceased to exist. The only existence it has for him comes from his ability to look at and manipulate it. He does not imagine it, picture it, think of it, remember it, or even forget it. There is nothing to forget. His only knowledge of it is what he is doing with it now.

At about two years of age, the child begins to develop grander schemes and to react to the similarities between experiences. He develops a scheme that might be stated, "If it feels the same, it is the

Figure 7.7

Drinking from a cup involves both assimilation and accommodation for this year-old child. She vigorously applies sucking and grasping schemes to the cup of milk, assimilating it well. Yet she must also learn to accommodate her schemes to the particular qualities of the cup—her grasp sometimes fails, and she appears to be puzzled by the fit of her mouth to the cup.

Figure 7.8

What is pictured in this photograph? As you look at it, you are trying to assimilate it to some scheme you already have. Now turn to Figure 7.16 on page 169 to see a more focused version of the picture.

Figure 7.9

This infant of about six months cannot yet understand that objects have an existence of their own, away from his presence. (a) The infant gazes intently at a toy elephant. (b) When the elephant is blocked from view, she gives no indication that she understands the toy still exists— she does not look for it. This thinking pattern changes by age two, as shown in Figure 7.10.

a  b

same." His toy has the same qualities of redness, squashiness, and squeakiness each time it comes into his world. The mother that keeps appearing and disappearing, he realizes, is not a succession of different objects, but one object.

Now the child is confronted with a contradiction: How can something cease to exist every time it disappears and still keep showing up again? The schemes he has will not work. The baby solves the problem by developing a new scheme—one that changes his entire understanding of the world. The new scheme, *object permanence,* might be expressed, "There is a thing out there that keeps existing independently of my interactions with it." This discovery is a huge accomplishment because it means that the baby conceives of a world around him separate from himself and his activities.

Before, he lived in a world made only of his own actions and sensations, but now he imagines another world of which he is only a part, a world in which there are things other than himself that have an existence of their own—his mother, his crib, his toys, and so on. This realization marks the beginning of *representational thought.* Up to this point, the infant has not really done any "thinking." But now he can imagine and remember (and forget), although he will go through many more changes before his intellect begins to work like that of an adult.

Piaget believes that as the child grows up he goes through a series of four mental stages before achieving adult-type thinking early in his

Figure 7.10
By the age of two, a child realizes that the disappearance of an object does not mean that it no longer exists. In fact, if an object is concealed from him, he will search for it because he knows that it still exists somewhere. This kind of understanding is called object permanence.

teens. At each stage the child builds on the stage before, increasing his abilities to see things from an objective point of view and to hold a number of factors in his mind at the same time. (Piaget's theory is further discussed in Chapter 8.)

THE DEVELOPMENT OF LANGUAGE

A child's ability to use speech develops closely with his ability to think. Both these abilities make use of symbols (as described in Chapter 3). Because words are symbols for things, language can be used to talk about objects that are not present or ideas that are not necessarily true. Because an infant cannot conceive of an object's permanence or use representational thought until the age of two, he does not have much use for symbols until then.

Can Animals Use Language?

The relationship between language and thought is one factor that prevents most animals from using language, although some scientists believe that porpoises and killer whales are exceptions. These sea animals have brains comparable to those of humans, and it is speculated that they, like man, make use of symbolic communications among themselves.

Another animal that shows some evidence of humanlike intelligence is the chimpanzee. Psychologists believe that chimpanzees must develop at least as far as a two-year-old human because they, like two-year-olds, will look for a toy or a bit of food that has disappeared. They can represent the existence of that toy or bit of food in their minds. Can they be taught to "talk" about it?

Many psychologists have tried to teach chimpanzees to use language, but only recently have such efforts been successful. One husband-and-wife-team, the Gardners, raised a baby chimp named Washoe in their home and taught her to use the American Sign Language for deaf people. At three and one-half years of age, Washoe knew eighty-seven signs, for words like "food," "dog," "toothbrush," "gimmee," "sweet," "more," and "hurry."

Making these signs at the appropriate times would not be enough to be called language, though. A dog or a parrot might make signs that its owner could interpret as demands for a walk or for food. Washoe's remarkable achievement was that some of her signs had abstract meanings and that she could put signs together in new ways to produce new meanings. For example, she learned the sign for "more" because she loved to be tickled. She learned to make the sign (putting her fingertips together over her head) to request more tickling. But she was not simply doing something like what a dog does when he rolls over to be tickled; she was able to use the same sign later in entirely new circumstances—asking for more food, or more hair brushing.

This ability to arrange symbols in new combinations to produce new meanings is especially well developed in the human brain. The

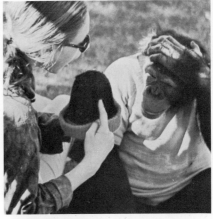

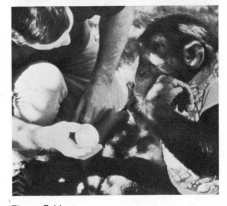

Figure 7.11

Washoe, a chimpanzee raised by Beatrice and Allen Gardner, was about five years old when these photographs were taken. She is demonstrating three of the many words she has learned in American Sign Language. At the top she is naming the object "hat"; in the middle she is making the sign for "sweet"; and at the bottom she is identifying the lemon as a "fruit."

rules for such organization of symbols are called *grammar.* Grammatical rules are what make the sentence "The boy roared at the rhinoceros" mean something different from "The rhinoceros roared at the boy," whereas such combinations as "The at rhinoceros the roared boy" mean nothing at all.

How Children Acquire Language

The example of Washoe shows that there are several steps in learning language. First, one must learn to make the signs; then, one must give them meaning; and finally, one must learn grammar. A child spends the first year of his life practicing making many sounds. He cuts down on crying and starts making mostly cooing sounds, which develop into a *babble* that includes every sound that humans can make—Chinese vowels, African clicks, German rolled r's, and English "o's."

Late in the first year, the strings of babbles begin to sound more like the language that the child is hearing around him. The child imitates the speech of his parents and his older brothers and sisters, and he is greeted with approval whenever he says something that sounds like a word to them. In this way he learns to speak their language, even though he could just as easily learn any other.

The leap to using sounds as symbols occurs some time in the second year. The infant's first real words usually refer to something he can see or touch, and they are usually used as labels or commands ("Dog!" "Cookie!"). The first words are primitive, and the sounds are incomplete: "Ball" usually sounds like "ba," and "cookie" may even sound like "doo-da."

By the time the child is two years old, he has a vocabulary of at least fifty words. Toward the end of the second year, the child begins to express himself more clearly by joining words into two-word phrases.

But at age two a child's grammar is still unlike that of an adult. He speaks in telegrams: "Where my apple?" "Daddy fall down." Nevertheless, as psychologists such as Roger Brown have discovered, the two-year-old already uses certain rules in his speech. He keeps his words in the same order as adults do, for example. Indeed, at one point in his learning of grammar he overdoes it, applying grammatical rules too consistently. For example, the usual rule for forming the past tense of English verbs is to add "ed." But many verbs are irregular: go/went, come/came, swim/swam, fall/fell. At first the child learns the correct form of the verb: "Daddy went yesterday." But once the child discovers the rule for forming past tenses, he replaces the correct form with sentences like "Daddy *goed* yesterday." Although he has never heard adults use this word, he constructs it in accordance with the regularities of grammar that he has extracted from the speech he hears.

By the age of four or five the child has mastered the basics of the

I Love Animals and Dogs

I love animals and dogs and everything.

But how can I do it when dogs are dead
and a hundred?

But here's the reason: If you put
a golden egg on them

They'll get better. But not if you put
a star or moon.

But the star-moon goes up

And the star-moon I love.

Figure 7.12
This poem was written by Hilary-Anne Farley, who was five years old at the time. It is an interesting example of the use of language because, grammatically, it is as correct as most adults', but the thoughts drift in a pattern that adults rarely use except in daydreaming.

language even though his ability to use it will continue to grow with his ability to think about and understand things.

THE GROWTH OF LOVE

While the child is developing his ability to use his body, to think, and to express himself, he is also developing emotionally and increasing his capacity for relationships with other people. All these aspects of the child are closely dependent on one another; they all grow together, and in the earliest part of life they all develop around one central figure—mother.

Experiments with Animals

The early attachment of a child to his mother and the far-reaching effects of this attachment provide a good example of the way in which maturation and learning work together in development. Experiments with baby birds and baby monkeys have shown that there is a maturationally determined time of readiness for attachment early in life. If the infant is too young or too old, the attachment cannot be formed. But the attachment itself is a kind of learning. If the attachment is not made, or if an unusual attachment is made, the infant will develop in an unusual way as a result of this experience.

Imprinting   A European psychologist, Konrad Lorenz, discovered that infant geese become attached to their mothers in a sudden, virtually permanent learning process called *imprinting*. A few hours after they struggle out of their shells, goslings are ready to start waddling after the first thing they see. Whatever it is, they stay with it and treat it as though it were their mother from that time on. Usually, of course, the first thing they see is the mother goose, but Lorenz found that if he substituted himself or some moving object like a green box being dragged along the ground, the goslings would follow that. The goslings are especially sensitive just after birth, and whatever they learn then makes a deep impression that is highly resistant to change. From this early experience with their mother— or mother substitute—the goslings form their idea of what a goose is. Later in life, if they have been imprinted with a human being instead of a goose, they will prefer the company of human beings to other geese and may even try to mate with humans.

Lorenz's experiments showed how experience with a mother can determine an infant bird's entire outlook on himself and on others. An American psychologist, Harry Harlow, went on to study the relationship between mother and child in a species closer to the human being.

Surrogate Mothers   Harlow studied the attachments formed between infant rhesus monkeys and their mothers. His first question was, what is it that makes the mother so important? He tried to

Figure 7.13
Imprinting. A few hours after they were hatched, these baby geese saw Dr. Konrad Lorenz instead of a mother goose. Because goslings have an inborn readiness to attach themselves to their mother within the first few hours of life, these goslings attached themselves to Dr. Lorenz. Thereafter, they followed him around as though he was their mother.

Figure 7.14

An infant rhesus monkey in one of Harry Harlow's experiments. The infant monkey got its food from the wire surrogate mother but maintained contact with the soft, terrycloth mother. Before these experiments were done psychologists believed that children loved their mothers because mother fed them. These experiments showed that, to monkeys at least, feeding is less important than touching. A rhesus monkey loves the mother who is soft and comfortable.

answer this question by taking baby monkeys away from their natural mothers as soon as they were born and raising each of them with two *surrogate,* or substitute, mothers. Each monkey could choose between a mother constructed of wood and wire and a mother who was constructed in the same way but covered with soft cuddly terrycloth. For some of the babies the wire mother had a nipple from which the baby could obtain milk by sucking; for other babies food could be obtained only from the cloth mother.

The purpose of the experiment was to see which surrogate made the better mother. The results were dramatic: The young monkeys became strongly attached to the cloth mother, whether she gave food or not, and for the most part ignored the wire mother. If a frightening object was placed in the monkey's cage, he would run to the terrycloth mother for security, not to the wire mother. It was the touching that mattered, not the feeding.

Effects Later in Life   In another set of experiments, Harlow discovered that monkeys raised without mothers grew up with serious emotional problems. As adults they seemed not to know how to mate, even though they tried; neither did they know how to play or defend themselves. In fact, when frightened by a strange human they often attacked their own bodies instead of making threatening signs of aggression as normal monkeys do.

The monkeys who had cloth mothers grew up more normally than the motherless ones, but even they were not well adjusted to normal monkey life. A partially adequate substitute for a mother turned out to be *peers*—other baby monkeys. Infant monkeys who played with other monkeys like themselves grew up fairly normally even if they never saw their mothers. To grow up completely

Figure 7.15

Harry Harlow performed one set of experiments with rhesus monkeys that showed the importance of early peer contact for normal development. Such contact can make up, at least in part, for lack of a mother, and these results seem to be true for human children as well.

normally, however, both mother *and* peers were necessary. Why were real mothers and other infant monkeys so essential in raising normal monkeys?

One possible answer is that no matter how much contact comfort the cloth mother could provide, "she" could not encourage independence. A normal mother, brother, or sister often becomes annoyed at an infant's clinging as he gets older, forcing him to stand on his own two feet. The cloth mother, however, remained always passively available. The encouragement of independence is, of course, only one factor. Interactions with mother and peers also allow the baby to see and learn from the behavior of other monkeys. The motionless surrogate provided no such opportunity.

Human Babies

A number of psychologists believe that these findings about mother-child relationships can be applied to human beings. John Bowlby, René Spitz, and others have investigated cases of children who, like Harlow's monkeys, were deprived of their mothers at an early age. They concluded that severe personality problems can develop when an attachment is not formed or when it is forcibly broken (as by death of the mother) before the age of seven.

Children need individual attention, warmth, comfort, security, and stimulation. Without a mother and family, they are less likely to

Figure 7.16
Can you tell yet what the photograph is showing? Make another attempt to accommodate your existing schemes, then turn to page 177 and check your new guess with the better resolution in Figure 7.25.

Figure 7.17
A warm and loving home environment helps to give a child the social and emotional basis he needs for normal psychological development.

receive it. Some infants in orphanages and other institutions may receive enough attention if the institution has a large staff of people who can give children love. More often, however, an institution has a cold, impersonal atmosphere in which children tend to become withdrawn and may literally waste away, even though their physical needs are adequately cared for.

SEX ROLES AND MORALITY

In his early family life the child establishes the roots of two of the most significant aspects of human life: sexual identity and morality. Children need to learn how to behave as a male or female; they also need to learn discipline, self-control, and respect for the rights of others. The most famous theory of how these two processes develop was proposed by Sigmund Freud.

Freud's Theory of Psychosexual Development

Freud believed that children have powerful urges and impulses that bring them into conflict with the rules and principles of civilization. (Freud's theory of personality is described in Chapter 12.) These urges and impulses, he thought, are mostly *erotic*. It is in learning to control and tame these impulses that children gain a sense of right and wrong. They do so by modeling themselves after their parents, who have already gained a moral sense. Boys model themselves after

Figure 7.18
Every child, no matter how he is brought up, has to learn to deal with his own bodily functions in a way that is acceptable to the adults around him. Toilet training and feeding may have more than practical significance for the child, because stresses between parents and children are often expressed in these fundamental situations. Some psychologists believe that adult character traits and emotional problems are determined by these early experiences.

their fathers, and girls model themselves after their mothers. In this way, they also learn how to behave like men and women.

In the first few years of life boys and girls have similar experiences. Their great erotic pleasures are obtained through the mouth, sucking at their mother's breast. Weaning is a period of frustration and conflict—it is the child's first experience with not getting what he wants. Freud called this the *oral* stage of development. Later the anus becomes the source of erotic pleasure, giving rise to what Freud called the *anal* stage. The child enjoys holding in or pushing out his feces until he is required, through toilet training, to curb this freedom.

The major conflict, however, comes between the ages of three and five, when the child discovers the pleasure he can obtain from his genitals. As a consequence, he becomes extremely aware of the differences between himself and the opposite sex. In this *phallic* stage, according to Freud, the child is like a little adult and wants to share adult pleasures, especially the pleasures of love. Each child becomes rival for the affections of his parent of the opposite sex. The boy wants to win his mother for himself and finds himself in hostile conflict with his father. The girl wants her father for herself and tries to shut out her mother.

In the boy, Freud called this crisis the *Oedipal conflict,* after Oedipus, the king in Greek tragedy who unknowingly killed his father and married his mother and later discovered with horror what he had done. Freud believed that the boy suffers great conflict about his feelings for his mother. The boy finds that he hates his father and wishes him gone or dead. But his father is far stronger than he is. The boy fears that his father will see how he feels and punish him, perhaps by castrating him. To prevent this fearful punishment, the boy buries his sexual feelings and tries to make himself "good." He tries to become as much like his father as possible so that his father will not want to hurt him. He satisfies himself with becoming *like* the person who possesses mother, instead of trying to possess her himself. In this process, which is called *identification,* the boy takes on all his father's values and moral principles. Thus, at the same time that he learns to behave like a man, he acquires his father's morality. His father's voice becomes a voice inside him, the voice of conscience.

Freud believed that a girl finds herself in the similarly dangerous position of wanting to possess her father and to exclude her mother. Freud's explanation of the girl's reasons for feeling this way was that the girl is driven by envy of her father's penis and by suspicion that her mother has already removed the penis the girl once had. The girl supposedly wants to make up for the situation as best she can by winning her father away from her mother.

Freud's theory of sex roles and moral development is now thought to have certain failings, but it does contain a general idea of great importance: Children have to learn to bring their desires in line with

Figure 7.19
The Oedipal conflict. Young boys, according to psychoanalytic theorists, go through a stage in which they wish they could get rid of their fathers and have their mothers all to themselves. Young girls experience a parallel conflict. Sigmund Freud believed that it is in resolving this conflict that children acquire a moral sense and a sexual identity. They bury their sexual feelings and model themselves on the parent of the same sex as themselves.

the rules of society. Freud believed that among the foremost of these desires was the desire for sexual love. The child learns that the society does not allow this desire to be satisfied in his own family.

The Social-Learning Approach

Freud's theory placed great emphasis on the *feelings* of children and on the importance of parents as models for the child to identify with. Later theorists have agreed with Freud that the child models himself on his parents, but they have emphasized the child's *behavior* or his *thinking,* rather than his feelings.

The group of theorists who emphasize behavior see moral and sex-role development as part of a gradual process of *social learning.* They believe that boys learn to behave like males and girls learn to behave like females because, in a thousand small ways, parents, teachers, and other children reward them when they act appropriately and punish them when they do not. Boys are rewarded for being tough and aggressive. Girls are likely to be punished for acting aggressively and to be rewarded for being sweet and shy.

Just as society shapes a child sexually, so it shapes him morally. A child learns to be obedient, for example, because his parents reward him with approval and love when he obeys and punish him with disapproval and anger when he does not. To avoid punishment and gain rewards from those around them, children learn to reward and

Figure 7.20
Social-learning theorists emphasize the fact that the growing child is rewarded for "good" behavior and for behavior that is appropriate to his or her sex. In addition, children learn to imitate the behaviors of important adults around them, particularly their parents.

punish themselves. A person might learn to mentally kick himself for making a mistake that in the past had led to punishment. The mistake might be a moral one—lying, for example. Or it might be a sexually inappropriate behavior. A boy might learn to be hard on himself for showing emotion because in the past his tears and blushes have met with derisive laughter.

In this theory, the *imitation of models* is also closely related to rewards and punishments. Psychologist Albert Bandura has shown how the process of imitation works. In his experiments he shows children movies of another child or an adult reacting to some situation; then he puts the children in the same situation to see how they will behave. In one experiment three groups of children watched films of an adult yelling at and punching a "Bobo" doll. For each group the film had a different ending. In one version the person who was attacking the Bobo doll was scolded afterward by an authority. In another version the authority praised the adult and rewarded him with candy and soft drinks. In the third version nothing happened.

When the children who had been watching the films were put in a room with Bobo dolls themselves, their reactions depended on which film they had seen. They acted as if they had been the person in the film. If they had seen the person punished, they tended not to hit the doll, but if they had seen the person rewarded, they attacked it

Figure 7.21
Imitation of aggression in children. (*top row*) Frames from one of the films that psychologist Albert Bandura showed to children. (*bottom two rows*) Behavior of children who watched the film and were given a chance to play with similar objects. As you can see, these children seem to be imitating the behavior they had watched. Such imitation was particularly likely if the adult in the film was rewarded for her aggressive actions.

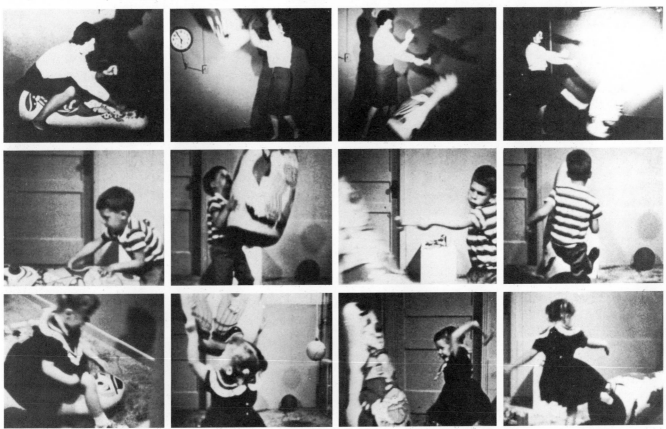

Figure 7.22
In the process of exploring his world and acting on the objects in it, the infant learns how reality is constructed. Sometimes, however, the learning process can be hazardous.

vigorously. The children who had seen the third version attacked the doll quite often, too. Bandura believes that children may learn to be violent from watching television heroes attack their enemies and from seeing one parent not fight back when attacked by the other. Of course, if the child models himself on the parent who does not fight back instead of the parent who attacks, then he learns skills of submission instead of aggression.

The Cognitive-Developmental Approach

The theorists who emphasize *thinking* (or cognition, as psychologists usually call it) in development see the child quite differently than do the Freudian or the social-learning theorists. Instead of viewing the child as driven by sexual urges into a clash with society, or as being gradually shaped by society's rewards, punishments, and examples, cognitive-developmental theorists see the child as a person in search of truth, understanding, and mastery of the world in which he finds himself. This theory is an offshoot of Piaget's theory of intellectual development.

What Freud called *identification* and social-learning theorists call *imitation* is called *role-taking* in cognitive-developmental theory. Children take on the roles of other people; they put themselves in the other person's position in order to gain a broader view of the world and to increase their mastery of the tasks they set for themselves. In moral development, for example, the child begins with only his own point of view. Later he sees things from the point of view of his own society and especially of certain adults—his parents and his teachers in particular. At an advanced stage (which not everyone reaches) he sees things from the point of view of all mankind. He feels that

Figure 7.23
According to cognitive-developmental theory, children imitate their parents for reasons other than approval. Instead, such imitation is an attempt to excel at being what they are, be it male or female. According to this theory, once a boy realizes he is a male, he will not want to be rewarded for female behaviors, even if he could be.

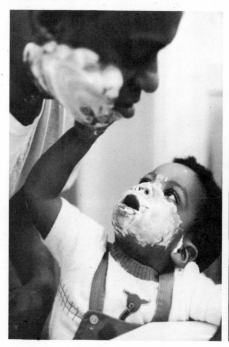

"good" is not what benefits just him, or just his parents and teachers, but what benefits the whole of humanity.

In sex-role development a girl decides to model herself on her mother because, realizing she has been born a girl, she decides she wants to do girl things and do them well. The same, of course, goes for boys. According to cognitive-developmental theory, this decision does not take place until about the age of five. Before that time, children do not realize that labels mean something permanent and unchangeable—they might think that a cat could turn into a dog, for example. Similarly, a four-year-old might think that a girl could become a boy by playing boys' games, wearing boys' clothes, or getting a haircut. But once the child realizes that he or she is a boy or girl no matter what, he or she does his or her best to fill that role.

The idealism of this theory is one of its most interesting aspects. This theory implies that in learning sex roles and morality the child is not simply adopting society's values but is trying to reach general truths about the nature of man, woman, and rightness.

IMPLICATIONS FOR CHILD REARING

It would be a serious mistake to think that one of these theories is correct and that the others are wrong. All of them contain elements of the truth, and they are best treated as different viewpoints of the same process. The most complete picture would contain all these points of view—the emotional, the behavioral, and the cognitive.

The three points of view have several practical implications for child rearing. The most obvious is that parents and older brothers and sisters should remember that they are being used as *models* by younger children. A child learns to behave as he sees others behaving, whether they want him to or not.

Second, it is important to recognize that the child is *trying to understand the world for himself*. A child who is given the freedom to figure out certain things on his own will begin to structure the world according to his individual needs. Many parents do not realize how important it is that the child develop skills on his own. A mother who tells her young child to color the sky blue instead of orange may not realize that she is inhibiting the child's natural tendency to experiment with his creativity. Or a mother who finds it more convenient to tie her five-year-old's shoelaces, instead of teaching him to do it himself, may not realize that she is depriving her child of the satisfaction and sense of accomplishment he could be deriving.

Third, it is important that the *rules for reward and punishment be clear and consistent*. A child who grows up with no boundaries has no framework within which to operate. He does not know what is possible and what is not possible. He may also feel that his parents do not really care about him because they do not seem sufficiently interested to direct his behavior.

Consistent rules are important because they allow the child to generalize from one situation to the next. If he is punished for hitting his younger brother or sister one day and not punished the next, he cannot be sure whether the behavior is permissible. And the rules must not require more of a child than he is capable of giving. If a two-year-old is punished for spilling his milk, he will begin to feel responsible for things he cannot control. If his parents consistently punish clumsy two-year-old behaviors, the child may eventually come to view himself as worthless—everything he does is bad.

Finally, one of the most important things that a parent can teach his child is *how to express his feelings.* In this sense, it is more to the child's advantage to grow up in a home where there is screaming and yelling when something goes wrong than in a home where there is nothing but bitter silence. It has been found that people who are able to express anger not only release feelings that can become destructive if repressed but are also able to express their positive feelings of joy and love. Parents should encourage their children to show their anger, their hurt, and their resentment, as well as their happy and positive feelings. Children need to know that their feelings are valid and important. Parents can give this confidence to their children simply by listening to them and responding with understanding. Children need to learn that they are responsible for controlling their actions but not their feelings.

Figure 7.24
A child's capacity for independence can at times be almost unbelievable to his parents because at other times he is so completely dependent on them.

SUMMARY

1. Even before birth, human babies are capable of simple responses. In the first months of life, infants exhibit a variety of rhythms and coordinated movement patterns, such as sucking and grasping.

2. Development is a combination of maturation and learning. Maturation is the process of internally programed growth: Babies tend to

develop at their own pace and on their own individual tracks. But the pattern of growth is also shaped by the individual's experience, through such mechanisms as association, reward, punishment, and imitation.

3. Jean Piaget has put forth the idea that a child's intelligence advances through qualitatively different stages. A child constructs and uses schemes, or plans for knowing, in dealing with the world. Through the process of assimilation, he tries to fit the world into his schemes; through accommodation, he tries to change his schemes to fit in with the world.

4. At about age two the child discovers the scheme of object permanence—the idea that objects continue to exist even when he is not perceiving them. This realization marks the beginning of representational thought—being able to think about the things that are not present.

5. Language is the use of symbols to communicate. Chimpanzees can be taught to use a simple language, but the ability to master complex grammatical rules seems to be unique to humans. Grammar allows people to create vast numbers of meanings from a relatively small number of symbols.

6. The earliest and most important emotional attachment animals have is to their mother. The process of attachment in birds takes the form of imprinting—baby birds become attached to the first moving object they see. Infant monkeys become attached to whatever provides comfort to them—even terrycloth-covered wire constructions that serve as surrogate mothers.

Figure 7.25
With this degree of focus, you are probably able to accommodate one of your schemes to successfully assimilate the picture. You can check your decision by turning to Figure 7.26 on page 179.

7. Human babies need human attention, comfort, and stimulation from an early age if they are to have normal emotional development.

8. Freud believed that the unconscious sexual conflicts of children must be resolved for them to have a productive relationship with society. Children develop a sex-role identity and a moral conscience by identifying with the appropriate parent.

9. The social-learning approach to sex roles and morality is based on the concepts of operant conditioning and imitation. A child's behavior is determined by rewards and punishments.

10. The cognitive-developmental approach to sex roles and morality derives from Piaget's theory of the stages of intellectual development. The child takes on those roles that aid him in the search for truth, understanding, and mastery of his world and that fit his cognitive stage.

11. The findings of developmental psychologists have several implications for child rearing. Parents should provide appropriate models for the child, allow him to figure out things on his own (develop his

own schemes), provide consistent rewards, and teach the child to express his feelings.

ACTIVITIES

1. Talk with children who are under five years old, paying particular attention to their grammar. What kinds of errors do they make? What kinds of grammatical rules do they already seem to know?

2. Do you and your parents share the same religious beliefs? Political orientation? Feelings about violence? Attitudes toward sex? Goals for living? Opinions about money? Views on drugs? Do you have similar tastes in: Clothing colors and styles? Music? Pets? Housing? Furniture? Foods? Cars? Entertainment? After asking yourself these questions, determine how well your beliefs, opinions, and tastes agree with those of your parents. How important do you think your early social training was for what you believe, think, and like? Compare your reactions to each of your parents with their reactions to each other—do you respond to your mother's anger the same way your father does, for example?

3. What is the most moral and the most immoral thing you have done or observed in your life? What are your reasons for these judgments? Can you explain why you, or the person you observed, acted in these ways?

4. How are sex roles communicated to people in American society? Look carefully through magazines and newspapers, watch television commercials, and listen to the radio. What activities, interests, worries, virtues, weaknesses, physical characteristics, and mannerisms are presented as attributes of typical men and women? Are sex roles portrayed differently in different media? Are there various stereotypes within each sex?

5. Make a log of a day in your life, or the life of a younger brother or sister, and take notes of every event that you think would come out differently for a person of the opposite sex. What are the reasons for these differences?

6. If you have a family album of photographs, look through it and try to remember how you felt and how you saw things at the times the pictures were taken. Look at childhood pictures of your parents and see if you can see their childhood personalities in them now.

7. Write a brief autobiography. What are the events that you feel have been the most significant in your life? What have been the main influences on your social and emotional development?

8. If you have an infant brother or sister, or a pet dog or cat, perform a simple experiment to test for object permanence. Be sure to use several different objects for your test, and be certain that the baby or animal is not afraid of, or uninterested in, the object. Most dogs or cats will probably search for vanished objects.

9. Ask children of different ages the following questions: Where does the sun go at night? Could you become a girl (a boy) if you wanted to?

Does your brother (sister) have any brothers (sisters)? What makes leaves fall off trees? If you find some of their theories interesting, it is easy to think of many other questions.

SUGGESTED READINGS

BECK, JOAN. *How to Raise a Brighter Child.* New York: Simon & Schuster, 1967. Beck presents the case for early cognitive stimulation of children and provides guidelines for rearing mentally well-functioning children.

BERRILL, N. J. *The Person in the Womb.* New York: Dodd, Mead, 1968 (paper). A beautifully written book that describes the development of the fetus and embryo in the womb.

BURNETT, FRANCES HODGSON. *The Secret Garden.* New York: Grosset & Dunlap, 1911 (paper). The unforgettable story of a plain, sour nine-year-old girl who, through her association with nature and her friendship with an unusual boy, grows and blossoms emotionally.

GINOTT, H. *Between Parent and Child.* New York: Macmillan, 1965 (paper). Ginott sees a child's behavior as a special way of communicating ideas he may not be able to verbalize. The author provides practical advice on how parents and children can understand and get along with one another.

HOLT, JOHN. *How Children Fail.* New York: Dell, 1964 (paper). A powerful description of the ways in which the American educational system stifles the development of children. As a teacher, Holt has many first-hand accounts to back up his criticisms.

HOLT, JOHN. *How Children Learn.* New York: Dell, 1967 (paper). In his follow-up to *How Children Fail,* Holt gives enchanting portraits of children learning to use language and ideas. He focuses particularly on preschoolers.

Figure 7.26
Finally, the picture is in full focus. Normally, the processes of assimilation and accommodation occur so quickly and so automatically that you are not aware of their existence.

LAING, R. D. *The Politics of Experience.* New York: Ballantine, 1967 (paper). Laing offers a probing expose of the individual and the family—the methods that family members use to manipulate and exploit one another in the name of socialization and protection.

LILLY, JOHN. *The Mind of the Dolphin: A Non-Human Intelligence.* Garden City, N.Y.: Doubleday, 1967. Very interesting account of Lilly's attempt to learn the language of dolphins and to teach them human language. Lilly believes that dolphins are easily as intelligent as humans and should be treated with respect.

SPOCK, B. *Baby and Child Care.* New York: Pocket Books, 1968 (paper), originally published, 1946. For decades this book has served as a handy and practical guide for parents. Spock speaks plainly on almost every conceivable issue of child rearing. In recent editions, Dr. Spock has recommended a less rigid approach to child rearing than he used to advocate.

8
Childhood and Beyond

There are two extraordinary periods of physical growth in human life—infancy and adolescence. During both these periods the individual undergoes rapid and dramatic spurts in development. But these two periods of life have more in common than physical changes: Infants and adolescents experience similar psychological changes as well.

If you have younger brothers or sisters or have watched other children growing up, you are probably familiar with the famous negativism of the two-year-old. A two-year-old spends a lot of time saying "no." The reason he does so is not because he has suddenly become obstinate or stubborn. Rather, it is because he has developed a sense of independence as a result of his newly acquired abilities to walk, to run, and to act on things in his environment.

The two-year-old uses "no" as a way of testing and confirming his independence. The adolescent is concerned with the same issue, but the independence he is seeking is on a higher level and has more final consequences than the two-year-old's. The adolescent is preparing to leave the security of home and parents. The stresses created by this adolescent drive toward independence will be explored later in this chapter. First, however, it is necessary to examine the ways in which an infant becomes a child and a child becomes an adolescent.

DEVELOPMENT OCCURS IN STAGES

In the process of psychological development, individuals necessarily pass through several *stages,* including infancy, childhood, adolescence, adulthood, and, eventually, old age. Many developmental psychologists believe that each stage is marked by the appearance of abilities that had not previously existed. They also believe that there are certain *developmental tasks,* or important changes, that must take place within each stage if the person is to successfully move into the next one. For example, Jean Piaget sees the achievement of object permanence as an important developmental task in infancy, and Sigmund Freud believed that resolution of the Oedipal conflict is

Figure 8.1
A child begins the long transition to adulthood when he or she first experiences the physiological changes of puberty. These changes bring a new kind of self-awareness that did not exist in childhood.

a major task for the five-year-old. (The theories of Piaget and Freud are discussed in Chapter 7.)

Another psychologist who has developed an influential theory of stages is Erik Erikson, who has based many of his ideas on Freud's theory. Erikson's view of human development takes into account both psychological and social factors, so his approach is referred to as *psychosocial.* Erikson believes that a person progresses through eight different stages in life and that the outcome of each stage has significant consequences for the individual's personality.

Erikson sees each stage as marked by a crisis or conflict of critical importance for the future. These eight crises are summarized in the names Erikson has given to them (such as basic trust versus mistrust), as shown in Figure 8.2. The two-year-old, for example, experiences a crisis in which he achieves *autonomy* (independence) if he is successful but suffers from *shame* and *doubt* if he fails. He wants to use his new-found physical skills and understanding to explore his surroundings, and just the fact that he has these new capacities adds to his self-esteem. But he also expects the adults around him to acknowledge his ability to walk and to confirm the sense of independence he has thereby gained. If those around him do not acknowledge his new status; if, in fact, they ignore him except to punish him for "getting into things," the child may begin to doubt the value of his new abilities and to suffer shame because he feels that his desire for independence is bad. If the outcome at this stage of life is shame and doubt, the child will be hampered in his development.

There is not enough room in this chapter to describe in detail all of the stages presented in Figure 8.2 (the alternatives at the adolescent stage are discussed later), but it is important to note that, unlike

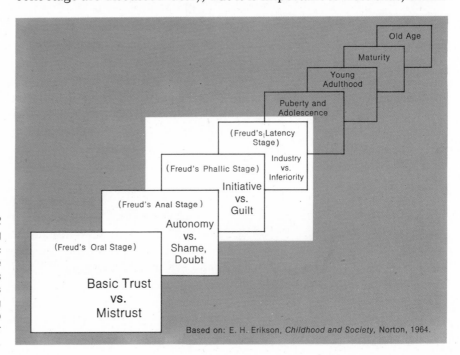

Figure 8.2
Erik Erikson's eight psychosocial stages, each of which contains a specific task to be accomplished. These stages are extensions of Freud's psychosexual stages referred to in Chapter 7. Erikson has elaborated on Freud's approach by adding the dimension of interpersonal relations to it. Erikson's eight stages are further described in Figures 8.3, 8.19, and 8.20.

Based on: E. H. Erikson, *Childhood and Society*, Norton, 1964.

Freud's stages, Erikson's do not stop with adolescence. Development is a lifelong process. Not only is change always possible, it is desirable and, as Erikson notes, necessary.

CHILDHOOD

Although the changes in children between the ages of six and twelve are not as dramatic as those in infants or adolescents, they are nonetheless significant. Besides new physical abilities, there are giant changes in the intellectual abilities of the child. Furthermore, the childhood years are probably the most important for learning how to live in society.

Growth of Thought and Emotion

The crowning achievement in the infant's cognitive development, as was explained in Chapter 7, is his ability to understand that objects and people continue to exist even when they are out of his sight. This

Figure 8.3
Erikson's first four stages.

(*top left*) Freud called the first stage the oral stage because the most important aspect of an infant's life is sucking. For Erikson, the crisis at this stage is basic trust versus mistrust. The infant needs to know that he will be looked after and that the world is an orderly place. If he experiences too much uncertainty to establish this confidence, he will thereafter tend to look at the world with fear and suspicion.

(*top right*) Freud's anal stage (the time of toilet training) is thought by Erikson to involve a crisis of autonomy versus shame and doubt. The child is learning self-control and self-assertion. But if he receives too much criticism, he will be ashamed of himself and doubt his right to be independent.

(*bottom left*) At about age three or four the child enters what Freud calls the phallic stage, a stage of sexual awareness. Erikson sees the issue here as initiative versus guilt. The child learns to make decisions with little worry about other people. If he is constantly discouraged or punished for going too far, he will feel guilty and mistakenly believe that his impulses are bad.

(*bottom right*) Freud believed that sexuality is temporarily forgotten, or latent, during the years from six to twelve. According to Erikson, at this stage the child struggles with industry versus inferiority. He gains mastery of skills that interest him, and he finds pride in his competence. But if people around him criticize his work as silly or useless, he will feel that he is somehow inferior.

Figure 8.4

According to Piaget, between the ages of five and seven every child masters the concepts of number, class, and order. Piaget believes that children can discover these principles for themselves, as this child is doing when she explores the properties of a deck of cards.

new understanding brings with it changes in emotional experience. When the infant realizes that all those mother figures that keep appearing to feed and comfort him are, in fact, one continuously existing mother, he also realizes that when this one (and only) mother leaves, she might not come back. So, for a while, he suffers *separation anxiety* and cries bitterly whenever his mother must go away for a while.

More complex cognitive abilities emerge as the infant grows into childhood. At some time between the ages of five and seven, most children come to understand what Jean Piaget calls *conservation*. For example, if you have two identical short, wide jars filled with water and you pour the contents of one into a tall, narrow jar, a child under five will say that the tall jar now contains more water than the short one. And even if you pour the water back into the short jar to show that the amount has not changed, the child will still maintain that there is "more" water in the tall jar if you repeat the experiment.

Within two years, however, the same child will be able to co-ordinate his perceptions of the height and width of the containers. He will be able to understand that pouring an amount of liquid from one container to another does not change the amount of liquid involved.

Many such cognitive advances take place between the years of five and ten. The child comes to have a rough understanding of *necessary truths*—some things simply have to be true because that is the way the world operates. This realization takes some of the magic away from the child's view of the world, but it allows him to operate more effectively because he is able to understand things as they are, rather than as they seem to be or as he wishes them to be.

The child's increasing sophistication also means that the objects of his fears change. Infants respond with fear most often to loud noises, falling, and strangers. But by the age of five, the child has an imagination, and many of his fears are ones that he has invented for himself. Fears of "things that go bump in the night" are remarkably persistent, sometimes lasting into adulthood, but they are generally displaced by more realistic fears as the child grows older. Fear of drowning, fire, or traffic accidents fills the mind of a seven-year-old. Fears related to social acceptability preoccupy him by the age of ten.

Learning to Live in Society

It is between the years of six and twelve that most of the process of *socialization* occurs—the child learns the rules of behavior necessary for living with the other people he finds around him. Although his parents remain important shapers of his personality, they are no longer the only influencers of his development. With his first full day of school, the child begins a period in which nearly half his waking hours are spent away from his family. (This process begins even earlier for those children who attend preschools.) His friends, schoolmates, and teachers enter the process of his learning about

Figure 8.5
Between the ages of five and ten, children not only develop physically and intellectually but also socially. They learn how to interact with one another, how to share enjoyment, and how to watch and appreciate as well as be the center of attention. They must also learn to deal with the negative experiences, such as anger and envy, that can occur in social relationships.

how the world works and how he should respond to its challenges and expectations.

Parents and Teachers Parents and teachers are important influences because children tend to imitate those adults who occupy large parts of their lives. Also, these adults have the power to reward and punish. They consciously and unconsciously reward the child, with praise or smiles or hugs, for expressing attitudes that back up their own beliefs, and they tend to ignore or be hostile toward the expression of opinions that are contrary to their own. In this way, both parents and teachers are powerful shapers. One of the most important things they teach children is sex roles.

Children who see their father go off every morning to an office or factory while their mother stays home to cook and clean come to understand that men work and earn money and women take care of their families. At home and in school, boys are encouraged to engage in athletics and be aggressive, whereas girls are discouraged from doing those things. One good illustration of how things are sorted out as boys' activities and girls' activities can be seen in what toys children are given. How many girls do you know who receive baseball mitts, footballs, or tool kits as gifts? And how many boys get miniature furniture or toy stoves?

Figure 8.6
Social rules in American society encourage males to be active and aggressive and females to be passive and supportive. These rules are reflected in many aspects of everyday life, such as this situation, in which the boy performs while the girl looks on in admiration.

One of the reasons for this differential treatment of children is that parents want their children to grow up behaving the way men and women are "supposed" to behave, and children themselves want to master the roles that they see adults playing. In addition to this social factor, some psychologists believe that there are activities and personality characteristics that are "natural" to each of the sexes. Along with bodily differences there are psychological differences; according to this view, women are more likely to be cooperative, caring, and submissive, whereas men are likely to be dominant and aggressive.

There is a good deal of controversy over this question. As will be seen later in this chapter, many characteristics that were thought to be "natural" to males and females have been found to be socially learned. At this point it is not clear what behavior, if any, is natural to one sex or the other. Certainly what society *expects* of the two sexes is beginning to change.

Friends and Schoolmates　　Socialization of the child is accomplished as much with peers as with elders. Among the most important ways in which children learn from each other is through *games.* Games in childhood are serious business. It is through game playing that children learn how to relate socially, test their own abilities, and try out aspects of adult life.

The games being discussed here are *not* those that adults organize for children. Little League baseball, for instance, is the opposite of the kinds of games children pass on to other children. In their own games—hopscotch or follow-the-leader—children spend a lot of time making the rules, and once they are made, they must be followed without deviation (although a leader may make some changes). This process lets children learn that an agreed-upon structure helps maintain social interactions. Also, once the structure has been established, a child can relax and enjoy the game without worrying about being rejected—as long as he does not break the rules.

Another function of most games is to let the child experience bits of adult life in a nonthreatening way. Children's games are different from most adult games because it is the experiencing of play, not the winning, that counts. A child can experience competition of various kinds, including testing himself against his outer limits, but he will not be hurt by comparison. In play, he can experience virtually all the incidents and emotions of life, from love to hate, without risk.

Through play, then, a child learns social roles, gathers information about what his peers expect of him, tests his strengths, and learns his weaknesses.

School　　Although teachers as well as parents shape and provide models for children's behavior, in general the school is a weaker influence in development than are family and peers. For many children, beginning in grade 4 or 5 and going on into high school, real life is lived outside the classroom. Although a few subjects or certain teachers may be valued, on the whole, school becomes something to be endured rather than enjoyed. Why should this be so? The answer may lie in two important organizational characteristics of public schools. For one, many teachers intentionally remain aloof from their students, especially in the later grades. They conceal what they personally like or what privately bores or enrages them. Where this emotional barrier exists, it is unlikely that children will imitate or identify with their teacher.

The other factor that lessens the school's impact on social development is its avoidance of controversial subjects. There are probably a number of reasons for sticking to safe topics—parent's

Figure 8.7
From the ages of six to seventeen, a large portion of everyone's life is spent in school. Individual responses to the school situation vary enormously. Because the school is one's main contact with society, the amount of satisfaction one finds in his school experiences is to some degree a measure of the amount of satisfaction he will find in society as a whole.

wishes, or tradition, or timidity, perhaps. But whatever the reason, schools have dealt with discussion of problems such as sex, prejudice, war, government, and pollution in such bland ways that the child often feels he must go to friends or family to learn about "real life."

ADOLESCENCE

The growing child might continue the process of social, emotional, and intellectual change toward adulthood smoothly and gradually if it were not for two factors. One, *puberty,* the startling biological transformation that begins in the early teens, makes a fairly abrupt break in the course of life an inevitability. This change is made sharper by a second factor: In Western society, adolescence is recognized as a separate stage of life distinct from childhood on the one hand and adulthood on the other. It has not always been so, nor is it so in all societies.

Even in Western industrial societies, adolescence was not set apart from adulthood until after World War I. Until then, most young people simply started working, some at age twelve or thirteen. Since then, a number of social changes have made it both impossible and unnecessary for most teenagers to work for a living in American society.

The American economy has become more industrial, more technologically sophisticated, and wealthier. It can afford to free middle- and upper-class young people from work, but it requires them to spend their time in high schools and colleges learning how to do the demanding jobs it needs them for later. Nevertheless,

Figure 8.8
Adolescence may be experienced quite differently depending on how a person has been brought up, what kind of community he lives in, and what his society expects from him. However, there are certain characteristics that seem to be common to all adolescents. Psychologist Edgar Friedenberg suggests that with adolescent sexuality comes a capacity for tenderness and understanding in personal relations that young children do not have. Furthermore, he says, adolescence brings a new kind of self-assurance and sense of freedom.

teenagers who do want to work find it difficult to get jobs, either because they lack skill and experience or because they are too young to be legally hired. This kind of contradiction is common in adolescent life. Some contradictions are inevitable at this stage, but it is interesting to keep in mind the fact that many of them are created by a society that tries to treat adolescents as children and as adults at the same time.

Contradiction, the existence of influences working in opposite directions, and a related experience, *ambivalence*, seems to be characteristic of adolescence. Ambivalence is the experience of conflicting feelings. One of the main causes of ambivalence in adolescence is the marked physical changes with which it begins.

Physical Changes

The growth spurt mentioned at the start of this chapter begins with puberty, the onset of hormonal changes that result in sexual maturity. These changes cause girls to start menstruating, to develop breasts, and to grow body hair. They cause boys to grow facial and body hair, to develop larger testes and penis, to have a deeper voice, and to become capable of ejaculation. With these changes, the individual becomes physically capable of engaging in sexual relations and of having children.

The age at which puberty begins is now about twelve for girls and about fourteen for boys. (These average ages have steadily decreased in Western societies with each generation.) Girls maintain the lead in physical maturity until near the end of adolescence. The difference between boys and girls in early adolescence is rather startling, especially because the girls are also more socially mature. Of course, there is a wide range in the average age at which puberty begins and in the subsequent rate of development. Some boys and girls mature early, some late. Reactions to the onset of puberty itself can range from pleasure and pride to shame or guilt. Adolescents whose parents have told them what to expect usually have few negative reactions. But individual differences in rate of maturation can cause some adolescents considerable worry and self-doubt because of their natural inclination to compare themselves with others.

Reactions to Growth   The sudden changes that occur in the adolescent often make him extremely self-conscious. He is changing too fast to get used to himself, and he wonders what others think of him. A girl whose breasts and hips fill out early may find herself the object of admiration or envy from her friends, but she may also feel herself out of place among them and ill at ease with older girls. A late-maturing girl is almost sure to feel inferior and childish for a while as her bosomed friends are joining adult society.

Males who mature early seem to be in a fortunate position: They are usually objects of admiration from their friends and from girls, who welcome them as more their equals. The self-esteem they gain

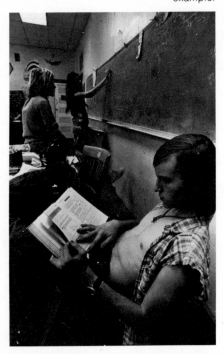

Figure 8.9
One of the most obvious results of the physical changes that accompany puberty is an increased awareness of one's physical appearance. This awareness may take the form of concern for personal cleanliness, of embarrassment or pride in one's differences from other people, or of taking pleasure in one's attractiveness, for example.

Figure 8.10
With new capacities for intensity and enjoyment of life comes a vulnerability to rejection and feelings of inadequacy. Such feelings of self-doubt are often associated with unsureness about one's sexual identity or about one's attractiveness to the opposite sex.

from this admiration appears to last well into adult life. Those who suffer most are the males who lag behind. Added to their own doubts about their physical adequacy are the jokes of classmates in locker rooms or on the athletic field. However, it is some consolation to men, especially late-maturing ones, to know that physical differences, such as in penis size, rarely, if ever, contribute to sexual problems. Furthermore, a study that followed early- and late-maturing boys into adulthood found that although the early maturers were poised, responsible, and successful men, they were rather conventional. The late maturers, although they were more impulsive men, were also explorative, insightful, and independent. There were, of course, individual differences.

Sexual Behavior   The female and male hormones that direct the physical changes of puberty also produce strong sexual feelings. Although there have been some changes in recent years in society's rules about how adolescents should deal with these feelings, the whole area of sex drives and sexual behavior in adolescence remains a confusing one. First, everyone knows the drive exists. It is especially pronounced in males, who can be aroused by pictures, words, and fantasies, as well as by touches and looks. The changing view of female sex roles makes it a little more difficult to define the force of the drive in women. Sex seems to be more romantic and emotional for women than for men, but there are indications that female sexuality has been widely misunderstood. For a long time, it was commonly thought that only "bad women" desired sexual relations, and until Masters and Johnson's studies, the physiological aspects of female sexuality were virtually unknown.

It is important to note that adolescents, although sexually mature, are not yet psychologically mature. An adolescent may feel at times that he has the personality of a child in the body of a man or woman. Most adolescents have a fierce desire to be independent yet need to be loved and cared for. They long to be self-directing but often have no idea about what direction to take. The process of creating an identity has just begun and may not be completed until well into adulthood. Ideally, sexual relations are the most intimate of personal interactions, and an adolescent often lacks the self-confidence and self-knowledge that such interactions require.

Social restrictions and personal doubts make sex a difficult problem in adolescence, but there may come a time when much of the confusion is removed. In the last ten or twenty years, there has been something like a sexual revolution. At least sex can be studied and discussed more openly and realistically. For example, before Alfred Kinsey's wide-ranging studies in the 1950s, it was not known that 90 percent of males and 40 percent of females masturbate by the age of fifteen. Knowing this information, one cannot rationally threaten children who masturbate with ideas that they will become insane or deplete their life forces—if such ideas were correct, almost all American men would be crazy and impotent.

Masturbation is one way in which adolescent men and women respond to their sex drives. Necking and petting are others. Intercourse, at least throughout most of adolescence, is not. A sampling of college students in 1969 showed that the average age of first intercourse for males is about eighteen and for females, about nineteen. This study also showed that half the women who had had intercourse expected to marry the man they were sleeping with. So the sexual revolution does not seem to mean that adolescents are becoming wildly promiscuous. The revolution seems to be more a matter of being more open about discussing sex.

Figure 8.11
Falling in love for the first time can be a revelation of a new world of caring, warmth, and happiness. With these feelings come physical desires that create considerable conflicts for adolescents. Because sex is both glorified and forbidden for the American adolescent, it is not always easy for an individual to resolve the conflict.

Sex is a highly variable experience. At its worst it can be a cold or fear-filled exchange that produces bitterness or guilt. At its best, a sexual relationship between two persons who wish to be open with each other, to give and take pleasure as an expression of love, is one of life's great rewards. Sexual experiences can easily be disappointing if one expects them to automatically produce the searing passion that novels and movies portray. Such disappointment is quite natural, simply because sex and love are experiences that have to be explored a good deal before such satisfaction can be achieved.

Social Development: Family and Friends

The ultimate aim for adolescents—and for their parents—is their independence from the family. Unfortunately, the means of achieving that status are not always clear, either to the teenagers or to their parents. First, there is ambivalence on both sides: Some parents have built their life styles around the family and are reluctant to let the child go. Such parents know they will soon have to find someone else on whom to shift their emotional dependence. Also, parents whose children are old enough to leave home sometimes have to wrestle with their own fears of advancing age. Many parents worry whether their children are really ready to cope with the harsh realities of life—and so do the adolescents. At the same time that a young person longs to get out on his own and try himself against the world, he worries a lot about failing there. This internal struggle is often mirrored in the adolescent's unpredictable behavior, which parents may interpret as "adolescent rebellion." Against this background of ambivalence, which is almost universal, there are various family styles of working toward autonomy.

Family Styles   By the time a person reaches his teens, he has been exposed to some parental pattern of discipline for many impressionable years. In some families, the pattern is a traditional, *authoritarian* one. The parent is "boss" and feels that he need not explain his actions. In fact, he feels that the child has no right to question parental decisions. These authoritarian parents tend to rely on punishment as a means of teaching children the right way to live.

Psychologists have found that this type of family structure is not too successful at producing independent adolescents. Such a family may seem to be marked by less conflict than other families, but the children seem to harbor resentment against their authoritarian parents. Nevertheless, the children seem unable to detach themselves easily from the family. They also tend to be docile and to accept or need other people's rules to control themselves, instead of developing self-control.

Other families involve the adolescents in decisions affecting them. These *democratic* families talk a lot about the whys of rules. Democratic parents ask their children to explain why they want to do something or go somewhere, and they explain their own reasons for saying yes or no. Children in families like this tend to develop their own controls earlier and are, toward the end of adolescence, good candidates for independence.

A third family style of dealing with adolescents is almost no style at all. Some parents just seem to give up their child-rearing responsibilities when children get older, and they make no rules about behavior, make no demands, voice no expectations. Home, for these adolescents, more or less resembles a boarding house. They sleep there most of the time and eat there sometimes. One of the most serious problems with this *laissez-faire* style is that the parents do not show much emotional attachment to the children. Although teenagers from homes like these may go out on their own relatively early, their struggle for real psychological maturity is usually a hard one.

Complications of Family Life   Several matters complicate the lives of all styles of families. One is the speed at which social change is taking place in the United States. Parents are afraid of being—or are—out of touch with the adolescent's world—his music, dress styles, dating patterns, attitudes toward drugs and sex, attitudes toward political activism. In dealing with such matters, parents are afraid that their own ideas may be so old-fashioned that they are unrealistic or so sophisticated that what they favor in theory may turn out to be harmful in practice.

Another complication is the necessity for parents to change rules and directions as the child moves through adolescence. The discipline applied to a thirteen-year-old is simply not appropriate for a seventeen-year-old. The parent must constantly make difficult decisions about his children's freedom and responsibility. The teenager's own confusion about these matters makes the situation even more complex. In his incomplete maturity, the adolescent often demands privileges or freedom, yet he may feel that the responsibilities that go with the privileges are somehow childish.

Friends   The people an adolescent *can* trust not to treat him like a child are his peers. Teenagers spend much of their time with friends—they need and use each other to define themselves. The patterns of social interaction have changed somewhat over the past decade or so. There is not the same emphasis on "dating." There seems to be more group and communal activity. And although the meaning of "being popular" has changed somewhat since the dating era, popularity is still extremely important.

High schools are important as places for adolescents to get together. And they do get together in fairly predictable ways. Most schools contain easily recognizable and well-defined *sets,* or crowds. And these sets are arranged in a fairly rigid social hierarchy—everyone knows who belongs to what set and what people in that set do with their time. Early in adolescence the sets are usually divided by sex, but later the sexes mix. It is not possible to define how all the

Figure 8.12
In early adolescence, close friendships are likely to develop between members of the same sex. Such friendships are crucial to future relationships, for they establish, for the first time, patterns of trust in which an individual can allow someone else to see him as he really is.

personal and social variables combine to decide what set or *clique* (a group within a set) a teenager decides to join. He is usually eligible for several. But, apart from a few "loners," who by necessity or by choice remain outside, most adolescents spend much of their time with a few chosen others. One thing is almost certain: The sets break down along class lines. Some school activities bring teenagers of different social classes together, but it is the exception rather than the rule that middle-class and lower-class adolescents are close friends.

Belonging to a clique gives the adolescent status and a means of defining himself. Although this is by no means the same thing as self-definition, which will be discussed later in the chapter, it is a handle the adolescent can hold onto while shaping an identity.

Of course, there are drawbacks to this kind of social organization. One of the greatest is that the fear of being disliked leads to *conformity.* A teenager's fear of wearing clothes that might set him apart from others is well known. But group pressures to conform often lead young people to do things that run contrary to their better judgment—or to do things they fear. One of the factors that undoubtedly made it possible for the use of drugs to become rapidly widespread in many American schools is the social pressure for adolescents to conform to the group.

Changing Patterns   These patterns of adolescent social inter-action have existed since soon after World War II. They are unlikely to change unless there is a basic change in American social structure. The fact that the adolescent is an economic dependent makes it likely that he will remain a social and emotional dependent. And there are no indications that adolescents will be badly needed in the work force

Figure 8.13

Although close friendships serve as sources for increased self-knowledge, interactions in larger groups are important for gaining a more general social knowledge and for exchanging ideas about acceptable behavior. Psychologists have found that an adolescent's popularity is largely determined by the degree to which he or she conforms to the standards, or norms, of the group. As discussed in Chapter 10, norms are common features of all groups at every age.

Figure 8.14
A summer job is one way in which an adolescent can develop the ability to make commitments. Without work experiences or tasks for which he is responsible, an adolescent cannot know what commitments he might be willing to make or whether he can live up to commitments if he does make them.

in the future. In fact, some psychologists have noted that there seems to be a prolongation of something like adolescence. Many young people are going to college, on and off, for a number of years. Many seem unable or unwilling to make the commitments that society traditionally expects of mature adults. It may be, however, that society's definition of maturity will change somewhat as a result of this phenomenon.

The Transition to Adult Thinking

In adolescence, the thinking patterns characteristic of adults emerge. From about the age of eleven or twelve, people are capable of *systematic experimentation;* that is, given a problem—in school, under the hood of a car, or in an art studio—the adolescent can consider all possible combinations of events and eliminate all the combinations that are irrelevant to the task until he discovers the correct one. One important side effect of this new ability is the ability to consider *hypothetical propositions* and reason from them. He can, for example, consider what would happen if there were another civil war or imagine what the world would be like without cars. Such situations would seem absurd to an eight-year-old because they are so contrary to his experience.

With comprehension of the hypothetical comes the ability to understand abstract principles. Not only is this capacity important for studying higher level science and mathematics, it leads the adolescent to deal with such abstractions in his own life as ethics, conformity, and phoniness. It allows him to be introspective, to examine his own motives and thoughts. One adolescent is quoted as saying, "I found myself thinking about my future, and then I began to think about why I was thinking about my future, and then I began to think about why I was thinking about why I was thinking about my future." These new cognitive abilities are very important to the development of ideals and the building of identity.

MATURITY: AN IDENTITY

What is maturity? How can one judge whether one has finally reached it? When Sigmund Freud was asked what the good adult life entailed, he said simply, "To love and to work." By love, he meant primarily the love that leads to marriage and parenthood, and love of one's children and friends. By work, he meant a self-satisfying commitment to some task that contributes to one's society.

The Search for Identity

Erik Erikson elaborated on Freud's statement considerably. In Figure 8.19, you can see what Erikson believes to be the great tests of adult life. To enter that life with the greatest chance of success, the necessary outcome of adolescence must be *identity*. What Erikson means by this term is a clear sense of who you are and what your goals are. The social facts of adolescent life make this kind of discovery one of the hardest that humans have to make. Conflicts with parents and pressure from peer groups make it difficult not to confuse one's own sense of self with what others expect and imagine one to be. The alternative to the achievement of identity is *role confusion.*

Erikson points out that although it is necessary to take your society into account in defining yourself, it is neither necessary nor desirable to let that society do the defining. For example, if through your search for identity you examined your needs, desires, and interests and decided to become a truck driver, you would have resolved the identity problem, in Erikson's terms. But if you made this same decision on the basis of urgings from your parents and because you have automatically accepted the idea that people from your background should not aspire to anything else, that would be an unsatisfactory resolution of the identity problem.

The difference emphasized here is the distinction that psychologists make between socialization and psychological growth. *Socialization* involves learning to understand the expectations of the social environment and to accommodate oneself to them. *Psychological growth* entails personality change, real autonomy and flexibility, and new capacities for self-determination.

Sexual Identity

A significant part of a person's self-definition and self-knowledge is his sexual identity. A sexual identity is related not only to one's personal relationships but also to the work one does, the opinions one holds, and the responsibilities one feels. American society appears to be undergoing major changes in its definition of the roles the sexes should play and in the attitudes it holds toward sexual behavior itself.

Changing Nature of Sex Roles   Today feminists (advocates of women's rights) are insisting that traditional sex-role definitions limit many natural abilities that women might have developed. There is a great deal of evidence that they are correct. It is known that until the last years in high school and the early years of college, American women do as well as or better than men in school. Their IQ scores are as high or higher. But in the space of a few years, those marks and scores suddenly drop, on the average. Why does this happen?

Obviously, women do not become less intelligent at this point in their lives. It is more likely that prevailing beliefs about the role of women in society are somehow responsible for the IQ score decline. One group of researchers has explored the idea that many women are actually afraid of success. These psychologists point out that, in today's society, intellectual or academic ability is associated with masculinity and that a successful, intelligent woman is often considered unfeminine. These researchers asked ninety women and eighty-eight men to complete a story about a fictitious student (see Figure 8.16). More than 65 percent of the women created stories that

Figure 8.15
The traditional American beauty queen exemplifies some of the most deeply held beliefs about sex roles in American society. According to this standard, an ideal woman is one who has a fresh, wholesome appearance, is charming and soft spoken, and has some artistic abilities. She is not supposed to appear to be aggressive, ambitious, or competitive because these are "unfeminine" characteristics.

Figure 8.16
If you are female, try writing a five- or ten-line story about Anne. If you are male, try to write a five- or ten-line story about John. When you have finished, turn the page to compare your responses with those of other men and women.

Complete the following story:

(*for women*) "After first-term finals, Anne finds herself at the top of her medical-school class."

(*for men*) "After first-term finals, John finds himself at the top of his medical-school class."

Figure 8.17

These stories were written by men and women who were given the directions presented in Figure 8.16. The stories women wrote about Anne are particularly revealing. The writer of the first story feels that Anne would suffer social rejection for her success. The second writer fears that Anne would lose her femininity from being too successful. The third denies that Anne could have been successful at all. Only the fourth woman is able to accept the idea that Anne could succeed and still be fulfilled as a woman. The typical stories written by men do not reveal such hidden fear of success.

Anne starts proclaiming her surprise and joy. Her fellow classmates are so disgusted with her behavior that they jump on her in a body and beat her. She is maimed for life.

Anne has a boyfriend Carl in the same class and they are quite serious. Anne met Carl at college and they started dating around their soph. years in undergraduate school. Anne is rather upset and so is Carl. She wants him to be higher scholastically than she is. Anne will deliberately lower her academic standing the next term, while she does all she subtly can to help Carl. . . . His grades come up and Anne soon drops out of med school. They marry and he goes on in school while she raises their family.

Anne is really happy she's on top, though Tom is higher than she—though that's as it should be . . . Anne doesn't mind Tom winning.

Congrats to her! Anne is quite a lady—not only is she tops academically, but she is liked and admired by her fellow students. Quite a trick in a man-dominated field. She is brilliant—but she is also a lady. A lot of hard work. She is pleased—yet humble and her fellow students (with the exception of a couple of sour pusses) are equally pleased. That's the kind of girl she is—you are always pleased when she is—never envious. She will continue to be at or near the top. She will be as fine practicing her field as she is studying it. And—always a lady.

John is a conscientious young man who worked hard. He is pleased with himself. John has always wanted to go into medicine and is very dedicated. His hard work has paid off. . . . John continues working hard and eventually graduates at the top of his class.

indicated fear of success, but fewer than 10 percent of the men did so. A good way to grasp the nature of the differences in the male and female responses is to read some of the typical stories, as presented in Figure 8.17.

This study revealed that many women are caught between the desire to succeed and the fear of being socially rejected for not filling the expected feminine role. A similar conflict occurs in men—many men want to be able to freely express their emotions, yet society treats emotional expression as unmasculine. Nevertheless, as society is structured now, American men have more power, prestige, and interesting work than women and, naturally, are not particularly dissatisfied with this situation.

Despite these conditions, certain social changes seem to be speeding up the redefinition of sex roles. For instance, the greatly increased divorce rate in the 1960s and 1970s has meant that many women entered the labor market as breadwinners for their families. Although discrimination in job opportunities has kept many women from reaching management levels, others have been able to overcome their fear of success and to discover that they are capable of doing competent work. And the children of these women are learning a markedly different definition of sex-appropriate behavior. Also, the ecological concerns of the past decade have made people aware of the dangers of overpopulation. This concern has decreased the emphasis on women's role as bearer of children. With the emergence of new, effective contraceptive techniques, couples can now choose whether or not they will have children. This deemphasis of motherhood may bring about the most dramatic changes in the redefinition of sex roles.

Homosexuality Identification of oneself as a male or female takes place very early. After that primary understanding, one goes on to learn—by trial and error, by watching and listening—what it is that men do and what it is that women do. One thing that becomes clear is that men desire sexual relations with women, and women with men. However, some small percentage of men and women end up preferring the company of their own sex. How does this happen?

No one really knows yet. Biologists have not been able to find any hormonal differences between heterosexual men and women and homosexuals. There is no evidence of genetic differences. Because no biological differences have been discovered, many psychologists have come up with explanations based on early childhood experiences. Some theorize that male homosexuals, by "loving" men, are trying to cover up intense hatred for their fathers or, by avoiding women, are reacting to a mother who tried to make them a "mama's boy." Other psychologists believe that homosexuality develops because of certain adolescent experiences. If a boy is rejected by most of his male peers—because he dislikes sports, for example—and is not attractive to girls, he may come to have serious doubts about his masculinity and prefer the companionship of men whom he sees as being like himself and who accept him more readily.

The factors that make a person prefer homosexual relations to heterosexual ones are not yet known. But certain things are known about homosexuality and sexuality in general that should be made clear: (1) Both male and female hormones exist in both sexes. Consequently, some capacity for homosexual feelings is possessed by everyone, and most people have had at least some sexual experience with someone of the same sex at some time in their lives. (2) A person's sexual preferences cannot be identified just by looking at him or her. Gay men are not necessarily effeminate and lesbians are not necessarily mannish. Nor are effeminate men and mannish women necessarily homosexuals. (3) Although most psychologists consider homosexuality abnormal, they do not consider homosexuals to have any worse problems than a great number of heterosexual people. (4) There is no one "homosexual" personality, just as there is no one "heterosexual" personality. Indeed, the only thing all homosexuals seem to have in common is their sexual preference. (5) A large proportion of a homosexual's difficulties in life are due to the fact that American society has treated homosexuals as outcasts and criminals. It is a myth that homosexuals are more likely than others to commit sex crimes against unwilling victims.

The reasons why homosexuals (especially male) are so dreaded and loathed in American society are no more understood than the reasons why people are homosexuals at all. One interesting theory is that because American society prohibits expressions of tenderness or delicacy in men, Americans fear those men who do express such characteristics. This subject is far too complex to be dealt with in

Figure 8.18

Like other matters pertaining to sex, homosexuality is now being discussed more openly and candidly than it has in the past. Homosexuals, like other minority groups, are beginning to demand the same rights and opportunities that are available to their more conventional peers. Negative social attitudes toward homosexuals have undoubtedly contributed to society's inability to understand sex roles and sexual preferences.

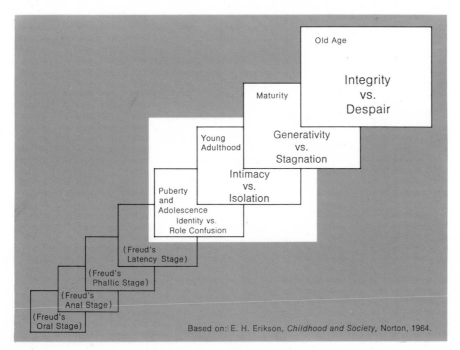

Based on: E. H. Erikson, *Childhood and Society*, Norton, 1964.

Figure 8.19

Although Freud's theory of psychosexual stages ends with the emergence of sexuality in adolescence, Erikson's stages continue on into adulthood and old age. Many personality theorists have stressed that psychological growth continues throughout the life cycle. Unfortunately, much less is known about the changes that take place in adulthood.

only a few paragraphs. All that can be said is that there is considerable confusion about sex in America, and an adolescent should not be surprised if he shares in this confusion.

Identity Resolution

Resolution of the identity problem is necessary to any further commitments to adult life. Without a clear sense of who one is, it is impossible to make a mature commitment in love. And without a clear sense of what one's goals are, it is difficult to choose work that will be fulfilling. It may be, with the prolongation of adolescence, that the resolution of the identity crisis does not take place until after the adolescent years. It is unlikely that anyone wakes up some time before his twentieth birthday and bounds out of bed saying, "Eureka!

Figure 8.20
Erikson's final four stages.

(*top left*) Identity versus role confusion is the central crisis of adolescence, and the question "Who am I?" assumes great importance. In answering this question, the individual considers such things as his race, religion, education, social class, sex, and nationality, as well as his personal ideals, styles, hopes, and experiences. This boy will answer the question quite differently than will most readers of this book, but no two of their answers will be alike, either.

(*top right*) In young adulthood, the crisis is intimacy versus isolation. The individual can unite himself with another person—in marriage or in a close friendship—or face the alternative of loneliness. The ways in which an individual seeks intimacy will depend in large part upon the way he has resolved the earlier identity conflict.

(*bottom left*) Generativity versus stagnation characterizes middle age. The individual at this stage must find a way to be productive or creative or will find himself bored, unsatisfied, and preoccupied with selfish interests.

(*bottom right*) In old age a person sums up the whole of his life and looks ahead into the unknown. The issue is integrity versus despair. If the individual feels that his life has been meaningful and useful, that he has been true to himself, and that he has taken responsibility for his own life, he feels proud and sure that existence is ordered and meaningful. Otherwise, the individual feels despair, because he feels that his life has been wasted.

I know who I am!" A few people do have a good sense of self early in life. For others, it may not come until late in life.

But of all human psychological processes, the knowledge of who one is—and a commitment to that self—is probably the most important.

SUMMARY

1. Most developmental psychologists, among them Erik Erikson, believe that there are stages in human development and that each stage is marked by the challenge of specific developmental tasks and by the appearance of abilities that had not previously existed.

2. As a child reaches school age, he develops new cognitive abilities, including an understanding of conservation and of necessary truths. These intellectual changes affect the child's emotional life; for example, the objects of his fears change.

3. Adults have a major impact on the child's social development, particularly in the learning of sex roles. Other agents of socialization include games, in which children learn to interact socially and to act out pieces of adult life, and school, which is less influential than family and peers because teachers are not easy to identify with and because schools often avoid controversy in subject matter.

4. Adolescence is characterized by contradiction and ambivalence. With puberty the adolescent experiences profound physical and sexual changes that create self-consciousness and sexual worries. Both males and females must learn to deal with sexual drives and with the constraints society places on sexual behaviors.

5. Adolescents are ambivalent about family life—they want to be independent, yet they also cling to the security of home. Parents faced with this problem may deal with it in an authoritarian, democratic, or laissez-faire style.

6. Adolescents place great importance on friendships and on the social groups, such as sets and cliques, to which they belong. These groups are used as a means of self-definition, but they also apply pressure to conform.

7. Cognitive changes in adolescence result in adultlike thinking abilities. The adolescent is capable of systematic experimentation, of considering hypothetical propositions, and of understanding abstract principles.

8. Erik Erikson has said that the ideal outcome of adolescence is ego identity—knowing who one is and what one's goals are, which involves both socialization and psychological growth.

9. Achieving an identity also involves knowing who one is sexually. The roles of men and women are changing in today's society, and people are redefining themselves in terms of these new roles. As male and female sex roles change, attitudes toward homosexuality are changing, too.

ACTIVITIES

1. Why do you choose certain people as friends, and how much influence do they have on you? Ask yourself the following questions: What would you feel if you were not allowed to be with your closest friend(s)? What need does approval from others satisfy in you?

2. If you were going to advise one of your peers on "how to win friends and influence people," what attributes would you list that make a person popular or unpopular? Pool your results with other people's to arrive at a single list (of perhaps ten or twelve items) of attributes.

3. Compare your approach to life at the age of twelve with your present approach to life. Include the following considerations: (1) the purpose of life, (2) moral values, (3) political beliefs, (4) religious beliefs, (5) desirable emotional and intellectual behavior, and (6) desirable educational and economic systems. What forces shaped the change in your attitudes? Based on these changes, can you make predictions about future changes?

4. List all the ways in which you now "conform"—in mode of dress, subjects you talk about frequently, hair style, and so on. How do you respond to fads? If you had the choice, what would you do instead of doing what others do?

5. What is the value of femininity in the modern "liberated" woman? If a method were perfected to develop (and fertilize) all babies in test tubes, would women and men become "true" equals and would the current concepts of femininity and masculinity become obsolete? Discuss this question with several of your (male and female) classmates.

6. Consider how "permission" to express emotions varies from culture to culture and even within a culture. Give examples. Is there any relation between a person's passivity or aggressiveness and the amount of emotional expression permitted in his culture?

7. How much of your femaleness/maleness is caused by biological differences? How much is learned from the culture? Make a list of those differences that you think are biologically caused in one column and those you think are learned in another column. Support your beliefs by comparing various cultures. If a particular characteristic is biological, it should remain constant between cultures.

8. List several magazines that seem to be directed solely toward adolescents. What aspects of these publications make them of interest to teenagers? Do you read any of them? Why?

SUGGESTED READINGS

ANDREAS, CAROL. *Sex and Caste in America.* Englewood Cliffs, N.J.: Prentice-Hall, 1971 (paper). This excellent, semi-textbook is a thorough and readable documentation of how and why sex-role stereotyping takes place in American society.

ERIKSON, ERIK. *Identity: Youth and Crisis.* New York: Norton, 1968 (paper). This book is heavy reading but of value for those who are interested in a thorough insight into Erikson's theories on adolescence. He sees the identity crisis as the crucial influencing force on the individual's future development.

FRANK, ANNE. *The Diary of a Young Girl.* New York: The Modern Library, 1952 (paper). This tender and tragic story is made even more remarkable by the realization that it is, in fact, a diary—a true account—written by a fourteen-year-old Dutch girl while she was in hiding from the Nazis.

FRIEDENBERG, EDGAR Z. *The Vanishing Adolescent.* Boston: Beacon, 1959. One of the best-known authorities on adolescence presents his views in an exciting and highly readable fashion. Friedenberg stresses the importance of adolescent conflict as a means of establishing a relationship between the individual and his society.

GORDON, SOL. *Facts About Sex—A Basic Guide.* New York: John Day, 1970. The author describes this book as "simple and brief—especially useful if you don't like to read too much and welcome lots of pictures."

HOFFMAN, MARTIN. *The Gay World.* New York: Basic Books, 1968. Hoffman gives a complete and readable account of male homosexuality in the United States, describing the lives of gay men, discussing homosexuality and the law, and providing theories of why some men are homosexual.

ROSZAK, T. *The Making of the Counter-Culture.* New York: Doubleday, 1969. A controversial and fascinating account of how values are instilled and enforced in American society.

SALINGER, J. D. *Catcher in the Rye.* New York: Bantam, 1951 (paper). A funny and poignant novel about a boy's search for meaning in the confusion and chaos of adolescence. This book has been a favorite on reading lists for more than twenty years.

TWAIN, MARK. *Huckleberry Finn.* New York: Dodd, Mead, 1953, originally published, 1885. This popular classic is not just a book for children—ask an adult who has re-read it. Huck's pains and joys, his problems with the "civilised" world, and his particular philosophies about life are as relevant now as they were 100 years ago.

Our only excuse
for reading books about people, is that we
cannot read people themselves.

A. R. Orage (1930)

Unit IV

Human Relations

How does one "read," or understand, another person? It is evident from news reports of conflicts between nations, racial groups, and individuals that humans have not yet discovered an answer to this question. Certainly books about people—including this one—do not provide the answer, but they can help move closer to one. By describing how people behave when they interact with one another, books contribute to our understanding of human relations, good and bad.

This unit presents some of the important findings that psychologists have made about the kinds of relations between people that occur on every level, from conflict between nations down to love between individuals. Chapter 9 deals with interpersonal relationships—the kinds of interactions that occur between two people, whether they are strangers meeting for the first time, friends, or lovers. Chapter 10 focuses on the kinds of interactions that occur within and between groups, from families to communities to corporations. Chapter 11 explores the roles that people play in influencing one another. Your friends and relatives, television producers, advertising executives, textbook publishers, and lawmakers all affect your thoughts, your feelings, and your actions. This chapter explains how and why they do.

This area of psychology, social psychology, is closely related to the field of sociology. In fact, some of the information in these chapters comes from sociologists. Although it is difficult to say where psychology leaves off and sociology begins, it is possible to note what each field emphasizes: Sociology emphasizes the overall society or group and how it affects the individuals in it; social psychology focuses on how and why individuals act the way they do in relation to one another and to society. Both these fields have produced valuable information that can lead to a better understanding of human relations.

9

Person to Person

Figure 9.1
The intimacy that can be shared
by a man and a woman is probably
the closest form of human contact, and yet
it is the least well understood by social
psychologists. But, as you will see toward
the end of the chapter, even this
relationship can be studied scientifically.

Human beings are social animals. From the first day of their lives they interact with others of their species—family, friends, neighbors, salespeople, doctors, teachers, fellow students, co-workers, entertainers. Such social interaction takes place in every kind of human activity, from playing checkers to running for President.

This chapter is about human interaction: why and how people interact, how people view themselves and others, and how people make friends and choose lovers.

THE NECESSITY FOR INTERACTION

Most animals interact with members of their own species in a more or less organized fashion. Bees and ants form huge, complex societies to gather food and reproduce; many species of birds and fish travel in groups; and baboons and chimpanzees roam the plains and forests of Africa in closely knit bands, playing, searching for food, and watching out for predators. Such gathering in groups seems to have contributed to the survival of certain species.

It is thought that some species of animals have an *instinctive* need to be with others of their own kind, just as they have instinctive needs for food and water and instinctive fears of strange objects. Many psychologists believe that humans are among the species that have such an instinctive need for company. But whether or not such an instinct exists, most psychologists agree that human beings have certain *emotional* needs that can be filled only by other humans. A person needs love, appreciation, and respect—he needs to know what other people think of him.

Humans also associate with one another for *economic* reasons. In every human society—and in some animal societies—each member is partially dependent on other members for food, shelter, or protection. In most modern societies the interdependence of people is high because individuals tend to concentrate on specific tasks, such

Figure 9.2
This famous passage, by English poet and essayist John Donne, eloquently states that human beings cannot exist in isolation from one another.

(From "Meditation XVII of Devotions upon Emergent Occasions," *The Norton Anthology of English Literature*, Vol. I. New York: W. W. Norton & Company, 1968, p. 917.)

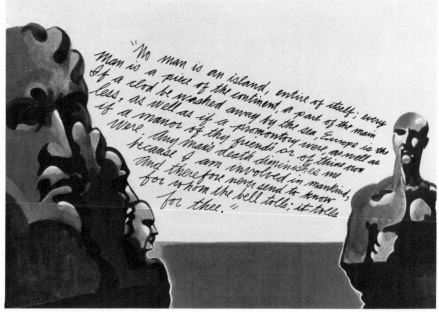

Figure 9.3
Certain social rules define the relationship of performers to their audiences and the status relationship of common men to rulers. When such rules are broken, the effects can be startling. The great jazz musician Louis Armstrong once violated both these sets of rules in a single brilliant stroke. In 1932 in the London Palladium, Armstrong was performing before King George VI of England. Toward the end of the performance he looked out toward the King and stunned the audience by introducing an encore with the words, "This one's for you, Rex!"

as building houses, growing food, caring for the sick, or providing entertainment. In order for a society to function in this way, its members have to cooperate with one another and to communicate their understanding of the parts they are supposed to play. What people communicate, and how, influences the ways in which others perceive them, feel about them, and act toward them.

INTERACTION AND COMMUNICATION

When one person comes in contact with another, he may be lonely and looking for a friend, boastful and needing an audience, or hungry and seeking something to eat. Whatever the reason, he will have to establish some relationship with the other person. This process of establishing relationships is made easier by social rules designed to help interpersonal relations run smoothly. A *social rule* is any agreement among members of a society about how people should act in particular situations.

Much of the communication between people is conducted according to such rules, and communication often serves the purpose of reminding everyone concerned of what the rules are. For example, communication is used to establish rules about *status* differences. In many situations in society one person has to acknowledge that he respects the other and that he is at least temporarily willing to obey the other. He communicates this agreement through the forms of address he uses. A waiter addresses a customer as "sir" or "ma'am"; a student addresses his teachers similarly. A judge is called "Your Honor," and a king or queen is addressed as "Your Majesty."

The communication of status differences is often indirect. A customer usually does not need to remind a waiter to act respectfully—the waiter's use of a polite form of address accomplishes the same

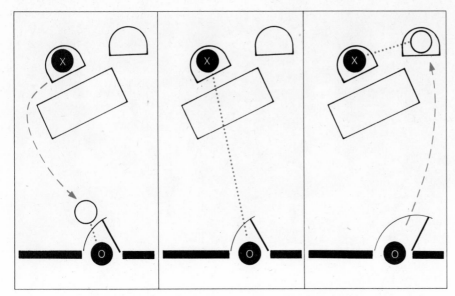

Figure 9.4
These diagrams illustrate how unwritten rules about occupational status are subtly communicated by physical position. A desk and two chairs are shown situated a short distance from the office door. O comes to visit X. The broken lines indicate movement; the dotted lines indicate conversation. See whether you can tell, before reading further, who has the superior status in each of these three cases. (*left*) X rises from his desk and moves to greet O. X's deference indicates that O is senior in rank. (*center*) O speaks from the doorway while X remains seated. O is deferring this time, suggesting that X is the superior. (*right*) O walks in, sits down beside X, and they start talking. This interaction indicates that X and O have roughly equal status.

purpose, with no embarrassment. Most interpersonal communication involves such indirect transmission of information—of telling people things about oneself and about one's relations with them without making direct statements. In fact, a good part of the communication process does not depend on words at all.

Nonverbal Communication

Most societies have rules about how distances communicate social relationships. Americans carry a two-foot bubble of privacy around them—if anyone comes closer than two feet, they feel uncomfortable. For Germans, the bubble is larger; for Arabs, it is much smaller. A person who violates this bubble is communicating *nonverbally* that he wants to be friendly or perhaps that he is "pushy" and insensitive to other people's feelings.

Other physical positions that people assume relative to one another convey different silent messages. People of high status, for example, generally place themselves above people of lower status— leaders sit or stand on platforms or balconies. King Arthur sat with his knights at a round table to symbolize his feeling that all were equal—no one sat at the head of the table. Nevertheless, status was communicated by the knights' distance from the king. Similarly, a corporation chairman sits at the head of the table, with his highest-ranking associates closest to him.

Nonverbal communication is even more important on the personal rather than the social level. You are probably familiar with the experience of listening to someone say one thing ("It doesn't matter") but show, by speaking in a low voice and looking away, that he really means something else ("My feelings are hurt"). Such nonverbal communication is usually more significant than what a person is actually saying.

Channels of nonverbal communication include posture, facial

Figure 9.5
Nonverbal communication has been made a high art by the famous mime Marcel Marceau. Relying solely on facial expression, gesture, and posture, Marceau is able to communicate any impression he wishes.

expression, tone of voice, gestures, and use of eyes. For example, a person speaking rapidly, loudly, and in a high voice communicates that he is excited or anxious. One talking slowly or in an unusually low voice indicates that he is depressed. The manner in which a sentence is said can affect its meaning: "Yes" can even become "no" if said hesitatingly, and "no" can mean "yes" if said provocatively.

Body Language

The way you carry your body communicates information about you. If you stand tall and erect, you convey the impression of self-assurance. If you sit and talk with your arms folded and legs crossed, you communicate that you are protecting yourself. But when you unfold your arms and stretch out, you are saying that you are open to people.

Body language includes gestures. Like all forms of communication, gestures can only be understood in context. A simple gesture such as waving your hand might mean you are saying goodbye or hello, depending on whether you are approaching or leaving. Another common gesture is the nod of the head. Americans nod their heads up and down to show agreement and shake them back and forth to show disagreement. But people of other cultures use different gestures for this purpose. The Semang of Malaya thrust their heads sharply forward to agree and lower their eyes to disagree. The Abyssinians rock their heads back and raise their eyebrows to

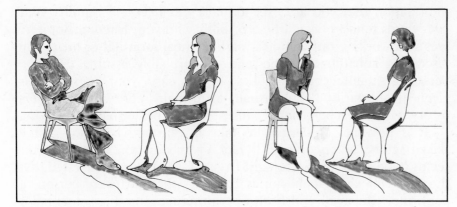

agree and jerk their heads to the right shoulder to disagree. And the Dayak of Borneo agree by raising their eyebrows and disagree by bringing them together slightly.

Facial Expressions

Unlike gestures, facial expressions seem to be universal. Expressions for anger, fear, sadness, happiness, surprise, disgust, and interest are similar everywhere. These expressions begin to develop in infancy and do not change much in adulthood. Along with gestures, facial expressions made it possible for silent film stars to communicate many things to their audiences around the world without the use of words. In fact, pantomime actors can tell entire stories and convey all the accompanying emotions and moods using only postures and facial expressions.

It has been said that the eyes are the windows to the soul. There is probably no stronger medium of nonverbal communication than eye movement and eye contact. Eye contact sustains the flow of communication. As one speaks, he watches his listener in order to obtain feedback. The listener can communicate that he agrees or that he wants to speak simply by raising his eyes. Prolonged eye contact can communicate either affection or anger, depending on the accompanying facial expressions.

HOW PEOPLE THINK ABOUT THEMSELVES

Most people are concerned about the impression they make on other people. They spend money on clothes, cars, deodorants, mouthwashes, and other such paraphernalia in order to convey special images of themselves. They try to hide their negative feelings and disguise their bad moods. You, too, have probably smiled at someone you dislike or have nodded in approval at times when you did not actually agree. People sometimes "fake" their real attitudes to create an impression that they feel is appropriate for the situation.

Creating Impressions

Impressions are given both voluntarily and involuntarily. For instance, you might want to impress someone by volunteering the

Figure 9.6
Bodily posture communicates a great deal about a person's emotional state and his attitudes toward others. In the drawing on the left the woman has adopted a fairly open posture, but the man, leaning back with folded arms and crossed legs, is distant and closed off. He is conveying to the woman, perhaps unintentionally, that he is bored or dislikes her. In contrast, the woman in the drawing on the right is conveying an active interest in her older companion: She is leaning forward and neither her legs nor her arms are crossed. Her companion is slightly withdrawn; the two are not quite facing one another. It appears that there is some caution and reserve at this point in their relationship.

Figure 9.7
A look can speak louder than words, as this photograph of a high-school vice-principal in Iowa shows. Among the components of nonverbal communication being displayed here are eye contact, posture, and facial expression.

information that you are exceptionally intelligent. Naturally, your own words tend to have little credibility with your listener. But if he sees you working out complex mathematical formulas or hears you discussing subatomic physics, he will probably assume that you possess great intellectual abilities. In this case, your impression is given involuntarily. People usually form their impressions of others by observing such behavior because it is more believable.

It is possible, of course, to fake involuntary behavior. Some skilled actors can cry on cue. In fact, everybody, to a certain extent, seems to be an actor. Sociologist Erving Goffman has suggested that the world of social behavior is truly a stage and every person, a performer. Behavior constitutes performances that the actors tailor to specific audiences. To succeed in social interaction, then, a person must be skilled in the techniques of creating and maintaining impressions.

Like professional actors, people in everyday life play a number of *roles*—they behave in different ways in different situations. You undoubtedly behave one way with your family, another way with

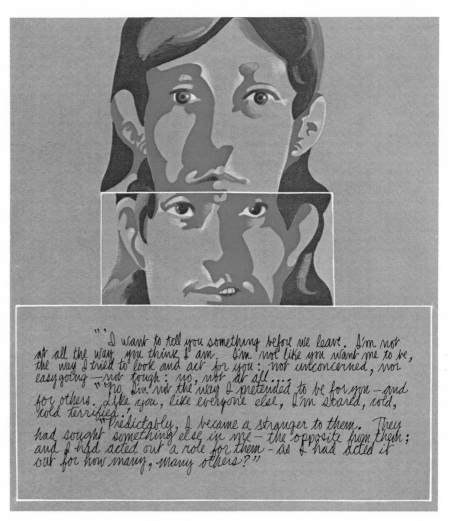

Figure 9.8
This young man, John Rechy, speaks about the mask he wears and its costs to him. His mask is that of a "cool customer" in the night world of downtown New York. His revelations confirm Erving Goffman's assertion that everyone is an actor, putting on a performance for others.
(From John Rechy, *City of Night*. New York: Grove Press, 1963, p. 369.)

friends, and still another way with teachers. In your life you may play many other roles, such as "worker," "parent," "customer," "athlete," "lover," and so on, and you will undoubtedly create a different impression in each one.

But people do not seem to go through life consciously and deliberately faking. Psychologists who studied people as they went from role to role found that most subjects felt that they were presenting true and accurate pictures of themselves from moment to moment. Apparently, individuals are capable of wide ranges of behavior depending on the context—they may appear dominant and powerful in one setting and weak and submissive in another. Yet, in all settings, people usually *feel* that they are honest and authentic. The implication is that people have many potential ways of being that are often inconsistent and unrelated to one another. At any particular moment they are aware of only a small number of these ways and are thereby able to feel true to themselves. People are convinced by their momentary thoughts and actions that they truly are what they seem to be. In effect, human beings tend to believe their own performances.

Motives for Impression Management

Why are people so interested in controlling and managing their impressions? The primary motive for this kind of behavior is the need for social approval. Acting in ways designed to gain approval fulfills an individual's need for security. If a person abandons his "act," he or she may face exclusion from certain areas of society. Many people feel that to "fit in" it becomes absolutely necessary to maintain a "front." For instance, a secretary who hates every boring minute at her typewriter may smile at her boss and act complacently in hopes of being promoted. In order to gain the approval of her boss, she feels she must play the role of a happy, competent employee.

Naturally, the secretary who behaves "properly" on the job may change her act the minute she leaves the office. Her work audience will probably never see how she behaves with her close friends and associates. There is, in other words, an inconsistency in her performance. In order to avoid a mix-up, she is careful to keep her two audiences separated. The important thing is that in both situations, work and play, she is giving the performance she feels will gain approval from the people around her.

Self-Concept

The idea that people are acting a good deal of the time is not hard to accept. But it is hard to accept that they are acting *all* the time. Surely, there is a person behind the act, a person who is being more or less truthful about himself.

But what is this true self? Psychologists have found this question difficult to answer. They have learned, however, that the way a person views himself—his *self-concept*—is affected by the perfor-

Figure 9.9
An individual's self-concept contains a number of components. This woman's "me" is probably a composite of all the aspects shown here. The reactions of others, the reactions she would like from others, the way she wishes to see herself, and the objective facts all enter into the overall "self."

As she sees herself: ten years younger than her age. Competent yet desirable.

As her husband sees her: older than she actually is.

As the camera sees her: she is thirty-seven and chic but looks inhibited.

As she thinks others see her: sophisticated and sexy, a focus of masculine approval.

Figure 9.10
This question from the French philosopher Jean-Paul Sartre confirms the observation made by some psychologists that the "I" is a person's direct experience of his own actions, and the "me" is his awareness of the reactions of others.

"Let us imagine that moved by jealousy, curiosity, or vice I have just glued my ear to the door and looked through a keyhole. I am alone.... This means first of all that there is no self to inhabit my consciousness, nothing therefore to which I can refer my acts in order to qualify them. They are in no way known: I am my acts....
"But all of a sudden I hear footsteps in the hall. Someone is looking at me! What does this mean? It means that I am suddenly affected in my being....
"I now exist as myself.... I see myself because somebody sees me..

mances he puts on and by the reactions other people have to those performances.

It seems that many people are only able to see themselves through the eyes of others. It is therefore not hard to understand why they have such a need for social approval: If they find themselves the frequent object of disapproval, they must inevitably think badly of themselves. To avoid such disapproval, they behave the way they think others expect them to behave.

When people put on performances, they often deceive themselves as well as their audiences. If someone tries to impress others with how intelligent and reliable he is and they react favorably, he will start thinking that he *is* smart, even though he may previously have felt that he was not very bright.

In addition, people try to fit their *self-concept* and their *roles* together. For example, a person who sees himself as a quiet, studious type will try to find an occupation—such as librarian—that fits this image. He will then act even more like a quiet, studious person because he feels that such behavior is expected of a librarian.

Psychologists who have tried to define the self have found that self-concept is only half the picture. They divide the self into an "I" and a "me." The "me" is the aspect of the self that is defined by self-concept; it is formed by looking at oneself through the eyes of others. The "I" is the self as experienced from the inside. The "I" is a process, the self in action—feeling, thinking, imagining, planning, listening, watching. It is believed that the "I" comes before the "me." For example, if you are riding a roller coaster, you may lose all sense of "me." Your entire consciousness is filled with the sensation of speed and flight, and you may scream with exhiliration or terror. But when the ride slows down you may become self-conscious. You think about the fact that you were screaming and wonder how you looked. You regain your sense of "me."

HOW PEOPLE THINK ABOUT ONE ANOTHER

It takes people very little time to make judgments about one another, even on the basis of the most limited contact. The impressions two people form of one another nevertheless influence the future of their relationship. If a stranger appears deep and interesting, he or she

Intelligent
Warm
Confident
Practical

Figure 9.11

What is your impression of this character? Do you think you would like him? What do you think of the way he is dressed? What sort of expression does he have on his face? When you have given your first impressions, turn to the drawing in Figure 9.12 and do the same.

may be a candidate for future interaction. People tend to be particularly sympathetic to someone who seems shy, to expect a lot from someone who impresses them as intelligent, and to be wary of one who strikes them as aggressive.

Forming an impression of a person is not a passive process in which certain characteristics of the individual are the input and a certain impression is the automatic outcome. If impressions varied only when input varied, then everyone meeting a particular stranger would form the same impression of him, which, of course, is not what happens. One individual may judge a newcomer to be "quiet," another might judge the same person to be "dull," and still another person might think the newcomer "mysterious." These various impressions lead to different expectations of the newcomer and to different patterns of interaction with him as well.

One reason that different people develop different impressions of the same stranger is that they form their impressions on the basis of their own *implicit personality theory*—their own set of assumptions about how people behave. Everyone has definite ideas about the behavior of others. For example, some people tend to distrust those who talk a lot. Their implicit theory is, "People who talk a great deal are usually hiding something." Others think that attractively dressed people are good workers. Their implicit theory is, "People who take good care of their appearance are likely to be thorough about other things, too."

People are always making guesses, judgments, or predictions about one another on the basis of limited information. As a result, they are sometimes highly accurate in their judgments and at other times inaccurate or completely in error. The methods they use to make their judgments are generalization, simplification, and emphasis of certain central traits.

Generalizations

Judgments of others are often inaccurate because they are broad *generalizations* based on only a few facts. The more general the judgment, the more necessary are specific facts in order for the judgment to be accurate.

Judgments of an emotional *state*—a person's condition at a particular moment—are easiest to make. If someone approaches you shaking his fist and shouting, you can be fairly confident in judging that he is angry. If this same person makes a frequent habit of carrying on in this way, you may judge him to be aggressive. Aggressiveness is a *trait,* an enduring aspect of a person's personality. Having judged a person as aggressive, you may predict that he is not likely to take things lying down, that he frequently gets into fights, and that he could be violent if provoked.

If you see a great deal of this aggressive person and find him to be intensely interested in certain subjects, very warm with his friends, and capable of crying over things that make him sad, you may describe him as a passionate type of person. A person's personality *type* is a composite of all his traits. By knowing a person's type, you may feel confident in making very general judgments about his behavior.

Simplification

Quite often people categorize others on the basis of their clothes, style of speech, occupation, or other such small bits of information. Once a person has been categorized, he is considered to have the characteristics associated with that category. This process is called *stereotyping.* The predictions made about the individual person on the basis of such categorization can be seriously in error.

The errors that result from stereotypes have had widespread effects in American society. Most people have had to face the fact that they have prejudged someone else on the basis of race, religion, or sex. But stereotypes exist at the personal level, too. A person may for some reason feel that all people with black hair are romantic. Another person may categorize all people who criticize him as "destructive" types.

Stereotyping is a way of simplifying the task of making judgments about people. This tendency to simplify causes what psychologists call the *halo effect.* Once you decide a particular person is good, you may find it difficult to see anything bad about him. On the other hand, if you feel negatively toward him, you may find it hard to see his good points.

Central Traits

Certain traits seem to weigh heavily in people's judgments of one another. For example, judging a person as warm or cold may have a

Intelligent
Cold
Confident
Practical

Figure 9.12
If your impressions of this character are different from your impressions of the fellow in Figure 9.11, the difference must be due to the change in a single word—the illustrations are otherwise identical. It seems to be impossible to see a person believed to be warm in the same way one sees a person believed to be cold. Such significant character traits are called central organizing traits.

significant effect on what other traits he will appear to have. One thinks quite differently about the generosity of someone who is warm than one does about someone who seems cold; in fact, it is almost impossible to think of a person as being both cold and generous. In comparison, the trait of politeness does not seem to be as basic as warmth. A person might easily seem generous and polite or generous and rude—the impression one has of his courtesy has little effect on one's impression of his generosity.

It is obvious that people often make mistakes in forming impressions of one another. Impressions are only educated guesses about how people are likely to behave, and as a result they often have to be changed as one gets to know a person better. The implicit personality theory that one uses to make judgments about people changes, too, as one learns more. Psychologists have found that people tend to judge others with the same assumptions and categories one uses to judge oneself. The implication is that by learning more about oneself one can learn to judge other people more accurately.

WHY DO PEOPLE WANT TO GET TOGETHER?
At the beginning of this chapter, the reasons for human interaction were described as both emotional and economic. Psychologists are particularly interested in the emotional aspect of people's desire to interact. They have discovered that the need to be with others is particularly strong in people who have been deprived of human contact over long periods.

Shipwrecked sailors, prisoners in solitary confinement, and monks in certain religious orders have reported strong feelings of insecurity when they had no contact with other human beings. They felt frightened and were unable to control the emotions that flooded them during their isolation. During such experiences they have often had striking religious visions. For example, Joshua Slocum, who sailed alone around the world, reported that a savior appeared to him during particularly perilous times.

The need for someone with whom to share one's fears and worries is an intense one. Some psychologists believe that this need is what motivates people to seek human contact, and they have conducted experiments to verify this belief.

Anxiety and the Need for Contact

Psychologist Stanley Schachter set up an experiment to prove the old saying, "Misery loves company." His experiment showed that people suffering a high level of anxiety are more likely to seek out company than those who suffer less anxiety. He arranged for a number of college women to come to his laboratory. Some of the women were greeted by a frightening-looking man in a white coat who identified himself as Dr. Gregor Zilstein of the medical school. Dr. Zilstein told each woman that she would be given electric shocks in order to study the effect of electricity on the body. He told the women, in an ominous tone, that the shocks would be extremely painful. He added, with a devilish smile, that the shocks would cause no permanent skin damage. For obvious reasons, this group of women was referred to as the *high-anxiety* group.

To the other women, the doctor was friendly. He told these women that the shocks would produce only ticklish, tingling sensa-

Figure 9.13
People may be separated from one another by only a few feet and yet feel themselves to be totally isolated. This situation is dramatically depicted in Edward Hopper's painting, *Nighthawks*. Social psychologists have investigated situations in which people feel a need to overcome isolation and interact with one another.
(Edward Hopper, *Nighthawks*. Courtesy of the Art Institute of Chicago, Friends of American Art Collection.)

tions, which they might even find pleasant. These women were considered the *low-anxiety* group.

Zilstein told each subject that she would have to leave the laboratory while he set up the equipment. He then asked each woman· to indicate on a questionnaire whether she wished to wait alone in a private room or with other subjects in a larger room. Most women in the low-anxiety group were satisfied to wait alone. However, the overwhelming majority of high-anxiety women preferred to wait with others.· Thus, the experiment demonstrated that high anxiety produces a need for human contact.

Did the high-anxiety women want to share their mutual fears with each other? Or were they perhaps hoping to organize a protest against the shocks? Although the experiment illustrated that misery loves company, it raised many more questions. Why, and with whom, do people prefer to share their misery?

Comparing Experiences

One theory of the anxious women's need for contact is that people like to get together with one another to reduce their uncertainties about themselves. For example, when you get exams back, you probably ask your friends how they did. You try to understand your own situation by comparing it to other people's. You learn your strengths and weaknesses by asking: Can other people do it, too? Do they do it better or worse? Many individuals use the performance of others as a basis for self-evaluation. According to this theory, the women in the shock experiment were eager to find out how they

Figure 9.14

Responses to intense emotional situations can be quite varied. These people have just seen a friend of theirs die in a freak accident (he was struck by a bolt of lightning). Some of them are huddling together to share their grief, while another is keeping his emotion to himself. Social psychologists believe that one reason people interact with one another is to share and compare their reactions. Intense feeling does not necessarily produce this result, however.

should respond to Dr. Zilstein. Should they feel fear or anger, or should they take the whole thing in stride? The only way to get this information was to talk to others.

People want to compare not only their anxieties, fears, and doubts but also their skills, opinions, personality traits, and even emotions. For just these reasons, casual conversation is one of the most widely practiced pastimes. Everyone wants to know what other people are thinking.

Another experiment was conducted to check this idea. It was essentially the same as the Dr. Zilstein experiment, but this time, *all* the women were made anxious. Half of them were then given the choice between waiting alone and waiting with other women about to take part in the same experiment. The other half were given the choice between waiting alone and passing the time in a room where students were waiting to see their academic advisers.

As you might expect, the women who had a chance to be with other women in the same predicament seized the opportunity. These women wanted to compare their dilemma with others. But the women in the second group usually chose to spend the time alone rather than with the unconcerned students. As the experimenter put it, "Misery doesn't love just any kind of company, it loves only miserable company."

If you consider the matter, however, you will probably remember times when you have acted in a way that contradicts this rule—when you have been under great stress and wanted to be alone. When a poll was taken a few days after the assassination of John F. Kennedy, many people said they would have preferred to be alone after hearing the news.

It seems that when a person is deeply moved, he often fears embarrassment. He may believe that other people will laugh at him or that they will think him peculiar. Instead of seeking social comparison in such situations, he avoids it. He doubts that other people find themselves in the same situation he does, and he has no desire to find out from them how he should cope with his distress.

CHOOSING FRIENDS

Most people feel they have a great deal of latitude in the friends they choose. The transportation, telephones, and spare time available to most North Americans would all seem to ease communication among them and, therefore, to permit them a wide range of individuals from whom to choose companions, friends, and lovers. However, the evidence is that people do not typically exercise this freedom of choice and that, in fact, they usually do not venture beyond the most convenient methods in making contact with others.

Proximity

The single most important factor in determining whether two people will become friends is *physical proximity*—the distance from one

Figure 9.15

A set of apartments such as this one was used in a study of friendship choice. It was found that the fewer doors there were between people, the more likely they were to become friends. It seems that "next door" is psychologically closer, because one does not have to pass by any other doors to get there. Also, social rules make one feel more compelled to say "hello" to someone coming out of a door two feet away than to speak to someone twenty feet away. Once people have exchanged hellos, there is at least a chance of their becoming friends.

another that they live or work. In general, the closer two individuals are geographically to one another, the more likely they will become attracted to each other. And it is more than just the opportunity for interaction that makes the difference.

Psychologists have found that even in a small two-story apartment building where each resident was in easy reach of everyone else, people were more likely to become close friends with the person next door than with anyone else.

Psychologists believe that this effect is a result of the fears and embarrassments most people have about making contact with strangers. When two people live next door to one another, go to the same class, or work in the same place, they are able to get used to one another and to find reasons to talk to one another without ever having to seriously risk rejection. To make friends with someone whom you do not see routinely is much more difficult. You have to make it clear that you are interested and thus run the risk of making a fool of yourself—either because the other person turns out to be less interesting than he seemed at a distance or because he expresses no interest in you. Of course, it may turn out that both of you are very glad someone spoke up.

Reward Values

Proximity helps people make friends, but it does not insure friendship. Sometimes people who are forced together in a situation take a dislike to one another that develops into hatred. Furthermore, once people have made friends, physical separation does not necessarily bring an end to their relationship. What are the factors that determine whether people will like each other, once they come into contact?

To some extent, friendships, sexual relationships, and marriages

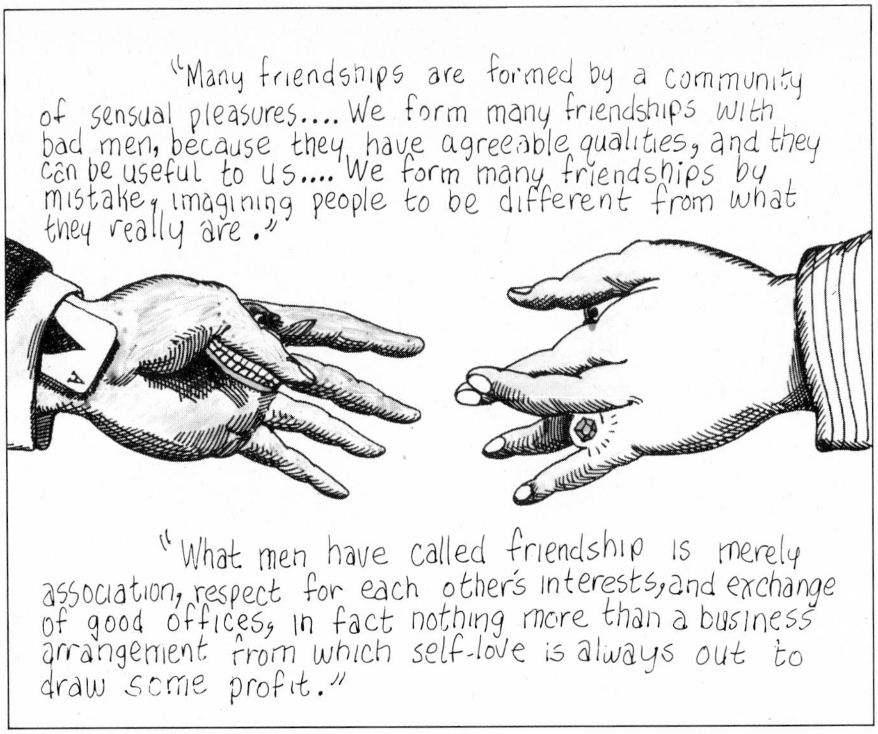

Figure 9.16

Both these cynical statements
(the top one by Samuel Johnson, 1772;
the bottom one by La Rochefoucauld, 1665)
make the point that friendships are always
formed for the purpose of obtaining some
reward. What these rewards are, however,
vary from friendship to friendship.

(Top quotation from James Boswell, *Life of Samuel
Johnson LL.D.* Chicago: Encyclopaedia Britannica, Great
Books of the Western World, Vol. 44, 1952, p. 193. Bottom
quotation from La Rochefoucauld, *Maxims.* L. W. Tancock,
trans. Baltimore, Md.: Penguin Books, 1959, p. 45.)

"Many friendships are formed by a community of sensual pleasures.... We form many friendships with bad men, because they have agreeable qualities, and they can be useful to us.... We form many friendships by mistake, imagining people to be different from what they really are."

"What men have called friendship is merely association, respect for each other's interests, and exchange of good offices, in fact nothing more than a business arrangement from which self-love is always out to draw some profit."

are like economic transactions—value is traded for value. In this sense people weigh the assets and liabilities of the people they meet—they do not wish to embark upon a relationship that will be painful or costly. Of course, the costs and rewards of friendship are quite different from those in economics. Each type of reward holds a particular emotional value.

One reward of friendship is stimulation. A friend has *stimulation value* if he is interesting or imaginative or if he can introduce you to new ideas or experiences. A friend who is cooperative and helpful, who seems willing to give his time and resources to help you achieve your goals, has *utility value.* A third type of value in friendship is *ego support value:* sympathy and encouragement when things go badly, appreciation and approval when things go well. These three kinds of reward—stimulation, utility, and ego support—are evaluated consciously or unconsciously in every friendship. A man may like another man because the second man is a witty conversationalist (stimulation value) and knows a lot about gardening (utility value). A woman may like a man because he respects her (ego support value) and because she has an exciting time with him (stimulation value).

By considering the three kinds of rewards that a person may look for in friendship, it is possible to understand other factors that affect liking and loving.

Physical Appearance   Everyone is aware to some extent of how much his impressions of others are influenced by their physical attractiveness. An attractive appearance has stimulation value and may also provide ego support. Psychologists have noted that different cultures have different definitions of what is beautiful—especially in women. In some cultures heavily built women are considered desirable, but in others, including middle-class America, small slender women are thought most attractive. From such observations psychologists have concluded that people are attracted to beauty as their society defines it. People feel better about themselves when they feel they have managed to associate themselves with what everyone agrees is desirable.

Conventional physical attractiveness is often misleading. Good-looking people are not necessarily the ones who will have the most stimulation value for you, and what society defines as good-looking may not be what you find attractive. Interestingly, psychologists have found that both men and women pay much less attention to physical appearances when choosing a marriage partner or a close friend than when choosing someone to go to a movie or a party with.

Approval   Another factor that affects a person's choice of friends is *approval*. A person tends to like people who say nice things about him because they make him feel better about himself—they provide ego support value.

In an experiment designed to study this factor, subjects were allowed to overhear a series of conversations between the experimenter and another subject. This second subject, in reality a confederate of the experimenter, made remarks about the subject who was listening in. For one-fourth of the real subjects, this woman made nothing but uncomplimentary remarks. For another one-fourth she made only complimentary remarks. For the third group, the fake subject began with favorable comments but ended up

Figure 9.17

These two men obviously enjoy each other's company. In addition to having stimulation value for each other, they probably provide considerable utility value: They are able to give each other business advice and exchange information on business opportunities.

making criticisms. The final one-fourth of the real subjects overheard the woman give negative comments at first and positive remarks toward the end.

After the real subjects had been allowed to overhear these analyses of themselves, they were asked how much they liked the woman who had been making the remarks. Not surprisingly, the subjects who had heard her make all positive comments liked her better than did the subjects who had heard her make all negative comments. But the subjects who liked her least were the ones who had heard her start positively and end negatively. Finally, the subjects who liked the woman most were the ones who heard her begin negatively and go toward the positive.

This experiment seems to show that other people's evaluations of oneself are more meaningful when they are a mixture of praise and criticism than when they are extreme in either direction. No one believes that he is all good or all bad. As a result, one can take more seriously a person who sees some good points and some bad points. But when the good points come first, hearing the bad can make one disappointed and angry at the person who made them. When the bad points come first, the effect is opposite. One thinks, "This person is perceptive and honest. At first she was critical but later she saw what I was really like."

Similarity   People tend to choose friends whose backgrounds, attitudes, and interests are similar to their own. It has been found

Figure 9.18
These two people find each other attractive partly because of a similarity of background and interests. They are both elderly, and both have seen a lifetime of family and work in the same society. Both have lost their former loved ones and are now turning to each other for companionship and warmth.

that most marriage partners share similar economic, religious, and educational backgrounds.

There are several explanations for the power of shared attitudes in attraction. First, agreement provides a basis for sharing activities. Friends are rewarded by being able to do things together that they enjoy. In other words, people who are similar have more utility value and more stimulation value because they can provide each other with help and with pleasant experiences.

Second, people who agree about things generally find it easier to communicate with each other. They have fewer arguments and misunderstandings, and they are better able to predict each other's actions. Third, a friend's agreement reinforces the notion that one's opinions are correct, thus contributing to one's self-esteem. Finally, people assume that others with similar backgrounds are less likely to reject them than are strangers with different backgrounds. In this way, similarity provides ego support value.

Complementarity

The reward theory of friendship makes it easy to see why people who are in a sense opposites are attracted to one another. Each person can fill in the needs of the other. The dominating person can satisfy his desire to direct and control things with a person who likes being directed and controlled.

Such filling in of needs is referred to as *complementarity*. Complementary roles include leader and follower, dominant and

Figure 9.19

The relationship between these two men suggests the role of complementarity in friendship. These men are rather different types in physical stature, in race, and probably in personality as well. But their differences enable them to enrich each other's lives. Their friendship is also supported by their similar situations in life and by their shared knowledge of city ways.

223

submissive, strong and weak. Psychologist Robert W. White provides a good example of how two different personalities complemented each other in the case of the friendship of two adolescent boys:

> Ben, whose school experience had been so unstimulating that he never read a book beyond those assigned, discovered in Jamie a lively spirit of intellectual inquiry and an exciting knowledge of politics and history. Here was a whole world to which his friend opened the door and provided guidance. Jamie discovered in Ben a world previously closed to him, that of confident interaction with other people. Each admired the other, each copied the other, each used the other for practice.

Many friendships, both same-sex and opposite-sex, seem to be built on such complementarity.

LOVE

There are many varieties of love—love between parent and child, between same-sex friends, between husband and wife. Although everybody has a feeling of what is meant by "romantic love," psychologists who wish to study it have tried to define it and to distinguish between what it means to like someone very much and what it means to love him or her.

People who like each other say favorable things about each other, have respect for and confidence in each other, and perceive each other as similar to themselves. But people in love, in addition to liking each other, feel highly attached, find it hard to imagine getting along without each other, and feel that they can confide anything to each other. Each feels that there is nothing he would not do for the other. People in love share an exclusive intimacy and often spend time just looking into each other's eyes.

The choice of a lover seems to follow the same principles as other kinds of interpersonal attraction. A person is most likely to fall in love

Figure 9.20
Eye contact is apparently one of the most significant forms of human interaction. Poets write about it, children often experiment with it (trying to "stare down" one another), and psychologists have used it as a measure of how much in love two people are. It is also interesting to note that children with a certain form of psychological disturbance known as autism tend to avoid eye contact entirely.

(From "The Look" by Sara Teasdale. In *Collected Poems*, copyright 1915 by the Macmillan Co., renewed 1943 by Mamie T. Wheless.)

"Strephon kissed me in the spring,
Robin in the fall,
But Colin only looked at me
And never kissed at all.

Strephon's kiss was lost in jest,
Robin's lost in play,
But the kiss in Colin's eyes
Haunts me night and day."

with another who is close by, whose background and attitudes resemble his own, whom he finds physically attractive, and who generally provides the rewards of stimulation, utility, and ego support. But loving seems to go beyond the cost-reward level of human interaction. Many psychologists have theorized that love is basic to man's existence—without it man could not realize his full human potential.

One psychologist who supports this view, Rollo May, has written, "To love means to open ourselves to the negative as well as the positive—to grief, sorrow, and disappointment as well as to joy, fulfillment, and an intensity of consciousness we did not know was possible before." According to May, it is this new "intensity of

Figure 9.21
It is easy to think of love in a narrow context and consider only the sexual relationship that exists between a man and a woman. But this view omits the kinds of love that exist between members of the same sex, between parents and children, between very young or very old people, and between some people and their animals.

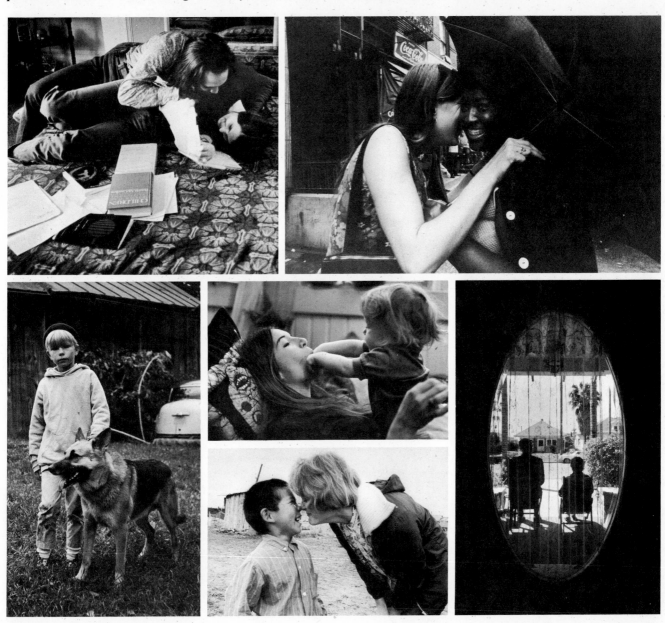

consciousness" that makes love an essential emotion. Love allows people to share and to be honest with one another. The deep intensity of love allows one to care for someone else's welfare more than one's own. Love is more than receiving rewards; it is the willingness and courage to make sacrifices for those whom one loves.

Another famous psychologist, Erich Fromm, has written that love is "the active concern for the life and growth of that which we love." Fromm views love as a basic need of man. He sees increasing isolation and loneliness as great dangers for man's future, but he feels that love can be the solution to this problem: Through love, the individual can reunite himself with other people and can feel a sense of belongingness and fellowship with the rest of humanity.

Figure 9.22
Poets and novelists have written about love for centuries, but only recently have psychologists tried to explore this phenomenon scientifically. Through theory and research psychologists may make the factors that help and hinder love more understandable, and they may be able to explain the behavior of people in love. But such knowledge is not meant to be substituted for the experience of love or to set limits on it; rather, it is meant to expand understanding of a phenomenon that is so important a part of life.
(From Sherwood Anderson, "Death," in *Winesburg, Ohio.* New York: Viking Press, 1964, p. 223.)

" *Love is like a wind stirring the grass beneath trees on a black night.... You must not try to make love definite. It is the divine accident of life.* "

SUMMARY

1. People have certain emotional and practical needs that can be satisfied only by interaction with other humans. The process of establishing social relationships is facilitated by communication. Much of the communication between people serves to clarify each person's status in relation to the other.

2. Nonverbal communication is as significant as verbal communication. Some of the ways in which people communicate nonverbally are through posture, gestures, facial expression, and tone of voice.

3. Most people are concerned about the impression they make on other people. They play roles according to what they think is appropriate to the situation and according to what they want other people to think of them.

4. The primary motive for giving a performance is the need for social approval. Acting in ways designed to gain approval fulfills an individual's need to think well of himself.

5. Most psychologists see the self as divided into an "I" and a "me." The "I" is the willing, experiencing, perceiving, feeling, imagining, planning part of the self, and the "me" is the self as seen through the eyes of others.

6. People form impressions of one another on the basis of their own implicit theory of personality. They cannot react to every action of another person, so judgments are made on the basis of generalizations about emotional states, personality traits, and personality types.

7. People often simplify the process of forming impressions of others by stereotyping them—categorizing them into groups and holding preconceived beliefs and expectations about what people in those groups are like. They also react toward people on the basis of central organizing traits, such as warmth or coldness.

8. Generally, a person seeks the company of others in order to compare himself to them and to determine if he is reacting correctly in a particular situation. However, if a person believes that his reactions will be disapproved of by others, he will usually prefer to remain alone.

9. Friends are selected on the basis of three types of rewards: stimulation value, utility value, and ego support value. Some of the factors favoring friendships are proximity, physical attractiveness, similarity, approval, and complementarity.

10. Love seems to go beyond the cost-reward level of human interaction. Love may be basic to man's existence—essential for self-realization and fellowship with humanity.

ACTIVITIES

1. Isolate yourself for one to five hours. No other people should be nearby and no entertainment, such as television or reading materials, should be available. Make notes of your thoughts and feelings as they unfold. After your experience, write a paragraph describing how you felt and what you discovered about yourself. Were you bored with your own company? If you were, how did you overcome the boredom? Do you think it is valuable for people to be able to be alone with themselves? Do you ever look forward to being alone?

2. One of the most difficult emotions to define is love. What is your own definition of love? Does this definition apply to love between family members and between friends as well as to romantic love?

3. What do you find physically attractive in the same sex and in the opposite sex? Ask your friends and relatives this question, and compare your answers. How important is physical attractiveness to you when it comes to choosing friends?

4. Examine the interactions between members of your family, your friends, or even strangers, paying as little attention as possible to verbal interaction and noting instead proximity, posture, gesture, facial expression, eye contact, relative position, and nonlinguistic verbal cues. Are you able to interpret this body language? Does this nonverbal communication conflict with what people communicate verbally? What happens if you reply verbally to nonverbal messages?

5. How do you analyze new instructors at the beginning of a term? On what do you base your impressions? How do your impressions affect how you behave toward each instructor? Have you ever changed your mind after getting the "wrong impression" about someone?

6. Cut out a variety of pictures of people from magazines. Mount the pictures on plain paper and identify each picture by number. Ask several friends to rate the people in the pictures as potential friends, dates, marriage partners, bosses, co-workers, and so on. Try to identify what characteristics in the pictures people respond to in making these judgments. (Ask your subjects, "What is it that makes you feel this way?") Write a brief summary of your results.

7. Organize a group of friends to put on a drama to observe how an individual communicates his status or role to another. Make the cast of characters diverse enough to observe a wide range of verbal and nonverbal behavior. (For instance, you might include a concerned doctor, an inquisitive plumber, a frightened child, a bored business-man, a harried teacher, and an angry housewife in your cast of characters.) Take notes on how each character communicates his social status and his individual personality through actions and words. After the drama, discuss your notes with the characters. How did each interpret his role? Was he aware of actually communicating the status or role of his character or were his reactions almost unconscious? What conclusions can you draw about social rules, status, and roles?

8. Have you ever felt like skipping, shouting, or dancing in a crowded public place but refrained because you anticipated social disapproval? Perhaps there was a time when you wanted to engage your parents in a serious discussion but found that they still thought of you as a small child whose thoughts regarding serious, "adult" matters were unimportant. In what other ways do social rules restrict you or keep you from behaving spontaneously?

9. Describe several situations in which you either "put on an act" or disguised your true feeling regarding a person or situation. Did your deception occur consciously or unconsciously?

10. List in detail the main criteria you use in choosing close friends. What are your reasons for rejecting certain people as either close friends or acquaintances?

11. If you knew that you and five other people would be the only survivors on Earth after an atomic holocaust, whom would you choose to be with? Why?

SUGGESTED READINGS

ARONSON, ELLIOT. *The Social Animal.* New York: Viking Press, 1972. A conversationally written textbook in social psychology. It is excellent reading for the person who wants to go deeper into the ideas presented in this and the next two chapters.

FAST, JULIUS. *Body Language.* New York: Evans, 1970. A good introduction to nonverbal communication.

FROMM, ERICH. *The Art of Loving.* New York: Harper & Row, 1956 (paper). Fromm suggests that there are different types of love and that love is an art that must be learned, just as one must learn any other art form.

GOFFMAN, ERVING. *The Presentation of Self in Everyday Life.* Garden City, N.Y.: Doubleday, 1959. A classic in the study of how impressions are made. Goffman describes everyday social interactions in terms of the acting out of roles.

HALL, EDWARD T. *The Hidden Dimension.* Garden City, N.Y.: Doubleday, 1966. A thorough and well-written book that describes the bubbles of privacy people carry about them and the purpose of personal space.

HALL, EDWARD T. *The Silent Language.* Garden City, N.Y.: Doubleday, 1959 (paper). Hall suggests that "communication occurs simultaneously on different levels of consciousness, ranging from full awareness to out-of-awareness." An excellent book on nonverbal communication.

HESSE, HERMANN. *Steppenwolf.* New York: Bantam, 1963 (paper), originally published, 1929. The myriad roles, or personalities, that reside in a single individual are examined in this profound novel.

JOURARD, SIDNEY M. *The Transparent Self.* New York: Van Nostrand, 1964 (paper). A thorough and straight-forward book about the choice between being authentic and playing a series of roles. Jourard contends that honesty "can literally be a health-insurance policy."

KELLER, HELEN. *The Story of My Life.* Garden City, N.Y.: Doubleday, 1902. A moving and very human account of how this remarkable woman, blind and deaf from infancy, became an expert in interpersonal communication.

10

People in Groups

THE NATURE OF GROUPS
HOW GROUPS ARE HELD TOGETHER:
Norms / Cohesiveness
MEANING OF GROUPS TO THEIR MEMBERS
INTERACTION WITHIN GROUPS:
Communication patterns / Leadership
WHEN THE GROUP PROCESS GOES WRONG:
Groupthink / Diffusion of responsibility
GROUPS IN CONFLICT
WAYS TO END GROUP CONFLICT

Each person feels himself to be different—an individual separate from the rest of humanity. And yet, he also has a feeling of being part of something larger than himself, of being a member of a profession, a nation, a race, or of humanity. The study of people as members of a larger whole is the study of *groups.*

One of the tasks of psychology is to try to understand how groups work and how they affect their members. What makes people loyal to a group? Why do people in groups sometimes act irrationally? How do hatreds develop between different groups in society? The answers psychologists have tentatively given to these questions are the subject of this chapter.

WHAT ARE GROUPS?

What is the difference between a random aggregate of people and a true group? How is it that three boys playing ball and the entire United States Army can both be classified as groups? In general, the features that distinguish a group from a nongroup are *interdependence* and *shared goals.*

Interdependence

All the people in the world who have red hair and freckles make up a category of people, but they are not a group. The people in this collection are not interdependent. People are said to be interdependent when any action by one of them will affect or influence the other members or when the same event will influence each member. For instance, in groups of athletes, entertainers, or roommates, each member has a certain responsibility to the rest of the group; if he does not fulfill his responsibility, the other members will

Figure 10.1
Group membership is a universal fact of life in human society. A marching band is a group, and so is a family, a business organization, or an entire community. Social psychologists assume that similar processes take place in individuals in all kinds of groups, and they try to identify these processes with a view toward explaining group structures, functions, and relations.

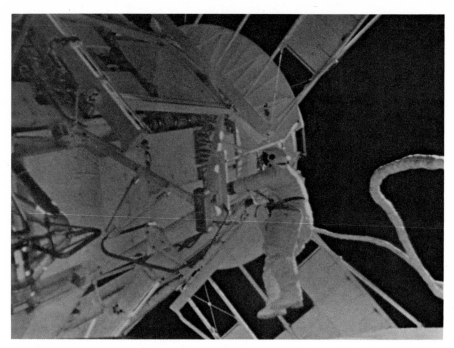

Figure 10.2
Toward the end of a twenty-eight day mission in space, a Skylab astronaut retrieves some film canisters from outside the module. This precarious situation is an extreme example of the interdependence that can exist between group members. One of the common goals these astronauts share is survival itself.

be affected. For the athletes, the consequence may be losing the game; for the entertainers, a bad show; for the roommates, a messy apartment.

In small groups the influence that members have on one another is usually direct. One person yells at another, smiles at him, or passes him a note. In larger groups, the influence may be highly indirect. The interdependence between you and the President of the United States is not a result of your personal contact with him. Nevertheless, one of the things that makes the people of the United States a group is the fact that the President's actions affect you and that your actions, together with those of many other Americans, affect him.

Common Goals

Group members become interdependent because they see themselves as sharing certain *common goals.* Groups are usually created to perform tasks or to organize activities that no individual could handle alone. Members of a consumer group, for example, share the common goal of working for consumer protection. Members of ethnic and religious groups desire to perpetuate a common heritage or set of beliefs.

The purposes that groups serve are of two general kinds: *task functions,* those directed toward getting some job done, and *social functions,* those that are directed toward filling the emotional needs of the members.

Political parties, teams of surgeons, and crews of construction workers are all task-oriented groups. Although social interactions occur within each of these groups, their main purpose is to complete a project or to achieve some change in the environment. Social functions are emphasized in more informal, temporary groups. When people take walks together, attend parties, or participate in conversations, they are forming groups to gain such social rewards as companionship and emotional support. Nevertheless, in most groups, task and social functions are naturally combined and cannot easily be separated.

An Example

The importance of interdependence and common goals in the formation of groups can be seen in the example of riders on the New York subway. They would usually not qualify as a group—there is little interdependence among them, nor do they share common goals. On the contrary, these people communicate as little as possible and are more likely to be pushing and shoving each other than to be cooperating in any way.

During the Northeast power failure of 1965, however, people stranded together in subways quickly became dependent on one another for emotional and physical support. Inside the darkened subway tunnels, passengers organized themselves into small brigades to preserve order and to protect one another. In the face of collective danger, group interdependence developed quickly. Task functions, such as preventing panic and finding ways to safety, were difficult to distinguish from social functions, such as providing the security and comfort of companionship.

HOW GROUPS ARE HELD TOGETHER

The maintenance of cooperative interdependence among group members is not always easy. Athletes may become angry with their teammates or try for their own individual glory at the expense of a team effort. Members of communes may become disillusioned by difficult work and by conflicts with other members over the division of labor. Soldiers may desert their companies if they lose faith in the army's purposes or in their commander's competence.

Norms

One way in which groups keep their members going in the same direction is by developing group *norms*. Norms are rules for the behavior and attitudes of group members. These rules are not necessarily rigid laws. They may be more like tendencies or habits. But group members are expected to act in accordance with them and are punished in some way if they do not. The punishment may take the form of coldness or criticism from other group members. If the norm is of high importance to the group, a member who violates it may receive a more severe punishment or may even be thrown out of the group.

Psychologists observed the operation of such norms in a group of assembly-line workers. The workers had developed among themselves a norm for the amount of work they should do. Workers who

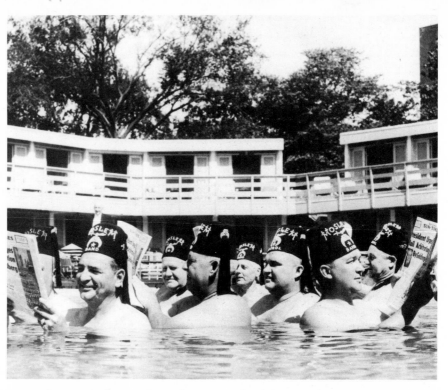

Figure 10.3

Shriners cool off as they read about a seven-hour Shriner parade held the day before. In addition to the wearing of fezzes, this group maintains norms that include benevolence, belief in God, and avoidance of any political discussion in their meetings. Part of the code of the Freemasons, norms such as these have bound together groups of people in many countries for more than two centuries.

went slower or faster than the prescribed rate endangered the whole group, either by making the management angry that too little work was being done or by giving management the idea that more work could be done by everyone. The work norm was enforced by "binging." Any worker who saw another worker going too fast or too slow could strike him painfully on the upper arm. "Binging" punished the violator and let everyone else in the group know about the misbehavior, and so preserved the norm.

Cohesiveness

Cohesiveness is the amount of "we" feeling among group members, or the amount of loyalty members feel to each other and to the group. If a group has high cohesiveness, the individual members will experience strong feelings of togetherness, of responsibility to one another, and of high motivation to remain in the group. A group with low cohesiveness is likely to have feelings of suspicion, hostility, and jealousy among its members.

Cohesiveness is particularly important in keeping the group together under conditions of stress. Military organizations, for instance, spend a great deal of time building cohesiveness in combat units. What would happen to a soldier if, during a battle, he suddenly decided that his group no longer served his interests? He might surrender to the enemy or he might desert, bringing danger to the goals of the group and probably to his own long-term goals as well. Even in less extreme situations, cohesiveness among group members gives the group greater power to accomplish its goals because members do not have to spend as much of their energy in working out disagreements and tensions.

Ideology and Symbols   For a group to be highly cohesive, the members' values should be identical to those of the group. This matching of values is achieved in several ways. First, the members arrive at agreement about the group *ideology*—the set of ideas, attitudes, and defined objectives for which the group stands. A black-power group, for example, might publish a newspaper and pamphlets to explain the purpose and goals of the group and to argue the rightness of its position on certain issues. Such publications not only reinforce the ideas of group members, they are likely to attract new members who agree with the ideology expressed.

The second way a group achieves agreement among its members is by adopting group values that are relevant to the individual member's well-being. Thus, the black-power organization might emphasize pride and accomplishment as benefits of membership and might stress the ways in which the accomplishment of group goals will improve each member's life—economically, socially, and psychologically.

Emotional attachment to a group and its ideology is often intensified by use of *symbols.* Symbols are usually simple, vivid things that can easily be recognized and kept in mind. Nations invariably have distinctive flags. Universities, colleges, and high schools maintain school colors, mascots, cheers, and songs. The American counter-culture has developed a unique handshake that symbolizes brotherhood. And groups devoted to ecology, peace, women's liberation and other political causes have developed special symbols to represent their ideology.

Commitment   A group's cohesiveness will be high if the members of the group are heavily committed to it. One factor that increases individual commitment is the requirement of *personal sacrifice.* If a person is willing to pay money, endure hardship, or undergo humiliation to belong to a group, he is likely to stick with it. For example, college students who undergo embarrassing initiation rites to join sororities or fraternities tend to develop a loyalty to the group that lasts well beyond their college years.

If a member wants to stay in a group and deeply believes in the group's ideals, he must be willing to conform to group norms, yield to group pressures, and make any sacrifice required. People may be so devoted to a group and to the ideals it represents that they are willing to sacrifice their lives to further the group or its goals.

The practice of using personal sacrifices as a method for building group solidarity has long been in use. Nineteenth-century utopian communes required personal sacrifice as a basic condition for membership. Social psychologists who studied these communes to better understand the group process found that some groups asked

Figure 10.4

Tommy Smith and John Carlos receiving the gold and bronze medals, respectively, for the 200 meter race at the 1968 Olympics. The two athletes raised their fists in a gesture symbolizing the Black Power movement. The significance of their gesture—the demand on the part of blacks for power to determine their own lives—was well understood by everyone. Nevertheless, many spectators found the action of Smith and Carlos inappropriate because the symbolism and ideology of the Games is that of fair and unprejudiced competition and therefore undeserving of such a defiant gesture.

Figure 10.5

A barn raising among the Amish people in Pennsylvania. The Amish choose to live apart from the mainstream of Americans in an attempt to preserve the Mennonite religion and a way of life that was common two centuries ago. Their adherence to strict group norms and their significant personal sacrifices (including severe dress style and avoidance of all frivolities and modern technological devices) have bound these people together into a tight-knit community. Helping one another with the tasks of living, as is exemplified in this barn raising, not only promotes group cohesiveness but enables members to retain their independence from society.

that their members give up such things as wearing jewelry and fine clothes, smoking tobacco, and eating meat. Others required members to renounce all outside ties, including family ones. Psychologists discovered that communes requiring such sacrifices tended to last much longer than ones that did not require sacrifices. They concluded that sacrifice makes membership in the group more costly, so membership becomes a valuable matter not to be given up lightly. The more one suffers, the more important the reason for suffering must be. (This phenomenon may be explained in terms of the theory of cognitive dissonance, which is described in Chapter 11.)

Another factor that strengthens group commitment is *participation*. When a person actively participates in group decisions and shares the rewards of the group's accomplishments, his feeling of group membership increases—he feels he has helped make the group what it is.

The failure of all group members to participate in group actions can create tremendous discontent. For example, in 1970 the majority of the members of the United Mine Workers Union felt that they were excluded from participation in union affairs. Group loyalty and strong "we" feelings among group members deteriorated rapidly. Many workers refused to attend union meetings. Others quit the union, feeling that they had been betrayed. When a democratic vote for union leadership was held, many workers abstained because they had lost faith in their ability to participate in the group. Eventually, the U.S. government intervened to try to restore the members' faith in the union.

As this example shows, the processes whereby a group is held together must work both ways. The individual must be responsive to the norms of the group, he must subscribe to its ideology, and he must be prepared to make sacrifices in order to be a part of it. But the group must also respond to the needs of its members. It cannot possibly achieve cohesiveness if its norms are unenforceable, if its ideology is inconsistent with the beliefs of its members, or if the rewards it offers do not outweigh the sacrifices it requires. Participation in the development of norms, ideology, and goals by all group members makes the group process possible.

MEANING OF GROUPS TO THE INDIVIDUAL

An individual's commitment to a group gives him a source of values and beliefs and a way of defining who he is. The groups with which a person identifies are called *reference groups*. Almost everyone uses large social groups such as their race, their religion, and their sex as ways to help establish their identities. A person is also likely to think of himself as a member of a certain nation, state, city, or neighborhood. People also identify themselves with other people who do the same type of work that they do. Not all reference groups are so large, however. A person may find his membership in a chess club, a swimming team, a social crowd, or a gang an important way of defining his own values and sense of self.

At times, a group to which someone does not belong becomes a powerful reference group for him. Many adolescents, for example, model themselves on the members of an in-crowd in hopes that they will be noticed and accepted by its members. Youth, in general, seems to be a desired reference group for many American adults. Similarly, immigrants or the children of immigrants are often more blindly accepting of the symbols and traditional ideology of the culture they are joining than are the country's settled inhabitants. Thus, paradoxically, the aspiring nonmember is often a group's most outspoken and uncompromising advocate of its ideology.

Once a person identifies with a group, he becomes proud of it. This pride may be seen in action when a person defends his group to outsiders. To illustrate pride in reference groups, psychologists experimented to see how much pain groups of Jewish and Christian college women would tolerate. A blood-pressure cuff with sharp rubber projections sewn into it was placed on each woman's upper arm and was inflated until she said the pain was intolerable. After this pain limit had been established, the experimenters told the subjects that they would take the measurement again in five minutes. In addition, the experimenters casually mentioned to Jewish subjects that Jews could endure less pain than Christians and told Christian subjects that Christians could endure less pain than Jews.

When the women were tested again, both Jewish and Christian women let the pressure go higher than they had on the first test. It seems that people tend to interpret "insults" to their religious reference groups as attacks on themselves and are prepared to defend the group publicly, even if doing so causes intense physical pain.

Thus, a group provides the individual with certain ways of behaving, with pride, and with a set of values and beliefs. If the

Figure 10.6
Cesar Chavez (*left*), leader of the United Farm Workers, and Walter Reuther (*center*), president of the United Auto Workers, lead a picket line of grape strikers in California. The unions represented by these men serve as reference groups for hundreds of thousands of working men and women. The common values and goals of unions and their members are strengthened and reinforced through the process of identification with such leaders.

person's or the group's values change, it is likely that he will leave the group, for it would no longer be providing him with what he needs.

INTERACTIONS WITHIN GROUPS

Providing an individual with values and a sense of identity is only one aspect of the group's meaning to him. The particular part he plays in the group's activities is also important. Each group member has certain unique abilities and interests, and the group has a number of different tasks that need to be performed. The study of the parts played in the group by various members, and of how these parts are interrelated, is the study of *group structure.*

As people interact in a group, each member comes to have a place in relation to every other member. And when members establish patterns of relating to one another, these patterns tend to determine the nature of future interactions.

There are many different aspects to group structure: The personal relationships between individual members, such as liking relationships and trusting relationships, are one aspect; another is the rank of each member on a particular dimension, such as power, popularity, status, or amount of resources. Think of the groups that you belong to and try to identify their structures according to the roles various members play. Typical group roles are easy to identify and may bring to mind roles that members of your groups occupy—leader, joker, black sheep and the silent member, to name a few.

One technique psychologists use in analyzing group structure is the *sociogram.* Researchers using this device ask all the members of a

Figure 10.7
A system of categorizing, such as the one shown here, enables psychologists to make detailed analyses of a group's structure and to observe the patterns of interaction among its members. For example, psychologists might observe a particular group in action, say a newspaper staff, and score the behavior of each member according to the twelve categories shown on the chart. The emerging profiles depict each member's role in the structure of the group. For instance, a member who scores high on 5 and 10 and low on 3 might be described as a "maverick," whereas a member who scores high on 1, 3, 8, and 11 could be characterized as "submissive." A person who scores high on 1, 5, and 7 is probably the group leader.

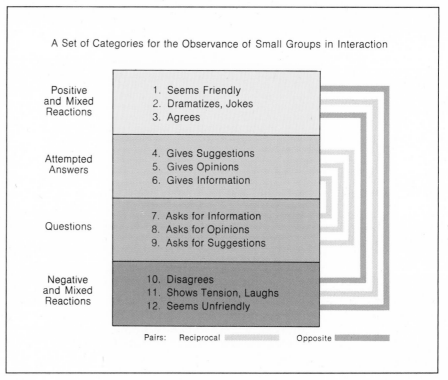

A Set of Categories for the Observance of Small Groups in Interaction

Positive and Mixed Reactions	1. Seems Friendly 2. Dramatizes, Jokes 3. Agrees
Attempted Answers	4. Gives Suggestions 5. Gives Opinions 6. Gives Information
Questions	7. Asks for Information 8. Asks for Opinions 9. Asks for Suggestions
Negative and Mixed Reactions	10. Disagrees 11. Shows Tension, Laughs 12. Seems Unfriendly

Pairs: Reciprocal   Opposite

group to name those people with whom they would like to interact on a given occasion or for a specific purpose, those they like best, and so on. For example, the members may be asked with whom they would like to go to a party, to share political ideas, to spend vacation time, or to complete an organizational task. Their choices can then be graphically plotted, as are the responses of the group members represented in Figure 10.8. Such sociograms can show a great deal about any one person's status in a group and can help to predict how that individual is likely to communicate with other group members.

Communication Patterns

Another way to find out the structure of a group is to examine the communication patterns in the group. Who says what to whom, and how often?

An experiment on communication patterns was done by Harold J. Leavitt in the 1950s. For his experiment, he gave a card with several symbols on it to each person in a group of five. The group's goal was to find which symbol appeared on everyone's card. Obviously the group members had to communicate with one another in order to solve this problem. Leavitt controlled their freedom by putting each person in a separate room or booth and allowing the members to communicate only by written messages. In this way he was able to create the networks shown in Figure 10.9. Each circle represents a person, and the lines represent open channels. Subjects placed in

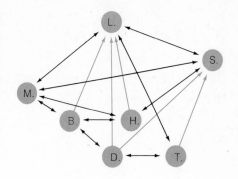

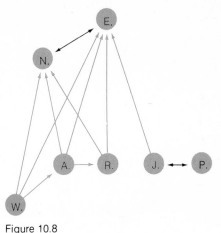

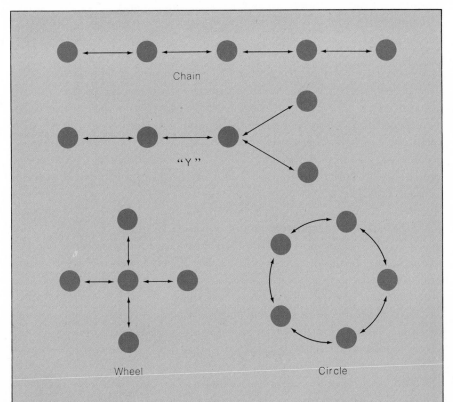

Figure 10.8
Patterns of friendship choices within two groups. The blue arrows indicate liking that is not returned; the black arrows indicate a two-way friendship. The more a person is liked, the higher in the pattern he appears. Patterns like these are called sociograms. Notice the difference between the two patterns. Whereas the pattern of the bottom group shows a hierarchical structure, with E and N clearly the leaders, the sociogram of the top group indicates strong group cohesiveness with even D and T, the two least-liked members, clearly tied in to the group and having friends who like them.

Figure 10.9
Harold Leavitt's communication networks. It is interesting to compare these structures, which were deliberately created by a person outside the group, with those structures shown in Figure 10.8, which spontaneously developed within groups. It is highly unlikely that such uncomplicated patterns as those imposed by Leavitt could develop naturally.

each position could exchange messages only with the persons to whom they were connected by channels.

The most interesting result of this experiment was that the people who were organized into a "circle" were the slowest at solving the problem but the happiest at doing it. In this group everyone sent and received a large number of messages until someone solved the problem and passed the information on. In the "wheel," by contrast, everyone sent a few messages to one center person, who figured out the answer and told the rest what it was. In this pattern, the solution was found quickly, but the people on the outside of the wheel did not particularly enjoy the job.

Following the experiment, the members in each group were asked to identify the leader of their group. In the centralized groups (wheel, Y, and chain), the person in the center was usually chosen as the group leader. But in the circle network half the group members said they thought there was no real leader, and those who did say there was a leader disagreed on who that leader was. Thus, a centralized organization seems more useful for task-oriented groups, whereas a decentralized network is more useful in socially oriented groups.

Leadership

All groups, whether made up of gangsters, soldiers, workers, or politicians, have leaders. A leader embodies the norms and ideals of the group and represents the group to outsiders. Within the group, a leader initiates action, gives orders, makes decisions, and settles disputes. In short, a leader is one who has a great deal of *influence* on the other members of the group.

Expertise   There are many ways in which a person can come to have enough influence to become the leader of a group. One kind of influence comes from being an *expert*. An expert directs the group's activity because he has the knowledge that the group needs to achieve its goals. Such a leader is usually someone who has a great deal of experience in the group's tasks. For example, a ship's captain must be someone who knows how to run a ship and how to meet an emergency at sea.

Charisma   Expertise is not enough by itself, however. Good leaders also possess a strong emotional appeal. Because of this appeal, or *charisma,* their approval or disapproval of other group members has a powerful effect. Nowhere is this kind of influence more apparent than in politics. President John F. Kennedy was a striking example of a political leader with a charisma that aroused strong feelings among both his followers and his enemies.

A leader must have qualities that enable his followers to identify with him. People often demand a leader who is similar to themselves or who represents what they would like to be. The importance of social attractiveness in leadership appeal can be seen in the recent

Figure 10.10
The Catholic pope is a leader whose influence over millions of people comes from several sources. In addition to the power and charisma inherent in his office, he is considered by Catholics to be the ultimate authority on matters of faith and morals.

emergence of entertainment celebrities on the political scene. Movie stars, television personalities, athletic performers, and astronauts have successfully achieved political leadership.

Power   Influence can also come from the power to control the rewards and punishments of group members. A president of a company, for instance, can give raises and promotions and can also fire people or give demotions. He is a leader not because members elected him but because he owns the most shares in the company or because he has been appointed by those who own shares. Similarly, a child who has special toys can influence members of his play group by giving and withdrawing the privilege of playing with his toys. In both cases leadership influence is determined not by group choice but by the leader's power to grant members the things they want.

Such power is often gained through appointment from outside the group. A person is simply placed in a position of authority and thereby assumes the role of leader. Appointed leaders include teachers, priests, and cabinet members. An appointed leader is usually less permanent and less respected than a leader chosen by the group. In some cases, the group may even refuse to recognize him as the legitimate leader. Obviously, leaders who are elected have potentially more influence than those who are appointed.

Machiavellian Techniques   There are some leaders who achieve their influence by deceit and manipulation. These leaders gain power through *Machiavellian* techniques—tactics based on emotional manipulation and the philosophy, "If it works, do it." This type of leader was named for Niccolò Machiavelli, who wrote a classic sixteenth-century book, *The Prince,* about the differences between people who manipulate and people who are manipulated. Psychologists have found that manipulators are the kind of people who can lie and cheat while still being able to convince people that they aren't lying and cheating. Such people feel that most people do not know what is really best for them and that they need to be given some direction.

The Machiavellian leader is always cool and collected and seems to exert particular influence in emotional situations. In competitions, the Machiavellian is expert at disrupting his opponents and interfering with their performance. The Machiavellian leader is least influential in situations where he cannot be face to face with group members, where there are many rules and regulations for behavior, and where there is little emotional arousal.

For whatever reason a member becomes a leader, his type of leadership will affect the structure of his group and the roles other members play. A powerful leader may make all the important decisions for the group and assign relatively unimportant tasks to other members. A more democratic leader may try to involve as many members as possible in the decision-making process.

Figure 10.11
The influence a leader has over other group members can be obtained by deceit and manipulation if a person is willing and able to play people off against one another and to keep his own emotions concealed.

MOBS, CROWDS, AND SUPERGROUPS

Do people in groups act more daringly or less rationally than they would if they were alone? The answer is yes, they often do. The great revolutions and wars of independence in America in 1776, in France in 1789, and in Russia in 1917, for example, were probably possible because of this fact. The marches and protests that changed the American scene in the 1960s were also dependent on the ability of people to find strength in numbers. But in other circumstances this tendency has had very different results. With a view to understanding how and why group processes go wrong and how such disasters can be prevented in the future, psychologists have studied several examples in detail.

Groupthink

Irving L. Janis has described a phenomenon he calls *groupthink,* using the famous "Bay of Pigs" incident as an example of how a group decision-making process can produce major errors, misinterpretations, and incorrect solutions. In 1961 President John F. Kennedy secretly assembled the top political policy makers of the country. They were reputed to be the most intelligent men ever to participate in such a tight-knit decision-making group.

This group met for three months in order to plan an invasion of Cuba. As a result, a brigade of 1,400 CIA-trained Cuban exiles, aided by the U.S. Navy and Air Force, was sent into Cuba. Within three days Fidel Castro's forces in Cuba had sunk the ships carrying the invaders' ammunition and supplies and had captured 1,000 invaders;

most of the rest had been killed. The President's high-echelon group had made one of the worst decisions in recent history. The group members attributed their failure to incomplete information and poor planning. Why, then, did they go ahead with the plan if they did not have the right information?

Janis studied the procedures of the group and found that the error was partly a product of overconfidence. The group was highly cohesive, and its members felt strongly committed to it; as a result, the members had become overly optimistic. This optimism created a dangerous illusion that the group was invulnerable, and it prevented the members from seriously examining the possibility of failure. They thought of themselves as a "supergroup."

The few group members who did have doubts did not want to upset the tight feelings of unanimity within the group. Furthermore, several of the doubters were afraid that dissent would damage their careers: They did not want to risk disapproval of other group members for expressing doubts. Everyone knew that an internal group disagreement was likely to create anxiety about possible failures, so instead of "rocking the boat," each member confirmed the positive feelings of every other member. In short, each member of the group was so busy making himself and everyone else feel good that the real problems of the group were avoided. In this case social functions were given precedence over task functions, with disastrous consequences.

Mob Action

The irrational behavior of an emotional and violent mob may also involve a kind of groupthink. The most disgraceful example of mob behavior in this country has been the lynching of black men by whites in many parts of the United States. Although lynchings are rare today, mob violence continues to occur in this and other countries.

When a collection of people engages in mob action, it becomes a group. A forming mob develops a sense of power comparable to the "supergroup" feeling that occurred during the planning of the Bay of Pigs invasion. The members of the mob believe that they are unanimous in their sentiments. Each individual confirms the feelings in those next to him that what they are doing is good and valuable.

Before a crowd can become a mob, its members must go through a slow, aimless *milling behavior.* In the milling process, people drift around transmitting and receiving information between each other. Thoughts and feelings spread rapidly through the crowd. It is by this process that the crowd becomes a collective entity in which each individual feels, thinks, and acts in a way different than he would if alone. Because the members of the crowd feel they are "one," they give little individual thought to the consequences of their actions.

People who form a mob lose their individuality and their sense of responsibility. Violence and other activities that are prohibited in

Figure 10.12

Groupthink. Mistakes can occur at any level of group decision making, from a family having to choose a spot for a vacation to high-level government statesmen formulating foreign policy. When people in a group create illusions of omnipotence and infallibility and make too many commitments to the maintenance of good feeling in the group, mistakes are even more likely to occur. When the errors are discovered, the group's cohesiveness may drop sharply.

Figure 10.13
Large groups generate powerful feelings, but it is not easy to predict which kinds of feelings will occur. People at the Woodstock festival maintained a feeling of community and cooperation despite hardships. But the results were different at a free concert in Altamont, California, where a throng gathered to hear the Rolling Stones. Members of the Hell's Angels, hired to protect the stage, beat people and committed a murder. One woman there said: "It wasn't just the Angels. It was everybody. There was no love, no joy. In twenty-four hours we created all the problems of our society in one place: congestion, violence, dehumanization. Is this what we want?"

other settings become norms in the mob because individuals are anonymous—they do not fear punishment from others for their behavior. Thus, people in mobs tend to behave similarly, to be prone to violence, and to emotionally overreact to their situation without thought for the outcome.

Diffusion of Responsibility

In some circumstances, being part of a crowd can produce an effect that is just the opposite of mob action but that is equally disturbing. This phenomenon might be called "group paralysis." A famous example occurred in the case of an eighteen-year-old girl who was raped and beaten in her New York office. She temporarily escaped her attacker and rushed out into the street, naked and bleeding. Thirty-eight neighbors looked on, but no one offered to help her and no one prevented the rapist from dragging her back into the building.

'NO MORE KITTY GENOVESES'
100 Corner Purse Snatchers After Assault on N.Y. Girl

NEW YORK (UPI)—One hundred New Yorkers chased three purse snatchers, surrounded the cab they tried to escape in, and kept it in place until police arrived.

Patrolman Peter Robinson, one of the first policemen to arrive at the scene Thursday night, said, "I've never seen anything like it. All these people just came out and stopped the cab."

Explaining their refusal to "look the other way" after a young woman was slapped and knocked down by the thieves, one of the pursuers said,

"We don't want any Kitty Genoveses in this neighborhood."

(Catherine Genovese was stabbed to death on a Queens street in 1964 while 38 neighbors looked on but did nothing as she screamed for help. Police said some of the neighbors said they "didn't want to get involved.")

According to police and witnesses, the West Side incident began when three men grabbed a black leather purse from a 19-year-old girl who was talking with a friend at a street corner.

When the girl, who asked not to be identified, began screaming for help, one of the three allegedly slapped her and knocked her to the ground.

Several passerby followed the purse snatchers as they fled. One of the pursuers threatened them with a tire iron.

The purse snatchers jumped into a taxi, but by this time 100 onlookers had joined in the chase. Shouting and shaking their fists, they surrounded the cab and refused to let it leave.

Figure 10.14
One of the encouraging outcomes of research in social psychology is that finding out how people behave—and telling them—often causes that behavior to change. The public condemnation of the crowd that watched silently as a murder was committed apparently created enough awareness to prevent such incidents from happening again.

She was saved only because two policemen happened by.

Why didn't the people act? Psychologists have tried to answer this question by studying artificial crises. In one experiment, college students were asked to wait in individual rooms, where they would soon be participating in a discussion of personal problems. Some of the students were told that they would be communicating with only one other person; others were given the impression that they would be talking with five other people. All communication, the psychologist told each student, was to take place over microphones so that everyone would remain anonymous and thus would speak more freely. Each person was to talk in turn.

In reality, there were no other people—all the voices heard by each subject were on a prerecorded tape. As the discussion progressed, the subject heard one of the participants go into an epileptic-like fit. The victim began to call for help, making choking sounds. The experimenters found that most of the people who thought they were alone with the victim came out of their rooms to help him. But of those who believed there were four other people nearby, less than half did anything to help.

The experimenters suggested that the cause of this behavior was *diffusion of responsibility.* In other words, because there were many people, each person waited for the others to offer help. They found that in similar experiments, where people could see the other participants, this same pattern emerged. In addition, bystanders reassured one another that it would not be a good idea to interfere. These findings on diffusion of responsibility suggest that the larger the crowd or group of bystanders, the more likely any given individual is to feel that he is not responsible for whatever is going on.

GROUPS IN CONFLICT

Conflicts between groups are a fact of everyday life: Some level of hostility exists between blacks and whites, women and men, young and old, workers and bosses, Catholics and Protestants, students and

*Some Parallels Between the Statuses
of Women and Black Americans*

Both have "high social visibility" because of physical appearance, dress, or both.

Originally both were considered property in Western culture and were controlled by male family heads.

Historically neither group could vote.

Neither historically had legal rights over property or guardianship of children.

Both were believed to have inferior mental capacities. At first only limited educational opportunities were provided for them; later, a special type of education was deemed appropriate.

Each has been assigned to a subordinate "place" in the social system. Social approval rests on their staying obediently in this subordinate status; any effort to alter this scheme is abhorred.

The myth of the "contented woman" who does not want to enjoy such civil rights as the right to vote and equal social and job opportunities serves the same social function as the myth of the "contented Negro."

It is difficult for either to take part in government by attaining important public office.

There have been certain jobs allocated to women and others to blacks. These jobs are usually low in salary and in prestige.

It is considered "unnatural" for white men to work under black supervisors or for males to work under female direction. In addition, women generally prefer not to have women bosses, and blacks have often felt the same way about working under other blacks.

A kindly paternalism such as a guardian feels for his ward has been thought of as the ideal solution.

Figure 10.15

These statements point out a number of similarities between the positions of women and blacks in American society. It is possible to extend these similarities to include such other groups as "hippies," students, and even children. It seems that a group does not have to be a minority in order to be assigned an inferior status.

teachers. Why do these conflicts exist, and why do they persist? The main contributing factors to conflict between groups seem to be oppression, stereotyping, prejudice, and discrimination.

Oppression

One common factor that can be found in group conflict is the *oppression* of one group by the other. It is not hard to see how such domination gives rise to feelings of hostility on the part of the oppressed group. In addition, the powerful group hates the oppressed group because it wants to justify its unfair actions and because it wants to stop the oppressed group from fighting back.

This is called a *master-slave* relationship, for obvious reasons. The present relationship between blacks and whites in America is a result of the fact that at one time blacks were literally the slaves and whites were literally the masters. The oppression of blacks by whites has only gradually been lessened, and that oppression has not ended yet. Psychologists are learning that the master-slave relationship exists between other groups, too. The freedom of women has been restricted by men; the freedom of students has been restricted by teachers, and so on.

Stereotypes and Roles

The existence of hostility between groups may in many cases have been caused by oppression, but it is strengthened and maintained by the existence of stereotypes and roles. As described in Chapter 9, a *stereotype* is an oversimplified, hard-to-change way of seeing people who belong to some group or category. Black people, businessmen, women, Mexicans, and the rich, for example, are often seen in certain rigid ways without appreciation for individuality. A *role* is an oversimplified, hard-to-change way of acting. Stereotypes and roles can act together in a way that makes them difficult to break down. For example, many whites have a stereotype of blacks. Blacks are believed to be irresponsible, superstitious, less intelligent, lazy, and good dancers. Whites who hold this stereotype expect blacks to act out a role that is consistent with it. Blacks are expected to be submissive, deferential, and respectful toward whites, who act out the role of the superior, condescending parent. In the past, both blacks and whites have accepted these roles and have seen themselves and each other according to these stereotypes. In recent years many blacks and whites have tried to step out of these roles and drop these stereotypes, and to some extent they are succeeding.

Most people use roles and stereotypes without questioning them. These devices serve as lazy ways for dealing with other people—if people stick to their roles, you know what to expect from them (as discussed in Chapter 9). Psychologists also believe that for some people stereotypes form a psychological crutch for personal insecurities. This type of person is called an *authoritarian personality*. Such a person fears his own aggressiveness and sexuality and instead claims

Figure 10.16
These lines from James Baldwin's novel *Nobody Knows My Name* express the impossible dilemma of being black in a white world and the way it feels to try and break free from the roles and stereotypes that are implicit in that situation. Baldwin's lines also point out that roles and stereotypes interlock with each other in such a way that they are self-perpetuating. Baldwin wrote this and several other powerful novels from his own experiences of what it was like to be a black man in Boston and New York during the 1940s and 1950s.

(From James Baldwin, *Nobody Knows My Name*. New York: Dell Publishing Co., 1969, pp. 73, 122–123.)

Figure 10.17
To understand how racism works, one must first distinguish between prejudice (racist attitudes) and discrimination (racist behavior). A person's behavior toward blacks, for example, may be either consistent with or contradictory to his attitudes toward them. (*top left*) This drawing represents a prejudiced discriminator, that is, one who both thinks and acts antiblack. (*top right*) A nonprejudiced discriminator: for example, a white person who thinks favorably of blacks but refuses to hire them in order to avoid his community's criticisms. (*bottom left*) A prejudiced nondiscriminator: for example, a person who recognizes his prejudices and tries not to act on them. (*bottom right*) A nonprejudiced nondiscriminator.

that it is Jews or blacks or hippies who are "animalistic" and who want to destroy society. In order to give up these irrational beliefs, the authoritarian person would have to admit his own fears and shortcomings to himself. Instead, he falls back on the use of stereotypes to keep from facing his own inadequacies.

Prejudice and Discrimination

Prejudice means, literally, prejudgment. It means deciding beforehand what a person will be like instead of withholding judgment until it can be based on his individual qualities. To hold stereotypes about a group of people is to be prejudiced about them. Prejudice is not necessarily negative—whites who are prejudiced against blacks are often equally prejudiced in favor of whites, for example.

There are many possible causes for prejudice. Psychologists have found that people tend to be prejudiced against those less well-off than themselves—they seem to justify being on top by assuming that anyone of lower status or income must be inferior. People who have suffered economic setbacks also tend to be prejudiced—they blame others for their misfortune.

Prejudice also arises from "guilt by association." People who dislike cities and urban living, for example, tend to distrust people

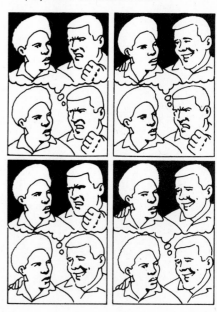

Figure 10.18

After the assassination of Martin Luther King in 1968, a third-grade teacher gave her students a lesson in discrimination. On the basis of eye color (blue and brown) the teacher divided the class into two groups and favored one group (the blue-eyed children) with such privileges as being leaders and having their choice of seats and activities. The next day she reversed the situation, favoring the brown-eyed children. On the day that they were favored, the blue-eyed children reportedly "took savage delight" in keeping "inferiors" in their place and said they felt "good inside," "smarter," and "stronger." On that day, one child drew the picture shown on the right. The next day, the same child, now one of the "inferiors," drew the picture on the left. The children who had felt "smart" and "strong" on their favored day became tense, lacked confidence, and did badly at their work on the day they were discriminated against. They said they felt angry, "like dying," and "like quitting school."

associated with cities, such as Jews and blacks. Also, people tend to be prejudiced *toward* those they see as similar to themselves and *against* those who seem different.

Whatever the original cause, prejudice seems to persist long afterward. One reason is that children who grow up in an atmosphere of prejudice conform to the prejudicial norm—at first because their parents do and later with the personal conviction that it is the right way to be. Children are socialized into the prejudicial culture of their parents—that is, they encounter numerous forces that induce them to conform to the thoughts and practices of their parents and other teachers, formal and informal.

Prejudice, the existence of an attitude, should be distinguished from *discrimination,* the unequal treatment of members of certain groups. *Personal* discrimination may take the form of refusing to rent to black people or allowing only men to frequent a particular bar or paying Mexican-Americans substandard wages. It is possible for a prejudiced person not to discriminate. He may recognize his prejudice and try not to act on it. Similarly, a person may discriminate, not out of prejudice, but in compliance to social pressures.

Many social *institutions* serve to reflect and preserve prejudice and discrimination. For example, many institutions, such as schools and businesses, maintain such discriminatory practices as segregation, unfair hiring, and unequal pay scales. Stereotypes are also preserved in the communications media, which have traditionally portrayed American Indians as villains, Italians as greasy gangsters, Jews as misers, and teenagers as car-crazy, fun-loving rock fans. Many of these stereotypes are changing now, but new ones have replaced them. For example, doctors on television are usually heroes, housewives are charming idiots, and so on. A critical look at television programs and movies reveals a lot about what is widely believed in American society.

WAYS TO END GROUP CONFLICT

Psychologists have tried in both experimental and natural settings to analyze group conflicts and to resolve them. Perhaps the most famous of these studies were done with boy campers in the 1950s and with integrated housing projects in the 1940s.

Conflict versus Cooperation

One group of psychologists created a boy's camp for the express purpose of studying intergroup relations. The camp offered all the usual activities, and the boys had no idea that they were part of an experiment.

From the beginning of the experiment, the boys were divided into two separate groups. The boys hiked, swam, and played baseball only with members of their own group, and friendships and group spirit soon developed. After a while, the experimenters (posing as counselors) brought the group together for a tournament. The psychologists had hypothesized that when these two groups of boys were placed in competitive situations, where one group could achieve its goals only at the expense of the other, hostility would soon develop. They were right.

Although the games began in a spirit of good sportsmanship, tension mounted as the tournament continued. Friendly competition soon gave way to name calling, fist fights, and raids on enemy cabins. The psychologists had demonstrated the ease with which they could produce unity within the two boys' groups and hatred between them.

After creating group antagonism, the experimenters then tried to see what might end the conflict and create harmony between the two groups. They tried to bring the groups together for enjoyable activities, such as a movie and a good meal. This approach totally failed to end the conflict—the campers shoved and pushed each other, threw food and insults, and generally used the opportunity to continue their attacks.

Next, the psychologists deliberately invented a series of "emergencies" designed so that the boys would either have to help each other or lose the chance to do or get something they all wanted. For instance, one morning someone reported that the water line to the camp had broken. The boys were told that unless they worked together to find the break and fix it, they would all have to leave camp. By afternoon, they had jointly found and fixed the damage. Gradually, through such cooperative activities, intergroup hostility and tensions lessened. Friendships began to develop between individuals of the opposing groups, and eventually the groups began to seek out occasions to mingle. At the end of the camp period,

Figure 10.19
These black inmates of Attica State Prison in New York rebelled in protest of unfair and abominable conditions. One of their complaints was that the prison authorities did not permit them to practice the Black Muslim religion. This restriction was only the last instance in a long string of such instances that led to the violent rebellion. Comparable practices in many institutions—in schools, in businesses, and particularly in the legal system—have contributed to the fact that there is a disproportionate number of black men in prisons.

Figure 10.20
Scenes from the Robber's Cave experiment, named after the Oklahoma location at which it was conducted. (a) Psychologists posing as camp counselors divided the boy campers into two groups and placed them in competition against one another in such sporting activities as a tug-of-war. (b) Considerable hostility developed between the two groups, the "Bulldogs" and the "Red Devils," which was expressed in drawings like the one shown here. (c) Hostility was also expressed in fights and in raids on enemy cabins. (d) The hostility was eliminated by contrived tasks that had to be performed jointly, such as pushing a heavy truck that supplied food to the camp.

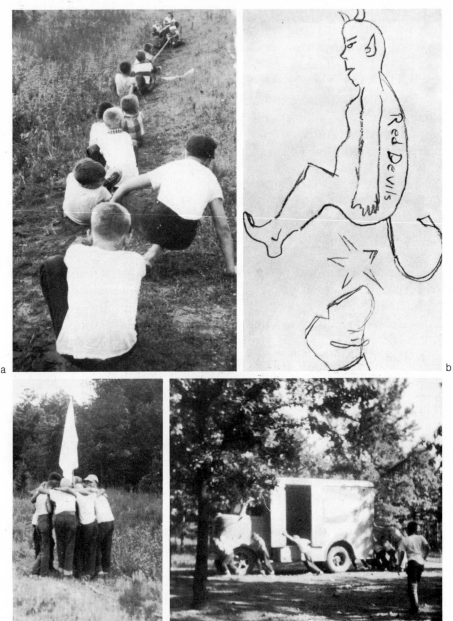

members of both groups requested that they ride home together on the same bus.

The results of this experiment were striking. A group of boys from identical backgrounds had developed considerable hostility toward each other, simply because they were placed in competition. The crucial factor in eliminating group hostility was cooperation.

Integration

The camping experiment demonstrated how easily group hatred can develop. None of the hostility between the two groups could be attributed to former prejudices or discrimination: All of the boys were of the same nationality, race, and class. When the campers resolved their hostility by working together to solve a mutual problem, they simply saw themselves as members of a larger group, the camp.

Centuries of racial prejudice in the United States and throughout the world seem to indicate that racial hatred poses a much more complicated problem. One barrier to cooperation between the races is *segregation.* One group of psychologists created an experiment to test whether racial prejudice could be overcome through desegregation. They reasoned that if people of different races had the opportunity to meet as equals they might come to recognize that their prejudices had no basis.

They interviewed people who had been placed in integrated and segregated buildings of a housing project just after World War II. The results of the interviews showed clearly that the amount and type of contact between black and white neighbors greatly influenced their opinions toward each other.

In the integrated buildings, more than 60 percent of the white housewives reported having "friendly relations" with blacks. In the segregated buildings, less than 10 percent reported friendships, and more than 80 percent reported no contact at all. In the integrated project, two out of three white women expressed a desire to be friendly with blacks. In the segregated projects, only one in eleven expressed such a desire. Similar effects occurred in the attitudes of black women toward whites.

The integrated housing situation gave the housewives a chance to have intimate contact with one another and to interact informally and casually. The housewives were likely to encounter each other in the elevators, hallways, and laundryroom. In this informal climate, the housewives did not have to worry that trying to strike up a conversation might be misinterpreted. In contrast, contact in the segregated buildings would have to be more deliberate and might be considered suspicious.

Another factor that facilitated formation of friendships in the integrated housing projects was the *climate of social approval.* People in the integrated housing felt that because they were integrated in the first place, it must be all right to mix. People in the segregated housing felt that for some reason it was not right to mix. Thus, the climate shaped the willingness to interact with other groups.

One last factor that can either break down or perpetuate racial barriers is *status.* Studies have shown that when blacks and whites work together and share equal status, intergroup liking and even friendships often develop.

Not surprisingly, contacts between blacks and whites in which blacks have lower status do little to change attitudes and behavior. For example, contact between an upper-middle-class white housewife and her black maid merely confirms the housewife's stereotype of the black as not too bright and suited only for menial jobs. In order to keep her job, the black maid may try to be pleasing and to

Figure 10.21
This basketball game netted $450 for a local antipollution program. The competitors were "the Heads" (long-haired students) and "the Feds" (short-haired highway patrolmen). Bringing such groups together and giving them equal status, initimate contact, a shared goal, and an approving audience has been found to be an effective way of reducing mutual distrust and hostility.

Figure 10.22
Most of the conditions that help to break down intergroup hostility are present at events like this casual backyard barbecue. There is evidence, however, that a gathering that is primarily oriented toward social functions is not by itself very effective in reducing hostility between opposing groups. Groups need to share task functions as well as social ones if they are to become friendly with each other.

superficially conform to the housewife's stereotype, thus reinforcing her own attitudes toward herself and toward whites.

This research thus shows that group prejudice, *and* group conflicts, can be broken down if four factors are allowed to work together: (1) cooperation to achieve a shared goal, (2) intimate contact, (3) contact in a climate of social acceptance, and (4) equal status of the groups.

SUMMARY

1. Groups are aggregates of people who are interdependent. Interdependence means that the actions of any one group member will affect or influence other members. Group members become interdependent because they see themselves as sharing common goals.

2. The two primary purposes of groups are to perform task functions and to perform social functions. Most groups serve both functions to some extent.

3. Group interdependence is maintained through the use of group norms that direct the behavior of members. Violation of group norms results in disapproval from other group members.

4. Group cohesiveness is the amount of "we" feeling, or loyalty, among group members. Group cohesiveness depends on individual commitment and is greatest when the members of the group adopt a common ideology and common symbols, make personal sacrifices to stay in the group, and participate in all group activities.

5. Reference groups are groups with which a person identifies. A reference group provides a set of attitudes and values and a sense of pride for the individual.

6. Group structure is the way in which individuals fit together into a whole unit. The way people interact in a group is studied through the use of sociograms and the analysis of communication patterns. An important element in the group's structure is leadership. A leader is the person who exerts the most influence in a group. Influence may come as a result of expertise, emotional and social appeal, or power. Leadership can also be gained by appointment or by manipulation.

7. People in groups often act less rationally than they might as individuals. In groupthink, members of a decision-making group make mistakes because they come to believe that the group is infallible and that disagreement is neither necessary nor worth the risk. A crowd becomes a mob when it holds irrational feelings or opinions strongly and unanimously and acts on them.

8. Diffusion of responsibility is similar to mob action in that people in a crowd seem to feel they are not responsible for whatever is going on. In a crisis, people often refrain from acting because they expect other people to act or because they do not want to be "different."

9. Conflict between groups is usually a result of oppression of one group by another. It is preserved by stereotyping, or perceiving people as belonging to a particular category. People often play the role for which they are stereotyped in order to avoid rejection.

10. Prejudice is judging people on the basis of stereotypes. Prejudice seems to have a number of causes, and it is perpetuated by social institutions. Discrimination is the unequal treatment given to people as a result of prejudice.

11. The experiment with boy campers demonstrated that prejudice can be broken down when members of opposing groups are forced to work together to solve a common problem.

12. Observations of integrated apartment buildings have shown that group conflict can also be alleviated by intimate contact in a climate of social acceptance and equal status of the groups.

Figure 10.23
The mass media (newspapers, magazines, radio, television, movies) have a major influence on people's perceptions of social roles and stereotypes. These stills suggest ways in which mass media have reflected racial and sexual roles in the past.

ACTIVITIES

1. You probably identify with many groups, including school, religious, work, racial, ethnic, national, political, family, and peer groups. Decide which ones are the most important and for each, consider: Are you a member of the group? Is it primarily a task-oriented or socially oriented group? What are its goals? What are its values? How does it respond to violations of its norms?

2. Experiments have shown that enforced integration in housing has resulted in less interracial hostility. What is your opinion of legally enforcing racial integration in housing, employment, and schools?

3. Write down the first ten or fifteen words or phrases that come to

Figure 10.24

These scenes from the popular television shows *Maude* (*top*) and *All in the Family* (*opposite*) show that the mass media have recently shifted their ways of portraying the roles and stereotypes of racial, occupational, sexual, and age groups.

mind when you ask yourself, "Who am I?" Stop. Now, categorize these items as either physical traits, psychological characteristics, or group affiliations. How much of your self-concept is built on your identification with groups?

4. Consider your primary (or most important) group. What sacrifices would you be willing to make in order to remain in the group? What sacrifices would you be unwilling to make? For what reason, if any, would you be willing to sacrifice your life for this group?

5. Do any of the groups to which you belong have rivals—other groups you compete against (for example, a rival team)? If so, what are the people like in the rival group? What information did you use to arrive at an answer to this question?

6. In the groups to which you belong (clubs, your school, and so on) you have undoubtedly had leaders or people with influence over you. Pick a few such leaders and try to analyze the sources of their influence. Are they experts? Do they have charisma? Are they socially attractive? How much power do they have? How have they obtained it?

7. Do you belong to any social or service clubs? Why or why not? Have you ever been rejected by a group you wished to join? Do you know why? What were your feelings on being rejected?

8. Make a list of ten or more nationalities, religions, races, and occupations. Have friends or family members list five things that come to mind when these groups are mentioned. What are your conclusions?

9. Ask one male and one female to reverse sex roles and discuss the following contentions: (1) Men need liberation as much as women. (2) Men are at least equally as vain as women. (3) Women do not mind being dominated as long as they are loved and cared for. (4) Women can never be as competent as men, or men as women, in which of the following occupations: scientist; child rearing; politician; construction worker; nurse; airplane pilot?

10. Pick a television program that is based on a set group of characters. Analyze the group by determining what goals the fictional characters share, how they are interdependent, and what maintains their cohesiveness. At the same time, consider what social roles and stereotypes, if any, the program perpetuates.

11. Most groups exercise some control over their members in ways that they are not aware of. Take any group you know well and analyze the controls that exist, the reasons for them, and how they are exercised. Obviously, an analysis of a group to which you belong will be more difficult, but it will also be more interesting.

SUGGESTED READINGS

ABRAMSON, MICHAEL, and YOUNG LORDS. *Palante*. New York: McGraw-Hill, 1971. A collection of writings and photographic studies of the struggle of young Puerto Ricans in New York to understand and change themselves and the conditions that oppress them.

ALINSKY, SAUL. *Reveille For Radicals.* Chicago: University of Chicago Press, 1946. Implicit in this radical's handbook are several psychologies—the psychology of organizing, the psychology of power, and the psychology of social conscience.

BROWN, TURNER. *Black Is.* New York: Grove Press, 1969 (paper). A powerful paperback book of cartoons of black men and women as seen through prejudiced white eyes.

GOLDING, WILLIAM. *Lord of the Flies.* New York: Coward, McCann, 1954 (paper). An absorbing and shocking novel about how the group process runs wild in a bunch of boys stranded on an island.

GREER, GERMAINE. *The Female Eunuch.* New York: Bantam, 1970 (paper). An excellent book on what it is like to be a female in contemporary society. Greer is an outspoken exponent of the Women's Liberation Movement, and she has an honest and straightforward writing style.

HOFFER, ERIC. *The True Believer.* New York: Harper & Row, 1951 (paper). Hoffer identifies and analyzes the characteristics of the "true believer"—the person who identifies so much with a group that he has no identity away from it.

KOESTLER, ARTHUR. *Darkness at Noon.* New York: Bantam, 1941 (paper). With personal knowledge and sensitivity, Koestler probes the literal and theoretical consequences of a political doctrine founded on the concept of Machiavellian techniques. A powerful novel.

MALCOM X, and ALEX HALEY. *The Autobiography of Malcom X.* New York: Grove Press, 1965 (paper). A highly dramatic and honest personal account of how this remarkable man evolved from a ghetto-raised criminal to a national leader of a powerful black political movement.

MORGAN, ROBIN (ed.). *Sisterhood is Powerful.* New York: Random House, 1970 (paper). Morgan has done a superb job in putting together an anthology of writings by and about women.

PARKINSON, C. NORTHCOTE. *Parkinson's Law and Other Studies in Administration.* New York: Ballantine, 1957 (paper). A clever analysis of organizations based on Parkinson's experience in the British civil service. Parkinson's Law says that work expands to fill the time available for its completion.

11
Attitudes and Social Influence

HOW ATTITUDES ARE FORMED:
Compliance / Identification / Internalization
ATTITUDES AND PERSONALITY
COGNITIVE CONSISTENCY
PERSUASION:
The communication process / The inoculation effect
THE POWER OF AUTHORITY
GROUP PRESSURE TO CONFORM
ATTITUDES AND ACTIONS:
Doing is believing / Self-fulfilling prophecy

Do you believe that sugar is bad for your health? How much sugar is in your diet?

Do you believe in honesty at all times? What would you do if your best friend made a fool of himself and then looked to you for approval?

How do you feel about war? Have you ever talked to a Vietnam veteran?

Each of these pairs of questions illustrates that there is a strong relationship between what you think and feel and how you behave. This chapter is about how people form their beliefs and how they change their feelings about, and actions toward, events and objects. It is also about how people's beliefs, feelings, and actions are continually influenced by teachers, parents, friends, advertisers, and other people around them.

WHERE ATTITUDES COME FROM

An *attitude* is a predisposition to respond in particular ways toward specific objects. It has three main elements: (1) a belief or opinion about something, (2) feelings about that thing, and (3) a tendency to act toward that thing in certain ways. For example, what is your attitude toward push-ups? Do you *believe* that they will strengthen your arms? Do you *like* or *hate* them? Do you ever *do* any?

You are continually forming and applying attitudes every day. Each time you meet someone, buy a record, watch a television show, or read a book you form an opinion. Attitudes are an inevitable consequence of moving about in your environment, for you must think, feel, and act in response to what you encounter.

An obvious source of attitudes is one's culture. Growing up in a certain family, ethnic group, class, and country provides a person with certain fundamental attitudes early in life. A simple example can be found in North American attitudes toward Mexican revolutionary Pancho Villa. In the United States, Villa is characterized as a

Figure 11.1
Richard Nixon holding a press conference, October 1973. Attitudes toward the President of the United States underwent enormous changes in 1973. Information about White House activities came to Americans through radio, television, news magazines, and newspapers; these reports influenced the minds of millions of Americans both favorably and unfavorably and had major effects on their subsequent actions.

Figure 11.2

Two of the many ways in which psychologists have tried to measure attitudes. (a) The person whose attitudes are being measured rates his feeling about a series of statements. Psychologists can infer some underlying attitudes about competitiveness, for example, from his responses. (b) The person is asked to rate some object or event, for example, "war," "father," or "supermarket," on a number of scales such as those shown. Analyses of responses to this test have revealed that underlying attitudes have three main components: active-passive, strong-weak, and good-bad.

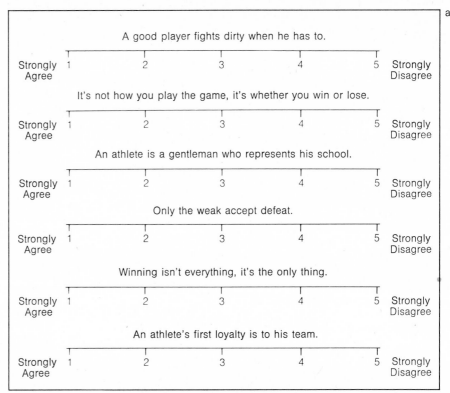

a

A good player fights dirty when he has to.

Strongly Agree　1　　2　　3　　4　　5　Strongly Disagree

It's not how you play the game, it's whether you win or lose.

Strongly Agree　1　　2　　3　　4　　5　Strongly Disagree

An athlete is a gentleman who represents his school.

Strongly Agree　1　　2　　3　　4　　5　Strongly Disagree

Only the weak accept defeat.

Strongly Agree　1　　2　　3　　4　　5　Strongly Disagree

Winning isn't everything, it's the only thing.

Strongly Agree　1　　2　　3　　4　　5　Strongly Disagree

An athlete's first loyalty is to his team.

Strongly Agree　1　　2　　3　　4　　5　Strongly Disagree

b

Rating

	1	2	3	4	5	6	7	
cruel								kind
active								passive
hard								soft
wise								foolish
good								bad
weak								strong
calm								excitable
beautiful								ugly
slow								fast
sweet								sour
worthless								valuable
difficult								easy
practical								theoretical
feminine								masculine
severe								lenient
serious								humorous

bandit; in Mexico, he is considered a national hero. (The idea that the groups to which one belongs, such as one's nation or family, can provide one with a set of attitudes is explored in Chapter 10.) The three main processes of attitude formation or change that will be described in this chapter are compliance, identification, and internalization.

Compliance

Attitudes are expressed in the ways people behave. Sometimes, however, people appear to change their attitudes or to have attitudes that they do not really hold. In certain situations one may feel compelled to present a false impression. Suppose, for example, that you must have dinner with relatives you dislike. In order to avoid strife, you make a point of dressing up, smiling, complimenting your hostess on the meal, and appearing to enjoy yourself. But beneath this facade you really dislike the food, feel uncomfortable, do not mean what you are saying, and look forward to leaving.

In such a situation your real feelings are temporarily outweighed by the circumstances. People often act in such ways to *comply* with the wishes of others in order to avoid discomfort or rejection and to gain approval. But their attitudes have not really changed—they are only complying temporarily. Compliance can have some unexpected effects on one's beliefs, as will be seen later in this chapter, but in general, it takes more than social pressure to change deeply held attitudes.

Identification

One way in which attitudes may really be formed or changed is through the process of *identification*. (This concept is also discussed in Chapters 7 and 10.) Suppose you have a favorite uncle who is everything you hope to be. He is a successful musician, has many famous friends, and seems to know a great deal about everything. In many ways you identify with him and copy his behavior. Now, suppose that during a conversation your uncle announces that he is an atheist. At first you are confused by this statement. You have had a religious upbringing and have always considered religious beliefs as essential. However, because you hold your uncle in such high esteem, you begin to reevaluate your attitude toward religion.

As you listen to your uncle expound on this topic, you find yourself starting to agree with him. If a person as knowledgeable and respectable as your uncle holds such beliefs, perhaps you should, too. Eventually, you join in the conversation, expressing a similar point of view. You have adopted a new attitude because of your identification with your uncle.

Identification is different than compliance because you actually believe the newly adopted views. But because these attitudes are based on an emotional attachment to another person or group, rather than accepted on their own merit, they are not always in accord with other attitudes and values that you may hold. For this reason they may be temporary: If your emotional attachment to the person or group loses its importance, the attitudes may also fade.

Internalization

The most deeply held attitudes are *internalized*—they become a part of the individual. Attitudes can only be internalized when they are consistent with a person's other basic beliefs and feelings. Internalized attitudes are based on their own merits, not on compliance or on identification.

If, for example, you decide to vote for a candidate because you are convinced his policies will lead to the world peace you are hoping for, your attitude toward him is based on internalization. You choose him because you believe his ideals are consistent with your ideals.

Internalization is the most durable of the three sources of attitude formation or change. Internalized attitudes will be more resistant to pressure from other people because your reasons for holding these attitudes have nothing to do with other people but, rather, are based on the merit of the attitudes themselves.

ATTITUDES AND PERSONALITY

Suppose you are trying to persuade someone to change his mind about something or to accept a new idea. You will find that some people are much more readily persuaded than others. Of course, agreement or disagreement with your ideas is partly determined by the nature of the information you are presenting. But to a considerable extent, a person's readiness to change his mind is dependent on his personality.

Apparently, to be persuaded about something is to admit that another person has more facts, more convincing arguments, greater expertise, or superior command of the issues. Some people are far too willing to make this admission; others are highly resistant.

Some people place a low value on their own opinions and attitudes; consequently, it is not difficult for them to part company with their ideas. They are easily influenced by those around them, both because they have few defenses for their ideas and because their ideas have been of little use to them. Such people often agree with others in order to gain their approval. Because they want to be liked, they do what they think others expect them to do.

At the other end of the spectrum is the person who has an inflated opinion of himself and of his ideas and is thus difficult to influence. Such a person is extremely closed-minded and will stick to his attitudes under all circumstances. He would consider any attempt to change his beliefs as an attack on his entire personality. This person clings to his attitudes as a way of defining himself. Without them, he fears loss of identity.

Still other people value their own opinions, but, if presented with convincing arguments, may alter their attitudes. This type of person tends to base his attitudes on knowledge, rather than on identification or social approval. In fact, he is likely to welcome the chance to examine new ideas and to accept or reject them. Personality factors that seem to influence attitude formation thus include a person's need for social approval, his belief in his own judgment, and the extent of his need to maintain his attitudes.

COGNITIVE CONSISTENCY

When people are put in new situations, they are likely to change or modify their attitudes. Many social psychologists, notably Fritz Heider and Leon Festinger, have theorized that peoples' attitudes change because they are always trying to get things to logically fit together inside themselves. It is possible for people to hold two conflicting attitudes, but it is uncomfortable. As a result, people are moved to change their ideas when such conflicts occur.

Suppose, for example, that you have always disliked mushrooms. One night you go to a friend's house for dinner and are served a delicious casserole, with flavors you have never before tasted. After

Figure 11.3

An example of cognitive dissonance. Mary has a positive attitude toward Bill and a negative attitude toward certain clothing styles. She can maintain both of these attitudes until a situation arises in which these attitudes are brought into conflict. Then she is faced with the same problem mentioned in the text regarding dislike for mushrooms. A state of dissonance exists that can only be reduced by some change in attitude. For example, Mary may decide that she does not care for Bill as much as she thought; she may decide that she really does like the new fashion; or she may resolve the conflict by deciding that Bill's "poor taste" is a minor fault compared to his many assets.

the meal, you congratulate your hostess on the fine dish and ask her what was in it. You learn that one of the main ingredients was mushrooms. You are now faced with an inconsistency between your antimushroom attitude and your enjoyment of the mushroom casserole. In this case, you are likely to change your attitude and become more of a mushroom eater. In addition, you may be more willing to try new things in the future.

Attitude change is not always this simple. Holding two opposing attitudes can create great conflict in an individual, and he must reconcile these attitudes to bring himself back into balance. A pacifist who has been drafted, a student who dislikes school, a doctor who smokes, and a parent who is uncomfortable with children all have one thing in common: They are in conflict.

According to Festinger, people in such conflict situations are experiencing *cognitive dissonance*—a term that might be translated as "thought conflict." To reduce dissonance, it is necessary to change one or both of the conflicting attitudes. A drafted pacifist, for example, is against violence and killing, but he may also feel that he must obey the law, even the draft law. This situation creates cognitive dissonance, and the young man is driven to reduce the conflict. One solution to his problem would be for him to decide that violence is acceptable when it comes to defending one's country. Another would be to decide that certain laws are wrong and should not be obeyed. Or, he might try to reduce the dissonance by attempting to convince the draft board that he should be placed in a job unconnected with violence. In this last case it is the situation that would change, not the attitudes.

Some people attempt to avoid dissonance altogether by avoiding situations or exposure to information that would create conflict. For example, they may make a point of subscribing to newspapers and magazines that uphold their political attitudes, of surrounding themselves with people who share the same ideas, and of attending only those speeches and lectures that support their views. It is not surprising that such people get quite upset when a piece of conflicting information finally does get through.

The process of dissonance reduction does not always take place consciously. Whether conscious or not, such conflict resolution appears to take place frequently in everyone's life.

PERSUASION

Persuasion is the direct attempt to influence attitudes through the process of communication. Everyone, at one time or another, engages in some kind of persuasion. When a smiling representative of the Acme brush company comes to your door, he tries to persuade you that you need his brushes. In return, you might try to persuade him that you already have a satisfactory supply of good brushes. A parent often attempts to persuade a son or daughter to conform to the parents' values about life, and the son or daughter tries to persuade the parent to see his or her point of view. In any case, the persuader's main hope is that by changing someone's attitudes he can change the person's behavior as well. The Acme man hopes you will buy; you hope he will leave. The parents hope the child will do as they ask; the child hopes the parents will stop badgering him.

Types of Persuasion

Persuasion is known by many names: salesmanship, political campaigning, and editorializing, to name a few. The most familiar form, however, is *advertising.* Americans are a sophisticated audience. After years of watching television, reading magazines and newspapers, and listening to radio, they like to think of themselves as immune to hard-sell tactics. Yet hard-sell advertising campaigns are usually accompanied by large jumps in sales, indicating that Americans are indeed susceptible to this method of persuasion.

Another form of persuasion is *propaganda.* Propaganda is persuasion designed to help or hinder some cause or group. Political parties, religious groups, governments, businesses, and other such organizations use propaganda techniques as ways of gaining support for themselves and their goals and of removing support from competing organizations.

Propaganda is usually more subtle and consequently less open to investigation than advertising. Propaganda techniques are particularly dangerous when they are aimed at defaming certain people or ideas. For example, not too many people openly refer to Jews in a hostile and negative manner, but creation and use of anti-Semitic jokes and the portrayal of stereotyped Jewish characters in literature and on film serve to maintain prejudice even more effectively than do open accusations.

Public service announcements are another form of persuasion. This type of persuasion is meant to inform the public of issues that are judged to be in its best interest. They urge people to contribute to charities, to get medical checkups, to report cases of venereal disease, to seek help for drug problems, and so on. Their major thrust is to urge certain action ("Put litter in trash cans"), to solicit funds ("Fight cancer with a checkup and a check"), or to provoke interest ("Send for this free pamphlet") for programs thought to be in the public interest.

The Communication Process

Much time, money, and effort go into the communication process, but changes in attitudes do not always result from it. One of the most practical questions that social psychologists have tried to answer is, what makes a persuasive communication effective?

The communication process can be broken down into four parts, and the factors that make a communication effective as a means to attitude change are quite different for each part. The *message* itself is only one part. It is also important to consider the *source* of the message, the *channel* that the message is delivered through, and the *audience* that receives it.

The Source   How a person sees the source, or the originator, of a message may be the critical factor in his acceptance of it. The person receiving the message asks himself several questions about its source: Is the person giving the message trustworthy and sincere? Does he know anything about the subject? If the source seems trustworthy and knowledgeable, the message is likely to be accepted. For instance, an advertisement for a new brand of aspirin would be more effective if it featured a fatherly looking man dressed in medical garments than if it featured a pushy man in a torn sweatshirt.

But the person receiving the message also asks: Do I like the source? If a communicator is respected and admired, people will tend to go along with his message, either because they believe in his judgment or because they want to be like him. This identification phenomenon explains the frequent use of athletes in advertisements. Football players and Olympic champions are not especially experts on the merits of deodorants, shaving equipment, or milk. In fact, when an athlete endorses a particular brand of deodorant on television, his audience knows that he is doing it for the money. Nevertheless, the process of identification still makes these sales pitches highly effective.

Similarly, people are much more likely to respond favorably to a physically attractive source than to one who does not make a good appearance. In the 1960 presidential campaign, Richard Nixon apparently lost many votes as a result of his poor appearance on a televised debate with John F. Kennedy. Such a negative response to a source is called the *boomerang effect:* The source alienates his audience instead of winning it over. People often respond to a source

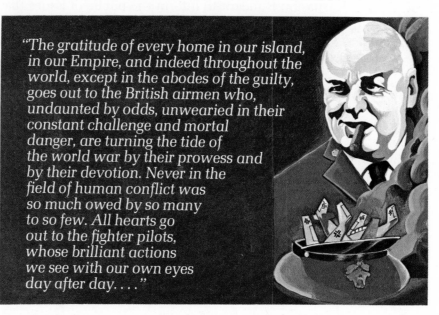

Figure 11.4
During World War II, Winston Churchill, a respected and trusted source, was consistently able to boost morale and to sustain the courage of the British people with speeches such as this one. Had Churchill communicated to the British populace only through the channel of newsprint, his messages would have had far less impact than they did. Because he was an eloquent speaker, the most effective channel was radio broadcasts directly into the homes of the people, a receptive audience united by war.

"*The gratitude of every home in our island, in our Empire, and indeed throughout the world, except in the abodes of the guilty, goes out to the British airmen who, undaunted by odds, unwearied in their constant challenge and mortal danger, are turning the tide of the world war by their prowess and by their devotion. Never in the field of human conflict was so much owed by so many to so few. All hearts go out to the fighter pilots, whose brilliant actions we see with our own eyes day after day. . . .*"

they dislike by taking an attitude opposite to that presented by the source. They may refuse to buy the source's product, or they may change their minds on a political point to keep from agreeing with a disliked official.

The Message   Suppose two people of opposing viewpoints are trying to persuade you to agree with them. Suppose further that you like and trust them equally. In this situation, the *message* becomes more important than the source. The persuasiveness of the message depends on the way in which it is composed and organized and on its actual content.

Should the message arouse emotion? Are people more likely to change their attitudes if they are afraid or angry or pleased? The answer is yes, but the most effective messages combine emotional appeal with factual information and argument. A message that emphasizes only the emotional side of an issue may be so overpowering that the viewer does not want to remember its content. On the other hand, a message that includes only logic and information may miss its mark because the viewer does not relate the facts to his personal life.

When presenting an argument, is it more effective to present both sides of an issue or only one side? For the most part, a two-sided communication is more effective because the audience will tend to believe that the speaker is objective and fair-minded on the issue. The hazard of presenting opposing arguments to one's views is that they might diminish one's argument, or they might suggest that the whole issue is too controversial to make a decision on.

A message may be so structured as to produce negative results. It may be so pushy and forceful that the audience feels pressured. For instance, if someone tried to persuade people that they boycott

Figure 11.5
Psychologists have found that a message is most effective when it combines an appeal to the emotions with solid facts. This advertisement presents a powerfully emotional picture and headline to shock the reader into attention and to arouse his concern. It then gives some hard facts to further involve him in the subject matter, and finally suggests that the reader subscribe to a certain journal for continuous information on such important matters. The reader might well have ignored the ad if it had simply said, "Doctors need to know about current issues relevant to the medical profession. Subscribe to *Medical World News.*"

certain stores by threatening the dangerous consequences of doing otherwise, his listeners would be unlikely to take him seriously, and they would resent his trying to make their decisions for them. If listeners infer from a message that they are being left with no choice but to adopt the speaker's views, they may resist his opinion rather than accept it.

The Channel   Where, when, and how a message is presented plays a smaller part in determining attitude change. Among the most common channels of communication are person-to-person exchanges, newspapers, magazines, radio, television, and film.

Marshall McLuhan, an unorthodox student of the communication process, is famous for saying, "The medium is the message." He meant *how* the message gets to you is more important than *what* the message is. It does seem to be true that the same message coming over television, over radio, or from a newspaper may have very different effects. People interact with a television set quite differently than they do with a newspaper. For this reason, most advertisers use different messages for each of these channels.

The Audience   The audience is composed of the people whose attitudes the communicator is trying to change. In preparing to persuade his audience, the communicator must think about their characteristics. Some people seem to be more easily persuaded than others, as was discussed earlier in this chapter. In addition, a given person is more susceptible to persuasion on certain issues than on others. Suppose, for instance, you want to persuade an audience that rugged exercise is necessary for good health. If your audience is a

Figure 11.6
Audiences change from generation to generation, so the means of persuading them must change, too. Attitudes toward the armed services, for example, have changed markedly since World War II, thus requiring army recruiters to radically alter their approach.

group of athletes, you will undoubtedly have little trouble. This kind of audience is already halfway in agreement with the message because they are already getting exercise in the course of their work. But suppose that the audience is a group of middle-aged business-men. You will probably have a problem in convincing them to take time out from their daily routine to do something they find difficult and taxing.

Certain audiences have deep emotional needs that can be capitalized on to maximize the chances for persuasion. For example, one advertising researcher was able to help the Red Cross collect blood donations from men by analyzing their fears. He thought that men associated blood loss with weakness and loss of manliness. He suggested that Red Cross advertisements should tell prospective donors how manly they are and that the Red Cross should offer donors pins shaped like drops of blood as medals for bravery. This campaign worked; blood donations from men increased sharply.

The Inoculation Effect

Is there anything you can do to resist persuasion? Research has shown that people can be educated to resist attitude change. This technique can be compared to an inoculation. Inoculation against persuasion works in much the same way as inoculation against certain diseases: When a person is vaccinated he is given a weakened or dead form of the disease-causing agent, which stimulates his body to manufacture defenses. Then, if he is attacked by a more potent form of the agent, his defenses make him immune to infection. Similarly, a person who has resisted a mild attack on his beliefs is ready to defend himself against an onslaught that might otherwise have overwhelmed him.

The inoculation effect can be explained in two ways: It motivates the person to defend his beliefs more strongly, and it gives him some practice in defending his beliefs. The most vulnerable attitudes you have, therefore, are the ones that you have never had to defend. For example, you might find yourself hard put to defend your faith in democracy or in the healthfulness of beefsteak if you have never had these beliefs questioned.

THE POWER OF AUTHORITY

The influence of other people on your own attitudes and actions is considerable. Sometimes this influence is indirect and subtle, but at other times it is quite direct. Other people may simply tell you what to believe and what to do. Under what conditions do you obey them?

Everyone in this society has had experiences with various authorities, such as parents, teachers, policemen, managers, judges, clergymen, and military officers. Obedience to these authorities can be either useful or destructive. For instance, obeying the orders of a doctor or fireman in an emergency would be constructive. Psychologists are more interested, however, in the negative aspects of

Figure 11.7

Stanley Milgram's experiment on obedience. (a) The fake "shock generator" used by the "teacher." (b) The "learner" is connected to the shock apparatus. (c) Milgram explains the procedure to the "teacher." (d) This subject refuses to shock the "learner" any further and angrily arises in protest. (e) Milgram explains the truth about the experiment.

(© 1965 by Stanley Milgram. From the film *Obedience*. Distributed by New York University Film Library.)

obedience. They know from such cases in history as German Nazism and American atrocities in Vietnam that individuals often obey irrational commands. In fact, people often obey authority even when obedience goes against their consciences and their whole system of morality.

Milgram's Experiment

The most famous investigation of obedience was conducted in 1963 by social psychologist Stanley Milgram. The experiment was set up as follows: Two volunteer subjects appeared for each session. They were told that they would be participating in an experiment to test the effects of punishment on memory. One of the subjects was to be the "teacher" and the other, the "learner." The teacher was to read a list of words into a microphone for the learner, who would be in a nearby room, to memorize. If the learner failed to read the list back correctly, the teacher was to administer an electric shock. The alleged purpose of the experiment was to test whether the shock would have any effect on learning. In actuality, however, Milgram wanted to discover how much shock the teacher would be willing to give a fellow human being.

As the experiment began, the learner, who was an accomplice of the experimenter, continually gave wrong answers, and the teacher began to administer the prescribed shocks from an impressive-looking shock generator. The generator had a dial that ranged from 15 volts, which was labeled "Slight Shock," to 450 volts, which was labeled "Danger: Severe Shock." After each of the learner's mistakes, the teacher was supposed to increase the voltage by one level, thus increasing the severity of the shock. The teacher believed that the learner was receiving these shocks because he had seen the learner being strapped into a chair in the other room and had watched electrodes being attached to the learner's hands. In reality, however, the accomplice was receiving no shocks at all from the equipment.

As the experiment progressed, the learner made many mistakes and the shocks became increasingly severe. At 300 volts, the learner pounded on the wall in protest and refused to provide any further answers. At this point, the experimenter instructed the subject to treat the absence of an answer as a wrong answer and to continue the procedure. The experiment ended either when the maximum of 450 volts was administered or when the teacher refused to administer any more shocks.

If at any point the teacher indicated that he wanted to stop, the experimenter calmly told him to continue: "Whether the learner likes it or not," the experimenter asserted, "you must go on until he has learned all the word pairs correctly. So please go on."

Milgram's Results

The results of the experiment were so startling that Milgram checked with forty psychiatrists in order to get their estimates of what might happen in such an experiment. These experts predicted that most people would not continue beyond the 150 volt level, and that only one in 1,000 would actually give the highest shock. Yet in Milgram's experiments more than half of the forty subjects gave the full shock!

These subjects were not sadists. Many of them showed signs of extreme tension and discomfort during the session, and they often told the experimenter that they would like to stop. But in spite of these feelings, they continued to obey the experimenter's commands. They were ordinary men—salesmen, engineers, postal workers—placed in an unusual situation.

What accounts for this surprisingly high level of obedience? A large part of the answer is that the experimenter represents a legitimate authority. People assume that such an authority knows what he is doing, even when his instructions seem to run counter to their own standards of moral behavior.

Milgram's subjects could have walked out at any time—they had already been paid and had nothing to lose by leaving. Nevertheless, social conditioning for obeying legitimate authorities is so strongly ingrained that people often lack the words or the ways to do otherwise. Simply getting up and leaving would have violated powerful unwritten rules of acceptable social behavior.

Subsequent experiments showed that there were three ways in which subjects could be helped to act more bravely in this situation. One was the removal of the physical presence of the experimenter. Even more effective was putting the subject face to face with his victim. The third and most effective variation of the experiment was to provide other "teachers" to support the subject's defiance of the experimenter.

GROUP PRESSURE TO CONFORM

Most Americans claim they would never have become supporters of Hitler if they had lived in Germany during World War II. Yet a nation of Germans did. Under pressure from others, individuals at least complied with the prevailing attitudes. Everyone conforms to group pressure in many ways. Have you ever come home and surprised your parents by wearing the latest fad in clothing? Possibly, the conversation that followed went something like this: "How can you go around looking like that?" "But everyone dresses like this." "Well, if everyone jumped off the Empire State Building, would you?" At this point you probably answered, "No, of course I wouldn't." But most people also claim that they would never give a painful electric shock to another person in the name of science. And yet Milgram demonstrated that one out of every two people probably would.

Psychologist Solomon Asch designed a famous experiment to test conformity to pressure from peers as opposed to from authority. He showed that people may conform to a lie that other people tell, even when there is no doubt in their minds as to the truth. The following is

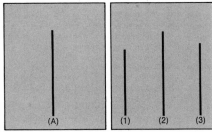

Standard Line   Comparison Lines

Figure 11.8

These two cards were shown to subjects in one trial of Asch's experiment on conformity. The actual discrimination involved is easy; those people not subjected to group pressure chose line 2 as the correct match in 99 out of 100 trials.

what you would have experienced if you had been a subject in this experiment.

You and seven other students come to a classroom for an experiment on visual judgment. You are shown a card with one line on it. You are then shown another card containing three lines and are asked to pick the one that is the same length as the first line. One of the three is exactly the same length and is easy to determine. The other two lines are obviously different. The experiment begins uneventfully. The subjects announce their answers in the order in which they are seated in the room. You happen to be seventh, and one person follows you. On the first comparison, every person chooses the same matching line. The second set of cards is displayed, and once again the group is unanimous. The discriminations seem easy, and you prepare for what you expect will be a rather boring experiment.

On the third trial, there is an unexpected disturbance. You are quite certain that Line 2 is the one that matches the standard. Yet the

Figure 11.9

Photographs taken during Asch's experiment on conformity. Subject 6 is the only real subject; the others are confederates of the experimenter (seen at the right in the first photograph). The subject listens to the others express identical judgments that differ from his own. He is in a dilemma: Does he express the judgment that he knows to be correct and risk being different from the group, or does he conform to the group's judgment? What do you think you would have done if you were a subject in the Asch experiment?

first person in the group announces confidently that Line 1 is the correct match. Then, the second person follows suit and he too, declares that the answer is Line 1. So do the third, fourth, fifth, and sixth subjects. Now it is your turn. You are suddenly faced with two contradictory pieces of information: The evidence of your own senses tells you that one answer is clearly correct, but the unanimous and confident judgments of the six preceding subjects tell you that you are wrong.

The dilemma with which you are faced persists through eighteen trials. On twelve of the trials, the other group members unanimously give an answer that differs from what you clearly perceive to be correct. It is only at the end of the experimental session that you learn the explanation for the confusion. The seven other subjects were all actors, and they had been instructed to answer falsely on those twelve trials.

How do most subjects react in this situation? Asch found that almost one-third of his fifty subjects conformed at least half the time. These conformers he called the "yielders." Most yielders explained to Asch afterward that they knew which line was correct but that they yielded to group pressure in order not to appear different from the others. Asch called those who did not conform "independents." They gave the correct answer despite group pressure.

Why so much conformity? Some sociologists argue that cultural forces toward conformist behavior are high in the United States. They contend that Americans are "other-directed." That is, Americans tend to overemphasize the importance of approval from others. At the same time, they neglect to develop a strong set of personal values and individual standards. Most American children are taught

Independent	Yielder
After a few trials he appeared puzzled, hesitant. He announced all disagreeing answers in the form of "Three, sir; two, sir." At Trial 4 he answered immediately after the first member of the group, shook his head, blinked, and whispered to his neighbor, "Can't help it, that's one." His later answers came in a whispered voice, accompanied by a deprecating smile. At one point he grinned embarrassedly and whispered explosively to his neighbor: "I always disagree—darn it!" Immediately after the experiment the majority engaged this subject in a brief discussion. When they pressed him to say whether the entire group was wrong and he alone right, he turned upon them defiantly, exclaiming: "You're *probably* right, but you *may* be wrong!" During the experimenter's later questioning, this subject's constant refrain was: "I called them as I saw them, sir."	This subject went along with the majority in eleven out of twelve trials. He appeared nervous and somewhat confused, but he did not attempt to evade discussion at the close of the experiment. He opened the discussion with the statement: "If I'd been first I probably would have responded differently." This was his way of saying that he had adopted the majority estimates. The primary factor in his case was loss of confidence. He perceived the majority as a decided group, acting without hesitation: "If they had been doubtful I probably would have changed, but they answered with such confidence." When the real purpose of the experiment was explained, the subject volunteered: "I suspected about the middle—but tried to push it out of my mind." It is of interest that his suspicion did not restore his confidence or diminish the power of the majority.

Figure 11.10

Descriptions of the behavior of two subjects in Asch's experiment: one who yielded to the group's judgment and one who remained independent.

the overriding importance of being liked and of being accepted. Conformity is the standard means of gaining this approval.

One of the most important findings of Asch's experiment was that if even one other person failed to conform to the group's judgment, the subject was able to adhere to his own perception. It seems that it is hardest to stand alone.

ATTITUDES AND ACTIONS

Social psychologists have discovered several interesting relationships between a person's attitudes and his actions. One obvious relationship is that attitudes affect actions: If you like Fords, you will buy a Ford. Some of the other relationships are not so obvious.

Doing Is Believing

It turns out, for example, that if you like Fords but buy a Chevrolet for some reason (perhaps you can get a better deal on a Chevy) you will end up liking Fords less. In other words, actions affect attitudes.

In many instances, if you act and speak as though you have certain beliefs and feelings, you may begin to *really* feel and believe this way. For example, prisoners accused of a crime have, under pressure of police interrogation, confessed to crimes they did not commit. They have confessed in order to relieve the pressure, but having said that they did the deed, they begin to believe that they really *are* guilty.

One explanation for this phenomenon comes from the theory of cognitive dissonance, discussed earlier in this chapter. If a person acts one way but thinks another, he will experience dissonance. To reduce the dissonance he will have to change either the behavior or the attitude. A similar explanation is that people have a need for *self-justification*—a need to justify their behavior.

In an experiment that demonstrated these principles, subjects were paid either $1.00 or $20.00 to tell another person that a boring experiment in which they both had to participate was really a lot of fun. Afterward, the experimenters asked the subjects how they felt about the experiment. They found that the subjects who had been paid $20.00 to lie about the experiment continued to believe that it had been boring. Those who had been paid $1.00, however, came to believe that the experiment had actually been fairly enjoyable. These last people had less reason to tell the lie, so they experienced more dissonance when they did so. In other words, in order to justify their lie, they had to believe that it was not a lie and that they had actually enjoyed the experiment.

The phenomenon of self-justification has serious implications. For example, how would you justify to yourself the fact that you had intentionally injured another human being? In another psychological experiment, subjects were led to believe that they had injured or hurt other subjects in some way. The aggressors were then asked how they felt about the victims they had just harmed. It was found that the

Figure 11.11
In communities throughout the People's Republic of China, small discussion groups meet daily to read the thoughts of Chairman Mao Tse-Tung. During these sessions, one person is assigned the role of "devil's advocate," which means he or she argues against Mao's statements while others defend them. This exercise strengthens the pro-Mao attitudes of all participants, because it promotes the process of internalization and produces the inoculation effect. The attitudes of the person playing "devil's advocate" are not threatened by his acting in opposition to them because he is playing a role that everyone expects of him.

aggressors had convinced themselves that they did not like the victim of their cruelty. In other words, the aggressors talked themselves into believing that their defenseless victims had deserved their injury. The aggressors also considered their victims to be less attractive after the experiment than before—their self-justification for hurting another person was something like, "Oh well, this person doesn't amount to much, anyway."

It is this type of self-justification that allows men to go to a country they have never before visited and kill other people they have never before seen. Without self-justification, armies of men would undoubtedly go crazy from their own guilt—and some war veterans return seriously disturbed for just this reason.

Self-Fulfilling Prophecy

Another relationship between attitudes and actions is rather sub-tle—but extremely pervasive. It is possible, it seems, for a person to act in such a way that he makes his attitudes come true. This phenomenon is called *self-fulfilling prophecy*. Suppose, for example, you are convinced that you are a bad cook. Every time you go into the kitchen, you start thinking poorly of yourself. Because you approach the task of baking a cake with great anxiety, you fumble the measurements, pour in too much milk, leave out an ingredient, and so on, and as a result, your cake is a flop. You thus confirm that you *are* a bad cook.

Self-fulfilling prophecies can influence all kinds of human activity. Suppose you believe that people are basically friendly and generous. Consequently, whenever you approach other people, you are armed with a friendly and open attitude yourself. Because of your warm smile and positive attitude toward yourself and the world, people like you. Thus, your attitude that people are friendly produces your friendly behavior, which in turn causes people to respond favorably toward you. But suppose you turn this example around. Imagine that you believe people are selfish and cold. Because of your negative attitude, you tend to avert your eyes from other people, to act gloomy, and to appear rather unfriendly. People think your actions are strange, and consequently, they act coldly toward you. Thus, your attitude has produced the kind of behavior that makes the attitude come true. (How self-fulfilling prophecy is used by teachers in the classroom is described in Chapter 15.)

Personal Applications

The psychological findings related to self-justification and self-fulfilling prophecy show that there is truth in the saying "Life is what you make it." What you do affects you directly, and it affects the way the world acts toward you. First, the fact that everyone tends to justify their actions by changing their attitudes has several practical consequences. If you give in to pressure and act against your better judgment, you will be undermining your own beliefs. The next time

Figure 11.12
The Red Queen's fatalistic attitude is likely to be confirmed if she behaves in this way. This common phenomenon is called self-fulfilling prophecy.

you are in a similar situation, you will find it even harder to stand up for what you believe in because you will have begun to wonder whether you believe it yourself. If you want to strengthen your convictions about something, it is a good idea to speak and act on your beliefs at every opportunity. If you do make a mistake and act against your beliefs, you should admit that you are wrong and not try to justify yourself.

Second, the phenomenon of self-fulfilling prophecy shows that the way the world seems to you may be a result of your own actions. Other people, who act differently, will have different experiences and produce different effects. When you find the world unsatisfactory, remember that to some extent, you are creating it. When you find the world a joyful place, remember, too, that it is making you happy partly because you believe that it can.

"I will not give in because I oppose it—I do—not my pride, not my spleen, nor any other of my appetites but I do—I!"

Figure 11.13
Sir Thomas More, a respected statesman and lord chancellor of England, defied his friend King Henry VIII and refused to agree to Parliament's Act of Supremacy. This Act had given Henry control of the Church of England (so that he could divorce his first wife). More's refusal, based on his determination to be true to his principles, cost him his job, his freedom, and, finally, his life. These lines are from the play *A Man for All Seasons*, based on More's life.
(From Robert Bolt, *A Man for All Seasons*. In *The New Theater of Europe*, Robert Corrigan, ed. New York: Dell Publishing Co., 1962, p. 111.)

SUMMARY

1. An attitude is an enduring set of beliefs, feelings, and tendencies to act toward people or things in predisposed ways. Processes involved in attitude change include compliance, identification, and internalization.

2. Compliance is acting as though one has a certain attitude in order to avoid discomfort or rejection or to gain approval. Identification is the adoption of new attitudes as a result of a strong emotional attachment to another person or group. Internalization is the deepest

kind of attitude change; it is the incorporation of attitudes into the person's entire belief system.

3. A person's readiness to change his mind is dependent in part on his personality. People who need social approval and have little confidence in their own judgment are easily susceptible to persuasion. People whose identities are based on their attitudes are highly resistant to change.

4. People have a need for cognitive consistency—that is, a need to fit their attitudes together into a nonconflicting set of beliefs. People who simultaneously hold two or more opposing attitudes experience cognitive dissonance. In order to reduce dissonance, one or more of the attitudes must change.

5. Persuasion is a direct attempt to change attitudes through the process of communication. Types of persuasion include advertising, salesmanship, political campaigning, and editorializing. Propaganda, another form of persuasion, is the spreading of information or ideas intended to promote or injure a cause, group, or nation.

6. Four components of the communication process are the source, the message, the channel, and the audience. For attitude change to occur, the source must be trustworthy and sincere, the message should combine fact and emotional arousal, the channel should be appropriate to the message, and the audience must be receptive.

7. One of the strongest ways in which social influence is exerted is through authority. Milgram's experiment showed that social conditioning produces such a strong tendency toward obeying legitimate authorities that people may easily be induced to do harm to others against their consciences or better judgment.

8. Asch's experiment showed that conformity to pressure from peers may be so strong that people will question or deny their own senses.

9. People's actions affect their attitudes. People often justify actions that go against their beliefs by changing their beliefs. Self-fulfilling prophecy is the phenomenon of acting in such a way as to make one's attitudes come true.

ACTIVITIES

1. How much have your parents influenced your life? Consider the areas of appearance, life style, sexual attitudes, academic performance, marriage plans, and political attitudes.

2. Collect samples of advertising that depict various techniques of persuasion—identification, social approval, fear of disaster, and so on. Analyze each ad on the basis of effectiveness and what type of person it might appeal to.

3. Does a researcher have the right to fool his subjects, even in the name of science? Consider, for example, the effects on Milgram's subjects of believing they had harmed a fellow subject by obliging the

order of a stranger. Do you think this experiment was valuable for allowing the subjects to realize the extent of their conformity? If you answered the first question no, and the second, yes, how would you reconcile these two conflicting attitudes?

4. Choose some issue on which you have a strong opinion. If you were given an unlimited budget, how would you go about persuading people to agree with you? Describe the sources you would employ, the channels you would use, the content of your message, and the audience you would try to reach.

5. To what extent does advertising influence the foods you like? Find several people who prefer butter to margarine. Ask them why they prefer butter. If they say it tastes better, then ask them to participate in an experiment to test their claims. Get several brands of both butter and margarine and spread them lightly on the same kind of crackers or toast. Blindfold your subjects and provide them with a glass of water to rinse their mouths whenever they wish. Ask them to identify the samples. Run through the series about four times, varying the order of presentation. Try similar experiments with people who prefer certain brands of milk, cola, or coffee.

6. Try this experiment to test the effects of self-fulfilling prophecy. Approach someone you vaguely dislike and whom you generally ignore and ask him or her to eat lunch with you, to go to the library, or to do some other socially oriented activity. Make a conscientious effort to get to know the person and see if your attitude of dislike is really justified or if the person's behavior was a function of the way you previously responded to him or her.

7. One of the primary objectives of advertising is to get the viewers/listeners to remember the product. To what extent do you think familiarity with brand names influences your choices in the market? How many television commercials do you find obnoxious? Do you find that you remember the products advertised in "obnoxious" commercials better than you remember products that appear in less offensive advertisements? Do you think there is a possibility that some commercials are deliberately offensive?

8. If any of your attitudes have recently changed, try to pinpoint what made you change your mind. What were the external factors, such as communications, involved? How were the other attitudes you already held involved?

9. Choose a controversial topic, such as abortion, drug abuse, or women's rights, and devise ten questions to measure people's attitudes toward this issue. Give the questionnaire to a number of different people and see whether your results make sense in terms of what you already know about these people. (Psychologists are greatly concerned with devising questionnaires that really tell something about how people tend to act.)

10. Clip editorials from different newspapers or magazines that take

opposite sides on an issue. Compare the attitudes expressed and the methods of persuasion used by the different editorial writers.

SUGGESTED READINGS

BEM, DARYL J. *Beliefs, Attitudes and Human Affairs*. Belmont, Calif.: Brooks/Cole, 1970. A well-written and enjoyable book on attitudes and their social implications.

DELLA FEMINA, J. *From Those Wonderful Folks Who Gave You Pearl Harbor*. New York: Simon & Schuster, 1970. A hilarious and insightful look at the world of advertising agencies through the eyes of a creative man with plenty of first-hand experience.

HELLER, JOSEPH. *Catch-22*. New York: Dell, 1961 (paper). One of the saddest and funniest novels ever written about war. But more than that a commentary about social influence—the factors that lead people into double binds, self-fulfilling prophecies, and unwilling obedience.

LIFTON, ROBERT JAY. *Home from the War*. New York: Simon & Schuster, 1973. An interesting account of how veterans of the Vietnam War have had to use self-justification for their wartime actions. Lifton points out that self-justification leads to new and different political consciousness unfelt in the men before their overseas experiences.

McGINNISS, JOE. *The Selling of the President, 1968*. New York: Trident, 1969 (paper). This book shows how advertising men manufacture, package, and market their most lucrative product: the President of the United States. The book is fascinating, frightening, and essential reading for anyone interested in the psychology of advertising and in the ways the public can be manipulated.

McLUHAN, MARSHALL. *Understanding Media*. New York: McGraw-Hill, 1964 (paper). A difficult but fascinating book that examines the effects of media on the recipient. McLuhan claims that content and programing are less influential factors than the medium itself.

ORWELL, GEORGE. *Nineteen Eighty-Four*. New York: Harcourt Brace Jovanovich, 1949. A frightening novel that takes a close look at a future in which attitudes are dictated by a totalitarian government from which there is little hope (or thought) of escape.

SHIRER, WILLIAM L. *The Rise and Fall of the Third Reich*. New York: Simon & Schuster, 1960 (paper). A fully detailed and documented account of the dynamics that created and destroyed the most evilly totalitarian political regime in modern history: Nazi Germany. A classic study of propaganda, obedience, and conformity. Heavy reading.

TRUMBO, DALTON. *Johnny Got His Gun*. New York: Bantam, 1970 (paper), originally published, 1939. A book about war: what people fight for and what they are willing to die for. Written originally about World War I, it is as applicable today as it was then.

ZIMBARDO, P. G., and E. B. EBBESEN. *Influencing Attitudes and Changing Behavior*. Reading, Mass.: Addison-Wesley, 1969. A short introduction to methodology, experimentation, and theory in the field of attitude change. Designed for readers without extensive background.

How glorious it is—
and also how painful—
to be an exception.

Alfred de Musset (1834)

Unit V
Personality and Emotional Life

There are millions upon millions of people in this world, and each one is unique. Each individual has not only a unique appearance and genetic background but also a unique way of dealing with the world, of viewing other people, and of viewing himself. You may have noticed that the other units in this book have for the most part ignored this individuality in order to explore the ways people are alike—in physiological functioning, in mental processes, in growth and development, and in interacting with one another. This unit, however, focuses on the ways in which people are different—and why.

Chapter 12 presents the theories of several psychologists who have tried to explain why individuals are different from one another. These men have addressed such questions as: How is character formed? To what extent can a person know himself? What determines a person's actions? How can a person be happy? Because it is difficult to know how much of any of these theories is correct, you may want to select parts from each theory to fit in with your own ideas about personality.

Chapter 13 discusses the problem of people who are so different from everyone else that they are considered abnormal. Such people are often painfully unhappy and are sometimes unable to handle the simplest tasks of everyday life. Chapter 14 focuses on the ways in which such people can be helped to achieve better contact with reality, with others, and with themselves.

In this area of individuality and exception, psychology can be said to touch upon medicine on the one hand and upon religion on the other. Medicine concerns itself with the welfare of the body; religion, with the welfare of the soul. Psychologists bridge the gap by sometimes acting as doctors, other times, as spiritual advisers, adapting themselves to meet the needs of the unique individual.

12
Personality Theory

THE PURPOSE OF PERSONALITY THEORIES

SIGMUND FREUD:
Id, ego, and superego / Defense mechanisms

CARL JUNG:
Archetypes / Individuation

ALFRED ADLER: THE STRUGGLE FOR MASTERY

ERICH FROMM: MAN AND SOCIETY

CARL ROGERS: SELF AND ORGANISM

ABRAHAM MASLOW: SELF-ACTUALIZATION

EXISTENTIALISM

BEHAVIORISM

Figure 12.1
French poet and philosopher Paul Valéry once remarked that the purpose of psychology is to present a completely different picture of one's most familiar experiences. This chapter explores the different views of six great psychologists, each of whom had his own ideas about the meaning behind the everyday experiences of life.

> . . . I stand once more beneath the sun, as I once stood as a small child. Nothing is mine, I know nothing, I possess nothing, I have learned nothing. How strange it is! Now, when I am no longer young, when my hair is fast growing gray, when strength begins to diminish, now I am beginning again like a child. He had to smile again. Yes, his destiny was strange! He was going backwards, and now he again stood empty and naked and ignorant in the world. But he did not grieve about it; no, he even felt a great desire to laugh, to laugh at himself, to laugh at this strange foolish world!
>
> from Hermann Hesse, *Siddhartha*

> I am a sick man. . . . I am a spiteful man. I am an unattractive man. I believe my liver is diseased. However, I know nothing at all about my disease, and do not know for certain what ails me. I don't consult a doctor for it, and never have, though I have a respect for medicine and doctors. Besides, I am extremely superstitious, sufficiently so to respect medicine, anyway (I am well-educated enough not to be superstitious, but I am superstitious). No, I refuse to consult a doctor from spite.
>
> from Feodor Dostoyevsky, *Notes from Underground*

These two characters have markedly different personalities. The way they talk, the things they know, their beliefs, their purposes, and their pleasures are all quite different. If you were to set a speech of your own alongside these, you would find that you, too, have a unique way of expressing yourself, as well as unique things to express. But could you explain just how and why you are different?

Describing or explaining human personality is difficult because people are anything but simple. Because the task is so formidable, only a few people have attempted it with much success. But these few people—psychologists who study personality—have changed the entire way that human beings think about themselves.

Most of these psychologists have lived emotionally intense lives themselves. They have based their theories on what they have learned from their own experiences, on what they have learned from the experiences of people they have tried to help, and on what they have learned from reading literature, philosophy, science, and the theories of other psychologists. This chapter presents the insights of several personality theorists into the nature of human life.

The work of these theorists is not described in complete detail here; this chapter describes only some of the most important parts of some of the most important theories. These are a few of the ideas that have increased man's understanding of man.

WHAT PERSONALITY THEORIES TRY TO DO

People often assume that theories about personality are likely to be difficult, uninteresting, and pointless. In fact, personality theories have many practical purposes. One of the purposes of a personality theory is to provide a way of organizing the many facts that you know about yourself and about other people. You know what you like or do not like, what makes you angry, how difficult it is for you to make decisions, how aggressive you are, how easily you cry. You also know some of these things about the people closest to you—you know what pleases them, what hurts them, how they are likely to act in certain situations. In describing a friend to someone who does not know her, you might say that she is outgoing or shy, bossy or meek, quick-tempered or calm, witty or dull, fun loving or gloomy, industrious or lazy, and so on. These words describe *traits,* general ways of behaving that characterize the individual's personality.

Personality theorists examine such personality traits and try to explain why some of them go together and why a person might have one trait and not another. The object is to find patterns in the ways people behave.

A second purpose of personality theories is to explain the differences between individuals. Some differences can be explained fairly easily. It is obvious that a man whose main aim in life is to please everyone he meets will behave differently from a woman who wants to become the editor of *The New York Times.* The motives of these people seem to explain a lot about them, but one might still wonder how they came to have different motives in the first place. A personality theorist might suggest that the man had parents who were hard to please or that the woman had shown an early talent for writing and organizing and had wanted to develop these abilities to the fullest.

A third purpose of a personality theory is to provide a set of guidelines to live by. Most personality theorists have devoted a good portion of their writings to the conduct of personal life. It is no accident that nearly every major personality theorist began as a psychotherapist, whose job is to help people with emotional problems. As therapists, they had to determine what it is to be free of emotional problems and to decide how a good or healthy personality might respond to certain standard situations in life.

Everyone, for example, feels puzzled about sex, finds it difficult to work hard, or feels unhappy and useless at certain times in his life. Personality theorists try to explain why such problems arise and what may be done about them.

Personality theorists are also concerned with determining how life should be improved. Most people are to some extent dissatisfied with themselves or with their parents, their children, their wives, or their husbands. Nearly everyone is dissatisfied to some extent with American society and with the political state of the world. Almost everyone recognizes that both the individual and society need to grow and to change. But what are the proper goals of growth and change? And how can they be achieved? Personality theorists try to provide answers to these questions.

SIGMUND FREUD: PSYCHOSEXUALITY AND THE UNCONSCIOUS MIND

Charming, spacious, homelike 1 rm. apts. Modern kitchenette. Hotel service. Weekly rats available.

from classified advertisement, *The New York Times*

This advertisement was recently received and typeset by someone at *The Times.* The person who set the ad probably did not leave the "e" out deliberately, but was it just a mistake?

Slips like these are common. People usually laugh at them, even if they are meaningful. But sometimes they are disturbing. Everyone has had the experience of making some personal remark that hurt a friend and later having asked himself, "Why did I say that? I didn't mean it . . . " Yet, when he thinks about it, he may realize that he was angry at his friend and wanted to "get back" at him.

Sigmund Freud was the first person to recognize that the little slips that people make, the things they mishear, and the odd misunderstandings they have are not usually mistakes at all. Freud believed that there was something behind these mistakes, even though people claimed they were just accidental and quickly corrected themselves. Similarly, when he listened to people describe their dreams, he believed that the dreams had some meaning, even though the people who dreamed them could not determine what they meant.

Freud was a medical doctor who practiced in Vienna, Austria in the early 1900s. At that time, most people thought, as many still do, that a person is aware of all his own motives and feelings. Freud decided that if people can say and dream things without knowing their meaning, they must not know as much about themselves as they think they do.

In his practice as a doctor of nervous diseases, Freud talked to a large number of people about their complaints, their thoughts, and their private lives. He eventually concluded that some of the most powerful influences in a person's life are things of which he is *not* conscious.

Freud was the first to suggest that every personality has a large *unconscious* component. This unconscious part, Freud believed,

Figure 12.2

Sigmund Freud was nearly forty when he began to formulate the psychoanalytic theories that made him famous. Before that time, he was a medical researcher and practitioner. Then, in the years between 1894 and 1900, he experienced what one writer has called a "creative illness" in which he analyzed his own psychological disturbances and emerged with the basic elements of his theory and a transformed personality. During these years, he wrote his most extraordinary book, *The Interpretation of Dreams.*

Figure 12.3 (*opposite*)
This illustration characterizes
the unruly id and the disciplined superego,
two of the three energy systems that Freud
believed exist within every individual. The
third system, the ego, is not represented
here, although the viewer might imagine
him or herself as the ego examining the
other parts of the personality. Freud
believed that these systems could vary
considerably from person to person in their
relative strengths, and in this illustration the
id is obviously the dominant system, just
barely being kept in check by the
superego.

may be more important than the conscious part. For example, an overweight person may be conscious only of the fact that he wants to eat and eat and eat. He may not realize that the reason for this excessive eating is that he is trying to get pleasure out of life by eating instead of by having friends or interesting work to do.

Life, from birth onward, includes both pleasurable and painful experiences. Freud believed that many of these experiences, particularly the painful ones, are forgotten or buried within the unconscious. Even though a person is not aware of many past experiences, they nevertheless influence much of his behavior. Perhaps you have a great liking for milk, potatoes, and rice pudding, or perhaps you are nervous when you have to talk to a stranger. Freud's theory would explain that these smooth white foods may make you feel good because they are like the food you enjoyed as a baby, or that strangers scare you because they remind you of times when your parents left you alone with someone you did not know and did not like.

The Id, Ego, and Superego

Freud tried to explain human personality by saying that it was a kind of energy system—like a steam engine, or an electric dynamo. The energy in human personality comes from two kinds of powerful instinctive urges, the life instincts and the death instincts. Freud theorized that all of life moves toward death and that the desire for a final end shows up in human personality as destructiveness and aggression. The life instincts were more important in Freud's theory, however. He saw them primarily as *erotic* urges to seek the pleasure found in sex and love.

These instinctive urges form the *id,* the lustful, driving part of the unconscious personality. The force of the id is felt consciously as a desire to touch one's lover, for example, or as an urge to hit someone who is being annoying.

The part of the personality that is mostly conscious is called the *ego.* The ego uses some of the energy of the id to deal with reality. The ego is the rational, thoughtful, realistic part of the personality. For example, if a person is hungry, his id might drive him to seek immediate satisfaction by dreaming of food or by eating all of the available food at once instead of keeping some of it for a later time. The ego is the part of the person that would recognize that the body needs real food and that it will continue to need food in the future; it would use the id's energy to preserve some of the food available now and to look for ways of finding more.

Suppose that the ego thought of stealing the desired food from someone else. The part of the personality that would stop the person from stealing is called the *superego.* The superego also uses energy from the id but transforms it into a different kind of force. The id is concerned with what the person *wants* to do and the ego is concerned with what he *can* do; the superego is concerned with what the

person *should* do. It is the moral part of personality, the source of conscience and of high ideals.

Obviously the id and the superego frequently come into conflict with each other, and because neither of them is concerned with reality, they may both come into conflict with the necessities of the outside world as well. Freud saw the ego as the part of the person that must resolve these conflicts. Somehow, the ego must find a way to satisfy the demands of the id in a fashion that works and that is acceptable to the superego. If the id is not satisfied, the person feels an intolerable tension of longing or anger or desire. If the superego is not obeyed, the person feels guilty and inferior. And if outside reality is ignored, the person suffers such results as starvation or dislike by other people. As Freud said, it is no wonder that people sometimes cry out: "Life is not easy."

Defense Mechanisms

The ego's task is so difficult that, for most people, it has to resort to a kind of psychological cheating. Its cheating methods are called *defense mechanisms* because they defend the ego from feeling anxiety over failing its task. Freud believed that some of these mechanisms are necessary if the individual is to live in society, but many of the theorists who have followed Freud doubt this pessimistic view. Generally, the defense mechanisms are considered harmful to the individual because they require some distortion of the truth. Freud identified many such mechanisms, a few of which are described here: displacement, repression, projection, and regression.

Displacement   Displacement is used when the id wants something that it cannot or must not have. The ego solves the problem by giving the id a substitute; it displaces the energy of the id from one object to another, more accessible, object. For example, if you were to hit your kid brother when you really wanted to hit your father, that would be a displacement. Freud believed that many adult activities are displacements of childhood pleasures; that, for example, an adult who enjoys keeping a house neat and clean may be enjoying the kind of pleasure that a child has in learning not to defecate in his pants.

Repression   When a person has some thought or urge that causes the ego too much anxiety, that thought or urge may be pushed out of consciousness down into the unconscious. This process is called *repression*. The person simply proceeds to "forget" the thing that disturbs him. For example, a person who has the impulse to say, "I hate you" may feel so afraid and anxious about having such an impulse that he convinces himself—without realizing what he is doing—that what he feels is not hatred. He replaces the feeling with apathy, a feeling of not caring at all. He says, "I don't hate you. I have no special feelings at all about you." Nevertheless, the feelings of anger, hatred, and hostility remain in the unconscious and may show themselves in cutting remarks or sarcastic jokes.

Projection   One of the tricks the ego uses in avoiding its problems is to pretend that the impulses coming from within the person are really coming from other people. For example, a feeling of physical attraction to someone of the same sex might make someone so uncomfortable that he might think, "I can't have feelings like that. That would make me a homosexual. But wait a minute! I'll bet *he's* a homosexual and that's why I get these feelings." This mechanism is called *projection* because inner feelings are thrown, or projected, outside. It is a common mechanism, which you have probably observed in yourself from time to time. Many people, for example, feel that others dislike them, when in reality they dislike themselves.

Regression   Regression means going back to an old pattern. When a person is under severe pressure and his other defenses are not working, he may start acting in ways that used to help him in the past. For example, he may throw a temper tantrum, make faces, cry loudly, or revert to eating and sleeping all the time the way he did as a small child. If you have ever been tempted to stick out your lower lip and pout when you know that you should really accept the fact that you cannot have your own way, you have experienced regression.

The recognition of the tremendous forces that exist in human personality and the difficulty of controlling and handling them was Freud's great contribution to understanding human life. After Freud, it became easier to understand why human life contains so much conflict. It is a matter, Freud thought, of a savage individual coming to terms with the rules of society. The id is the savage part, and the superego, the representative of society. In a healthy person the ego, the "I," is strong enough to handle the struggle.

CARL JUNG: MYTH AND RELIGION

It was like a voyage to the moon, or a descent into empty space.
First came the image of a crater, and I had the feeling that I was
in the land of the dead. The atmosphere was that of the other
world. Near the steep slope of a rock I caught sight of two figures,
an old man with a white beard and a beautiful young girl.

from Carl Jung, *Memories, Dreams, Reflections*

These words describe one of the many visions that Carl Jung had in his life. In this vision the man turned out to be the Old Testament prophet Elijah, and the girl was Salome, who danced for the head of John the Baptist, as related in the New Testament.

Such visions are probably the best example of Jung's unusual approach to the problems of personality theory. Although Jung openly disagreed with Freud, he did borrow from and was influenced by him. One of Jung's most interesting ideas was that the uncon-

Figure 12.4
Carl G. Jung was a Swiss psychiatrist who formed a close association with Freud after their first meeting in 1906. Later, they split over several differences in opinion as to the direction that psychoanalytic theory should take, and Jung formed his own school of psychoanalytic thought. One of the most mystical and metaphysical of the pioneer theorists, Jung has had, until recently, a wider acceptance in Europe than in America.

scious mind contains more than personal impulses and memories. Jung thought that there is a *collective unconscious* that contains the instincts, urges, and memories of the entire human race.

He called these unconscious deposits *archetypes*. The same archetypes are present in every person, and they shape experience the way a dried-up riverbed shapes the flow of running water after a storm. Jung thought that these archetypes arose from the common experiences of all humanity: experiences with Mothers, Fathers, War, Nature, and so on. These archetypes show up in myths and dreams, in paintings and poetry, in ghost stories and religious beliefs. Jung thought that the religious characters in his vision, for example, were symbols of Wisdom (Elijah) and Erotic Excitement (Salome).

To take another example, consider the similarity of the stories of Jack and the Beanstalk and David and Goliath. Every person who hears these stories can understand them easily. They tell how a small, weak, good person triumphs over a big, strong, bad person. Jung believed that such stories are common and easy to understand because the situations they describe have occurred over and over again in the history of mankind and have been remembered as archetypes in the unconscious of every human being.

The Polarities of Personality

The David and Goliath story is a good example of a conflict between opposites. Jung was very interested in the idea of opposites. He thought that the energy of personality is made up of the tension between opposites—like the poles of a magnet. He pointed out, for example, that each sex contains characteristics of the opposite sex. Men have a feminine side to their natures, and women have a masculine side.

Another pair of opposites that Jung described was *extraversion* and *introversion*. These are two different ways of looking at the world, and every person is capable of both. A person who is strongly extraverted looks outward. He is objective, practical, and sociable. An introverted person tends to look inward. He is concerned with his own feelings, and he has vivid dreams and fantasies.

The Achievement of Wholeness

Jung's belief was that every person wants to bring the opposite parts of himself together. A man wishes to express his feminine side—to work by intuition and emotion. A woman wishes to express her masculine side—to work by reason and concrete awareness. Similarly, an extraverted person wants to become more aware of himself and of his own ideals, and an introverted person wants to become more aware of the outside world and of practical realities.

But most people have not achieved these goals. They are fragmented or broken apart. They concentrate on certain parts of themselves and hide certain others. Bringing out both sides and working

Figure 12.5 (*opposite*)
Any symmetrical arrangement around a central point can be called a mandala. Simple mandalas are often found in children's paintings, and complex mandalas are common in Eastern art. Jung believed that the mandala form is a symbol for the polarities, or opposites, in human nature and that the central point represents the point of unity or wholeness. This mandala shows the entire panorama of life on Earth, unfolding from primordial atoms. One of the central polarities emphasized here is the contrast between the murky depths below, containing mysterious horrors, and the warm green light above, where man and woman are enshrined. Recent evidence from experiments with altered states of consciousness have suggested that the collective unconscious contains material from man's biological origins, as well as from his uniquely human history.

Figure 12.6

Alfred Adler's considerable influence on modern psychological theory is often overlooked by many who feel his contributions were overshadowed by the impact of Freud and Jung. Unlike Freud, who had a gift for writing and who was inspired both by Shakespeare and the Greek playwrights, or Jung, whose inspiration came from mystical and religious studies, Adler was an intensely practical man who did not possess the dynamic personality of either of these two contemporaries. Nevertheless, Adler's writings on psychotherapy offer more optimism and practicality than those of Freud or Jung. Furthermore, his intuitive and commonsense approach to human life has greatly affected the thinking of later psychologists interested in the existential approach (presented at the end of this chapter).

on them until they balance each other is part of a process that Jung called *individuation*. Individuation is a "journey of the soul" that not everyone makes. It means becoming more and more aware of yourself and understanding what parts of yourself you show to the outside world (which Jung called the *persona*) and what parts you hide even from yourself (the *shadow*, in Jung's terminology).

ALFRED ADLER: THE STRUGGLE FOR MASTERY

I had a case of a medical student who wanted to commit suicide, an undersized man, who consequently wanted to be tall. He was very much spoiled by his mother, who was the wife of a physician, a tyrannical husband with whom she was not happy. One day the cook came into the room screaming and crying out that the father had made a sexual assault upon her. From this time the mother went into a depression and cried continually. The boy could not understand this. . . . He had already asked his mother how she could be so much depressed by the unfaithfulness of a husband for whom she neither had nor professed any affection: but she interrupted his question by screaming, "You cannot possibly understand this!" The student [when asked whether] the father's behaviour was as brutal or rough as before, [said] that on the contrary he was very quiet, calm, and considerate.

"Do you think?" I then asked, "that your mother will give up her only means of taming this tyrant? She pays the price with her depression, but she feels that she is the conqueror. You are doing something very similar. You used to be your mother's favourite, but now you are alone in a foreign city, deprived of the attentions of your mother, who is so busy taming your father. You are failing in your work at the university, and are not prepared to be independent, so you wish to impress your mother with your suicidal impulses just as your mother impresses your father with her depression. You have been trained, as pampered children often are, to succeed by a display of weakness."

from Alfred Adler, *Problems of Neurosis*

You may find this analysis by Alfred Adler, another of the best-known personality theorists, a bit difficult to understand at first, but it illustrates some of Adler's chief ideas. Like Jung, Adler was an early and intimate associate of Freud. In 1911, Adler broke with Freud to develop his own approach to personality.

Adler believed that the driving force in people's lives is a desire to overcome their weaknesses. Classic examples are Demosthenes, a famous Greek orator who overcame a speech impediment by practicing with pebbles in his mouth, Napoleon, a short man who became conqueror of Europe in the early 1800s, and Glenn Cunningham, an Olympic runner who lost his toes in a fire as a child and had to plead with doctors who wanted to amputate his legs because they thought he would never use them again.

Everyone struggles with inferiority, said Adler. A child first feels inferior because he is so little and so dependent on adults. Gradually he learns to do the things that older people can do. The satisfaction that comes from even such simple acts as walking or learning to use a spoon sets up a pattern of overcoming inadequacies, a pattern that lasts throughout life.

Such patterns were called *styles of life* by Adler. The medical-student patient, Adler felt, had developed a poor style of life. He was not really overcoming his weaknesses at all. Instead he was trying to get his mother to feel sorry for him so that he would not have to struggle for himself. Adler described such a person, who continually tries to cover up and avoid his feelings of inadequacy, as having an *inferiority complex.*

The way parents treat their children has a great influence on the styles of life they choose. Overpampering, in which the parents attempt to satisfy the child's every whim, tends to produce a self-centered person who has little regard for others and who expects everyone else to do what he wants. On the other hand, the child who is neglected by his parents may seek revenge by becoming an angry, hostile person. Both the pampered and the neglected child tend to grow up into adults who have a lack of confidence in their ability to meet the demands of life. Ideally, said Adler, a child should learn self-reliance and courage from his father and generosity and a feeling for others from his mother.

Adler placed great importance on *social interest,* or a feeling for others. He thought that it is proper and natural for people to feel a responsibility toward others and that no one could be happy unless willingly and actively engaged in improving life for everyone, not just for himself.

ERICH FROMM: MAN AND SOCIETY

You tell me it's the institution . . . you better free your mind instead.

from John Lennon, "Revolution"

In these lines, John Lennon addresses people who try to resolve their problems by attacking the Establishment. If you want to change the world, he suggests, you had better start with yourself.

Do men make societies or do societies make men? Lennon is criticizing those who give easy answers, but the question is a difficult one. Obviously, the effects go in both directions. The personality theorist who has had most to say on this subject is Erich Fromm. Like Adler, Fromm minimizes the influence of instincts and stresses the effect of the social environment, especially the family.

Society and Character

Fromm believes that the individual's relationship to society is a difficult one. A person is dependent on the society in which he lives to meet certain basic needs. A person needs to be *related*—he needs

Figure 12.7
Erich Fromm has enriched modern personality theory by combining a psychoanalytic perspective with sociological and existential viewpoints. Fromm has been largely influenced by two men: Freud and Karl Marx. Freud explained human personality in terms of unconscious instincts; Marx explained human history in terms of economic pressures. Fromm believes that both factors should be taken into account in explaining and understanding human personality. Fromm's writings are far less obscure than those of Freud, Jung, and Adler, and, consequently, his books have enjoyed much popular success.

to feel that he is part of humanity by having friends and loved ones. A person needs to be *rooted*—he must feel that he belongs, to his family, to his community, to his church, for example.

In addition, a person needs a *frame of reference*—he needs ideals, beliefs, and purposes that give his life meaning, that suggest the direction he should take. A person also needs an *identity*—he must have a sense of himself as distinctive and unique. Finally a person needs to *transcend*—he needs to rise above all the influences life has on him, he needs to have some control over his life, some power to create new things, to be more than an animal.

Fromm believes that different societies meet these needs in different ways and that societies often use these needs to control people. The ways in which a society responds to the needs of individuals has a considerable effect on their personalities. He identified the United States, for example, as a capitalistic society. He believes that in such a society one way to satisfy the need for personal identity is to become rich and that one way to achieve rootedness is to become a trusted employee in a large business.

Fromm thinks that most societies mold personality in ways that are damaging to the individual. Capitalistic societies, for example, produce a certain number of people who are hoarders. They achieve a sense of security by holding on to what they already have and never letting go. Another capitalistic type is the receiver, who depends on being supported by others in order to feel secure.

Fromm called such character types *nonproductive*. The nonproductive person feels that the source of all that is good in life is outside himself. The only way he can get what he wants is by receiving, taking, keeping, or buying it from other people. Fromm thought that what a person should be is *productive*. A productive person feels that the source of what is good is inside himself. As a result, he can be a loving, giving, generous person.

Freedom and Loneliness

People create societies in which it is difficult to be creative, loving, and free, Fromm says, because freedom carries with it the terrible price of loneliness and isolation. Every child faces this problem as he grows up and becomes independent of his family's support. People are anxious, Fromm says, to *escape from freedom*. One way for them to escape is to find someone else to do their worrying. They welcome a government or a ruler or a system that tells them just what to do and that looks after them, even though they lose their freedom and opportunity to be creative.

Fromm points to the success of Nazism in Germany in the 1930s as an example of a mass escape from freedom. The German people had been living in a society in which selfish striving for personal gain took the place of love, brotherhood, and unity. Hitler took advantage of the fact that the German people were, as a result, desperate for

Figure 12.8
A number of personality theorists besides Erich Fromm have emphasized what Fromm calls the desire to escape from freedom. One theorist, for example, has suggested that there exists in each person both a fear of life (a fear of the uncertainty and loneliness of too much freedom) and a fear of death (a fear of the dullness and restriction of too little freedom). Another theorist has suggested that people are constantly making choices that leave them either feeling anxious because they have chosen the unknown or guilty because they have chosen the safe and familiar. This illustration represents the conflict between these two aspects of human life and the need of each person to find a balance between them.

something that would guide them and weld them together. He built a society that was unified and purposeful—but based on hatred and fear instead of love.

Love and Work

The true escape from the insecurity of freedom is not into tyranny but into love and work. In this way, man can become a part of mankind and nature again, without losing himself and his freedom. Fromm says that many people are confused about what real love and work are. They think that owning a person or being owned by one is love. They think that work is a chance to get away from feelings of loneliness, or a chance to enjoy conquering nature. But real love and real work mean a sensitivity and respect for the other person and for nature. The object is to join another person and become a part of

Figure 12.9
Carl Rogers' theories have had a considerable impact upon modern psychology and upon society in general. His views about personality were the first to seriously rival Freudian theory. Rogers has emphasized the personal experiences of humans rather than their drives and instincts, and he believes that psychology is being held back by those who retain an old-fashioned concept of science.

nature, without losing one's own individuality. One should not need to mold oneself, nature, or the person one loves in order to have relationships.

CARL ROGERS: YOUR SELF AND YOUR ORGANISM

O wad some Power the giftie gie us
To see oursels as ithers see us!
It wad frae monie a blunder free us,
    An' foolish notion . . .

from Robert Burns, To a Louse

You have probably felt this same way at times, though you might not have expressed your frustration in quite these accents. You may also have felt what the English poet Rudyard Kipling expressed in the lines: "If you can trust yourself when all men doubt you . . . "

These are points of view about personality that would interest psychologist Carl Rogers. Rogers believes that a conflict between what you truly value in yourself and what you learn about other people's evaluation of you is the basic problem in human life.

A personality has two systems regulating its behavior, Rogers says. One is the *organism,* which is the whole of a person, including his body. Rogers believes that the organism is constantly struggling to become more and more complete and perfect. Anything that furthers this end is good. The organism wants to become everything that it can possibly be. For example, children want to learn to walk and run because their bodies are built for these activities. People want to shout and dance and sing because their organisms contain the potential for these behaviors. Different people have different potentialities, but every person wants to realize them, to make them real, whatever they are. It is of no value to be able to paint and not to do it. It is of no value to be able to make witty jokes and not to do so. Whatever you can do, you want to do—and to do as well as possible.

The second system in a person is the *self.* The self is your experience of you, your actions, your thoughts, your feelings in relation to others. You form a picture of this self from the reactions of others, and one of the crucial questions, Rogers says, is whether this picture is positive or negative. A person needs to see himself in a favorable light, or as Rogers puts it, he needs *positive regard.* The trouble is that positive regard cannot come from inside. It must come from outside. A child's first experience of positive regard is his mother's love. He asks himself, "How does she see me?" and it is very important to him that the answer be, "She loves me. She likes what I am and what I do." If he sees that his mother does not feel this way about him, he will decide that the things she dislikes are bad. These decisions become part of his view of himself. He says to himself: "When I do this, I am bad," even if he really likes doing it. He develops what Rogers calls *conditions of worth.* That is, he can see himself as good only if he acts in certain ways and avoids acting in

Figure 12.10
A representation of the two systems that Carl Rogers believes exist in human personality. One is the organism, which values whatever leads to its own growth and perfection. The other is the self, which takes into account the reactions of other people in deciding what is good and bad, and which can therefore be misled.

certain other ways. He has learned from his mother and from other people who matter to him that unless he meets these conditions he will not be loved.

This, Rogers believes, is what happens to most people. The conditions of worth come into conflict with the values of the organism. The self is seen as bad when the organism wants to act in certain ways. For example, suppose that a person has a capacity for anger and feels right about becoming very angry when someone is doing him wrong. Suppose, also, that during his childhood this person's mother and family were frightened of his anger and considered it to be bad. Because the people around him as a child felt this way, he now sees himself as bad when he gets angry. Consequently, he tries never to get angry, even though he has a great potential for anger that he very much wants to express when it is aroused.

There is now a state of disharmony between the self and the organism. The self cannot admit that certain things about the organism are true. It pretends that the organism is wrong, or that it does not exist. When a person is in such a state, he cannot be what Rogers calls *fully functioning*. To return to such a state a person must get rid of the conditions of worth and learn to give himself positive regard. Then he can accept his organism and become open to all his own experiences and hence to other people.

ABRAHAM MASLOW: GROWTH AND SELF-ACTUALIZATION

. . . it is precisely the god-like in ourselves that we are ambivalent about, fascinated by and fearful of, motivated to and defensive against. This is one aspect of the basic human predicament, that we are simultaneously worms and gods . . .

from Abraham Maslow, *Toward a Psychology of Being*

Figure 12.11

Abraham Maslow was deeply interested in the study of human growth, or, in his terms, "self-actualization." The work of Maslow, Rogers, and others has helped to create a humanistic orientation toward the study of human behavior by emphasizing the actualization of an individual's full potentialities.

Figure 12.12

A representation of Maslow's view of human life as beginning humbly but growing magnificently. Maslow was deeply interested in the ability and need of all human beings to grow toward greater creativity, greater wisdom, and greater devotion to beauty and goodness.

Psychologists who stress the uniqueness of the individual, who focus on the value, dignity, and worth of the person, and who feel that healthy living is the result of realizing one's full potential are known as *humanists*. Erich Fromm and Carl Rogers are humanists, but in the words above, Abraham Maslow makes the point of humanism as clearly as it can be made in a few words.

Growth Needs and Deficiency Needs

Maslow believes that human beings are capable of two kinds of needs, *deficiency* needs and *growth* needs. Maslow says that deficiency needs are like holes that must be filled. If they are not filled, you get sick. You must have food, water, and shelter, for example. You must also have protection from disaster. If you do not, you will never be free from worry. In addition, you need to feel that you belong, that you are loved, that you are respected, and you need to be able to respect yourself. Maslow says that all these things are basic; you need love, admiration, sunlight, and vitamin C all in just the same way. Without them you are crippled, stunted, or sick.

The other kinds of needs, growth needs, are quite different. These are the needs that make man godlike, in Maslow's opinion. They are needs to become more and more yourself. They are like the values of the organism described by Rogers. A person wants to develop the abilities and talents he finds in himself; to fulfill his destiny, his fate, or his calling; to know more and more of himself; and to bring the parts of himself into greater harmony, so that he no longer suffers from self-doubt, inner conflict, or confusion.

Maslow points out that it is difficult to work on growth needs if one has deficiency needs. Growth cannot proceed if one has to spend time just trying to survive. The strain, for instance, on a child who must compete or fight for love from his parents will make it extremely difficult for him to concentrate on becoming a warm and generous person himself.

Self-actualization

But whatever the conditions, people continue to need to grow and to strive for perfection and expression. Maslow speaks of an inner nature that speaks softly but insistently in every person. This inner core is never bad or evil. It is either good or merely neutral. It is not a strong force. To discover and uncover it is hard, and it is sometimes extremely painful.

A person who is uncovering, expressing, and developing his inner nature, a person who is moved by his need to grow, is in the process of *self-actualizing*. Self-actualization is not a process that has an end; it is a way of being, by continuously becoming more yourself, more human, and more godlike than you are now.

Maslow believed that relatively few people become highly self-actualized. He counted a few among his friends, and he thought that such historical figures as Abraham Lincoln, Henry David Thoreau,

Ludwig van Beethoven, Eleanor Roosevelt, and Albert Einstein were good examples. Maslow characterized such people as follows:

1. They *perceive reality* very accurately, unlike most people who, because of prejudices, and wishful thinking, perceive it rather inaccurately.

2. They *accept themselves, other people* and the *natural world* for what they are, instead of rejecting them or trying to change them to what they would like them to be, as many people do. Such a person would feel no shame, for example, about his sexual desires.

3. They are *spontaneous.* They trust their impulses and act freely on them.

4. They are *problem-centered* rather than self-centered: They concentrate their attention on something outside themselves, a problem to be solved, a mystery to be penetrated, rather than thinking selfishly about themselves and their own feelings.

5. They are *detached* and *desire privacy.* They are not always interested in what is going on around them, though they are aware of it, and they often feel a need to be by themselves, away from all distractions.

6. They are *autonomous* and *resist conformity to the culture.* They do not go along with the crowd or seek support from it.

7. They *appreciate* people and things freshly and richly. They do not become jaded or habitual or lukewarm in their reactions. Ecstasy is a common experience to them, as is agony.

8. Most of them have had profound *mystical* or *spiritual* experiences, although not necessarily religious in character.

9. They *identify with mankind.* They can see things from the point of view of a human being—not just from the point of view of a student or a teacher, a white or a black, an American or a Chinese.

10. They have *intimate, deeply emotional relationships* with a few special people, rather than many superficial relationships.

11. Their values and attitudes are *democratic.*

12. They are highly *creative* and *original.*

13. They have a strong *sense of humor,* but the things they find amusing are never things that hurt other people, put other people down, or embarrass them.

Maslow's self-actualized person is a rare and valuable one. But each person, by making the hard decision to realize his own inner nature and goodness to the fullest, and by sticking to that decision, can move toward that goal.

PERSONALITY THEORY: DEEP PHILOSOPHY OR HARD SCIENCE?

As one moves from the pessimistic picture painted by Freud, who saw an instinct-driven organism clashing with society, to the optimistic views of Maslow, in which man is in the act of making himself free, one realizes that there are many remarkably different ways of looking at human personality.

In recent years, two diverse approaches to the study of human personality have become popular—*existentialism* and *behaviorism.* A comparison of the two reveals some of the basic issues with which personality theorists must deal. Neither of these approaches is really a theory of personality so much as it is an attitude toward human life.

Existentialism

Existentialism had its start in a chaotic, war-torn Europe and grew out of a philosophical wondering about the nature of man and the meaning of existence to the individual. It is, by definition, a *subjective* approach, and only recently have existentialist ideas been incorporated into a personality-theory context. Existentialist psychologists approach human behavior from the standpoint of *free will.* That means that human action is a result of choice and is not determined by physical or divine forces over which the individual has no control. Existentialists maintain that man creates himself every time he makes a decision; that is, you are who you are because of what you choose to do and who you choose to be.

As a result of this emphasis, existential psychology treats personality on the basis of the decisions that a person makes. It emphasizes the present situation of the individual and how he goes about making decisions for his future. The psychologically healthy individual is the person who makes rational choices and shows the courage to live and act at his best even in the face of possible death. The famous French philosopher Jean Paul Sartre once said, "Freedom is what you do with what's been done to you."

Behaviorism

Behaviorial psychologists maintain that the freedom and dignity championed by the existentialists are illusions. They say that personality is determined by what the person is born with (hereditary characteristics) and what has happened to him since (environmental factors). Unlike the existentialists, behaviorists look at the individual *objectively,* that is, from the outside. Behavioral psychologists are concerned with aspects of human behavior that are dependent upon factors outside the individual's area of control. For this reason, behaviorism takes a *deterministic* attitude toward human action— that is, it emphasizes that all choice and action are determined by external causes.

This line of reasoning is based on the concepts and principles of learning theory (described in Chapter 6). B. F. Skinner, the most famous living behaviorist, has stated that he objects to the idea of an inner man, or self, that causes one to behave in certain ways. He maintains that people behave as they do because they have been rewarded or punished for their behaviors. Therefore, any un-

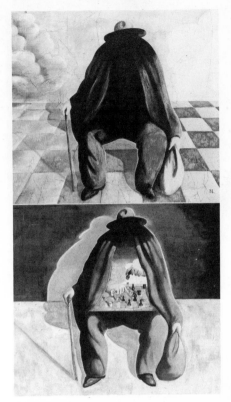

Figure 12.13
An interpretation of existential theory. Existentialists emphasize that a person must assume responsibility for his own actions because only through accepting responsibility can he create meaning in his own life. They stress that the individual learn to "control his own chessboard" rather than be a "pawn of fate."

Figure 12.14
B. F. Skinner is the most famous living behaviorist; he is not considered to be a theorist of personality. Nevertheless, behaviorism, which emphasizes the development of personality through conditioning and learning, is now a major force in the area of personality theory. Skinner believes that external forces rather than inner choices make people what they are.

Figure 12.15
Jean-Paul Sartre is the major force in modern existential thought. He believes that the exercising of free will is what makes humans unique and that because of this free will, man can become anything he wishes. According to Sartre, it is a mistake to think that man is forced by his instincts or by his environment to behave one way rather than another.

desirable behavior can be changed by applying new rewards or punishments.

Both these theories have implications for how you should live your life. According to the behaviorists, if you want to change yourself, you must change your environment—the things that reward and punish you. According to the existentialists, the environment is not something that can be controlled, so any changes must come from within yourself.

Modern personality theory is a product of the twentieth century and of the experiences and thoughts of men such as Freud, Fromm, and Maslow. Freud developed his theory in a medical context, from the experiences of his patients and his own self-analysis. A great man in the field, he both attracted and repelled his contemporaries, including Jung. Other psychologists, such as Adler and Maslow, developed theories to balance Freud's image of man as a mass of sexual impulses.

Existentialism developed in a European society in which man's roots and personal relationships were torn apart. Behaviorism developed in a relatively safe, industrial and mechanical society in which alienation, rather than brotherhood or a sense of community, is the prevailing way of life. As society changes, so, too, will theories of personality, for new information will be learned, new problems will be faced, and new approaches will be needed.

SUMMARY

1. Personality theories provide a way of organizing information about oneself and other people; they can be used to explain similarities and differences between people; they provide a set of guidelines for setting up an approach to life; and they provide a means for recognizing goals and achieving growth.

2. Freudian theory centers around the unconscious and the important role it plays in an individual's personality. The conscious and unconscious mind is like a powerful energy system. Energy from the id is diverted into two other areas: the ego and the superego.

3. Defense mechanisms are unconscious solutions to conflict situations. Stress and anxiety are reduced by denial, falsification, or distortion of reality. Some common defense mechanisms are displacement, repression, projection, and regression.

4. Jung believed that personality is made up of opposites and that the tension between these opposites is the source of mental energy. The collective unconscious is a universally shared inheritance of instincts, urges, and memories called archetypes.

5. Extraversion and introversion are terms Jung used to describe two opposite ways of looking at the world. Extraverted people look outward; introverted people look inward.

6. Individuation is Jung's term for the process by which man integrates the strong and weak fragments of his personality. It is a "journey of the soul" that leads to true understanding of oneself.

7. Adler believed that the main motivating force in the development of personality is the effort to overcome feelings of inferiority. Childhood experiences such as overpampering or neglect set the pattern for adult life styles. The healthy personality is one that is built on an effective life style, which includes a strong social interest.

8. Fromm's theory of personality centers around the conflict between man's need for a unique and separate identity and his need for relatedness with society and all mankind.

9. Fromm distinguishes between two types of character, the productive and the nonproductive. He believes that the price of freedom is loneliness and the loss of the sense of belonging and of purpose, and the only way out of this dilemma is not through escaping from freedom but through real love and real work.

10. Rogers' theory focuses on the organism and the self and the person's need for positive regard. Anxiety and maladjustment occur when the person experiences a conflict between his own idea of his worth and how other people experience him.

11. Maslow's theory of personality and his characteristics of a self-actualized person are based on man's ability to satisfy his growth needs as well as his deficiency needs.

12. Existential theories of personality place heavy emphasis on man's freedom of choice and on his responsibility for his decisions and actions.

13. Behaviorism, based on the principles of learning theory, views personality in terms of scientific laws of behavior. Skinner and his followers believe that people can be trained to live effectively and happily through the application of conditioning principles to the individual and to his society.

Figure 12.16
Several personality theorists have developed modified versions of Freud's theory. Two such theorists who have gained prominence are Karen Horney (*top*) and Erik Erikson (*bottom*). Horney identified three basic social patterns in human personality: moving *toward* people, moving *against* them, and moving *away* from them. She also considered Freud's views about women to be mistaken; she has suggested that psychological differences between the sexes are due more to cultural than to biological factors. Erikson's theories are described in Chapter 8.

ACTIVITIES

1. Make a list of the qualities and characteristics that you think should compose an ideal person. Now rate a few of your friends on each item on a scale of 1 to 7. Ask them to do the same for you, then compare the analyses. Do different people have different ideas about what is ideal? Do you see yourself in the same way that your friends see you?

2. What are the key features of your own personality? What are the key features of the personalities of each of your parents? Compare your personality with that of your parents. There will be both similarities and differences. Because one's parents are necessarily such highly influential forces in a child's development, it may be of greater interest to note the chief differences in personalities. Then try

Figure 12.17
Harry Stack Sullivan, another influential personality theorist, was a psychiatrist who worked with young people considered to be schizophrenic. He believed that it is incorrect to view personality as something within the individual; he proposed, instead, that it be viewed as the pattern of interactions between an individual and others. Sullivan presented this view in his book *An Interpersonal Theory of Psychiatry*.

to identify the factors responsible for those differences. For example, what key individuals or events have influenced or redirected the course of your life or changed your habits of living? How have society's institutions affected you?

3. Which psychologist or theory of personality presented in this chapter seems to hold the most value for you in terms of usefulness or relevance to your life? Write a brief summary of the appropriate theory, explaining how and why you find it of value.

4. The text contains a list of characteristics that Maslow found to be representative of people whom he described as "self-actualized." Choose from among your acquaintances a few whom you especially respect or admire for "doing their own thing," people who achieve satisfaction by being who and what they are. Ask them to list what they see as their distinguishing personality characteristics. Compare their answers and your observations with Maslow's list. In addition, compare this information with Jung's idea of individuation, Fromm's productive person, and Rogers' fully-functioning person. Do the theories adequately describe the characteristics you admire? Are they consistent with them?

5. Jung believed that people are unconsciously linked to their ancestral past. Can you think of any evidence for or against the "collective unconscious" Jung described? Which, if any, of your own experiences lend support to or deny this theory?

6. Make a collage that depicts your particular personality, using pictures and words from magazines and newspapers. For example, include your likes, dislikes, hobbies, personality traits, appearance, and so on.

7. Look and listen for "Freudian slips." Write them down and try to determine the relevance of each slip.

8. Listen to conversations of several friends, relatives, teachers, and so on. Try to identify their use of defense mechanisms and write down the circumstances surrounding their use. Try to listen to your own conversations and do the same for yourself. Why do you think people use defense mechanisms?

9. Adler placed great importance on social interest, or a feeling for others. You can explore this idea in your own life. Make a two-column chart titled "Things I Do for Others," and "Things Others Do for Me." Keep a record of these events for a week. Your social interest depends on your life style. What do the entries on this chart tell you about your life style?

10. Erich Fromm wrote about specific needs, such as the need to be rooted, to have a frame of reference, to have an identity, and to transcend. What do you think Fromm would say about the current trend for more ethnic courses in high school and colleges? Do these courses meet these needs? At what expense to the concept of

humanity? Are the desires for such courses a result of needs not met? Which ones?

SUGGESTED READINGS

FROMM, ERICH. *Escape from Freedom.* New York: Holt, Rinehart and Winston, 1941. In this important work, Fromm explores the problems of freedom and loneliness. He develops the thesis that man can resolve his dilemma through love and work.

FROMM, ERICH. *Man for Himself—An Inquiry into the Psychology of Ethics.* New York: Holt, Rinehart and Winston, 1947. An interesting, well-written book that discusses in depth the relationship between psychology and morality.

HALL, CALVIN S. *Primer of Freudian Psychology.* Cleveland: World Publishing, 1954 (paper). A good introduction to Freudian theory. The book is clearly written and emphasizes Freud's contributions to the psychology of "normal" people.

JUNG, CARL. *Memories, Dreams, Reflections.* New York: Vintage, 1961 (paper). A beautifully written autobiography that is bound to leave any reader with deep respect and admiration for this highly original thinker and writer.

MASLOW, ABRAHAM. *Toward a Psychology of Being.* New York: Van Nostrand, 1968. Maslow, one of the founders of humanistic psychology, directs current thinking away from its obsession with the "normal" person and focuses on the "healthy" person.

MAY, ROLLO. *Love and Will.* New York: Norton, 1969. May views therapy not as an attempt to cure but as assistance in self-exploration. He emphasizes the forces of love and the daimonic—the natural functions that contain vitality and creativity but that also have the power to possess a person. He also emphasizes the will because it contains consciousness, intentionality, and hence, meaning.

PERLS, FREDERICK S. *In and Out the Garbage Pail.* Lafayette, Calif.: Real People Press, 1969. This unique book combines autobiography, theory, and practical application to form a thoroughly enjoyable and painless introduction to the foremost exponent of Gestalt psychology.

ROGERS, CARL. *On Becoming a Person.* Boston: Houghton Mifflin, 1961. Rogers presents a clear and thorough description of the humanistic theory of personality. This is an important work in that it was the first major rival to traditional Freudian theory.

SKINNER, B. F. *Beyond Freedom and Dignity.* New York: Knopf, 1971. Skinner proposes a solution to the world's problems based on the deliberate manipulation of behavior by conditioning techniques.

Figure 12.18
Gordon Allport, one of the most famous American theorists, emphasized the study of normal, productive adults as opposed to animals, children, or mental patients. He felt that most personalities could be described by a few significant traits, such as desire to simplify or love of gardening. Allport was one of the first psychologists to emphasize the role of the self.

13
Disturbance and Breakdown

DEFINING ABNORMALITY
THE PROBLEM OF CLASSIFICATION
NEUROSIS:
Anxiety / Phobias / Obsessions and compulsions / Hysteria / Depression and suicide
PSYCHOSIS:
Schizophrenia / Affective reactions / Possible causes
PERSONALITY DISORDERS
MENTAL RETARDATION
ALCOHOLISM AND DRUG ADDICTION

Figure 13.1
The experiences and actions of people who are called "disturbed," or "mentally ill," are often only extreme forms of the depressed moods, irrational fears, and self-doubts that disturb everyone from time to time. This man was playing baseball on the grounds of a mental hospital when, in the middle of a play, he left the game, lay down, and withdrew himself under his coat. You have probably felt so depressed at times that you have wanted to withdraw in a similar fashion.

Humans invent labels for other humans, groups, movements, or objects because labels provide a handy way to briefly describe something that would otherwise take several sentences to explain. But one of the problems with using labels is that most of them do not provide everyone with the same mental picture. Most people will agree, for example, that a "mutt" is a dog of mixed breeds, but few will picture the same dog. The English language provides many words, or labels, to describe people who seem different from the ordinary: Words such as "abnormal," "crazy," "insane," and "lunatic" are freely used among people in Western society. And all these words have negative associations. What no one seems to agree upon, however, is what these labels mean. Psychological disturbance is not an all-or-nothing phenomenon. Disorder exists in degrees, from mild to very severe, and few people are entirely free from psychological problems. But many people are unwilling to consider the idea of their own "abnormality" because of the overwhelmingly negative feelings attached to that particular label.

Psychologists at Stanford University tried to find out what it means to be labeled as abnormal. They asked eight ordinary people to attempt to get themselves admitted to twelve different mental hospitals around the country. Among the eight people were a psychology graduate student, three psychologists, a pediatrician, a psychiatrist, a painter, and a housewife.

Each phony patient told the admissions officers of the hospitals the truth about his family background and his present feelings and lied only about his name and his real reason for being there. Each fake patient complained of being bothered by disembodied voices that said things like "empty," "hollow," and "thud." Apart from mak-

Figure 13.2
When a person is judged "abnormal,"
it often means that the person does not fit
into the society of those who judge him.
Thus, although almost everyone would
agree that a man convicted of several
senseless murders is "sick," not everyone
would agree that a drug-taking hippie is
"crazy" or that a hippie-hating construction
worker is "inhuman."

ing this complaint, each patient acted quite normally. In every case but one, the patient was diagnosed as mentally ill and was admitted to the hospital.

Once inside the institutions, the people stopped pretending that they heard voices and began taking notes about their surroundings. Staff members considered the note-taking to be part of the patient's sickness. The only people who were able to tell that these patients were faking were the real patients. In some cases, as many as one-third of the real patients voiced their suspicions. One patient told a faker, "You're not crazy. You're a journalist or a professor. You're checking up on the hospital."

The phony patients were all released from the hospital after a few days or weeks but not because they were discovered to be fakers. The hospital records simply said that they had stopped showing the symptoms of their illness. They were still labeled as "mentally ill." Apparently, once hospital staff members decided that the people were "crazy," they assumed that all their behavior must be "crazy."

This study raises many important questions: On what basis did the officials diagnose mental illness? How could the real patients tell that the phony patients were faking? What is the difference between a real mental patient and a normal person who has simply been labeled as mentally ill? What makes one person "normal" and another "abnormal"? In short, what is a psychological disorder or abnormality, how can it be identified, and how should it be dealt with? These questions are the subject of this chapter and of Chapter 14.

DEFINING ABNORMALITY

Psychologists use the word *abnormal* to refer to the wide range of behaviors that have traditionally been referred to as "insane," "sick," "crazy," "disturbed," and so on. There are a number of ways to define abnormality, but, unfortunately, none of them seems to be entirely satisfactory. The major approaches to such a definition include the deviance approach, the adjustment approach, the legal approach, and the psychological health model.

Deviation from Normality

One approach to defining abnormality is to say that whatever most people do is normal; thus, abnormality is any *deviation* from the average or from the majority. Following this line of reasoning, it is normal to bathe periodically, to get turned on to the opposite sex, and to laugh when tickled, because most people do so. But because few people take ten showers a day, find horses sexually attractive, or laugh when a loved one dies, these behaviors may be considered abnormal.

On closer examination, however, this definition of abnormality presents several difficulties. If the majority of people smoke cigarettes, are nonsmokers abnormal? If most people cheat on their income tax returns, are honest taxpayers abnormal? If most people are noncreative, is the brilliant artist abnormal? Because the majority is not always right, the deviance approach to defining abnormality is not really useful.

Adjustment

Another attempt at a solution to the problem is to say that the normal person is one who is able to get along in the world—physically, emotionally, and socially. He is able to feed and clothe himself, to work, to find friends, and to live by the rules of society. By this definition, an abnormal person is one who fails to *adjust*. He may be so unhappy that he refuses to eat or so lethargic that he cannot hold a job. Contact with other people may make him so anxious that he avoids them and lives in a lonely world of his own. Or he may be so filled with anger and hate that he is in frequent conflict with parents, teachers, and the police.

The idea that the psychologically healthy person is one who can adjust to his environment seems to make good sense. But a disturbing question arises: Just what is it that he is adjusting to? For example, were the people that adjusted to the Nazism of Hitler's Germany normal? Is it normal to adjust to the air in Los Angeles or to the crime in New York? In some cases, it seems that the normal, healthy person is the one who fails to adjust and who, in fact, fights back.

The Legal Approach

The terms "sane" and "insane" are not used by psychologists but rather are *legal* distinctions. A person is called legally insane if it is judged that he cannot understand the difference between right and wrong or that he is unable to control his own actions. If normality is defined in terms of sanity, then the normal person is one who is able to exercise a certain amount of judgment and who is able to take responsibility for his own actions. A person who is unable to judge the rightness or wrongness of his behavior or who cannot control what he does is considered potentially dangerous to others and is considered insane or at least incompetent in the eyes of the law.

This approach raises many questions, however. How does one account for the numerous people in mental hospitals who are obviously psychologically disturbed but who are also obviously harmless? How does one distinguish between legal "wrong" and moral "wrong"? And how can one *know* that the individual in question cannot distinguish right from wrong or that his behavior is out of his control?

Psychological Health

The terms "mental illness" and "mental health" imply that psychological disturbance or abnormality is like a physical sickness—such as the flu or tuberculosis. Although many psychologists are beginning to think that "mental illness" is a completely different sort of thing from physical illness, the idea remains that there is some ideal way

Figure 13.3

A still from the film *Who's Afraid of Virginia Woolf?* This powerfully emotional drama (based on Edward Albee's play) portrays one night in the lives of two couples: George and Martha (Richard Burton and Elizabeth Taylor) and Nick and Honey (George Segal and Sandy Dennis). This play won wide critical acclaim because Albee so accurately (and painfully) exposed the inner conflicts of a "normal" and "stable" marriage to reveal nightmares that are recognizable to millions. What is frightening is that this play is not about "mental illness"—it is about the people next door.

for people to function psychologically, just as there is physically. Some psychologists feel that the normal or healthy person would be one who is functioning ideally or who at least is striving toward ideal functioning.

Personality theorists such as Carl Jung and Abraham Maslow (see Chapter 12) have tried to describe this striving process, which is often referred to as *self-actualization*. According to this approach, being normal or healthy involves full acceptance and expression of one's own individuality and humanness. Accomplishing this task is difficult, and some psychiatrists think that for some people, going "crazy" for a while may actually be part of the growth process. It is thought that such people find major problems in their lives impossible to solve, so they "drop out" of life for a while in order to reorganize their personalities. During this period of reorganization they act peculiarly, but they eventually emerge better equipped to face the world than ever before.

One problem with this approach to defining abnormality is that it is difficult to determine whether or not a person is doing a good job of actualizing himself. How can you tell when a person is doing his best? What are the signs that he is losing the struggle? Answers to such questions must often be arbitrary.

The fact that it is difficult to define abnormality does not mean that there is no such thing as abnormality or that no one is mentally disturbed. It does imply, however, that one should be cautious about judging a person to be abnormal just because he acts in an unexpected or unexplained manner. It should also be kept in mind that mild psychological disorders are common. It is when a psychological problem becomes severe enough to disrupt everyday life that it becomes thought of as "abnormality" or "illness."

THE PROBLEM OF CLASSIFICATION

There obviously are people who are hopelessly unhappy, whose minds are confused and chaotic, who have a difficult time doing the simple things in life, or who act in ways that are harmful to other people. For years psychiatrists and other scientists have been seeking a logical and useful method for classifying such problems. So far, they have not been particularly successful, mostly because psychological problems do not lend themselves to the same sort of categorizing that physical illnesses do.

The classification scheme presently in use contains hundreds of categories and subcategories of psychological disorders. This scheme has many drawbacks. For one, two psychologists may give completely different diagnoses of the same patient. For another, few patients fit nicely into the scheme; most disturbed people exhibit behavior typical of several different categories. Nevertheless, this scheme is the best anyone has managed to develop, and it does permit psychologists and psychiatrists to share information about symptoms and treatment and to compare notes on possible causes.

The scheme distinguishes two main types of disorders: neurosis and psychosis. *Neurosis* is a disorder in which the individual frequently experiences anxiety to such an extent that it reduces his ability to deal with reality. *Psychosis* is a disorder in which the individual is often unable to deal with reality at all. Psychosis is not an advanced stage of neurosis—they are considered as two distinct types of psychological disturbance.

The rest of this chapter will be devoted to a discussion of the varieties of neuroses and psychoses and to some of the other categories of psychological problems, including personality disorders, mental retardation, alcoholism, and drug addiction.

NEUROSIS

As you read the rest of this chapter, you should not be surprised if you feel that some of the descriptions could be applied to yourself at times—they probably could. A psychologically disturbed person is one who turns ordinary reactions into extreme and distorted patterns of behavior, and as has been mentioned, mild forms of psychological problems are not uncommon, particularly in neurosis.

The world of a neurotic person is real but painful. Such a person seldom acts in an alarmingly unusual fashion, but he is discomforted with life and deals with it inefficiently. His inner anxiety may be expressed in the form of worry and concern, or in depression or mood swings, or in any of a variety of bodily symptoms (headache, sweating, muscle tightness, weakness, fatigue). His anxiety makes him live a life marked by continuous upset and few periods of true tranquility.

Anxiety

Where does such anxiety come from? Neurotic *anxiety* is a generalized apprehension—a vague feeling that one is in danger. Unlike fear, which is a frank reaction to a real and identifiable danger, anxiety is a reaction to vague or imagined dangers. Most psychologists believe that neurotic anxiety is caused by internal feelings,

Figure 13.4
Anxiety and tension are the overriding features of neurosis. The neurotic has created a trap from which he does not know how to escape. His attempts to escape cause him to act in ways that other people find annoying or disturbing, and these responses of annoyance in turn produce further anxiety.

desires, or impulses that are so disturbing to the individual that he must pretend to himself that they are not there. It is the continuous (unconscious) effort to hide these feelings that causes the person to feel anxious. Every once in a while, everyone feels a vague nervousness that he is unable to explain; but a severely neurotic person feels this way practically all the time.

Such anxiety feelings are painful, and the more a person suffers from them, the less he can truly enjoy life. Most people manage to cope with such anxiety, however, as long as their feelings remain bearable. But if the anxiety increases, the neurotic individual must take increasing steps to cope with it. He begins to focus so much on his internal problems that he neglects his social relationships. The people he sees every day recognize that he is anxious and uptight, but they are unable to see the source of his fears.

Such a person has trouble in relating to his family and friends and in upholding his responsibilities, and he begins to worry about these social troubles, thereby adding to his anxieties. He is trapped in a vicious circle. The more he worries, the more difficulty he has, and the more difficulty he has, the more he worries. If the neurotic can find no way to stop this cycle, it may end in a "nervous breakdown": The person is temporarily forced to give up his struggle with everyday life and find other people to look after him for a while.

Neurotics may develop a number of unusual behaviors as a result of anxiety. They may suffer from phobias, obsessions, compulsions, hysteria, or depression.

Phobias

When severe anxiety is focused on a particular object or situation, it is called a *phobia.* A phobia can focus on almost any object: high places (acrophobia), crowds (ocholophobia), closed places (claustrophobia), open spaces (agoraphobia), darkness (nyctophobia), and so on. The person with a phobia has a persistent, irrational, unwholesome fear of such objects or situations.

The neurotic builds an elaborate life plan to avoid that which he fears. For example, there are cases of people who have developed such a fear of crowds that they stop going to movies or shopping in busy stores. In some cases, such people have reached the point where they will not leave their houses at all.

There are a number of theories as to how a phobia develops. It is thought that some phobias are the result of frightening experiences in the past. For example, a person's claustrophobia may have been caused by having been locked in a closet as a child. The person realizes that closets are not harmful, yet he feels a distinct dread of enclosed places. Most people have similar fearful feelings about objects associated with past unhappiness.

Neurotic fears, however, do not always have such straightforward explanations. A phobia may often be explained in terms of *projection*—what is really feared is an impulse inside oneself; to avoid this

Figure 13.5
Phobias, or irrational fears, are useful tools for the neurotic. They provide him with an outlet for his anxiety without forcing him to confront the real source of the anxiety. For example, the man in the illustration who is exhibiting a phobia about ladybugs may in fact be frightened of women. By releasing his fear in this way, he spares himself the ordeal of having to face his real problem. A second function that phobias serve is to command the attention and sympathy that the neurotic individual cannot get (or thinks he cannot get) in more direct ways.

fear one projects it onto some object outside himself (see Chapter 12). For example, a person who fears heights may really fear an inner impulse to destroy himself. By concentrating on avoiding heights, he hopes to foil his self-destructive urges.

Obsessions and Compulsions

When a person is suffering from severe anxiety, he may find himself thinking certain thoughts over and over again, even though he finds them distasteful. Such an uncontrollable pattern of *thoughts* is called an *obsession*. When a person finds himself engaging repeatedly in irrational *actions,* he is said to have a *compulsion*. Obsessions and compulsions often go together.

A compulsive person may feel compelled to carefully wash his hands twenty or thirty times a day, or he may feel a need to avoid stepping on cracks in the sidewalk when he goes out. A person with an obsession may be unable to rid himself of unpleasant thoughts of death or of a recurring impulse to make obscene remarks in public.

Everyone is capable of obsessions and compulsions. Love has been described as an obsession, and people's hobbies are sometimes described in the same way. Striving to do something "perfectly" is often considered to be a compulsion. But if the person who is engrossed in his hobby or who aims for perfection is trying to further his life and improve himself, he is usually not considered neurotic. It is only when such interests crowd out necessities like having friends or earning a living that they are described as abnormal.

The neurotically obsessive or compulsive person is regularly laden with worry and doubt. He fears that he has failed to do something that is important to his welfare and to the well-being of his loved ones, and he may spend so much time double-checking everything he does that he accomplishes very little.

It is thought that obsessions and compulsions help the neurotic to reduce his anxiety over his real fears because they serve as diversions from the real origins. In addition, compulsions provide the neurotic with the evidence that he is doing something well, even if it is being able to avoid cracks in the sidewalk. Thus, there is a logic in his illogical behavior.

Hysteria

Neurotic anxiety can also create a wide variety of physical symptoms with no apparent physical causes. This phenomenon is known as *hysteria*. Hysteria is divided into two types: *conversion reactions* and *dissociative reactions*.

Conversion Reactions   In conversion reactions, emotional difficulties are said to be converted into loss of a specific physiological function. Many people occasionally experience mild forms of hysteria, as when someone is so scared that he is "frozen stiff." But neurotic hysteria is more enduring than a brief experience of fright. A hysteric

Figure 13.6

A still from the film *The Caine Mutiny*, in which Humphrey Bogart convincingly portrayed Captain Queeg, an individual who was obsessed with order. Any disruption of Queeg's established routine (as when some strawberries disappeared) sent him into panic and produced the compulsive behavior of continually rolling ball bearings in his hand. Queeg's odd behavior led his officers to label him "mentally ill" and to mutiny against him.

experiences a real loss of hearing, speech, touch, or the ability to move his muscles.

He might awaken one morning and find himself paralyzed from the waist down, deaf, or blind. A normal reaction to such a traumatic event would be violent upset, but the hysteric often accepts his condition with relatively little concern. It is thought that he has unconsciously invented the physical symptoms to provide freedom from the anxiety that has been making life miserable for him.

Hysteria should be distinguished from *hypochondria,* in which a person, despite good health, preoccupies himself with imaginary ailments and blames all his problems on them. Hysteria should also be distinguished from *psychosomatic* illnesses, in which emotional problems have produced real physical damage (see Chapter 5). Something real has happened to the hysteric, but not physically. It is interesting to note that Sigmund Freud's first cases were hysterics. Such disorders were common in his day but are rather rare now.

Dissociative Reactions   Hysteria may take the form of dissociative states, in which the person experiences a loss of memory or identity or exhibits two or more identities. These states are extremely interesting and revealing about the nature of human personality, and as a result one hears a good deal about them. But they are, in fact, quite rare, even more so than conversion reactions.

Loss of memory, or *amnesia,* is an all-out escape from the problems of life by simply blotting them out completely. The amnesiac remembers how to speak and use language and usually retains his

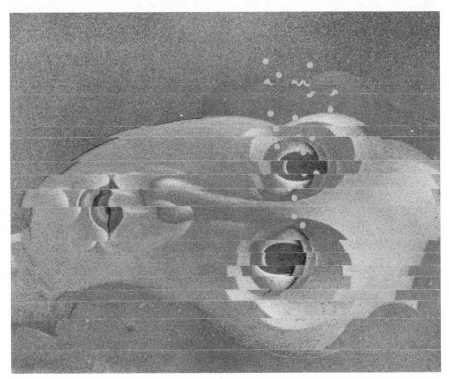

Figure 13.7

People suffering from hysterical dissociation usually experience considerable confusion, yet they seem unbothered by anxiety. In fact, the dissociation has developed precisely for that reason: to escape anxiety. If the individual is reminded of the anxiety-causing difficulties, his anxiety is likely to reappear.

fund of general knowledge of things like geography. But he usually denies knowing who he is, where he lives and works, and to whom he is related.

In the *fugue state,* the individual combines amnesia with a move to a new environment. He may establish a new, sometimes radically different identity in a new geographical location and deny all knowledge of his previous life. Fugue states seem to have the same psychological function as amnesia.

In *multiple personality,* another type of dissociative reaction, the individual seems to have two or more distinct identities that are unaware of each other. It is thought that such "alter egos" allow the individual to temporarily express parts of his personality that he has been trying to hide and to escape parts that he dislikes. An interesting case of this rare phenomenon is described in Chapter 4.

Depression

Depression is a pattern of sadness, anxiety, fatigue, insomnia, agitated behavior, and a reduced ability to function and work with others. It may range from a mild feeling of uneasiness and sadness to intense suicidal despair.

Depression is an experience common to everyone. When a healthy person suffers a severe loss, such as the death of a loved one, he is naturally saddened. And, from time to time, everyone feels "blue" for what seems to be no reason. But frequent, severe depression may be an escape from the responsibilities of life and of interpersonal relations. The neurotically depressed person may even seek out catastrophes to reinforce his notion that life is miserable and that he is not really responsible for the way things happen.

Depression may reflect guilt or a need for self-punishment. A depressed person may be unconsciously accepting the blame for some tragedy over which he had no control, such as the death of a loved one he feels he has neglected. Or he may use depression as an excuse for avoiding enjoyable activities in order to punish himself for some unconscious feeling of wrongdoing. In any case, depression often accompanies neurosis, and it is the most common complaint of people seeking psychiatric help.

Depression and Suicide

Some severely depressed people struggle on desperately. Others choose suicide as a permanent way out of a seemingly impossible life. Between 20,000 and 30,000 Americans (more men than women) kill themselves each year. Suicide is most common among the elderly, but it also ranks as the third leading cause of death among college students.

Everyone thinks about suicide sometime in his life, but comparatively few people give it serious consideration. Suicide is a fascinating but disturbing subject, and there are a number of misconceptions about it. It is commonly thought, for example, that people who

Figure 13.8
Neurotic depression frequently takes the form of apathy and withdrawal. The individual in this state simply stops caring about what is going on around him and may spend days or weeks at a time sitting or lying in a darkened room with nothing on his mind but his own feelings of gloom and despair. This state is typically produced by an overreaction to an experience that would be only a minor setback to a nonneurotic individual.

threaten suicide or who make an unsuccessful attempt are not really serious about taking their own lives. But studies show that about 70 percent of all persons who successfully commit suicide had threatened to do so within three months of the act and that an unsuccessful attempt often serves as a trial run.

The single factor most often associated with suicide is the individual's sense of helplessness. He sees his problems as unsolvable, with suicide as the only alternative. The elderly, for example, often conclude that suicide is a better alternative than a slow death from failing health.

Suicidal individuals tend to have such a low opinion of themselves that it becomes impossible for them to see how anyone else could care whether they live or die. They lose the ability to love themselves and come to believe that no one else could possibly love them either. Failure to communicate with others about his problems may confirm the person's suspicions. If he can talk to someone, even a stranger, about his suicidal mood, he may be able to realize that his problems are not as overwhelming as they seem.

Encouraging a depressed person to talk about his suicidal ideas often helps him to overcome them. A depressed person is usually unsure of his life and of his feelings. He may be equally unsure of whether or not he wants to kill himself. Such discussions provide him with an opportunity to talk about his problems and gives others information about the best ways to help him.

Depression, anxiety, phobias, obsessions, compulsions, hysteria—all are ways people use, in various combinations, to escape problems in themselves or the real world. But these neurotic reactions do not completely remove people from real life. Other kinds of reactions do. They are the psychoses.

PSYCHOSIS

The person with a neurosis was described as one who is emotionally crippled by anxiety but who continues to slug it out with life as best he can. The psychotic person is thought to be one whose distortions of perception and behavior reach such an irrational, fantastic, and fear-laden level that he withdraws completely from normal life. It has been said that the neurotic dreams in an unreal way about life, whereas the psychotic lives life as an unreal dream.

Like neurosis, psychosis is not a single problem; therefore, it has no single cause or single cure. It is, rather, a collection of symptoms that indicate that the individual is in serious trouble trying to meet the demands of life. Two of the major categories of psychosis are *schizophrenia* and *affective reactions*.

Schizophrenia

Schizophrenia is a condition in which the individual's thoughts, emotions, and perceptions are confused and disconnected. Of all the people staying in hospitals for psychiatric care, about one-third are

Figure 13.9
Feelings of helplessness and despair may be so overwhelming to a person that he or she feels that suicide is the only way out of a miserable and meaningless existence. For some people, suicide may be the final attempt to communicate a desperate need for love, help, or understanding.

("The Last Resort" by Käthe Kollwitz; courtesy of the National Gallery of Art, Washington, D.C., Rosenwald Collections.)

Figure 13.10

These illustrations were painted by a young man who exhibited behavior patterns characteristic of schizophrenia. Some of these patterns are revealed in his paintings. The illustration of a partially faceless woman alone in a desertlike setting suggests the withdrawal and absence of emotion that is common in schizophrenia. The painting of a globe being split apart seems to symbolically express the violence of the split the patient has experienced in himself. The last painting shows another feeling common in schizophrenia: a sense of sinister watchfulness. Schizophrenics often feel that they are being watched and that they, in turn, are watching the world.

Figure 13.11

These illustrations were painted by a male patient considered to be a chronic schizophrenic. Throughout, there are references to the therapist and the hospital staff, and there is a persistent use of intense colors to depict mythical, biblical, and historical events to express the feelings, attitudes, and concerns of the patient. The first painting (*top*) depicts the biblical story of Jonah and the whale, with implications of punishment and persecution. Also portrayed is the historical event of Washington crossing the Delaware. The second illustration (*bottom left*) portrays the mythical story of Romulus and Remus, and animals become a symbolic substitute for people. In the last painting (*bottom right*), a biblical theme as well as animals are again used to express the individual's psychological needs. An interesting example of the unusual and creative use of language in schizophrenia is shown in the first and last paintings. The religious, sexual, and historical themes are highly characteristic of schizophrenia.

Figure 13.12

The frantic excitement expressed in this painting by Joan Miró is reminiscent of the excitement and frenzy characteristic of some patient art. Although no one has suggested that Miró was mentally ill, it is interesting to consider how Miró himself describes the way he paints. The first stage, he says, is free and unconscious. He begins painting without knowing consciously what he is going to express. He lets the picture form itself. However, in the second stage, he uses careful, conscious control to continue and completes the form that appeared in the first stage. Many psychologists believe that schizophrenics similarly express their unconscious feelings in their art and their behavior but are unable to direct these feelings consciously and with restraint.

labeled schizophrenic. Although schizophrenia is common and although it has been the subject of extensive research and investigation, its nature is still poorly understood, its causes are not clear, and its cure is most uncertain.

One of the chief difficulties in understanding schizophrenia is the wide range of unusual behaviors exhibited by people who fall into this category. Symptoms can vary from apathy and withdrawal to silliness and bursts of rage.

People with simple forms of schizophrenia are not usually subject to hallucinations or delusions, nor do they commonly act in bizarre ways. Rather, they are dreary, apathetic human beings who make little or no contact with other people and who feel insecure in any but the most uncomplicated and undemanding situations. Most of the time they are emotionally indifferent and listless, but they may react aggressively toward family members or friends who comment on their apathy. They can sometimes hold jobs, particularly ones requiring unskilled labor and few interpersonal contacts, but they are generally described as "drifters."

Only in severe cases does the behavior of a schizophrenic become dramatically unusual. One such pattern of behavior is called *hebephrenia*. The speech of a hebephrenic person may be incoherent or unintelligible, or he may giggle or laugh unexpectedly. He lives in a private world dominated by hallucination, delusion, and fantasy, and his behavior is highly unpredictable. He may believe he is a famous person, such as Napoleon or Jesus, or he may be convinced that the world has come to an end and that he is its only survivor. A minute

Figure 13.13
The catatonic schizophrenic patient may spend a great deal of time in positions such as these, apparently oblivious of the world around him. However, this appearance of total withdrawal can be misleading. For example, when one group of visitors to a mental hospital was told by a staff member that the patient they were observing had not spoken for twenty years, the patient looked up and said, "What do you want me to say?"

later, he may urinate and defecate in his clothes and act like an infant.

Another kind of severe schizophrenic reaction is called *catatonia.* A catatonic person lives in a stuporous state. He can hold himself in painful postures for hours on end and not show any response to the physical discomfort that others would find impossible to bear. He may be mute and sit unmoving and unresponsive in the hospital ward. It is as if the catatonic is paralyzed by fear that any action or reaction on his part will jeopardize his already shaky, threatened security. His periods of inaction, however, may alternate with periods of violent activity, dangerous to himself and to others.

A third type of schizophrenic reaction is *paranoia.* The paranoid schizophrenic trusts no one and is constantly watchful, for he is convinced that others are plotting against him, sometimes out of the belief that they are jealous and envious of his superior ability or special status. Paranoia arises out of the general inability to correctly perceive reality that characterizes all types of schizophrenia.

Affective Reactions

Another common kind of psychosis is one in which individuals are excessively and inappropriately happy or unhappy. These *affective reactions* may take the form of high elation, hopeless depression, or an alternating combination of the two.

The *manic,* or highly elated, type of reaction is characterized by extreme confusion, disorientation, and incoherence. The patient's world is much like a movie that has been speeded up until the figures

317

Figure 13.14
Physical manifestations of depression have been characterized for centuries by physicians, novelists, and other observers. Some psychologists believe that chemical changes in the bodies of depressed people cause them to become incapable of receiving pleasure from their environment. As a result, psychologists have had some success in relieving depression by administering certain drugs or by applying electric shock to the brain.

Figure 13.14
Physical manifestations of depression have been characterized for centuries by physicians, novelists, and other observers. Some psychologists believe that chemical changes in the bodies of depressed people cause them to become incapable of receiving pleasure from their environment. As a result, psychologists have had some success in relieving depression by administering certain drugs or by applying electric shock to the brain.

and events are no more than a blur of purposeless movement. In the *depressive* reaction, the patient is overcome by feelings of failure, sinfulness, worthlessness, and despair. He may cut off all communication with others and descend to such a stuporous level of mental and physical inactivity that he is bedridden and has to be fed forcibly.

In some cases, referred to as *manic-depressive* psychosis, a patient will alternate between moods of frantic action and motionless despair. Theorists have suggested that the manic periods serve as a futile attempt to ward off the underlying hopelessness.

Causes of Psychosis

A small proportion of all people diagnosed as psychotic are known to have physical brain damage. The rest have nothing so obviously wrong with them. Their problems are the result of the interaction of many different factors, most of which are not well understood.

The difficulty of understanding or pinpointing a cause for psychosis is impressively illustrated by the problem of *autism,* a childhood psychosis that seems to be present from birth. From the earliest age, autistic children are aloof and uncommunicative. Often, they do not even cry or coo like other babies. They act as if other people do not exist, and they spend much of their time rocking back and forth, hitting themselves methodically, or examining spots on the floor. They become very upset over any change in their environment—they want things to be kept as much the same as possible.

These children are usually physically healthy; in fact, they are often quite beautiful, and their movements are quick and skillful. Psychologists have been at a loss to explain autistic behavior in a satisfactory way. Are these children born this way, or are they reacting unusually quickly to some peculiarity in their parents? Do they have some mysterious brain defect? Do their bodies produce too much or too little of certain vital chemicals? Have their parents given them some insoluble problem? Or are they suffering from some

Figure 13.15
Autistic children. Autism seems to be a complete withdrawal into another world. Persons who attempt to interact with a severely autistic child often feel that, at best, the child treats them as objects to be investigated or moved aside and, at worst, as though they were inhuman enemies. One mother described life with her autistic boy, Billy, as a nightmare. Billy would attack anything he could get his hands on, from his mother's dresses to his baby brother. When Billy's mother finally discovered that the one thing Billy feared was Alfred Hitchcock, she put Hitchcock's picture on the bathroom door to protect herself when she wanted some peace.

overpowering anxiety? Although this set of questions has been applied to autism, it could be applied to almost any psychosis. Most psychologists believe that all these factors play some part in mental disturbance.

Hereditary Factors   There is some evidence that a tendency toward mental illness can be inherited. Close relatives of schizophrenics, for example, are more likely to become schizophrenic than are other people. Just how such a tendency could be inherited is a matter of speculation. According to one theory, people are born with different kinds of nervous systems. Some respond strongly and persistently to outside stimulation; others respond less strongly. Some form new reactions extremely quickly; others, more slowly. If a person has inherited an extreme type of nervous system, he may overreact or underreact to stress or complexity and begin to behave crazily. A situation that might be only mildly upsetting to one person might be enough to cause a psychotic reaction in an extremely sensitive person. If this or some similar theory is correct, it could be possible for certain individuals to inherit a *tendency* to become disturbed. Whether one actually does develop a disorder, however, depends on the amount of stress and complexity he must deal with. Given a relatively simple, pressure-free environment, he may never experience disorder.

Biochemical Factors   The proper working of the brain depends on the presence of the right amounts of many different chemicals, from oxygen to proteins. Some psychologists believe that abnormal behavior is due to chemical imbalances or irregularities in the body. They believe that certain drugs are helpful in treating mental patients because they help to bring the body's chemicals back into balance.

Some researchers have actually been able to find unusual concentrations of certain chemicals in the bodies of schizophrenic patients. However, it is hard to tell if these chemicals are the cause of the disorder or a result of it. Also, mental patients may show a different biochemistry simply because they all eat the same food, get little exercise, and are given various drugs daily.

Conflict   It has been suggested that many mental problems, particularly those that involve confusion of thought and isolation from other people, are due to conflicts in communication. The psychologists who subscribe to this theory believe that a child's ability to think and to communicate with others can be undermined by parents who repeatedly communicate contradictory messages. For example, a mother may resent her child and feel uncomfortable around him yet also feel obligated to act lovingly toward him. She may therefore tell her child how much she loves him but stiffen her body whenever he touches her or wants to hug her. Thus, the child is given one message in words and another in action. He is said to be caught in a *double bind* because no matter what he does, it is wrong.

The double bind is commonly expressed as "damned if you do, and damned if you don't." The child is in an impossible situation. If he reaches out to his mother, she shows him (in her actions) that she dislikes it. If he avoids her, she tells him (in words) that she dislikes that. He wants very much to please her but finds it impossible.

According to the double-bind theory, a childhood full of such contradictory messages causes the individual to believe that the

Figure 13.16
This figure represents a paradox—a contradiction in which there is no way one can win. Paradoxes are called double binds when one is forced to accept the terms. Frequent exposure to such situations may be a cause of schizophrenia.

world is a confusing, disconnected place and that his words and actions have little significance or meaning. He thus develops the bizarre language and social ineptness of the mentally disturbed.

PERSONALITY DISORDERS

Some individuals develop unusual ways of behaving that are not so bizarre as those of psychoses or so involved with anxiety as those of neuroses. People who are diagnosed as having such *personality disorders* seem unable to develop appropriate relationships with work or with other people.

There are a number of patterns of personality disorder that all share the characteristics of being lifelong maladaptive ways of behavior that are difficult to change and that are not caused by physical factors. Here, the focus will be on one such pattern, the *antisocial personality.*

The antisocial individual, often referred to as a psychopath or sociopath, is characterized by a lack of conscience and an inability to feel guilt. Such people are often irresponsible, emotionally shallow humans who are frequently in trouble with authorities. Some are in aggressive and open rebellion against society; others are criminals that prey on others as a way of life. The antisocial personality is further characterized by selfishness, impulsivity, an intolerance of the normal frustrations that others usually take for granted, and seeking of immediate gratification at the expense of more important and valuable long-term goals.

The person with an antisocial personality may be intelligent and charming, but his relationships with others are emotionless—without depth, love, or loyalty. He mimics human emotions that he cannot feel, and he cannot organize his life past the pleasures of the moment and the lure of immediate temptation. Moreover, he has little insight into the kind of person he is, and he seems unable to profit from past errors in his style of life. Dictators, gangsters, ruthless businessmen, and tough, calculating politicians often fall into this category.

MENTAL RETARDATION

Mental retardation is what used to be called "feeblemindedness." The term "mentally retarded" is applied to people who have since childhood been less able to learn and understand things than most people of the same age. A retarded child has difficulty learning to tie his shoes, finds it impossible to keep up in school, and cannot join in the games that other children his age enjoy.

Mental retardation is not a type of psychosis or neurosis. Nevertheless, a neurotic or psychotic person may sometimes act as if he is mentally retarded, and it is possible for a retarded person to find the world so unpleasant that he withdraws from it in a neurotic or psychotic manner. In general, however, mental retardation is an intellectual disability rather than an emotional one.

Retarded people are often made worse by the way other people

Figure 13.17
Scenes from the family life of Annie, a mentally retarded Mongoloid child. (Mongoloid children are so called because their facial features have a superficial resemblance to those of the Mongolian people of Asia.) During the day, twelve-year-old Annie attends a school that specializes in the education of retarded children. At home, she handles chores and responsibilities suited to her capabilities. Annie has remained an integral part of the family structure and partakes in a full range of activities with her parents, siblings, and pets. As a result, she is an active, happy child. Mongolism, one of a variety of forms that are classified under mental retardation, is believed to be caused by an abnormality in the genes.

treat them. Most retarded people are capable of living normal lives if given the chance. They must, however, be given special attention, affection, and understanding if they are to reach their full potential as human beings.

Unfortunately, retardates are often treated as if they were unseeing, unhearing, uncomprehending "objects" devoid of human responses. The presence of a retarded child in a household may cause a great deal of friction and resentment among members of the family. This situation does not go unnoticed by the retarded child. Despite his intellectual handicaps, the child is a sensitive human being who understands the meaning of anger and resentment, as well as of love and acceptance. Conflict and rejection can rob the child of the supportive environment necessary for his maximum development.

Only about one-fourth of the 6 million people who are called retarded in the United States actually have something physically wrong with their brains. Their retardation is due to diseases contracted before birth or during early infancy, to brain injuries, to poor nutrition in childhood, or to some other physical factor.

The majority of people who are called retarded are people who seem never to have learned to use their minds. They may have been brought up in lonely, dull, or frightening environments in which there was no opportunity or reward for thinking. This situation occurs most often with children born into poor or unstable families and reared in slums or orphanages. If such children are given the opportunity and the encouragement to use their minds early enough, they are almost always able to live normal lives.

ALCOHOLISM AND DRUG ADDICTION

In American society, drug abuse has become a major psychological problem. Millions of Americans depend so heavily on drugs that they hurt themselves physically, socially, and psychologically.

Abuse of drugs invariably involves *psychological dependence.* The user comes to depend so much on the feeling of well-being created by the drug that he is compelled to continue using it. People can become psychologically dependent on a wide variety of drugs, including alcohol, caffeine, nicotine (in cigarettes), opium, marijuana, and amphetamines. When deprived of his drug, the psychologically dependent person becomes restless, irritable, uneasy, or anxious. Drug abuse may also involve *tolerance,* the need for an increased dosage in order to produce the same effect. With sedatives such as sleeping pills, for example, tolerance of up to fifteen times the usual dose can rapidly develop.

The three most widely used and abused drugs in the United States are alcohol, heroin, and the barbiturates. All three of these drugs are *depressants*—drugs that slow down the activity of the brain instead of speeding it up like stimulants, such as amphetamines, caffeine, and nicotine, do. In addition to producing psychological dependence and tolerance, depressants can cause *addiction.* In addiction, the per-

Figure 13.18
Alcoholics tend to be people who experience greater extremes of psychological discomfort than most other people; they have deep-seated feelings of inadequacy or are frequently anxious and depressed. They often experience unbearable psychological or social stress, and drinking provides temporary relief. Yet repeated intoxication invariably causes physical, psychological, or social problems that, in the long run, can only increase the very stress the alcoholic seeks to reduce by drinking and may help to perpetuate his drinking.

son's body requires continual doses of a particular drug in order to avoid an extremely painful illness, known as *withdrawal syndrome.* The delirium tremens attacks (DTs) of the alcoholic represent a withdrawal syndrome: Convulsions, hallucinations, nausea, vomiting, and the shakes are principal symptoms. Heroin carries with it the greatest risk of addiction, followed by alcohol and barbiturates; however, the withdrawal illness from heroin, although excruciating, is less severe than that for alcohol or barbiturates.

Heroin Addiction

Heroin users report that this narcotic drug reduces their feelings of anxiety and brings them sensations of warmth, calm, and inner peace. People who become addicted to heroin are generally those who wish to contract their consciousness and to blur out the external world. They turn to heroin as a way of avoiding the anxiety and tension in their lives.

The heroin addict must spend a great portion of his life trying to procure more of his drug. By alternating between periods of getting high and hustling, the addict avoids having to think about the aspects of life that cause him to feel anxiety and tension. Even after going

Figure 13.19

A heroin addict in a drug treatment center in London mainlines (injects a solution into a vein) the dosage of heroin allotted to him in this program of gradual withdrawal. The administration of controlled amounts of heroin or taking a heroinlike drug called methadone are recent approaches to the problem of narcotics addiction. These approaches have the advantage of making it unnecessary for the addict to steal in order to support his habit and of reducing his risk of disease or death from dirty needles and overdoses. Whether such treatments can eventually "cure" the addict is uncertain.

through a long and painful withdrawal from drugs, the heroin abuser frequently chooses to return to drugs rather than face the problems of life in the real world.

Alcoholism

People use alcohol to relax, to reduce tensions, and to loosen inhibitions. Unlike heroin, which reduces all drives, alcohol makes it easier for people to act on their drives—usually those drives toward aggression, dependency, or sex.

Many people drink to excess on occasion, but only when intoxication occurs repeatedly, causing problems of personal health or interfering with psychological or social functioning, is the drinker considered an *alcoholic.* Alcoholics tend to be people who are selfish, dependent on the emotional support of others, and prone to blame other people for their deep-seated feelings of inadequacy. Most alcoholics have turned to drinking as a temporary relief from what they find to be unbearable stresses in their lives.

The Barbiturates

Next to alcohol, the most widely used group of depressants is the barbiturates, which are more commonly referred to as "downers," or sleeping pills. The behavioral effects of these drugs are quite similar to those of alcohol. They reduce anxiety, slur speech, and eventually bring drowsiness and sleep.

Many people begin taking barbiturates for insomnia. They slowly increase their nightly doses, and after a while start taking a few capsules at stressful times during the day. Eventually, the drug becomes a major focus of their lives. Like the severe alcoholic, the barbiturate addict cannot usually function adequately in his daily activities, often becomes mentally confused, and frequently is obstinate, irritable, and abusive. This behavior is in marked contrast to that of the heroin addict, who usually remains passive and able to function moderately well.

Most psychologists feel that drug abuse reflects an underlying emotional disorder that ultimately would have been expressed in some other way if the person had not turned to drugs. Individuals who are able to cope with the stresses, strains, frustrations, and disappointments of living are unlikely to become drug abusers.

This chapter has focused on the kinds of behaviors people exhibit when they are psychologically distressed. The next chapter focuses on how their distress can be dealt with.

Figure 13.20
More than 10 million Americans use prescription sedatives (barbiturates and tranquilizers) and stimulants (amphetamines). It is estimated that several hundred thousand of these people are drug abusers. The barbiturates ("reds," "blue devils," "rainbows") are physically addicting. A surprisingly large proportion of barbiturate addicts are middle-class housewives who begin using "sleeping pills" but who gradually resort to taking the drug to calm down during the day.

SUMMARY

1. Abnormality has been defined in terms of deviation from the average; in terms of maladjustment, or inability to get along in the world; in terms of legal insanity, or inability to take responsibility for one's own behavior; and in terms of models of ideal functioning. Classification of psychological disorders carries with it many problems, but it does provide some basis for looking at abnormal behavior.

2. Neurosis is a broad category of mental disorder that is characterized by chronic anxiety. Severe neurotic anxiety may produce such symptoms as phobias, obsessions, compulsions, hysteria, and depression. Hysteria may involve conversion reactions or such dissociative states as amnesia, fugue, and multiple personality.

3. Suicide is a last-resort measure taken by people who are severely depressed and hopeless about their future. Contrary to popular belief, most suicide victims have previously threatened to take their lives, and most unsuccessful attempts are usually followed by a successful one.

4. Psychosis is another major category of mental disorder and is characterized by behavior that is so unreasonable as to virtually eliminate the individual's capacity to meet the demands of life.

5. Schizophrenia is a type of psychosis in which the individual's thoughts, emotions, and perceptions are confused and disconnected. Schizophrenia may occur in a simple or a severe form, and it may include such reactions as hebephrenia, catatonia, or paranoia.

6. Affective reactions are another major category of psychosis. They are characterized by excessive and inappropriate changes in mood, from manic to depressive.

7. Psychoses are caused by a variety of factors. A small number of disorders are caused by organic brain damage. It is thought that some

people inherit a tendency to become disturbed. Biochemistry may also be a factor in causing psychoses.

8. Recently, some psychologists have suggested that mental disorders are due to conflicts in communication. The double-bind theory states that prolonged exposure to contradictory messages can produce psychological disturbances.

9. Personality disorders are diagnosed in people who have an ongoing maladaptive behavior and who are unable to develop appropriate relationships with their environment or with other people. The antisocial personality is characterized by lack of conscience and the inability to experience deep emotions.

10. Mental retardation is a condition of very low intellectual development. It may be caused by any number of genetic or environmental factors and may be worsened by poor treatment of the individual.

11. The three most widely used and abused drugs are alcohol, heroin, and the barbiturates. All three of these drugs are depressants, and all are addictive; that is, they cause psychological dependence, tolerance, and a severe withdrawal illness that occurs when the drug is not present in the body.

ACTIVITIES

1. Formulate a definition of mental illness. Is your definition free of social values, or are values a necessary part of the definition? Would a person who lives in a tormented world of sound and sights that other people cannot sense be called schizophrenic? What if great art, literature, or music were the outcome?

2. Study a book of paintings and drawings by Vincent Van Gogh. Can you tell which were done when he was mentally healthy and which were done when he was suffering from severe psychological disorder? How?

3. It is thought that one of the conditions that produces mental disorders is overexposure to double-bind situations. Everyone has faced these situations at various times. How many examples from your own experiences can you think of that illustrate various forms of the double-bind situation? How did you resolve the conflicts? Can you see patterns of behavior responses developing?

4. Labeling of mental disorders presents huge problems for patients and therapists. But the problems of labeling are not limited to this area. Whenever you dismiss certain people as "creeps" or "ninnies," for example, you are really saying more about yourself than about the people you are labeling. For example, people who are nervous in social gatherings usually cannot stand other people who are nervous in social gatherings. For a good indication of your own problems, make a list of people you don't like and the reason(s) why you don't

like them. Take a hard, honest look at those traits you have written down and see how many of them apply to you as well.

5. Write a detailed description of your morning routine—what you do from the time you wake up until the time you leave. Include such things as how you get out of bed, how you brush your teeth, what clothes you put on first, when you look in the mirror, and so on. Chances are that you, like most people, have an extremely rigid routine that varies little from day to day. What is the difference between this type of behavior and the behavior patterns of people who are labeled compulsive or obsessive? What about recurring thoughts such as songs that you cannot get out of your head?

6. Cut out about fifteen pictures of people from magazines and paste them on a large piece of paper. Include among the pictures several of people with long or mussed up hair and untidy clothes. Ask several friends or classmates if they can determine which of the people in the pictures are mentally ill. How many select the people with unkempt appearances? What conclusions can you draw from this experiment?

7. Discuss how smoking can be considered neurotic behavior.

8. Consider yourself in a strange city, totally alone and with no money. You have eaten nothing for three days and now find yourself next to an unattended food stand. What would you do? Would you act any differently if you had not eaten in six days? If, instead of being alone, you were carrying a small hungry child, would your actions be different? What would you regard as antisocial behavior in these situations? How do you think neurosis would effect the actions of a person in such a situation? Can you describe the double-bind conflict in these situations?

9. What are you afraid of? Do you fear high places, or water, or maybe snakes or spiders? Try to think back to when you first had these fears. Can you state rationally why you have each of your fears?

SUGGESTED READINGS

ALBEE, EDWARD. *Who's Afraid of Virginia Woolf?* New York: Atheneum, 1962 (paper). Albee, a famous contemporary playwright, describes the horribly fascinating, extremely neurotic relationship of a husband and wife living in a small academic community in the United States.

ALVAREZ, A. *The Savage God: A Study of Suicide.* New York: Random House, 1970. A well-researched yet highly personal and emotional study of suicide. Alvarez explores the way that thoughts of suicide color the world of creative persons, recounts his own attempt at suicide, and traces the history of myths surrounding the phenomenon.

BARNES, MARY, and JOSEPH BERKE. *Mary Barnes: Two Accounts of a Journey Through Madness.* New York: Harcourt Brace Jovanovich, 1971. This book consists of interspersed chapters by Mary Barnes, who went on a journey into and through madness, and by Joseph Berke, the psychiatrist who helped Mary through her "down years" and into her "up years."

BATESON, GREGORY. *Steps to an Ecology of Mind.* New York: Ballantine, 1972 (paper). Bateson argues that neurosis and psychosis are stages of deterioration in communication and that the major cause of schizophrenia is prolonged exposure to double binds. Very difficult reading.

GREEN, HANNAH. *I Never Promised You a Rose Garden.* New York: New American Library, 1964 (paper). A moving and compelling story about the inner world of an adolescent girl who has been labeled schizophrenic. A well-written and thoughtful novel.

KAPLAN, BERT (ed.). *The Inner World of Mental Illness.* New York: Harper & Row, 1964 (paper). A fascinating collection of first-person accounts of what it is like to experience severe mental disturbance. The last section of the book consists of excerpts from literary classics and from the diaries of well-known writers and thinkers.

KEYES, DANIEL. *Flowers for Algernon.* New York: Bantam, 1966 (paper). A beautifully done novel charting a man's psychological changes as he progresses from a retardate to supergenius and back again.

LAING, R. D. *The Divided Self.* Baltimore: Penguin, 1959 (paper). Laing questions the entire social context that labels a person mentally ill. He believes that psychoses and neuroses make sense if the experience of the person is understood. Presently accepted "normality" is in fact pathological. Psychosis, in a way, is a step toward sanity.

PLATH, SYLVIA. *The Bell Jar.* New York: Bantam, 1971 (paper). An autobiographical novel about a young woman's struggle with madness. Plath is an excellent writer and the book is especially powerful because she is able to articulate her feelings so well.

RUBIN, THEODORE. *Jordi/Lisa and David.* New York: Ballantine, 1971. The characters are David and Lisa, two schizophrenic adolescents who have insulated themselves from reality. This is a short, dramatic case history of how their mutual affection became an avenue to recovery.

STEINBECK, JOHN. *Of Mice and Men.* New York: Viking Press, 1937 (paper). Lenny and George are drifters with complementary personalities and a common aspiration. Lenny, a retardate, relies upon George to structure his life; George finds meaning in his role as protector. Steinbeck's graphic novel explores this human relationship with compassion and sensitivity.

14
Therapy and Change

At certain times of transition and crisis in a person's life, he feels an urgent need to find someone trustworthy with whom he can share his doubts and problems. A parent, relative, or close friend is often helpful in such times of need. But many psychological problems are too bewildering and complex to be solved in this way. When a person finds life unbearable and suspects that the reason lies inside himself, he is likely to seek help from someone with training and experience in such matters. People who deal with the psychological problems of others include clergymen, teachers, counselors, social workers, physicians, psychologists, and psychiatrists. The special kind of help they provide is called *psychotherapy*.

This chapter will present some of the major approaches to therapy and will describe what it is like to undergo therapy. It will also explore various types of group therapy, probe the current situation in America's mental institutions, and touch on the trend toward community mental health.

WHAT IS PSYCHOTHERAPY?

Psychotherapy literally means "healing of the soul," and in early times psychological disturbances were often thought to be some sort of moral or religious problem. Madmen were sometimes viewed as being inhabited by devils or demons, and treatment consisted of exorcism, the driving out of these demons by religious ceremonies or by physical punishment (see Chapter 1). Within the last two hundred years, however, views of psychological disorders have changed.

Figure 14.1
A person who is overwhelmed by his troubles, feelings of inadequacy, and unhappiness reaches for help in a number of ways, sometimes by appealing to friends and relatives, at other times seeking professional guidance. Anyone who tries to help such a person in his or her time of need is acting as a therapist.

331

Mental disorders have slowly come to be thought of as types of diseases, and the term "mental illness" is now popularly applied to psychological problems.

This medical view of psychological disturbance has helped withdraw some of the stigma associated with such problems, and it has done much to convince society that troubled people need care and treatment. Nevertheless, several psychologists feel that the term "mental illness" has outlived its usefulness and that, in fact, it may now be doing more harm than good.

One of these psychologists, Thomas Szasz, has argued that people with psychological problems should not be treated in the same way that doctors treat people with physical problems. He believes that a disturbed person should be viewed not as a person with an illness but as a person who is having *problems in living.* Szasz sees the disturbed individual as one who is perhaps confused about his values, who is playing certain games with himself and those around him, or who is communicating to others in an indirect, self-protecting way.

According to Szasz, the trouble with letting a person think of himself as mentally ill is that he sees himself in a passive, helpless position. He sees his troubles as being caused by forces over which he has no control. By thinking of himself in this way, the person can avoid taking responsibility for his own situation and for helping himself change.

One of the functions of psychotherapy, then, is to help people realize that they are responsible for their own problems and that, even more importantly, they are the only ones who can really solve

Figure 14.2
The series of paintings shown here was executed by Joanne, a gifted and artistic adolescent who had never received formal art training. Joanne was a mental patient and was being treated for psychotic behavior. At times she believed herself to be Shakespeare's Richard II. Five of the paintings are self-portraits, and one is of a friend whom she met in the hospital (*bottom right*). Joanne told the therapist that she depicted the "true colors" that only she could see beneath her subject's skin. The first painting (*top left*) reveals Joanne's fear that she would lose control and go mad. The next painting (*top center*) was done shortly after she entered the hospital and began art therapy. The third and fourth paintings also reflect her fear and depression, but to a lesser extent. In the last painting (*bottom center*), Joanne has represented herself in a more relaxed state, and the natural tones indicate her greater calm.

these problems. This approach does not imply that people become disturbed on purpose or that no one should need outside help. People often adopt certain techniques for getting along in life that seem appropriate at the time but that lead to trouble in the long run. Such patterns can be difficult for the individual to see or change. The major task of the therapist, therefore, is to help people examine their way of living, to understand how their present way of living causes problems, and to start living in new, more beneficial ways.

The new trend thus seems to be away from viewing the psychotherapist as a "healer" who makes the "patient" well. Rather, the trend is more toward viewing the therapist as a guide who is hired by the individual to help him find the source of his problems and some possible solutions.

Characteristics of Psychotherapy

There are many different kinds of therapy, only a few of which will be described in this chapter. Each one is based on different theories about how human personality works, and each one is carried out in a different style. Some psychotherapists stick rigorously to one style and consider the others useless. Other psychotherapists pick and choose methods from many different kinds of therapy and use whatever works best. But whatever the style or philosophy, all types of psychotherapy have certain characteristics in common. In all cases, obviously, there is a *patient:* a person who is no longer able to function happily or constructively in everyday life. This troubled person goes (or is taken by others) to an individual of recognized knowledge and power—someone with prestige. This person, someone considered to be an expert in human problems, is the *therapist.* The relationship that develops between these two is crucial to solving the patient's problem.

The primary goal of all patient-therapist relationships is to create *positive change* in the life of the patient. In order to change, it is necessary for the patient to achieve some *understanding* of his troubles. One of the first tasks of therapy, therefore, is to closely examine the patient's problem. Another major task of therapy is to help the patient find meaningful *alternatives* to his present unsatisfactory ways of behaving.

One of the most important factors in effective treatment is the patient's belief or hope that he *can* change. The influence that a patient's hopes and expectations have on his improvement is often called the *placebo effect.* This name comes from giving medical patients *placebos*—harmless sugar pills—when they complain of ailments that do not seem to have any physiological basis. The patient takes the tablets, his symptoms disappear, and he considers himself cured.

The placebo effect does not imply that problems can be solved simply by fooling the patient. It does demonstrate, however, the tremendous importance of the patient's attitude in finding a way to

Figure 14.3

Many people have a mental picture of psychotherapy as taking place with the patient reclining on a comfortable couch while a middle-aged, bearded man sits taking notes in a chair behind the patient. Actually, few therapeutic settings fit this picture nowadays. Therapists are more likely to talk to their patients in a face-to-face position. Furthermore, the therapist is likely to employ a variety of techniques rather than adhere to a strictly psychoanalytic approach. Several of these varied techniques are discussed in this chapter.

Psychotherapy is practiced by a considerable variety of people with a wide range of training and experience. Just what credentials a psychotherapist should have before he or she can practice is still an open question. What is clear, however, is that the credential is less important than the character of the therapist and the amount of experience he or she has had.

Psychiatrists are medical doctors who specialize in the treatment of mental illness. They generally take a post-M.D. internship in a mental institution. Because of their medical background, psychiatrists tend to be more biologically oriented than psychologists.

Psychoanalysts are psychiatrists who have taken special training in the theory of personality and techniques of psychotherapy of Sigmund Freud, usually from an established psychoanalyst. They must themselves be psychoanalyzed before they can practice.

Lay Analysts are psychoanalysts who do not have degrees in medicine but who have studied with established psychoanalysts.

Clinical Psychologists are therapists with a Ph.D. degree. They are the product of a three-to-four-year research-oriented program in the social sciences, plus a one-year predoctoral or postdoctoral internship in psychotherapy and psychological assessment.

Counselors generally have a master's or doctor's degree in counseling psychology. They usually work in educational institutions where they are available for consultation about personal problems. They customarily refer clients with serious problems to psychiatrists or psychologists.

Psychiatric Social Workers are people with a graduate degree in psychiatric social work. They generally recieve supervised practical training coupled with two years of courses in psychology.

Nonprofessionals include clergymen, physicians, teachers, and others who dispense a great deal of advice despite the fact that they have had no formal training in therapy or counseling. Nevertheless, more troubled people turn to nonprofessionals than to professionals—and they seem to be more satisfied with the therapy they receive.

change. A patient who does not believe he can be helped probably cannot be. A patient who believes he can change and believes he has the power to change will find a way. Therapy is professional guidance, not a placebo.

What Makes a Good Therapist?

In American society, there are many people who do psychotherapy. Some, such as psychiatrists and psychoanalysts, are highly trained in psychology and medicine; others, such as counselors and clergymen, have considerably less formal training. The different kinds of professional therapists and the training that each goes through before practicing psychotherapy are shown in Figure 14.4.

Before going to a professional therapist, most people first turn to a friend or other nonprofessional for help and advice. Such nonprofessionals sometimes tell the individual exactly what he wants to hear—that "it's not your fault, you couldn't help it." They provide sympathy and an understanding ear. Professional therapists, on the other hand, are more likely to tell the person things he does not want to hear. In the process of therapy, the patient may feel frustrated because he cannot push the burden of responsibility onto someone else the way he can with a friend.

The process of therapy is always difficult and upsetting, and the patient often becomes heavily dependent on the therapist while they are trying to make changes. A patient may become angry or hurt, for example, if his therapist suddenly goes on vacation. The therapist, therefore, has to be careful not to betray the trust that the patient has placed in him. On the other hand, he must not let the patient lean on him or take out his problems on him. Patients often try to avoid their problems by using the therapist as a substitute parent or by blaming him for their misfortunes.

In recent years, some researchers have questioned whether professional psychotherapy really works. They have gathered statistics that seem to bear out their contention that just as many people improve without psychotherapy as with it. Subsequent studies have shown, however, that these original statistics were misleading. A good number of people, it is true, improve whether they see a trained psychotherapist or not, but in most of these cases the person has obtained help from someone else—a clergyman or the family doctor, for example. Furthermore, there is evidence that formal psychotherapy, rather than having no effect, is a powerful experience for good in many cases but has bad effects in some others.

Whether psychotherapy will be beneficial to a person depends on both the patient and the therapist. The patients who get the most out of psychotherapy are people with high intelligence, good educations, and middle-class backgrounds. Such people have much in common with most therapists, and this similarity seems to help. In addition, the people who benefit most from psychotherapy are those who have relatively mild problems about which they have considerable anxiety or depression. Severely disturbed apathetic patients are much more difficult to change.

The characteristics that are found in effective therapists are of three kinds: First, a therapist needs to be reasonably *healthy* himself. A therapist who is himself anxious, defensive, and withdrawn will not be able to see his patient's problems clearly. A second important characteristic is a capacity for *warmth* and *understanding*. Troubled people are usually fearful and confused about explaining their problems. The therapist needs to be able to give the patient confidence that he is capable of caring and understanding.

Finally, a good therapist must be *experienced* in dealing with people—in understanding their complexities, seeing through the "games" they play to trick the therapist and themselves, and judging their strengths and weaknesses. Only by having worked with many people can a therapist learn when to give support, when to insist that the patient stand on his own feet, and how to make sense of the things people say.

KINDS OF THERAPY

Although there are many approaches to psychotherapy (several are included in the suggested readings at the end of this chapter), only the three major influential approaches will be discussed here: traditional psychoanalysis, client-centered therapy, and behavior therapy. In addition to these types of individual therapy, several kinds of group therapy will be described.

Psychoanalysis

For a long time *psychoanalysis* was the only kind of psychotherapy practiced in Western society. It was this type of therapy that gave rise to the classic picture of a bearded Viennese doctor seated behind a patient on a couch.

Psychoanalysis is based on the theories of Sigmund Freud. According to Freud's views, psychological disturbances are due to anxiety about hidden conflicts between one's conscious and unconscious desires. (Freud's theory of personality is described in Chapters 7 and 12.) The job of the psychoanalyst, therefore, is to help make the patient aware of the unconscious impulses, desires, and fears that are causing the anxiety. Psychoanalysts believe that if the patient can understand his unconscious motives, he can gain control over his behavior and free himself of his problems. Such understanding is called *insight*.

Psychoanalysis is a slow procedure. It may take years of fifty-minute sessions several times a week before the patient is able to make fundamental changes in his life. Throughout this time, the analyst assists his patient in a thorough examination of the unconscious parts of his mind. This task begins with the analyst telling the patient to relax and talk about everything that comes into his mind. This method is called *free association*. The patient may consider his passing thoughts to be too unimportant or too embarrassing to mention. But the analyst suggests that he express everything—the thought that seems most inconsequential may, in fact, be the most meaningful upon closer examination.

As the patient lies on the couch, he may describe his dreams, talk about his private life, or recall long-forgotten experiences. The psychoanalyst sits out of sight behind the patient and often says nothing for long periods of time. He occasionally makes remarks or asks questions that guide the patient, or he may suggest an interpretation of something the patient has been talking about, but most of the work is done by the patient himself.

The patient is understandably reluctant to reveal painful feelings and to examine lifelong patterns that need to be changed, and as the analysis proceeds, he is likely to try to hold back the flow of information. This phenomenon is called *resistance*. The patient may have agreed to cooperate fully, yet he finds at times that his mind is blank, that he feels powerless and can no longer think of anything to say. At such times the analyst will simply point out what is happening and wait for the patient to continue. The analyst may also suggest another line of approach to the area of resistance.

Sooner or later, the analyst himself begins to appear in the patient's associations and dreams. The patient may begin feeling toward the analyst the way he feels toward some other important figure in his life. This process is called *transference*.

If the patient can recognize what is happening, transference may allow him to experience his true feelings toward the important

Figure 14.5
Although the traditional couch has disappeared from modern psychoanalytic therapy, the phenomena of resistance and transference remain central. Here the patient's resistance is shown in the fact that he is seeing the therapist as a menacing dentist. At the same time, he is transferring: The "dentist" seems to him like an impersonal, frightening mother. Such images arise in the patient's dreams and free associations; the therapist tells the patient to discuss and examine these images and symbols thoroughly.

person. But often, instead of experiencing and understanding his feelings, the patient simply begins acting toward the therapist in the same way he used to act toward the important person, usually one of his parents.

The therapist does not allow the patient to resort to these tactics. He remains impersonal and anonymous. He always directs the patient back to himself. The therapist may ask, for example, "What do you see when you imagine my face?" The patient may reply that he sees the therapist as an angry, frowning, unpleasant figure. The therapist never takes this personally. Instead, he may calmly say, "What does this make you think of?" Gradually, it will become clear to both patient and therapist that the patient is reacting to the neutral therapist as though he were a threatening father.

Through this kind of process, the patient becomes aware of his real feelings and motivations. He may begin to understand, for example, why he has trouble with his boss at work—he may be seeing his boss, his therapist, and indeed any man in a position of authority in the same way that as a child he saw his father.

Traditional psychoanalysis has changed a good deal over the years, although its basic principles remain the same. Few psychoanalysts use a couch any longer. They sit face to face with their patients and talk to them. They also place more emphasis on the conscious decisions of the individual rather than focusing exclusively on his unconscious motivations. These changes have helped to make the process faster and less anxiety provoking.

Client-Centered Therapy

A newer and quite popular type of psychotherapy is *client-centered therapy,* in which the role of the therapist is considerably different from his role in traditional psychoanalysis. In client-centered therapy, the therapist is no longer a distant, faceless, authority figure. There is much more of a feeling that the therapist is there to serve the patient.

Client-centered therapy is based on the theories of Carl Rogers (see Chapter 12). The use of the term "client" instead of "patient" gives one an insight into the reasoning behind Rogers' method. "Patient" is a negative, passive word that suggests inferiority, whereas "client" implies an equal relationship between the therapist and the person seeking help.

Client-centered therapists assume that people are basically good and that they are capable of handling their own lives. Psychological problems arise when the true self becomes lost and the individual comes to view himself according to the standards of others. One of the goals of therapy, therefore, is to help the client to recognize his own strength and confidence so that he can learn to be true to his own standards and ideas about how to live effectively.

In the course of an interview, the client is encouraged to speak freely about intimate matters that may be bothering him. He is told

Figure 14.6

The role of the client-centered therapist is rather different from that of a psychoanalyst. Because the client-centered therapist often restates what he considers to be the emotional content of the client's communication, he tends to be like a mirror for the client's feelings. In this way, he provides understanding and positive regard, without making value judgments. The client-centered therapist gives the impression of being more "human" than the "blank wall" appearance of his psychoanalytic counterpart.

that it is up to him what he talks about. The therapist listens and encourages conversation but tries to avoid giving opinions. Instead, he tries to echo back as clearly as possible the feelings that the client has expressed. He may try to extract the main points from the client's hesitant or rambling explanations. For example, a male client may tell a long story about an incident with his father, and the therapist may respond by saying, "This kind of thing makes you feel very stupid." The client may in turn say, "No, not stupid, angry. It's really him that is being stupid, " and the therapist will say, "Oh, I see, you really feel angry at him when he acts this way." Between them, they form a clearer and clearer picture of how the client really feels about himself, his life, and the people around him.

Client-centered therapy is conducted in an atmosphere of emotional support that Rogers calls *unconditional positive regard.* The therapist never says that he thinks the client or what the client has said is good or bad. But he shows the client that he will accept anything that is said without embarrassment, reservation, or anger. His primary responsibility is to create a warm and accepting relationship between himself and his client.

This acceptance makes it easier for the client to explore thoughts about himself and his experiences. He is able to abandon old values without fear of disapproval, and he can begin to see himself, his situation, and his relationships with others in a new light.

As he reduces his tensions and releases his emotions, the client feels that he is becoming a more complete person. He gains the courage to accept parts of his personality that he had formerly considered weak or bad, and, by recognizing his own self-worth, he can set up realistic goals and consider the steps necessary to reach them. The client's movement toward independence signals the end of the need for therapy—he can assume the final steps to independence on his own.

Behavior Therapy

Psychoanalysts and client-centered therapists have sometimes been criticized for being "all talk and no action." In *behavior therapy,* there is much more emphasis on action. Rather than spending large amounts of time going into the patient's past history or the details of his dreams, the behavior therapist concentrates on finding out what is specifically wrong with the patient's current life and takes steps to change it. By working on specific problems with direct methods, behavior therapists have been able to demonstrate the success of their methods more clearly than can other therapies.

The idea behind behavior therapy is that a disturbed person is one who has *learned* to behave in the wrong way. The therapist's job, therefore, is to "re-educate" the patient. The reasons for the patient's undesirable behavior are not important; what is important is to change the behavior itself. To bring about such changes, the therapist uses certain conditioning techniques that were first discovered in animal laboratories. (The principles of conditioning are explained in Chapter 6.)

One technique used by behavior therapists is *systematic desensitization*. This method is used to overcome irrational fears and anxieties that the patient has learned. The goal of desensitization therapy is to teach the patient to associate a pleasant feeling, rather than anxiety, with certain feared objects or events. For example, suppose a student is terrified of speaking in front of large groups of people—that, in fact, his stage fright is so tremendous that he is unable to speak when called upon in class. How would desensitization therapy effectively change this person's behavior?

To begin with, the therapist might have the student make a list of all the aspects of talking to others that he finds frightening. Perhaps the most frightening aspect is actually standing before an audience, whereas the least frightening is speaking to a single other person. The patient ranks his fears in order, from the most frightening on down. First, the therapist begins teaching the patient to relax. As he relaxes, the patient tries to imagine as vividly as possible the least-disurbing scene on his list. As he thinks about speaking to a single stranger, the student may feel a mild anxiety. But because the therapist has taught him how to relax, the patient is soon able to think about the experience without feeling afraid. The basic logic is that two opposite feelings cannot exist at the same time. The therapist attempts to replace anxiety with its opposite, relaxation.

This procedure is followed step by step up the list of anxiety-

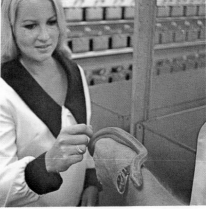

Figure 14.7

These photographs illustrate the desensitization of a snake phobia. To overcome her fear, this woman is slowly going through a series of stages in which she learns to be calm in fearful situations. First, she simply observes the snake in the hands of the attendant, who is on the other side of a screen. Just seeing another person handling the snake helps decrease her fear. (The importance of imitation and modeling in learning is discussed in Chapters 6 and 7.) Next, she gradually gets closer to the snake until she is able to touch it without fear.

arousing events. The patient finally reaches a point where he is able to imagine the situations that threaten him the most without feeling anxiety. Now the therapist starts to expose the person to real-life situations that have previously frightened him. Therapy finally reaches the point where the stage-frightened student is able to get up and deliver an unrehearsed speech before a full auditorium.

Another form of behavior therapy is called *contingency management.* In this method, the therapist and patient decide what old, undesirable behavior needs to be eliminated and what new, desirable behavior needs to appear. Arrangements are then made for the old behavior to go unrewarded and for the desired behavior to be reinforced. In its simplest form, contingency management consists of the therapist agreeing with the patient, "If you do X, I will give you Y." This form of agreement is similar to systems of reward that people often use on themselves. For instance, a college student may say to himself, "If I get a good grade on the exam, I'll treat myself to a great dinner." The reward is *contingent* (dependent) upon getting a good grade.

Contingency management is used in prisons, mental hospitals, schools, and army bases as well as with individual patients. In these institutions it is possible to set up whole miniature systems of rewards, called *token economies.* For example, psychologists in some mental hospitals select behavior they judge desirable. Patients are then rewarded for these behaviors with "hospital," or token, money. Thus, if a patient cleans his room or works in the hospital garden, he is rewarded with token money. The patients are able to cash in their

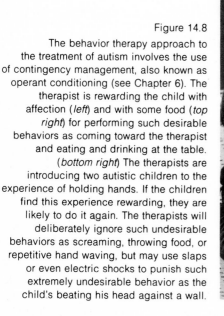

Figure 14.8
The behavior therapy approach to the treatment of autism involves the use of contingency management, also known as operant conditioning (see Chapter 6). The therapist is rewarding the child with affection (*left*) and with some food (*top right*) for performing such desirable behaviors as coming toward the therapist and eating and drinking at the table. (*bottom right*) The therapists are introducing two autistic children to the experience of holding hands. If the children find this experience rewarding, they are likely to do it again. The therapists will deliberately ignore such undesirable behaviors as screaming, throwing food, or repetitive hand waving, but may use slaps or even electric shocks to punish such extremely undesirable behavior as the child's beating his head against a wall.

token money for things they want, such as candy or cigarettes, or for certain privileges, such as time away from the ward. These methods are successful in inducing mental patients, who often sit around doing nothing day after day, to begin leading active lives. They learn to take care of themselves and to take on responsibility instead of having to be constantly cared for.

Group Therapy

In the forms of therapy described thus far, the troubled person is usually alone with the therapist. In *group* therapy, however, he is in the company of others. There are several advantages to this situation. Group therapy gives the troubled person practical experience with one of his biggest problems—getting along with other people. A person in group therapy also has a chance to see how other people are struggling with problems similar to his own, and he discovers what other people think of him. He, in turn, can express what he thinks of them, and in this exchange he discovers where he is mistaken in his views of himself and of other people and where he is correct.

Another advantage to group therapy is the fact that one therapist can help a large number of people. Most group therapy sessions are led by a trained therapist who makes suggestions, clarifies points, and keeps activities from getting out of hand. In this way, his training and experience are used to help as many as twenty people at once.

Not all group therapies are run by professionals, however. Some of the most successful examples are provided in nonprofessional organizations, such as Alcoholics Anonymous and Synanon.

Alcoholics Anonymous The purpose of Alcoholics Anonymous is "to carry the AA message to the sick alcoholic who wants it." According to AA, the only way for an alcoholic to change is to admit

Figure 14.9

In Alcoholics Anonymous, one of the main emphases is on the alcoholic's responsibility for his actions, both in his personal life and in his efforts to make the organization work. The man at the lectern is recounting his experiences with alcoholism and how his life has improved with the help of AA. All of the people in the room can empathize with his story, and sooner or later they will all tell their stories to the group. This autobiographical storytelling is a technique utilized by AA to build a feeling of cohesiveness and solidarity among group members.

Figure 14.10
Explanations of various methods
and approaches currently being used
in group therapy.

Encounter Group   A group whose purpose is to allow people to meet, experience, and interact with each other as persons, as directly as possible. All usual manners, restrictions, inhibitions, pressures, and unspoken rules that normally prevent direct interaction are actively discouraged.

T-Group   "T" stands for training: This approach was devised by Kurt Lewin to train people in the skills of task-oriented human relations. Group members examine and discuss the processes that occur in the group, thereby discovering how they operate and affect one another.

Marathon Group   An encounter group continued nonstop for up to 36 hours. The object is to place group members in a situation in which they are unable to maintain their usual fronts.

Sensitivity Training   The use of encounter principles and techniques to increase the effectiveness of such people as business managers, policemen, and teachers. Based on the idea that people in traditional roles can learn to do their jobs better and have better effects on other people if they understand more about themselves and how other people react to them.

Body-Oriented Therapy   A theory and method of therapy based on the principle that psychological problems are often expressed physically. If the body can be freed from tension, knottedness, strained posture, and so on by any of a variety of methods, the person can experience his feelings more fully, can become more aware and sensitive.

Psychodrama   A method of therapy, devised by Jacob Moreno, in which participants take parts in an improvised play. The script provides only general outlines; the actors fill in the details of dialogue and action as their feelings lead them.

Gestalt Therapy   A theory and method of therapy developed by Fritz Perls. It is based on the idea that a person can change if he becomes aware of how he is living his life in the here and now. With the guidance of the therapist, each person in the group imagines himself talking to or being various objects and characters in his dreams, being parts of his body, and so on in order to bring parts of himself together into a unified whole.

that he is powerless over alcohol and that his life has become unmanageable. He must come to believe that only some power greater than himself can help him. The drinker who thinks he can battle out his own problem will not be successful.

Members of AA usually meet at least once a week to discuss the meaning of this message, to talk about the horrors of their experiences with alcohol, and to describe the new hope they have found with AA. Mutual encouragement, friendship, and an emphasis on personal responsibility are the main techniques used to keep an individual "on the wagon." Every member must be willing to come to the aid of another member who is the tempted to take a drink.

Most psychologists are unable to explain why AA works, but there is no doubt that it is effective: One study showed that of the people who went to seven or more AA meetings 75 percent never took another drink.

Synanon   Synanon is an organization that deals with the problem of heroin addiction. Synanon members spend weeks, months, and even years living together in an effort to overcome drug addiction and to create a new and lasting life style.

Synanon is a total experience. During the day everybody works together; in the evenings, members make use of a unique therapeutic device called the Synanon Game, which all members are required to play. One at a time, members sit in the "hot seat" and receive the harshest possible personal criticism from their fellows. No matter what the target person says or does, he is likely to be fiercely attacked.

These games serve several purposes. They force the individual to see the personal weaknesses that have led him to drug addiction, and they teach him that it is useless to try to defend these weaknesses. He learns that he must overcome them, but he also learns to tolerate and stand up to personal criticism. For many people the game is the first situation in which they learn to respect their own ability to accept criticism and to live with themselves.

For those who can stick with it, the Synanon group is a highly effective method of therapy, but about half the people who try Synanon drop out. Synanon has also been heavily criticized for failing to prepare people to deal with the outside world. But its founder, Chuck Dedrick, sees it as an alternative to traditional American life. "Synanon just happens to be a better way for people to live together, both with themselves and others," he has pointed out.

Encounter Groups   The power of group interaction to affect and change people has given rise to the controversial *encounter group*. Encounter groups are primarily for people who function adequately in everday life but who, for some reason, feel unhappy, dissatisfied, or stagnant.

The purpose of encounter groups is to provide experiences that will help people live more intense lives. Being in a small group (between five and fifteen people) for this express purpose is bound to teach one something about interpersonal relations. Techniques are often used in groups to overcome the restrictions that people live by in everyday life. A typical exercise requires each person to say something to every other person and at the same time to touch him in some way. Such methods are intended to increase sensitivity, openness, and honesty.

Role playing is another common encounter-group technique. It is a form of theater in which the goal is to help the people expose and understand themselves. A person may try acting out the role of a character in one of his dreams; another person may pretend to be himself as a child talking to his mother, played by another member. By switching roles and placing themselves in each other's situation, group members are better able to see themselves as others see them.

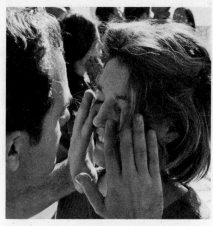

Figure 14.11
Exercises that increase physical sensitivity are often used in groups. The people in this photograph have been asked by the group leader to touch each other's faces without looking or speaking. This exercise forces the participants to communicate with each other in ways that do not rely on conventional habits. The purpose of this exercise is to help group members learn to become aware of themselves and one another in new and often more direct ways.

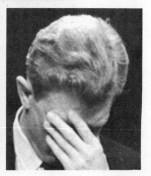

Figure 14.12
Carl Rogers is shown here (on the left, top photograph) leading an encounter group in front of film cameras. Many encounter group leaders, including Rogers, feel that their role in the group is the same as that of any other member. The only exception is that if the group as a whole or any one of its members gets into trouble, the leader is the person who (as a result of his experience) can perhaps best rescue the situation. Typically, other group members will exhibit leadership or therapeutic skills and the designated leader will remain in the background, letting the group process determine itself but continuing to provide direction when necessary.

Figure 14.13

A popular technique employed by family therapists is to have all the family members produce a joint creative effort, such as a drawing. By watching the interactions of the family during the creative process, the therapist can usually obtain a fairly representative picture of their typical relationship patterns. For example, if the husband/father dominates the artistic endeavor, and the suggestions and contributions of the wife/mother and children are timid and relegated to the background, it is likely that this relationship carries through to all levels of family interactions. Using this as a starting point, the therapist can point out what he or she sees happening and thereby begin a dialogue with all members participating.

Acting out a past experience or playing the role of another person can do much to bring out a person's hidden and true feelings.

Regardless of the type of therapy, all groups require experienced leaders who are qualified to take responsibility for the group. In a few cases, people who have been unprepared for the intense emotional exposure that occurs in groups have suffered long-lasting psychological distress from the experience. In most of these cases, it has been found that a particular leader was insensitive and misjudged the vulnerability and stability of the group members.

Such casualties are rare, but in general the claims made for the benefits of encounter groups should be carefully examined. There is no doubt that groups can introduce a person to positive aspects of life of which he may have been unaware, but so far there is no guarantee that such experiences will have lasting effects. Groups offer intense and useful experiences but they are not sure routes to happiness any more than are other new experiences.

Family Therapy Recently therapists have begun to suggest, after talking to a patient, that his entire family unit should work at group therapy. This method is particularly useful because the members of the group are all people of great importance in one another's lives. In family therapy it is possible to untangle the twisted web of relationships that have led one or more members in the family to experience emotional suffering.

Often family members are unhappy because they are mistreating or are being mistreated by other family members in ways that no one understands or wants to talk about. The family therapist can point out what is going wrong from an objective viewpoint and can suggest ways of improving communication and fairness in the family.

MENTAL INSTITUTIONS

When the demands of everyday life cannot be met, the mentally disturbed individual may face the prospect of institutionalization. There are institutions to handle many different social problems: prisons for criminals, hospitals for the physically ill, and mental institutions for people who are considered unable to function in normal society.

Commitment

The process of placing a person in a mental hospital is called *commitment.* About one-half of all mental patients commit themselves voluntarily or have their friends or family commit them. However, many individuals are committed against their will. Involuntary commitment is a controversial legal and ethical issue. It has been argued that a committed mental patient has fewer rights than a convicted criminal.

Many people have been placed in mental institutions simply because they do not have the money to go elsewhere. People with plenty of money can afford to see a private therapist at $50.00 an hour. A person with average or below average income is more likely to go to someone associated with a public institution—a clinic, general hospital, or mental hospital. It is standard procedure at such places to interview potential patients and to commit those who are thought to be seriously disturbed. By this process a poor person may end up in an institution, whereas his rich and equally disturbed counterpart is simply seen by a psychotherapist four times a week.

Conditions

The quality of care in mental hospitals varies greatly. If the individual can afford it, he can be committed to a private institution with all the comforts of a country club. While paying as much as $150.00 a day,

Figure 14.14

Nine out of ten patients in mental hospitals are housed in institutions financed and administered by state or county governments. More often than not, these institutions lack sufficient space, personnel, funds, and effective therapeutic programs to make them useful treatment centers. These institutions tend to prolong hospitalization by fostering dependence and docility. Yet research has shown that, in general, mentally disturbed people benefit greatly when they are actively involved in work and when they have frequent contact with other patients and with therapists.

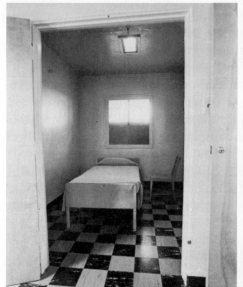

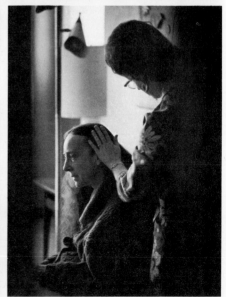

he can enjoy the use of swimming pools, tennis courts, and good food while he considers his problems. But the majority of people go to state mental hospitals or cheaper private institutions. The quality of treatment in these hospitals varies tremendously. It is possible, in fact, for a patient's condition to worsen or remain unchanged because his hospital environment is unconducive to improvement. And because the patient fails to improve, he remains institutionalized year after year. This situation exists because most public hospitals lack funds for adequate nursing staffs, equipment, and trained therapists. In many cases the patient's day-to-day care is left to attendants who do little more than clean and feed the patients and keep order.

Ideally, a mental hospital should be a place where the patient is temporarily freed from social pressures that he cannot bear. Limited and carefully planned demands should be made by a staff capable of understanding and concern for the individual. Unfortunately, the reality of many state hospitals does not fit this ideal. Patients in a typical public hospital are dressed in dull uniforms, stripped of all individuality. They become molded into a pattern of obedience, dependence, and conformity by a deadening routine of sleep, meals, ping pong, and other ways of filling time.

As the patients become increasingly apathetic and resigned, they lose all ties with the outside world. In order to survive the boredom of each day, they rely on fantasy, dreams, and sleep, and they stop giving thought to a return to outside life. Nevertheless, many patients welcome this routine—they prefer to be taken care of and to thus avoid the responsibilities of the outside world.

Therapy in Mental Hospitals

Individual and group psychotherapy are provided in mental hospitals, but this type of therapy is slow and expensive, and it does not work well with people who are often beyond caring whether they improve or not.

Some traditional treatments in mental hospitals are more physical than psychological. A good example is the use of *electroconvulsive shock* in the treatment of depression. No one knows why it works, but the delivery of an electric current to the brain sufficient to produce convulsions is often effective in reversing severe depression. This result has been compared to the personality changes sometimes seen in people after a bad car accident or a severe physical illness. This treatment is no longer in common use.

Recently, administration of drugs has become the most widely used and most effective form of treatment. A wide variety of drugs have been developed to deal with specific psychological symptoms. *Tranquilizers* have proven to be remarkably effective in alleviating anxiety, and *antidepressants* have been used successfully with extremely depressed patients. Specific drugs are also given to physically violent patients. It used to be necessary to lock such people in bare

rooms, tie them in straight-jackets, or wrap them in wet sheets. Now they can be chemically rather than physically restrained. Drugs do not make any lasting changes in a person, but they can relieve his anxiety, his depression, or his overexcitement. They enable many people to carry on life outside the hospital instead of being confined for months or years.

There are certain dangers inherent in the use of psychiatric drugs. They are often administered to make up for the lack of staff at mental hospitals. In many institutions it is common policy to administer a tranquilizer to every patient early in the morning, so that throughout the day there is very little activity among patients, thus reducing the workload required of an already overworked staff.

Most psychiatric drugs have undesirable side effects, such as extreme lethargy or peculiar losses of coordination when given in high doses over long periods. For such reasons, it is not uncommon for mental patients to flush some of their drugs down the toilet.

COMMUNITY MENTAL HEALTH

Community mental health programs have been created as an alternative to expensive private therapy and inadequate public institutions. These programs are meant not only to help those who are already troubled and disturbed but also to change conditions that are making people this way.

Community Centers

Emotional problems are often caused or made worse by conditions in the community. People who are treated unfairly by police, school authorities, landlords, or shopkeepers feel resentment and anger that cannot readily be expressed. So do people who have trouble feeding and clothing their families.

Conditions that create emotional problems are not confined to slums or ghettoes, however. Colleges create pressures that drive

Figure 14.15

These drawings, titled "My Life in the Hospital," were made by a woman considered to be psychotic and depict her self-perceptions during hospitalization. In the first series (*left*) she shows herself as she had entered the hospital, bent over and depressed. Then, as she became involved in such activities as cooking and art therapy, she regained a measure of self-confidence, which is reflected in her erect posture and outstretched arms. The series ends with a relapse of the depression and her attempts to deal with questions and fears. The second series of drawings (*right*) initially shows the patient's interaction with the hospital chaplain, who seems to have answered some of her questions and dispelled some of her fears. After the chaplain was transferred to another post, the woman experienced a sense of loss and regression. Once again she shows herself bent over; the rest of the world—her bed and her home—has been crossed out, lost; the last drawing is as the first.

Figure 14.16
An organization called the "Young Lords" sponsors hot breakfasts and recreational activities for ghetto children in a church basement in Upper East Side New York. Community projects such as these are therapeutic—both mentally and physically. They create conditions that prevent the depression and feelings of helplessness that contribute to mental disorder.

some students to suicide. Suburban homes and schools contain restraints and pressures that lead to divorce, "delinquency," and severe parent-child conflicts.

The aim of community mental health programs is to provide local centers where personal and community problems can be attacked. Because these centers are community organizations, they can attract people who might never before have dreamed of having psychological help.

The basic idea behind these programs is to establish community clinics staffed by psychiatrists, psychologists, social workers, and trained nonprofessionals who work as a team. Individual patients are charged fees according to their ability to pay. Applicants to a program are evaluated by the entire team. The patient is then assigned to a specially skilled member of the clinic, depending upon his history, needs, and goals. He may receive treatment or counseling or may participate in local group activities.

Crisis Centers

Crisis centers have been established in many communities to perform services for people who suffer a sudden emotional crisis, such as a death in the family, a divorce, a frightening drug experience, or an urge to commit suicide.

The telephone hotline is a special tool of crisis-center treatment. The hotline is for people who need help but who want to remain anonymous. By calling a local crisis center, a person with suicidal feelings, for example, can receive advice and reassurance that, under regular circumstances, would be almost impossible to acquire.

The crisis center is a preventive measure designed to keep people from acting on their panic. Prevention techniques are also used with entire communities to help people feel that they can become useful and effective in dealing with community problems. For example, a

Figure 14.17
A Los Angeles crisis center where trained volunteers are available to receive calls twenty-four hours a day. This telephone emergency service, or hotline, eliminates the long delays and necessity for dealing with authorities that so often frighten people away from seeking help. Note the chart of common drugs in the window on the right: This chart helps the volunteers to identify drugs that have been taken by a caller who has overdosed or is on a bad trip.

psychologist might teach people to organize and gain some political control over the conditions in their neighborhood.

Halfway Houses

There are thousands of people who spend time in mental hospitals, prisons, and homes for delinquents and who, when finally released, are psychologically unprepared to return to life in society: They may be able to behave well under structured conditions, but they find the freedom and immensity of society confusing and overwhelming. Such people can ease back into society through *halfway houses.*

Halfway houses give their inhabitants the support they need in order to build enough confidence to reenter society. Unwritten rules and informal social pressures guide the members in their efforts to readjust to the larger world.

One of the ways in which community mental health programs are changing the way in which psychotherapy is done in the United States is by recognizing the ability of nonprofessional people to give help. Housewives, policemen, teachers, and nurses are being given short periods of training in psychology. For many of the problems of everyday life, they are just as helpful as a highly trained professional.

Psychotherapy is limited in solving mental problems because human problems are not always limited to individuals, and even an individual's problems are difficult to understand unless his home and neighborhood are well understood. The greatest contribution of community mental health programs is that they recognize the important relation of a community's environments and resources to the emotional well-being of its people.

Community mental health programs have been severely criticized by some psychologists, such as Thomas Szasz, who say these programs are a means of converting social misfits into socially useful citizens with little attention to the person's own psychological needs.

These critics point out that such programs are designed to fulfill the goals of the community, not those of the individual. Community mental health programs also suffer from low budgets and understaffing, thus preventing the programs from adequately doing the job they are designed to do.

In conclusion, psychotherapy and treatment of people with psychological problems, whatever the setting they are conducted in, must fulfill two primary goals: They must provide the troubled person with an understanding of himself and his problems, and they must help him find a way to overcome these difficulties and become a responsible, whole person.

Figure 14.18
Psychologist Albert Ellis has developed an unusual therapeutic approach that he calls "rational-emotive therapy." This method is based on the idea that disturbed people *act* rationally but that their *assumptions* about the world are irrational. Ellis insists that his patients abandon their faulty assumptions.

Figure 14.19
Frederick "Fritz" Perls, the founder of Gestalt therapy, had a major influence on modern psychology and group therapy. Perls believed that the goal of therapy is to unify the fragmented person into a single whole, or Gestalt. He emphasized the necessity of total self-awareness and the destructive aspects of behaving on the basis of "shoulds."

SUMMARY

1. Psychotherapy is the practice of helping people find solutions to mental, emotional, or behavioral problems through the use of psychological techniques.

2. The popular view of "mental illness," which equates mental disorders with physical disorders, is currently undergoing considerable change. The mental illness concept is being replaced by the "problems in living" concept, which places emphasis on the patient's ability to help himself.

3. Psychotherapy is practiced both by highly trained specialists and by people with little or no formal training. Successful therapy depends on a therapist's ability to be warm, compassionate, and intelligent in his relationship with the patient. Patients with mild disorders and with backgrounds similar to the therapist's are likely to benefit most.

4. Psychoanalysis, a form of therapy based on the theories of Sigmund Freud, utilizes the techniques of transference and free association. The primary task of a psychoanalyst is to help the patient become conscious of impulses, desires, and fears that are causing his problems.

5. In client-centered therapy, based on the theories of Carl Rogers, the therapist creates an atmosphere of acceptance, refrains from directing the client, and reflects back what the client has said.

6. Behavior therapy, based upon the principles of learning theory, takes the position that people have psychological problems because they have acquired faulty behavior patterns or have failed to learn effective responses. Systematic desensitization and contingency management are two general kinds of behavior therapy.

7. Group therapy treats several people at the same time, which has the advantage of allowing people to interact with others who share similar problems. Alcoholics Anonymous and Synanon have provided successful group approaches to helping people with problems.

8. Encounter groups are the most popular form of group therapy and are designed for people who do not have serious adjustment problems. These groups encourage openness, honesty, emotional expression, and sensitivity. Family therapy enables family members to better communicate with each other.

9. Commitment to a mental institution can be either voluntary or involuntary. In either case, public mental institutions have serious drawbacks in treatment of mental disorders. Tranquilizers and other drugs are widely used in connection with mental disorders. They are effective in alleviating certain symptoms but do not treat the cause of the disorder.

10. Community mental health programs have been created as an alternative to expensive private therapy and inadequate public institutions. These programs provide both treatment for and prevention of serious problems in living. Community mental health programs include community centers, crisis centers, and halfway houses.

ACTIVITIES

1. Try the following encounter-group technique. Stare at a friend's eyes for several minutes, without explaining (until afterward) why you are doing so. How long were you able to sustain eye contact? Was it a disturbing experience? If possible, try this with several friends. What does the encounter tell you about each friendship?

2. On a sheet of paper draw a large thermometer ranging from 0 to 100 degrees. Think of the most fearful thing you can imagine and write it down at the hundred-degree mark. Write down the least fearful thing you can think of at the zero-degree mark. Continue to list your fears on the thermometer according to their severity. Have several friends make similar lists of their fears. Compare lists, looking for differences and similarities. Do you think any of your fears are based on conditioning? Can you think of a method of reconditioning that would remove the fear or make it less intense?

3. Try this therapeutic technique to release conscious or unconscious anger. Lie down on your bed on your back. Kick your legs and pound your fists on the bed as hard as you can, throwing your whole body into the movement. Your head should be flopping around loosely with the rhythm of the movements. While you are kicking and pounding, use your voice to emit any words or sounds that want to come out. Try yelling "I won't, I won't" over and over again. Keep it up for about ten minutes. (It might be a good idea to warn the people in the house that you will be making a good deal of noise before beginning the exercise.) Afterward, continue lying down for another ten minutes or so, letting your thoughts and emotions wander where they will. You will be surprised at the amount of feelings this exercise can evoke.

4. Psychotherapists use several techniques to get their patients to talk about particular subjects. You can "play" therapist by trying the

Figure 14.20
The existential views described in Chapter 12 have also had a significant impact on the field of psychotherapy. Two of the foremost existential therapists are Victor Frankl (*top*) and Rollo May (*bottom*). After surviving the German concentration camp at Auschwitz, Frankl wrote his famous book, *Man's Search for Meaning.* May, who has had training in both psychoanalysis and theology, emphasizes the irrational, devilish aspect in people that, he feels, must be recognized and accepted if it is not to become evil.

following simple experiment. Mentally select an attitude, or even particular words that you want your subject to express. Then, during the course of an "ordinary" conversation, say "um-mm-mmm" whenever he or she makes the proper response. Try this out on several people and see how effective you are at getting them to say what you want them to say. Write a brief report of your results.

5. Recommend a treatment for the following problems: compulsive overeating, inability to finish work, severe depression. Think of real examples as much as possible. How do the techniques you suggest resemble the therapies described in this chapter?

6. Ask several people in different lines of business if they would hire someone whom they knew had undergone psychotherapy. Do their responses indicate to you that society has matured to where it now understands and accepts emotional problems in the same way it accepts medical problems? Do you believe a person should be barred from high public office because he has sought psychotherapy?

7. Get a few people together to role play a therapy situation. Have one person play the part of a client, another the part of a therapist, with the others serving as evaluators. The group might select some problem for the client to present. After a spontaneous session is played through, have the client and therapist reverse roles to approach the same problem. The evaluators will then point out the techniques observed that they believe would be used by a good therapist.

8. Assume the role of a person with an emotional, alcohol, or drug problem. Find out what program(s) exist in your community to deal with such a problem. Note how long it takes you to find this information, then ask yourself, "If I really needed this help, would I have found it in time?" If no such programs can be found in your area, how might you help start something of this type?

9. One way to lessen feelings of frustration and hostility is to talk about whatever is disturbing you with a close friend or relative. Think about the last time that you talked out a problem with someone. Did the person sympathize with you? If so, what kind of feelings did their sympathy arouse? Did the person try to help you understand the problem, or did he/she simply uphold your point of view? What approach would have been more helpful?

SUGGESTED READINGS

BRANDEN, NATHANIEL. *Breaking Free*. Los Angeles: Nash, 1970. Branden, a practicing psychotherapist, has developed a list of questions posed to clients to help them break through to repressed childhood feelings. Each question is dramatized through interesting case histories.

GLASSER, WILLIAM. *Reality Therapy*. New York: Harper & Row, 1965. A presentation of psychotherapy based on the principle that people do not act irresponsibly because they are "ill," they are "ill" because they act irresponsibly.

Figure 14.21
The writings of British psychiatrist R. D. Laing have been characterized as "anti-psychiatric." Laing believes that the so-called "insane" person makes perfect sense within his own frame of reference and that some kinds of "insanity" may be the only sane response to an insane society.

GOFFMAN, ERVING. *Asylums*. Garden City, N.Y.: Doubleday, 1961 (paper). A highly original sociological analysis of institutions; it presents mental illness as an act played out to fulfill the expectations of institutional custodians.

JANOV, ARTHUR. *The Primal Scream: A Revolutionary Cure for Neurosis*. New York: Putnam, 1970. Janov believes that people are neurotic because they are anesthesized to pain. He insists that re-experiencing traumatic events of the past and reliving the pain of those experiences are the only means for opening up the reservoir of feelings that are trapped inside.

KESEY, KEN. *One Flew Over the Cuckoo's Nest*. New York: Viking, 1964 (paper). A sometimes funny and often frightening novel about one man's experience inside a mental institution. An important work because it forces the reader to confront the issue of the value of therapy on a deeply emotional level.

LINDNER, ROBERT. *The Fifty-Minute Hour*. New York: Bantam, 1954 (paper). A psychologist has put together a collection of short "stories" that are actually adopted from case histories of people he has treated in therapy. Fascinating and informative reading.

LOWEN, ALEXANDER. *The Betrayal of the Body*. New York: Macmillan, 1969 (paper). Based on the theories of Wilhelm Reich, Lowen has developed a form of therapy called *bioenergetics*. He believes that neurotic problems are manifested in the body, and therapy, therefore, must consist of acting out emotional problems in body language.

PERLS, FREDERICK S. *Gestalt Therapy Verbatim*. Lafayette, Calif.: Real People Press, 1969 (paper). Gestalt therapy consists of building awareness of the here and now, rather than concentrating on the past. The goal is to help the patient integrate experiences in order to achieve a wholly functioning personality. Perls has a dynamic writing style, and the book is both funny and informative.

ROGERS, CARL, and BARRY STEVENS. *Person to Person: The Problem of Being Human*. Lafayette, Calif.: Real People Press, 1967 (paper). A good analysis of the dynamics of client-centered therapy. The authors describe the meaning of, and the conditions for, positive growth, with emphasis on the relationship between client and therapist.

ROLF, IDA P. *Structural Integration*. Available from The Guild for Structural Integration, 1776 Union St., San Francisco, Calif., 1963. Rolf has developed a form of therapy popularly known as Rolfing. The book describes the rationale behind her therapy and the techniques employed in accomplishing a flowing, unhampered, and graceful movement.

SZASZ, THOMAS (ed.). *The Age of Madness*. Garden City, N.Y.: Anchor Books, 1973 (paper). Szasz has compiled personal accounts by mental patients, historical writings, excerpts from novels, and a variety of similar pieces all related in some way to involuntary commitment. Fascinating and often horrifying reading.

Figure 14.22
Karl Menninger, a well-known figure in psychiatry, has had considerable influence on the direction of American psychotherapy. Some of his theories are suggested by the titles of the books he has written: *Man Against Himself, Love Against Hate, The Crime of Punishment*, and *Whatever Became of Sin?*

*I wished, by treating
Psychology <u>like</u> a natural science,
to help her become one.*

William James (1892)

Unit VI
Methods in Psychology

Until recently, man's search for knowledge was neatly divided into three distinct areas of study: the natural sciences, the social sciences, and the humanities. The natural sciences involved the objective study of natural phenomena, such as stars, cells, magnetism, and combustion. The social sciences were devoted to man's study of himself and of such aspects of his life as government, revolution, custom, and education. The humanities were concerned with the products of man's mind: ideas and creations, philosophy and religion, poetry and art.

As man's knowledge of his world has increased, however, these divisions have become less distinct. Where, for example, does psychology fit into this scheme? Because of its focus on thought, feeling, and human purpose, psychology was originally considered to be one of the humanities. Yet, because it studies man, it has more recently been classified as a social science. But the human mind and human behavior are certainly natural phenomena, so why should psychology not be considered a natural science? Because the natural sciences have been tremendously successful in revealing the nature of a number of complex phenomena, it seems reasonable that the same methods can provide insight into psychological phenomena as well.

This last unit presents two of the most important features of natural science as it applies to psychology. Chapter 15 discusses the problem of measurement: Can scientists measure the dimensions of the human mind? In Chapter 16, the focus broadens to encompass a presentation of all the various ways psychologists conduct scientific research. Some of these methods are identical to those used in the natural sciences; others are unique to psychology because the object of study—human behavior and experience—is unique. Where these research methods will lead, whether they will remain useful or will change into something currently unimaginable, is something you will probably observe and even influence in your lifetime.

15
Mental Measurement

BASIC CHARACTERISTICS OF TESTS:
Reliability / Validity / Standardization
INTELLIGENCE TESTING:
Widely used tests / Use of IQ scores / Controversy over IQ
APTITUDE AND ACHIEVEMENT TESTS
PERSONALITY TESTING:
Interest tests / Clinical tests / Graphology
SITUATIONAL TESTS
USE AND ABUSE OF TESTS

It is a fact that, on the average, poor Americans and black Americans score lower on standard intelligence tests than do rich Americans and white Americans. Does this mean that poor people and Negroes are naturally inferior to rich people and to whites?

It is a fact that psychotics score differently from normal persons on many personality tests. Does this mean that people whose scores are similar to that of the average psychotic should be hospitalized?

It is a fact that many large corporations have designed personality and aptitude tests that allow them to determine which job applicants are likely to do well and which are not. Does this mean that an applicant should be refused a job on the basis of his scores on a personality test?

If you were to compare your answers to these questions with the answers supplied by others, you would begin to see the enormity and complexity of mental measurement, or testing. One conclusion all would agree on is that people rely heavily on test scores and on test results.

Over the years, psychologists have devised a wide range of tools for measuring intelligence, interests, skills, aptitudes, and personality patterns. The educational, military, industrial, and clinical uses of testing are enormous. Furthermore, the use of psychological testing has steadily increased in the modern world, although many ethical issues have recently been raised about their use. This chapter will describe the major types of tests in current use and will also present some of the controversial aspects of testing.

Figure 15.1
Is it possible to accurately measure such psychological attributes as reasoning ability, depression, or artistic interest in the way a ruler measures length or a thermometer measures heat? Psychological testing, or mental measurement, has been widely studied over the last sixty years, and the results show that the answer is "no." Psychological tests can be helpful, but they do not measure anything as clearly or as accurately as do rulers or thermometers. Nevertheless, psychological tests continue to be extensively used by psychologists, schools, businesses, and government agencies.

BASIC CHARACTERISTICS OF TESTS

All tests have one characteristic in common that makes them both fascinating and remarkably useful: They promise to make it possible to find out a great deal about a person in a very short time. Tests are intended to be useful in predicting how well a person might do in a particular career, in assessing his desires, interests, and attitudes, and in revealing his deep psychological problems. With the use of some tests psychologists can help people to understand things about themselves more clearly than before.

One of the great dangers of testing, however, is that people tend to forget that tests are tools for measuring and predicting human behavior. They start to think about test results as ends in themselves. It is important, therefore, to always keep in mind what a test score means—that it is only a number representing how a person responded to a particular set of questions or problems on a particular day under a particular set of circumstances.

The justification for using a test to make decisions about a person's future depends on whether the decision would be more fair and more accurate based on test scores than on any other criteria. The fairness and usefulness of a test depend on its reliability, on its validity, and on how it has been standardized.

Test Reliability

The ability of a test to give the same results when given to the same person under the same circumstances on several different occasions is known as *reliability*. Imagine, for example, a thermometer that gives you a reading of 95 degrees one minute and 102 degrees five minutes later, even though your temperature stays the same. Such a measuring device, which gives different results from moment to moment, is not of much use. To be reliable, a testing instrument must yield results with consistency.

All kinds of chance factors can influence test scores. People may react differently to the test situation at different times—sometimes trying too hard, sometimes not trying hard enough. They may be anxious, or they may be preoccupied with problems that have nothing to do with the test. An individual may be so worried about what his answers reveal or how high he can score that his emotions interfere with his performance.

Another chance factor is that particular items on the test may influence an individual's score in unexpected ways. For example, if the word "philately" is an item in the vocabulary section of an intelligence test, people who happened to have watched a television program on stamp collecting the night before would probably give the right answer, whether they are "intelligent" or not.

To be reliable, then, a test must be relatively free of the influence of such unpredictable factors. It should be long enough that only a few items will be responded to in a unique and unexpected way by the individual test taker. The questions should be worded clearly and simply so that anxiety or disinterest cannot easily result in confusion for certain individuals. The test should be given with a certain standard set of instructions in a standard set of circumstances so that,

Figure 15.2
Regardless of what is being tested, the test situation is an unpleasant and even traumatic event to many people. A person's emotional and physical well-being at the time of the test can influence his or her performance, as can the environment in which the test is taken. The casual atmosphere (*top*) and the formal atmosphere (*bottom*) are likely to influence the mood and performance of the individuals involved. Test administrators need to be aware of these factors in evaluating the reliability of test scores.

as much as possible, every person is presented with exactly the same situation.

Test Validity

A test may be reliable but still not be valid. *Validity* is the ability of a test to measure what it is supposed to measure. Using a thermometer to determine illness in frogs or lizards would be useless because variations in temperature are not good indicators of illness in cold-blooded animals. Similarly, giving students a test that contains only questions on American history will not measure their mathematical reasoning abilities. For a test to be valid, it must measure what it claims to measure.

Establishing the validity of a test is a more complex problem than assessing its reliability. One of the chief methods for establishing a

Figure 15.3

If one were to construct a test of intelligence by measuring head size and equating bigger measurements with higher IQ, one would have a test with high reliability. That is, all the people who independently measure Leonardo's head would come up with much the same results. However, the test would have little validity because large head size simply does not correspond with high IQ in the real world. The tape-measure test would, however, be a valid test for predicting hat size. A test's validity can only be judged on whether it serves the purpose for which it is intended.

test's validity is to find out how well it predicts some future performance. For example, a test may be designed to measure teaching ability. It may ask questions about teaching methods, attitudes toward students, and so on. But do people who score high on this test really make good teachers?

Suppose that the test makers decide that a good way to check on teaching ability is to find out how much a teacher's students improve their reading in one year. If most teachers who score high on the test later have students who greatly improve in their reading abilities, the test may be considered valid for identifying "good" teachers. School districts may then adopt this test as one way of deciding who to hire to teach in their schools.

But what if a teacher's students are already good readers and have no need to improve? Or what if the students detest reading and refuse to work at it even though they learn rapidly from movies, tapes, and television? Or, what if teachers who can raise reading ability are terrible at teaching anything else? In such cases, would a test that predicts the raising of reading ability still be a test of "teaching ability"? These are the kinds of difficulties that psychologists experience in trying to make a test valid. This example shows that nothing can be said about a test's validity until the *purpose* of the test is perfectly clear.

Standardization

Once a test result or score is obtained, the examiner must translate it into something meaningful and applicable. Because all tests are ways of comparing an individual with other people, a score by itself tells one very little. One needs to know what kinds of scores other people have made. For example, if you are told that your score on a test of one hundred items is 50, you do not know whether you have done well or poorly in relation to other people. Perhaps most other people scored 60 or higher, but, then, most of them may have scored below 30. Test scores, in other words, are not absolute measures. They tell you how you scored in relation to others—how different or how similar you are.

In order to interpret test scores meaningfully, psychologists must develop standards for comparison by giving the test to a large and well-defined group of people. This process is called *standardization.* Once it is completed, all future results can be looked at in light of the results obtained by the standardization group. For example, if you receive the highest score on a test that has previously been tried out on only three other people, you would not consider it to be nearly as significant as receiving the highest score on a test given to 10,000 others. Similarly, you would find more meaning in a test score if you knew it reflected a comparison with other students like yourself than if it resulted from comparison with, say, fishermen.

One method used by psychologists to transform actual (raw) scores into figures that reflect a comparison with others is the

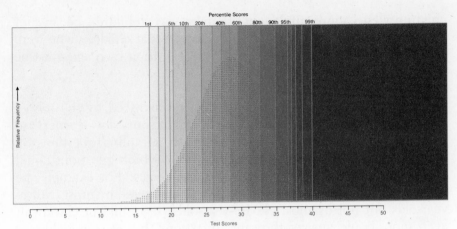

Figure 15.4
The meaning of percentile scores. The range of possible raw scores on a test is shown in relation to an idealized curve that indicates the proportion of people who achieved each score. The vertical lines on the curves indicate percentiles, or proportions of the curve below certain points. Thus the line indicated as the 1st percentile is the line below which only 1 percent of the curve lies; similarly, 99 percent of the curve lies below the 99th percentile line. Percentiles cluster more closely toward the center of the curve because that is where the majority of raw scores occur.

percentile system. Suppose, for example, that you take a test that contains fifty questions. When the results are tabulated, you find that your score is 32—you missed eighteen of the questions. However, you still do not know what this score means.

You are then told that this score places you in the 75th percentile. You now know that 75 percent of the people who took the test when it was standardized scored the same or lower than you did and that 25 percent scored higher. If you scored in the 32nd percentile, it would mean that 32 percent scored the same or below you, and 68 percent, above you. The way in which test scores are translated into percentiles is shown in Figure 15.4.

Thus, when you take a test and obtain a certain score, you should consider the following questions in deciding the significance of the results: (1) Was the test a reliable one, or was it the kind of test whose results could easily have been influenced by chance factors? In other words, if you took that test or a similar one again, would you respond to it in about the same way as you did this time? (2) Was this test a valid one? Are your performances on the test and on the matter it is supposed to measure really related? (3) How was this test standardized? In other words, what group of people are you being compared with by the scores on this test?

INTELLIGENCE TESTING

The most widely used tests in America today are those designed to measure "intelligence" and that yield an "IQ" score. This section will describe some of the major intelligence tests and will present some of the issues raised over the use of IQ scores.

Development of Tests

Alfred Binet, a French psychologist, was the first to develop a useful intelligence test. Binet was unable to define intelligence, but he felt that it was reflected in such things as the abilities to make common-sense judgments, to tell the meanings of words, and to solve problems and puzzles. He was particularly interested in the fact that these abilities seemed to change with age, and he assumed that older children were "more intelligent" than younger children because of these differences in ability. He also assumed that children who were better at answering questions than others of their own age must be more intelligent than their peers.

The Stanford-Binet   In 1904, Binet was asked by the school authorities in Paris to devise a means of picking out "slow learners" so they could be placed in special classes. By sampling questions on many children, Binet was able to determine which questions could usually be answered by children at certain ages. For example, he discovered that certain questions could be answered by most twelve-year-olds but not by most eleven-year-olds. If a child of eleven, or even nine, could answer the same questions that were possible for most twelve-year-olds, he was said to have a *mental age* of twelve. If a child could adequately answer the questions on the test for nine-year-olds but not the more difficult ones, his mental age was nine.

Binet's intelligence test has been revised many times since he developed it. The Binet test currently in widespread use in the United States is a revision created at Stanford University, and it is known as the Stanford-Binet Intelligence Test. The Stanford-Binet test follows Binet's pattern of grouping test items by age level. To stimulate and maintain the child's interest, a variety of tasks are included, ranging from explaining word meanings to drawing pictures to explaining events in daily life. Children are tested one at a time, and for each one the examiner must carry out the standardized instructions exactly. At the same time, he must put the child at ease,

Figure 15.5

A clinical psychologist administers three parts of the Stanford-Binet Intelligence Scale to a five-year-old boy. (a) The tester points to one of the shapes (circle, star, or the like) shown on a page of the notebook and asks the child to pick out the card that contains the same shape. (b) The child is shown the objects attached to the cardboard and is asked to point to each object as the tester names it; for example, "Show me the ball, which one is the ball?" (c) The child is asked to build a tower of blocks to match the tower just constructed by the tester. The child is given credit if he builds a tower of four or more blocks. These parts of the test are easy for most five-year-olds and are usually not given unless the child has difficulty with more advanced items, such as explaining the meanings of words.

a

b
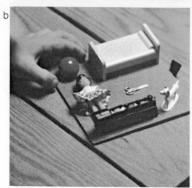

c

make friends with him, and get him to pay attention and to try as hard as he can.

In the final scoring, the mental age indicates how high a level the person has reached. If his performance is as high as the average twelve-year-old's, he is said to have a mental age of twelve. The *IQ*, or *intelligence quotient,* is called a quotient because it used to be computed by dividing mental age by actual (chronological) age and multiplying the result by 100 to eliminate any decimals. Although the term "IQ" has stuck, the actual computation is now made on a basis similar to the percentile system. One reason for this change is that mental age stops increasing at about age seventeen, so adult IQ, if computed as a quotient, would decline steadily, reaching an average value of 50 by the age of thirty-four. The meaning of IQ scores in terms of percentiles will be described shortly.

The Wechsler Tests   Other frequently used individual intelligence tests are the Wechsler Intelligence Scale for Children (WISC) and the Wechsler Adult Intelligence Scale (WAIS). The Wechsler tests differ from the Stanford-Binet in several important ways. For example, the Wechsler tests place more emphasis on performance tasks (such as doing puzzles) than does the Stanford-Binet, so that test

Figure 15.6

Test items similar to those included in the various Wechsler intelligence scales. (a) A sampling of questions from five of the verbal subtests. (b) A problem in block design, one of the performance subtests. The subject is asked to arrange the blocks to match the pattern on a card that he is briefly shown in the notebook. (c) Another example of a performance subtest. The subject is asked to put together puzzle pieces to form a familiar object, such as a duck.
(Test items courtesy The Psychological Corporation, New York.)

a

General Information
1. How many wings does a bird have?
2. How many nickels make a dime?
3. What is steam made of?
4. Who wrote "Paradise Lost"?
5. What is pepper?

General Comprehension
1. What should you do if you see someone forget his book when he leaves his seat in a restaurant?
2. What is the advantage of keeping money in a bank?
3. Why is copper often used in electrical wires?

Arithmetic
1. Sam had three pieces of candy and Joe gave him four more. How many pieces of candy did Sam have altogether?
2. Three men divided eighteen golf balls equally among themselves. How many golf balls did each man receive?
3. If two apples cost 15¢, what will be the cost of a dozen apples?

Similarities
1. In what way are a lion and a tiger alike?
2. In what way are a saw and a hammer alike?
3. In what way are an hour and a week alike?
4. In what way are a circle and a triangle alike?

Vocabulary
"What is a puzzle?"
"What does 'addition' mean?"

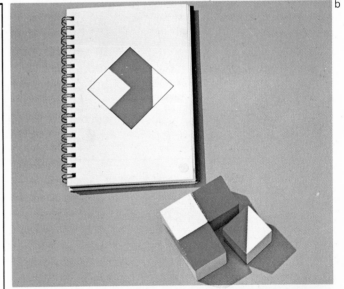

takers who are less skilled in the use of words will not inevitably achieve low IQ scores.

Also, instead of yielding one overall IQ score, the Wechsler tests produce separate percentile scores in several areas—vocabulary, information, arithmetic, picture arrangement, and so on. These separate scores are then combined into separate IQ scores for verbal and performance abilities. This type of scoring provides a more detailed picture of the individual's strengths and weaknesses than one single score could.

Group Tests   Both the Wechsler and Stanford-Binet are costly and time-consuming tests to administer because they are given individually. Paper-and-pencil intelligence tests that could be administered to large groups of people were developed during World War I, when the United States Army found it necessary to test nearly 2 million men.

Group IQ tests, such as the Army Alpha and Beta, have proved to be convenient and economical and are used extensively in schools, employment offices, and many other such situations. A major drawback of group tests is that they are generally not as reliable as individual tests. Chance factors, such as misunderstanding of the instructions, are more likely to influence an individual's score.

The Uses of IQ Scores

In general, intelligence tests are fixed so that most people score near 100. They are designed so that about seventeen people in one hundred score above 115 or below 85, and three in one hundred score above 130 or below 70. In other words, a score of 130 corresponds to the 97th percentile and a score of 70 corresponds to the 3rd. These scores seem to be most useful if related to school

Figure 15.7
Pencil-and-paper tests of intelligence. (a) Items of the type that appear on the School and College Ability Test (SCAT) are shown. The purpose of this test is to estimate high-school students' ability to do college-level work. This test provides a measurement similar to that of a general intelligence test; that is, your SCAT score would be about the same as your Wechsler or Stanford-Binet score. (b) Sample items from the Army General Classification Test (AGCT). This test was developed to select army recruits in World War II and is rather out-of-date. It has since been replaced by the Armed Forces Qualification Test.

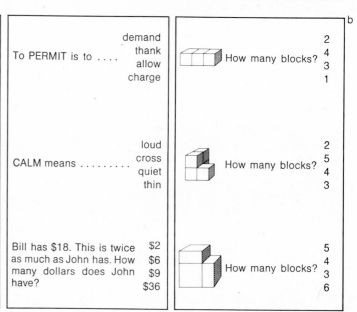

a

Select the missing word by deciding which one of the five words *best* fits in with the meaning of the sentence.

To make you understand my point I must go back a bit and seem to change the subject, but the (   ) will soon be plain.

A correction   **B** effect   **C** origin   **D** controversy
E connection

Choose the correct answer, using scratch paper if necessary.

$\frac{.7}{.05}$ is equal to which of the following?

F $\frac{7}{50}$ **G** $\frac{7}{5}$ **H** 14   **J** 35   **K** None of these

Pick the word or phrase whose meaning is closest to the word in large letters.

induce

A grant   **B** prolong   **C** mix   **D** persuade   **E** convict

To PERMIT is to .... demand / thank / allow / charge

CALM means .... loud / cross / quiet / thin

Bill has $18. This is twice as much as John has. How many dollars does John have? $2 / $6 / $9 / $36

How many blocks?   2 / 4 / 3 / 1

How many blocks?   2 / 5 / 4 / 3

How many blocks?   5 / 4 / 3 / 6

b

achievement—they are quite accurate at predicting which people will do well in schools, in colleges, or in universities.

The increasing number of people who are critical of IQ testing do not question the accuracy of this predictive ability. They do wonder, however, whether such tests actually measure "intelligence." Is school success or the ability to take a test a real indication of intelligence? Generally, IQ tests measure the ability to solve certain types of problems; they do not measure the ability to pose those problems or to question the validity of problems set by others.

Intelligence tests are regularly used in schools to determine what to expect of students: A child with a high IQ score is expected to do better and have fewer academic difficulties than a child with a lower score. Unfortunately, educators sometimes place so much importance on IQ scores that they ignore a student's day-to-day performance in school. If a student scores high, he is expected to do well, and if he scores low, he is expected to do poorly.

In a classic study on teacher expectations for students, researchers told teachers that they were testing students to obtain data on "late bloomers" and that the tests would reveal which of the students were most likely to show an academic spurt later in the year. After pretending to process the test results, the investigators gave the teachers lists of the late bloomers in their classes. In reality, the investigators had randomly picked 20 percent of the children and labeled them "potential academic spurters." Thus, the only real difference between the so-called bloomers and the other students was in what their teachers expected of them. The teachers expected the "spurters" to spurt and the "regular students" to be regular.

This study showed that children from whom teachers expected intellectual gains did, in fact, show gains. In other words, the teachers' preconceived attitudes and expectations about the children actually shaped their development. The conclusion of the researchers was that the teachers' attitude probably caused them to unconsciously communicate their expectations of good work to the "spurters." This communication was done nonverbally, through facial expressions, tone of voice, touch, and posture. The students whom the teacher considered to be "regular" were deprived of the special attention given to the spurters. Their academic performance was average because they were expected to be average. (This is a famous example of the "self-fulfilling prophecy" that is described in Chapter 11.)

The conscious use of IQ scores to decide what kinds of classes students should be placed in or to determine whether they should be given preparation for college has lessened in recent years, but the IQ score remains significant in many people's minds.

Controversy over IQ

Many people have tried to use intelligence tests to prove the existence or nonexistence of inborn intellectual differences between groups. So far, however, no reliable conclusions have been reached about such differences. It has been shown that people whose childhood environment has been quite different from that of the majority of American and European children tend to have lower scores on tests developed in the United States and in Europe. But it is impossible to tell how much of this difference reflects genetic (inborn) potential for intellectual development and how much of it reflects the individual's experience and learning in his environment.

Recently, psychologist Arthur Jensen has argued that intelligence is 80 percent inherited and that environmental changes can do little to raise an individual's IQ score. Jensen has further suggested that the intelligence of blacks in America is probably inferior to that of whites. Needless to say, Jensen's ideas have raised a storm of protest. Many people fighting for racial equality argue that differences in average IQs among different races and ethnic groups are due to inferior opportunity and that therefore the environment of those groups who score poorly should be improved. Other people have argued that intelligence is inherited and the races are basically different and should be taught separately.

In the midst of this controversy, a number of Jensen's assumptions have been questioned. First, he assumed that conclusions based on research on the intelligence of whites can be generalized to blacks, even though the inheritance of intelligence in blacks has received little study. Second, Jensen assumed that middle-class blacks and middle-class whites and lower-class blacks and lower-class whites grow up in similar environments. Jensen's critics argue that these environments do, in fact, differ in important ways. Third, Jensen assumed that the bias of tests in favor of middle-class whites is

Figure 15.8
Items from a test designed by Adrian Dove, a social worker in an urban black community. She developed the test (which has never been scientifically validated) to demonstrate that an intelligence test measures a person's familiarity with his culture as much as it measures his ability to learn and understand. What kind of IQ scores do you think middle-class white suburbanites would get on such a test?

The Dove Counterbalance Intelligence Test
by Adrian Dove

In "C. C. Rider," what does "C. C." stand for?
(a) Civil Service
(b) Church Council
(c) County Circuit, preacher of an old-time rambler
(d) Country Club
(e) "Cheating Charley" (the "Boxcar Gunsel")

Cheap "chitlings" (not the kind you purchase at the frozen-food counter) will taste rubbery unless they are cooked long enough. How soon can you quit cooking them to eat and enjoy them?
(a) 15 minutes   (b) 2 hours
(c) 24 hours
(d) 1 week (on a low flame)
(e) 1 hour

A "Handkerchief Head" is
(a) A cool cat   (b) A porter
(c) An "Uncle Tom"   (d) A hoddi
(e) A "preacher"

A "Gas Head" is a person who has a
(a) Fast-moving car
(b) Stable of "lace"   (c) Process
(d) Habit of stealing cars
(e) Long jail record for arson

If a man is called a "Blood," then he is a
(a) Fighter   (b) Mexican-American
(c) Negro   (d) Hungry Hemophile
(e) Redman or Indian

If they throw the dice and "7" is showing on the top, what is facing down?
(a) "Seven"   (b) "Snake eyes"
(c) "Boxcars"   (d) "Little Joes"
(e) "Eleven"

(Answers: "c" is correct for all but the last question, which is "a.")

Figure 15.9
Project SEED (Special Elementary Education for the Disadvantaged) is designed to teach high-level mathematics to disadvantaged elementary-school students. Its goal is to teach children that they can be successful in learning and that intellectual work can be rewarding. Another aim is to counter the argument that black children are genetically intellectually inferior to white children. Evaluation studies show that black SEED children score the same as white children of the same age.

unimportant, even though many items on the test obviously depend on familiarity with middle-class white culture.

Jensen's critics point out that if a test is developed for people with a specific cultural background, it cannot legitimately be used for people with a quite different background. For example, of all the various kinds of items on intelligence tests, vocabulary provides the best single estimate of IQ scores. Yet vocabulary clearly depends on cultural background. If someone has never heard words like "sonata" or "ingenuous," he will perform poorly on verbal intelligence tests. And if he has grown up in a community in which English is not the primary language, he will be handicapped even further.

Although this controversy still rages, it is probably best not to think of IQ scores in terms of heredity or environment but instead to use them cautiously in making predictions about individual capabilities. For example, test scores may alert a seventh-grade teacher to the fact that one student is equipped at the outset of a course to do excellent work and should be held to a high standard but that another student may have more difficulty in grasping the main ideas and should be given special help.

MEASURING ABILITIES AND EXPERIENCE

Intelligence tests are designed to measure the overall ability to solve problems that involve symbols (such as words, numbers, and pictures). Other tests have been developed to assess the special abilities and experiences unique to the individual. These include aptitude tests and achievement tests.

Aptitude tests attempt to predict how well a person will be able to learn a new skill or ability and to determine what sort of job or career he is "talented" for. The most widely used aptitude test is the General Aptitude Test Battery (GATB). Actually, the GATB comprises nine different tests from vocabulary to manual dexterity. Test results are used to determine whether a person meets minimum standards for each of a large number of occupations. In addition to GATB, there are aptitude tests in music, language, art, mathematics, and other specific fields. Most prospective college students take a test called the SAT (Scholastic Aptitude Test), a test that is good at predicting college success.

Whereas aptitude tests are designed to predict how well a person will be able to learn a new skill or ability, *achievement tests* are supposed to measure how well he has already done in some area. All educational tests and exams are achievement tests. These tests, however, serve many purposes besides an instructor's assessment of a student's knowledge. They also help the student assess his knowledge for himself.

Most individuals are unable to evaluate the contents of their memories or estimate the state of their learned skills. People often underestimate how much they know. If a person has a chance to answer questions about the South American geography he learned many years before, he may find that much of the information comes back to him, even though, if asked beforehand, he might have doubted that he could recall a scrap of knowledge in this area.

At other times, however, people think they know more than they

Figure 15.10

Items from aptitude tests. (a) The General Aptitude Test Battery (GATB) includes a test for the ability to take small shapes apart and put them back together again as well as the pencil-and-paper items of the type shown here. These tests, used extensively by the U.S. Employment Service, make it possible for a person to find out whether he meets minimum standards for each of a considerable number of occupations. (b) Sample items similar to those used in the Differential Aptitude Test (DAT), which serves a similar purpose to the GATB but has only pencil-and-paper items and is used more with students than is the GATB.

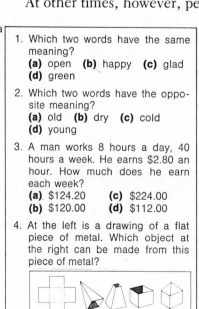

a

1. Which two words have the same meaning?
   (a) open **(b)** happy **(c)** glad **(d)** green

2. Which two words have the opposite meaning?
   (a) old **(b)** dry **(c)** cold **(d)** young

3. A man works 8 hours a day, 40 hours a week. He earns $2.80 an hour. How much does he earn each week?
   (a) $124.20   **(c)** $224.00
   (b) $120.00   **(d)** $112.00

4. At the left is a drawing of a flat piece of metal. Which object at the right can be made from this piece of metal?

   A B C D

b

MECHANICAL REASONING.
Which man in this picture has the heavier load?

A   B

LANGUAGE USAGE: II. SENTENCES.
Decide which of the lettered parts of each sentence contain errors, if any, and mark the corresponding letters on the answer sheet.

Ain't we / going to the / office / next week / at all.

A   B   C   D   E

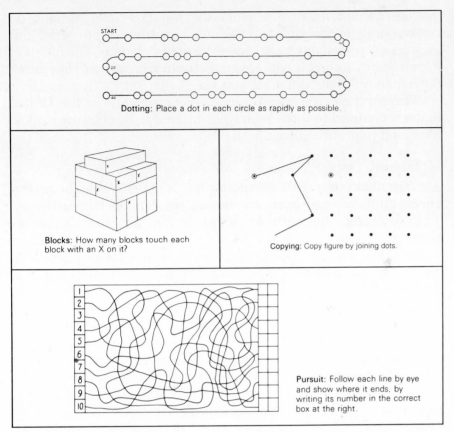

START

Dotting: Place a dot in each circle as rapidly as possible.

Blocks: How many blocks touch each block with an X on it?

Copying: Copy figure by joining dots.

Pursuit: Follow each line by eye and show where it ends, by writing its number in the correct box at the right.

Figure 15.11

Sample items from the MacQuarrie Test for Mechanical Ability (MTMA), which was designed to measure several aspects of mechanical aptitude. Auto mechanics and lathe operators would score well on this test. So, probably, would architects and engineers.

do. Having taken a course and studied sporadically, many students feel they understand material that they do not really command. Periodic, systematic, and comprehensive achievement testing can tell a student what he knows, how well he knows it, what to review, and what to skip. If he tries to study the things he already knows, he will waste his time; if he skips things that he has not mastered, he will be in even worse trouble.

The distinction between achievement tests and aptitude tests has become somewhat blurred. What psychologists had at first thought were tests of aptitude—defined as *innate* ability or talent—turned out to partly measure different kinds of experience, so that they had to be considered in some sense achievement tests. On the other hand, achievement tests often turned out to be the best predictors of many kinds of occupational abilities, so that they were in some sense aptitude tests. Because of this confusion, psychologists have agreed that the distinction between the two types of tests rests more on purpose than on content. Thus, if a test is used to predict future ability, it is considered an aptitude test; if it is used to assess what a person has already learned, it is an achievement test.

PERSONALITY TESTING

The instruments for measuring personality characteristics differ from instruments for measuring abilities. Answers to questions on an

1	Actor	L	I	D
2	Advertising Man	L	I	D
3	Architect	L	I	D
4	Military Officer	L	I	D
5	Artist	L	I	D
6	Astronomer	L	I	D
7	Athletic Director	L	I	D
8	Auctioneer	L	I	D
9	Author of novel	L	I	D
10	Author of technical book	L	I	D
11	Auto Salesman	L	I	D
12	Auto Racer	L	I	D
13	Auto Mechanic	L	I	D
14	Airplane Pilot	L	I	D
15	Bank Teller	L	I	D
16	Designer, Electronic Equipment	L	I	D
17	Building Contractor..	L	I	D
18	Buyer of merchandise	L	I	D
19	Carpenter	L	I	D
20	Cartoonist	L	I	D
21	Cashier in bank	L	I	D
22	Electronics Technician	L	I	D

Figure 15.12

A few items from part of the Strong Vocational Interest Blank (SVIB). In this phase of the test the subject indicates whether he thinks he would like (L), dislike (D), or be indifferent to (I) working in each occupation. Later in the test the person is asked to react similarly to lists of activities and types of people.

Figure 15.13

The Strong Vocational Interest Blank exists in two forms, one for men and one for women. Both forms yield scores on a set of basic interests. Patterns for scores on the male version of the test are shown here.

The test is arranged so that a random selection of fifty-two-year-old men provides the standard, or average, against which all other scores are compared. Their scoring pattern appears as the blue line through the 50 mark on every scale. Also shown here are the scoring patterns produced by a group of astronauts and a group of sixteen-year-old males. According to the test, neither of these groups has as much interest in business management as the standard group and both have more interest in adventure. Astronauts appear to be more interested than the sixteen-year-olds in practically every kind of work, particularly mathematics, science, public speaking, and teaching.

intelligence test indicate whether the test taker can, in fact, do certain kinds of thinking and solve certain kinds of problems. But answers on personality tests cannot be right or wrong. The question in personality testing is not "How much can you do?" or "How much do you know?" but "What are you like?"

The psychological measurement of personality in the United States is confined to three main types: interest tests, objective clinical tests, and projective clinical tests.

Interest Tests

The essential purpose of an interest test is to determine the preferences, attitudes, and interests one has regarding certain activities. The taker's responses to the test items are compared to the responses given by people in clearly defined groups, such as professions or occupations. The more his answers correspond to those of people in a particular occupation, the more likely it is that he would enjoy that profession.

In constructing the most widely used device for measuring interests, the Strong Vocational Interest Blank, psychologists took the responses of people who are successfully employed in a particular occupation and compared them to the responses of a group of "people in general." Suppose, for instance, that most engineers responded that they liked the idea of becoming an astronomer but did not like the idea of becoming an athletic director. If the group of people in general had responded that they did not particularly favor or disfavor either of these possibilities, the item was included in the test. Another test constructed in this way is the Kuder Preference Record.

This system allows psychologists to construct a series of questions and appropriate responses that directly correspond to responses of most people in a specific occupation. Research has shown that people who do give responses similar to those given by doctors, for example, are less likely to drop out of medical school than those who

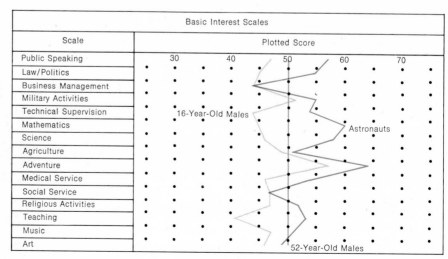

	Basic Interest Scales				
Scale	Plotted Score				
Public Speaking	30	40	50	60	70
Law/Politics					
Business Management					
Military Activities					
Technical Supervision	16-Year-Old Males				
Mathematics					
Science				Astronauts	
Agriculture					
Adventure					
Medical Service					
Social Service					
Religious Activities					
Teaching					
Music					
Art	52-Year-Old Males				

		Most		Least
G.	Read a love story	●	G.	●
H.	Read a mystery	●	H.	●
I.	Read science fiction	●	I.	●
J.	Visit an art gallery	●	J.	●
K.	Browse in a library	●	K.	●
L.	Visit a museum	●	L.	●
M.	Collect autographs	●	M.	●
N.	Collect coins	●	N.	●
O.	Collect butterflies	●	O.	●
P.	Watch television	●	P.	●
Q.	Go for a walk	●	Q.	●
R.	Listen to music	●	R.	●

Figure 15.14

Items from the Kuder Preference Record (KPR), a test that works similarly to the Strong Vocational Interest Blank. The person taking the test is asked to pick from among three possible activities the one he would most like to do and the one he would least like to do. The test provides numerous sets of such alternatives.

give other responses. One purpose of these tests, then, is to predict how successful one might be in a particular career.

Clinical Tests

Clinical tests are those used by psychiatrists and psychologists to help in psychotherapy. Some of these tests are *objective,* or forced-choice; that is, a person must select one out of a small number of possible choices. Other clinical tests are *projective*—they are wide open and encourage the test taker to respond freely and give his own interpretations of various test stimuli.

Objective Type   The most widely used forced-choice personality test is the *Minnesota Multiphasic Personality Inventory* (MMPI). Like other personality tests, the MMPI has no right or wrong answers. The test is arranged in the form of 550 statements to which the test taker can respond "true," "false," or "cannot say." Items vary from statements like "I like tall women" to "I daydream very little."

The items in the MMPI are designed to reveal sexual attitudes, delusions, habits, fears, religious feelings, social attitudes, and symptoms of mental problems. Although all the statements that are related to any given characteristic (such as depression) are scattered throughout the test, the answers to them can be pulled out and organized into a single depression scale. There are nine such clinical scales to the MMPI, as well as a masculine-feminine scale.

One unique aspect of the MMPI is that it has a built-in lie detector. If a person attempts to deceive the tester by giving inaccurate answers, his lying will be reflected in a series of questions planted throughout the test. If, for example, a test taker answers "true" to questions such as "I never tell a lie," the psychologist scoring the test may reasonably suspect that he is trying to create a false impression. The MMPI is also designed to detect misunderstanding of items,

Figure 15.15

Four items of the kind that appear in the Minnesota Multiphasic Personality Inventory (MMPI). There are 550 such items on the test, each item appearing on a separate card that the test taker sorts into piles of True, False, and Cannot Say. This test is valid in the sense that patients in mental hospitals score much higher on most of the scales than do other people, but scoring high on any particular scale does not necessarily mean that one is mentally disturbed.

(Reproduced by permission. © 1943 renewed 1970 by the University of Minnesota. Published by The Psychological Corporation, New York. All rights reserved.)

T.		F.	
☐	☐	☐	I have never indulged in any unusual sex practices.
☐	☐	☐	Someone has been trying to poison me.
☐	☐	☐	I am afraid of losing my mind.
☐	☐	☐	I feel anxiety about something or someone all the time.

consistent failure to reply to questions, tendencies to deny symptoms, and tendencies to give unusual answers.

The MMPI has proved to be useful in diagnosing various forms of mental disturbance and in providing data for personality research. It has also been used for such purposes as employment screening and college counseling—but because it is possible for quite capable people to obtain highly unusual scores on this test, there is considerable question as to whether such uses are wise.

Projective Type   Projective tests are open-ended examinations in which personality characteristics are revealed by the way people tell stories about or otherwise interpret ambiguous material. The idea is that because there is no established meaning in the material, any meaning that the person puts into his story must come from his own needs, wishes, fears, and other aspects of his personality.

Perhaps the best-known and most widely discussed projective technique is the *Rorschach Inkblot Test.* This famous test was developed by Hermann Rorschach, a Swiss psychiatrist. Rorschach created ten inkblot designs and a system for scoring responses to them. To administer the inkblot test, a psychologist hands the inkblots one by one to the person being tested and instructs him to report what he sees. Administration is divided into a free-association period and an inquiry period. During the free association, the person simply identifies what he sees. He might say, for example, that a certain area of a blot resembles an airplane or an animal head. During the inquiry, the examiner asks certain general questions in an attempt to discover what aspects of the inkblot determined the person's response.

In general, three categories are involved in scoring a person's

Figure 15.16
Symmetrical inkblots similar to those used in the Rorschach Inkblot Test. Psychologists skilled in the Rorschach test can derive a great deal of information about a person not only from his responses to the cards but also from his behavior during the test. Test results are frequently inconsistent and have not been shown to relate highly to a person's other characteristics. Nevertheless, the Rorschach is by far the most popular test ever devised—about 1 million Americans take it every year. It seems that both psychologists and test takers find this test as interesting and mysterious as their own personalities.

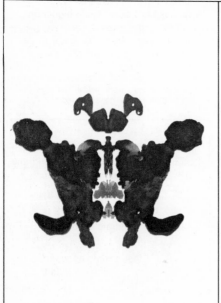
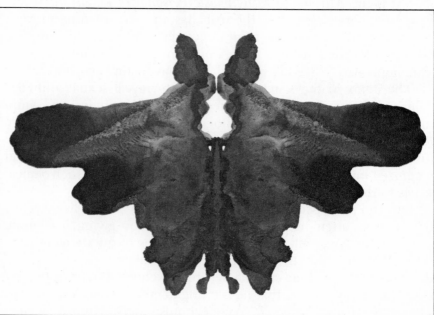

response. The first category indicates the location or part of the blot with which the subject associates each response. The second category relates to whether the subject responds primarily to form, color, shading, or movement. The third category is content (human, animal, scenery, and so on).

The lack of structure involved in the Rorschach technique is both a strength and a weakness. It is a strength in the sense that it provides the opportunity for a person to reveal important unconscious aspects of himself that might not emerge otherwise. The disadvantage is that interpretation is left open to the biases of the particular examiner.

The second most widely used projective test, called the *Thematic Apperception Test* (TAT), consists of a series of twenty cards containing pictures of a variety of vague but suggestive situations. The test taker is asked to tell a story about the picture, including what led up to the situation, what the characters are thinking and feeling, and how it will end.

Each TAT story is evaluated on the basis of a standard scoring system. The examiner pays close attention to themes that emerge in the individual's invented plots. The interpreter looks for the hero or leading figure of the story and determines the needs of the story's characters. Are the characters aggressive? Do they seem to have needs for achievement, love, or sex? Are they being attacked or

Figure 15.17
Three cards similar to those used in the Thematic Apperception Test (TAT). The scenes depicted in the drawings permit a variety of interpretations, and the person taking the test is therefore assumed to project his own needs, wishes, defenses, and other personality factors into the story. One problem with analyzing the responses to the TAT cards is that the story a person tells might occur to him because of some incident that recently happened rather than because of a basic attitude about life that he holds.

Figure 15.18
The Children's Apperception Test (CAT) works the same way as the TAT but uses pictures of animals instead of people. Animals were chosen for this version of the TAT because children supposedly identify more readily with animals—although researchers later found that this is not true. Like the Rorschach, the TAT and CAT are very popular tests. They both seem to be helpful devices in giving a psychologist more material to consider in making his evaluation of a person, but they do not seem to be valid, reliable measuring tools in themselves.

Figure 15.19

Other popular projective techniques are the Draw-a-Person, House-Tree-Person, and Draw-a-Family tests. The drawings shown here were made by a thirteen-year-old girl named Chris. The first drawing was produced when Chris was asked to draw a person. The off-center design of the blouse and the precision of the drawing were at first thought to indicate that Chris was a rigid and overly careful person. The flat chest and the pantskirt were thought to show that she wanted to pretend that she had no sexuality. Similiar interpretations were made of the second picture that she drew after being asked to draw a family. Notice the apathetic expression and the pock marks on the father's face. The cross-hatching of Chris's sweater were thought again to indicate rigidity and a denial (or crossing out) of sexuality. The interpretion of such drawings is practically impossible unless the psychologist also knows something about the rest of the life of the person he is testing. The above interpretations were reinforced by the fact that Chris's father was in a mental hospital and, according to Chris's mother, had sexually molested all the children in the family before being put there.

criticized by another person, or are they receiving affection and comfort? But even though psychologists may agree to general answers for these questions, there are still wide differences in the way these answers are interpreted.

A number of other projective tests have been developed that require a person to draw pictures of people, to construct miniature situations out of toys or out of pictures, to make figures from clay, or to act out social roles. One such measurement device is the *Draw-a-Person Test,* in which the individual is instructed simply to draw a person and then to draw a second person of the opposite sex from the first one. By studying the form and content of each drawing, a psychologist is able to measure a person's tendency to be analytical and to structure his environment. People who are analytical tend to include many details in their drawings, to differentiate clearly between the sexes, and to avoid simplification.

Graphology

One kind of testing that is closely related to projective testing is handwriting analysis, or *graphology*. Graphology is not widely accepted in the United States and is regarded more as a fanciful game than as a method of personality analysis, but in Europe psychologists take it seriously—more seriously, indeed, than the Rorschach.

Graphologists believe that a person's handwriting style is greatly influenced by unconscious forces. They further believe that a person's handwriting style is fixed, consistent, and measurable. How does graphology work? Essentially, it measures how an individual's handwriting changes from the way he was taught. Almost everyone was taught a standard type of writing, but only a few adhere to the standard form. It is in analyzing differences between personal and standard styles that the graphologist develops a portrait of the writer's personality. The graphologist looks at such things as letter size, slant, and form, at the flow and design of words and phrases, and at the

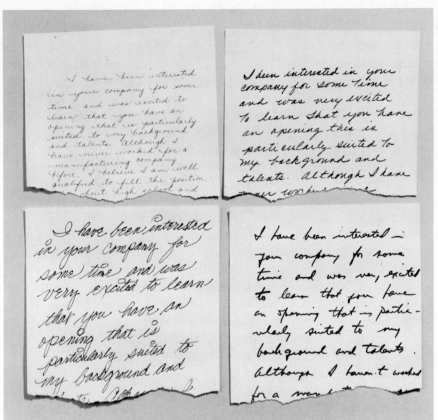

Figure 15.20
On the basis of these handwriting samples, which writer would you hire to sell insurance policies for your company? Which one would you hire to keep your financial records? Handwriting analysis has been used effectively in making decisions like these, but no one has yet been able to establish firm rules for using graphology to reliably and validly measure personality.

strength of stroke. From these studies he purports to measure creativity, individuality, and general adjustment.

SITUATIONAL TESTS

The controversies that arise over the use of most psychological tests, particularly projective tests, are caused by doubts about validity. There is usually no obvious relation between a person's responses to the test and his behavior in everyday life. Do a person's perceptions in an inkblot really tell something about his ability to keep calm under pressure or his problems with sex? Such difficulties can be eliminated by the use of a rather different kind of test.

In general, the closer a test is to the actual situation that the tester wants to know about, the more useful the results will be. A test that measures an individual's performance in terms of emotional, attitudinal, and physical responses to "true life" situations is called a *situational test*. For example, a test required for getting a driver's license involves actual driving.

An interesting example of a situational test was developed by the Office of Strategic Services (oss) during World War II. The oss decided that it needed to measure candidates for assignment to military intelligence. In order to evaluate the candidates, the oss set up a three-day session of intensive testing in which highly complicated and frustrating problems were presented to the candidates. By actually placing candidates in situations similar to those they would encounter as agents, the examiners were able to observe more "true-to-life" reactions.

During the test period the candidates lived together in small groups under inspection by members of the assessment staff. Nearly everything they said, did, or felt was visible to the examiners. In one procedure, an assessment staff member suggested that the candidate build a certain type of construction cube out of wooden poles, blocks, and pegs. The candidate was told that because it would be impossible for one man to complete the job within the ten-minute time allotted, he would be given two helpers. Actually, the helpers were psychologists who played prearranged roles. One assistant was extremely lazy and passive, engaged in projects of his own, and offered no advice. The other interfered with the work by making impractical suggestions, harassing the candidate, and asking embarrassing questions.

The assistants succeeded so well in frustrating the candidates that in the whole history of the program the construction was never completed. The emotional reactions elicited by this task provide a good measure of the candidates' tolerance for frustration. Some men were so shaken by this experience that they asked to be released from

Figure 15.20
Using this airplane flight simulator, pilots are trained and tested before they are given the responsibility of flying a real airliner. Emergency situations can be created in the simulator to test how a pilot reacts in a crisis. None of the standard psychological tests described in this chapter could predict accurately whether a pilot would panic in such a situation—that's why this type of test can be extremely valuable.
(United Air Lines photo.)

the program and from their assignment. Obviously, this test was extremely effective in finding out who could really do the job.

THE USE OF TESTS IN WESTERN SOCIETY

As was mentioned at the beginning of this chapter, psychological testing has become an extremely widespread activity in Western society. Testing is probably the biggest single contribution that the science of psychology has made to Western culture.

Testing has been developed to a high art and a big business. (One of the main businesses of a company called the Psychological Corporation, for example, is to publish tests.) Psychological tests of the kind that now exist probably do as good a job as they are ever likely to. The difficult question has become not, how can tests be made better, but, how should tests be used?

The main benefits of psychological testing have been benefits of efficiency. In fact, efficiency was the original motivation for the development of IQ testing. Tests have provided help in identifying people who will and will not do well in school, who will and will not make good mechanics, soldiers, typists, or salesmen. Schools use tests so that they will not waste time having brilliant children read *Dick and Jane* for a year or having retarded children struggling to make sense out of algebra books. Businesses use tests so that they will not put clumsy people into jobs requiring great care or highly trained people into jobs that are dull. Individuals have psychologists give them tests in hopes of finding out something about themselves that they might otherwise have to learn by years of hard experience.

But although tests do help in these ways, there also are disadvantages to their use. For one thing, tests are imperfect. Bright, able people sometimes get low IQ scores; perfectly sane people sometimes make unusual responses to inkblots; incompetent workers sometimes do well on aptitude tests; and highly disturbed people sometimes show no sign of their problems in writing answers on a personality test form. Tests usually turn out to measure much less than most people think they do, and they never supply absolutely certain information. *The results of all tests are always a matter of probability*—at best they supply only good clues that should be followed up.

Another drawback of psychological testing is that tests compare an individual with others in his society according to accepted social standards. Because psychologists do not agree on exactly what intelligence and emotional disturbance are, they cannot measure them perfectly; what they can do is devise questions that are answered differently by people whom society calls "smart" than by people whom society calls "dumb" or that are answered differently by people whom society calls "stable" than by people whom society calls "crazy." Tests results thus reflect social judgments, and if society is wrong or unfair about something, tests are likely to be, too.

Such considerations lead to doubts about the use of tests in making major decisions about individual lives. Should people be denied a college education or be confined to a mental institution on the basis of test results? Should people be required to take tests at all, when many find it a traumatic, demanding experience of questionable value? Do governments or businesses have any right to use tests to probe into the personal lives of potential employees? The answers to these questions are not easy. Psychological tests, like other technological advances, have their uses and their limitations. Like automobiles, tranquilizers, and nuclear power, tests can be overused and badly used. But, as is the case with other technologies, they can be used well if people understand them.

Figure 15.21
Psychological testing has been sharply criticized in recent years, but certain forms of testing are unlikely to be subjected to such questioning. For example, to obtain a driver's license in most states, you must take three different kinds of psychological tests: a test of visual acuity, a written test of driving knowledge, and a situational test of driving skill. Few people suggest that this method of driver selection be abolished.

SUMMARY

1. All tests are designed to find out a great deal about a person in a very short time. Test scores are not ends in themselves; they are simply numbers indicating how a person responded to a situation.

2. Reliability is the ability of a test to give the same results upon

repetition. Validity is the extent to which a test measures what it is supposed to measure.

3. Standardization allows a test score to be interpreted in light of other people's scores. The percentile system is a method for comparing scores—it lets you know how your score ranks with the scores of others.

4. The first intelligence test was designed by Alfred Binet as a means of picking out slow learners. The test currently in widespread use is a revision of Binet's test known as the Stanford-Binet. The results of this test yield an IQ score. The Wechsler tests differ from the Stanford-Binet in that they place more emphasis on performance tasks than on verbal skills.

5. IQ tests are good at measuring how well children will do in school, but how much this measurement has to do with "intelligence" is not clear because intelligence has never been well defined.

6. It is generally thought that differences in IQ scores are a reflection of cultural and environmental differences as well as of certain hereditary tendencies that are common among all groups of people.

7. Aptitude and achievement tests are virtually identical in content, so the distinction between the two is based primarily on their purpose. Aptitude tests are used to predict how well a person will be able to learn a new skill. Achievement tests are supposed to measure how well the person has already done in some area.

8. Personality tests have no right or wrong answers; they attempt to find out what a person is like. Interest tests are designed to determine the preferences, attitudes, and degree of interest one has toward certain activities. The results of these tests are used to predict how successful one might be in a particular career.

9. Clinical tests are used primarily as an aid in psychotherapy. The most widely used of these tests are the MMPI and such projective tests as the Rorschach Inkblot Test, the Thematic Apperception Test, and the Draw-a-Person Test.

10. A situational test, such as a driving test, is designed to measure how well a person performs in specific, "real-life" situations.

11. Tests can be useful tools for many purposes in a variety of situations, but they also have drawbacks and limitations. Many people are beginning to question the desirability of testing because they are not sure that testing's usefulness in many situations outweighs its disadvantages.

ACTIVITIES

1. The chapter discusses a wide range of devices used to measure intelligence, aptitudes, personality traits, and so on. Think about and write down the criteria by which *you* "test" others. How crucial are these "tests" in determining whether or not you decide to pursue a friendship? Think about the ways in which you "test" yourself. Are

the criteria you use for yourself the same as those you use for others? If not, what are the differences?

2. *Barnumisms* are broad generalizations or clinical truisms that apply to nearly everyone (such as "you have a strong need to be liked"). Because they apply to a broad spectrum of any population, they are of little assistance in psychological testing. To become more aware of the various testing techniques, you might consult a college testing service or a clinical psychologist and take one or more of the various psychological tests. While you are taking the test, and with the permission of the person administering the test, jot down any comments regarding the questions and record the numbers of questions you consider to be Barnumisms. Discuss any questions or comments with the test administrator.

3. If you were asked to rate people on an intelligence scale of your own making, what criteria would you use, and how would you make your decision? What roles would such factors as memory, emotional maturity, creativity, morality, and intuition play in formulating your intelligence scale? How would you "test" for these factors?

4. Make your own inkblot test. Take a sheet of paper and fold it in half. Place three drops of liquid ink along the crease of the paper. Fold the paper and spread the ink. When you open the paper, you should have an inkblot. Show the inkblot to three or four people and write down the ages and responses of those viewers.

5. Psychological testing has been considered an invasion of privacy by some people. Defend or refute the use of psychological testing. Discuss this question with your classmates—perhaps you can organize a classroom discussion on the subject.

6. What kind of test would you devise as an entrance exam to a college or university? Would you use a test at all? If not, what criteria would you use to make a decision?

7. As discussed in this chapter, graphologists attempt to assess an individual's personality on the basis of his handwriting. Collect samples of handwriting from a wide variety of individuals that you know (family, friends, teachers, and so on). Code the samples so that only you know which samples belong to which person, then have several subjects guess the personality that goes with each sample. Analyze your data. What do they seem to show, if anything?

8. The experiment on teachers' expectations described in this chapter has some far-reaching implications. In light of this experiment, do you think it is a good idea for teachers to be informed of their students' IQ scores? What good uses might be made of this knowledge? Do you think students should be told their IQ scores? What about their parents? Discuss the positive and negative aspects of these questions.

9. Call or write for one of the questionnaires available from a computer dating service (they usually place advertisements in the

classified sections of newspapers). Fill out or just look over the questionnaire. What general categories do the questions seem to fall into? What does the questionnaire seek to measure? Do you think it might be a useful way to obtain meaningful information about people?

SUGGESTED READINGS

EYSENCK, H. J. *Know Your Own I.Q.* London: Penguin, 1968. You can use this book, which contains eight tests and scoring keys, to get a rough estimate of how you would score on an IQ test, but you will also discover the cultural biases that are inevitably built into such tests—this book was written for a British audience.

FITTS, P. M., and M. I. POSNER. *Human Performance.* Belmont, Calif.: Brooks/Cole, 1967. A nontechnical book about the differences in human skills and abilities. Especially interesting when read with regard to practical implications for vocational and aptitude testing.

GARCIA, JOHN. "IQ: The Conspiracy," *Psychology Today* (September 1972). A provocative and well-written article about the abuses of IQ testing.

GROSS, MARVIN. *The Brain Watchers.* New York: Random House, 1962. This book is an outspoken and well-written criticism of personality testing as inaccurate and immoral. Worth reading as a signal to the dangers of their excessive and improper use.

HOFFMANN, BANESH. *The Tyranny of Testing.* New York: Collier Books, 1962 (paper). Hoffmann contends that objective tests "reward superficiality, ignore creativity, and penalize the person with a probing, subtle mind." In this readable little book, he criticizes the massive role that tests play in society today.

ROSENTHAL, R. "Self-Fulfilling Prophecy," *Psychology Today* (September 1968). An interesting article about the effects of teachers' expectations on students' progress, as described in this chapter. This important experiment is described in a clear, easy-to-read style.

SEREBRIAKOFF, VICTOR. *How Intelligent Are You?* New York: Signet, 1968. The author, a leader in Mensa (the high IQ club), describes this book as giving people "a harmless opportunity to have fun by checking their intelligence and personality on tests which are parallel with and illustrative of scientific tests."

WILCOX, ROGER (ed.). *The Psychological Consequences of Being a Black American.* New York: Wiley, 1971. A good anthology of articles on testing intelligence in blacks, cultural disadvantages of minority groups, intelligence and achievement, attitudes and emotional characteristics of blacks, and the black psychologist in America.

16
How to Do Research

DEVISING RESEARCH QUESTIONS:
Samples and data / Observer effects

COLLECTING AND INTERPRETING DATA:
Simple observation / Correlation / Experimentation

STATISTICS AND WHY THEY MATTER:
Descriptive statistics / Inferential statistics

WRITING AND READING RESEARCH ARTICLES

WRITING REVIEW PAPERS

THEORY AND PROOF

Psychological researchers are trained knowledge-seekers. They use certain tried-and-true methods to find out something about how humans and other animals behave. There is nothing magical or mysterious about these methods. They are careful applications of common sense that you, too, can use to investigate how and why people (or animals) behave and feel as they do. This chapter will describe how the experts go about seeking psychological knowledge and how they often encounter pitfalls and make mistakes in their efforts. At the same time, it explains how to go about doing your own research on any matter that may happen to interest you.

ASKING QUESTIONS

One of the most important steps in the knowledge-seeking process is the careful formulation of the proper questions. If you know what to ask and how to ask it, you are halfway to the answer.

If a prosecuter in a court case were to ask the defendant, "Do you still beat your wife?" the defendant might rightly find it difficult to answer. This question is unfair and improper because it assumes that the defendant habitually beats his wife. A question phrased in this manner is loaded to make the defendant look bad whatever reply he gives. The only way the defendant can avoid giving the answer that the prosecuter wants to hear is to reject the question.

The "defendant" in the case of research, however, is usually a person or animal who does not even know—or care—that a question is being asked. As a result, it is easy for psychologists to make the mistake of designing experiments guaranteed to prove their assumptions. The tendency for psychologists to load their experimental

Figure 16.1
Careful observation made under controlled conditions forms the basis of the scientific method. However, it is not easy to maintain complete objectivity; one is always tempted to interpret the data in accordance with one's own preconceived notions. This temptation is particularly strong in psychology.

Figure 16.2
German psychologist Wolfgang Köhler, required apes to use objects as tools to reach their goal (food). He observed that they solved the problem by first thinking and then acting. He concluded that learning consists of reorganizing perceptions.

Figure 16.3
American psychologist Edward Thorndike placed cats inside puzzle boxes from which they could escape only by tripping the right levers. He observed that they roamed about continuously until they hit the lever, and he concluded that learning is a matter of random trial and error. Neither Köhler nor Thorndike was wrong, but because each man had asked his question according to his preconceptions, each received only part of the answer.

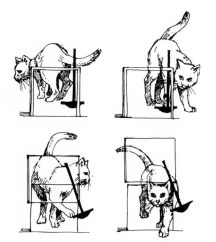

approaches in favor of the answers they want to find was commented on by philosopher Bertrand Russell:

> . . . all animals that have been carefully observed have behaved so as to confirm the philosophy in which the observer believed before his observation began. Nay, more, they have all displayed the national characteristics of the observer. Animals studied by Americans rush about frantically with an incredible display of bustle and pep, and at last achieve the desired result by chance. Animals observed by Germans sit still and think, and at last evolve solutions out of their own inner consciousness.

(The experiments Russell was referring to are those done by the American Edward Thorndike and the German Wolfgang Köhler that are described in Chapter 3.)

The first step in formulating a question, then, is to examine your assumptions: Make sure that your question is not designed to force an answer that will support your own preconceived notions.

Samples and Data

The pieces of information that a researcher collects in order to answer his question are called *data.* Because of the huge amount of information available for answering even a simple question, a researcher is limited to examining only a small part of it. This small segment of information is known as a *sample.* With data from a properly chosen sample, the researcher can make a good estimate of what data he might get if he were able to examine every piece of information instead of just some of it.

Most of the statistics reported in newspapers, government publications, and magazines are based on samples. The sampling procedure is fairly simple. For example, in order to determine the proportion of blue marbles to green marbles in a large sack containing both, it would probably be adequate to pull out a handful and count them. This method would provide an approximate idea of the proportion of blue marbles to green ones in the bag. The larger the sample, the more accurate your estimate is likely to be. But if you were to choose only four marbles, for instance, they might all turn out to be green, and you might erroneously conclude that few, if any, of the rest of the marbles are another color.

Bias   In addition to being of adequate *size,* a sample must be *representative* of the whole range of available data. If you wanted to know how tall American men tend to be, for example, you would want to make certain that your sample was not drawn from a group of basketball players. Even if you sampled thousands of them, your data would be misleading. Such a sample would be *biased* because it would not represent the range of all men.

Bias can creep into the sampling of data in a number of ways. In 1936, for example, a telephone poll was taken by *Literary Digest* magazine to predict the outcome of the Roosevelt-Landon presidential election. The poll predicted a massive victory for Republican Alf

Landon, but when the votes were counted, Roosevelt had won by a landslide. The problem was that the magazine had polled its own subscribers and had collected its information by telephone. In those depression days, people who had telephones and who subscribed to literary journals were far from a cross-section of the voters. These people tended to be affluent Republicans. Roosevelt's victory was delivered precisely by the people omitted from the sample.

Such bias can be eliminated by taking a purely *random sample,* that is, one that gives an equal chance of being collected to every piece of data within the scope of the research. An almost random sampling of people in a city may be achieved by taking every twentieth name in the phone book, for example. (Note that even then, people with unlisted numbers or without phones are excluded.)

Bias can also be reduced by *deliberately* making the sample as representative as possible. If one were interested in the opinions of the people in a city, one might be careful to interview people from all parts of the city, equal numbers of each sex, people of different ages, and so on. This is what pollsters such as the people who publish ratings on television programs do. Psychologists are more likely to

Figure 16.4

The sampling problem. An area full of unknowns confronts the researcher. Because he can collect only a limited amount of the information, he must use what he gets to make educated guesses about the rest. In the first frames of this sequence, the researcher obtains misleading information: His first sampling technique produces a biased sample. He then takes a random sample and correctly concludes that most of the unknowns are cubes and spheres. On the basis of the first sample he might have concluded that pyramid shapes were equally as common.

take a random sample from a particular group—all the students at some college, for example—and assume that this group is similar to other groups in which they are interested.

Relevance of Data   Even if a researcher formulates a question that contains no hidden assumptions, collects a large sample of data, and insures that his sample is unbiased, he may still come up with a misleading answer if he collects data that are irrelevant or meaningless. It can be difficult even after you have phrased a question and decided *where* to collect data, to know exactly *what* data to collect.

Suppose, for example, that you wished to find out something about people and paintings. You might decide to collect data at a museum or an art gallery. How would you go about finding out, for example, which paintings are the most popular?

How would you know whether a person likes or dislikes a painting? How would you separate genuine interest from casual inspection? Perhaps you would note the amount of time people spend lingering in front of a particular painting. Or you might examine the condition of the floor near each painting to see how worn it is. Or you may want to ask certain questions of each person who looks at the paintings.

Once you finished collecting your data, what would they mean? Do people stare at some paintings simply because they were painted by famous artists? Are the paintings most viewed the ones by entrances and exits, or by benches? Do people truthfully answer questions about their tastes in art? If so, can they put their feelings into words? In this situation there are many kinds of data you could gather; the difficulty is in deciding which data would really be relevant to your question.

The Effects of Observation

In gathering data from a given source, the person doing the gathering invariably influences the data. The experimenter is a complex human being, with attitudes, feelings, and ideas of his own. These components of his makeup may easily shade, alter, or distort what he sees or reports. Obviously, a racially prejudiced person would not be the ideal observer to describe the behavior of black Americans. Similarly, a revolutionary leftist might not be the best person to observe white middle-class behavior.

Furthermore, the observer's tools and techniques may be inadequate to deal fully with all of the elements that enter into the situation under study. For example, the earth was thought to be the center of the universe until the telescope and advances in astronomy proved otherwise. It is therefore more than likely that the experimenter may be handicapped by factors unapparent to him.

This problem is expressed in the familiar saying, "He can't see the forest for the trees." If the researcher is too close to his subject, he will fail to notice certain patterns, but if he moves back, he will be too

Setting: A psychologist is seated at his desk.	There is a knock on his office door.	After the student has completed the experiment, he leaves. There is another knock at the door.	The only difference between the two episodes is the smile! Can a smile affect the results of an experiment?
	Psychologist: **Come in.** (A male student enters) **Sit down, please.** I am going to read you a set of instructions. I am not permitted to say anything which is not in the instructions nor can I answer any questions about this experiment. OK? We are developing a test of . . .	Psychologist: **Come in.** (A female student enters) **Sit down, please.** (The psychologist smiles) I am going to read you a set of instructions. I am not permitted to say anything which is not in the instructions nor can I answer any questions about this experiment. OK? We are developing a test of . . .	

far away to see certain other patterns. He must choose—is it the forest or the trees in it that interests him?

A researcher, like a photographer, must decide the "angle" and "distance" from which to "shoot" his subject. He uses his own judgment as to what merits attention. By focusing on one aspect of the subject, the observer ignores various other perspectives that might radically alter the overall picture. To account for this type of bias, the researcher must remember that there are angles besides his own and that he should study them if he can.

Observer effects also result from the fact that subjects may behave differently than they might otherwise just because they know they are being studied. The presence of the observer causes them to change their behavior, just as the presence of a photographer can change a bunch of unruly children into a peaceful, smiling group. Under observation, people are apt to try to please or impress the observer—to act as they think they are expected to act. For this reason, researchers must constantly be aware that their contacts and involvement with the people whom they are observing can easily influence the results of their investigations.

COLLECTING AND INTERPRETING DATA

There are three main approaches to gathering and organizing data. *Simple observation* involves watching, listening to, or even touching

Figure 16.5
Yes, and so can any number of other factors that may have escaped the researcher's attention. Not surprisingly, this researcher will probably find that females are more friendly and cooperative than are males. Other researchers, even when working with animals, have obtained the results they anticipated by unconsciously handling the animals in such ways that produce the expected behaviors.

and smelling the subject of one's investigation. *Correlation* entails making two sets of observations and seeing how they are related. In *experimentation* the researcher controls or manipulates certain aspects of the situation he is studying and observes other aspects to see what happens.

Simple Observation

Observation is the most simple method of research, and it is a basic part of the more complex research methods. Careful observation is not easy; getting the facts and describing them accurately can be a real challenge. It can be useful and extremely interesting, for example, to simply sit in a place like a park or a restaurant and observe how people act in some standard situation, such as buying an ice cream cone for a small child or waiting to be served a meal.

Observational techniques are commonly used in the study of animals (as in bird watching) but not so much with humans because observation of many human behaviors is often impossible. Suppose, for example, that you wanted to find out what brand of toothpaste people use. Making a direct observation would require your presence in the bathroom—a request that is likely to be denied. In such a case you would be driven to more indirect methods. You might look for empty toothpaste cartons in people's trash, watch to see what they buy in the supermarket, or ask them what they use and assume they will tell the truth.

Describing the results of simple observation is another problem. How do you describe how a person walks or waits, for example? Researchers often try to assign some number or value to each observation—to *measure* it. Even assigning observations to categories is a kind of measurement. You might classify each person you see walking past as either a strider, a strutter, a foot dragger, or a racer depending on his walking style.

This measurement would not allow you to easily compare different people, however. To obtain such a measurement you might, instead, use a stopwatch and note down the time it takes different people to cover the ground between two parking signs. You might find out in this way that big people move faster than little people. You should not assume, however, that numerical measurements are necessarily better than categories. Sorting people into different walking-style categories might tell you more about people and walking than timing them would. Thus, the kind of measuring you do depends very much on what question you are trying to answer.

Correlation: Relationships Between Observations

The term *correlation* is used to indicate a degree of relatedness between two sets of data. Psychologists try to understand certain data by determining how well they correlate with other data. A psychologist might compare a student's grades with his study habits or a child's alertness with the number of hours he sleeps.

In some instances, the relationship between two things is very close—there is a high correlation between IQ scores and academic success. Such a relationship is called a *positive* correlation: a higher IQ score goes with higher academic performance; a lower IQ score goes with a lower academic performance. In other cases, a relationship is nonexistent—there is no correlation between eye color and academic success. By knowing that a high correlation exists, it is possible to predict that, for example, a person with a high IQ score will do well in school.

Suppose you wanted to see what sort of relationship exists between music preferences and age. In taking an opinion poll, you might find out that most young people prefer rock music—that age and taste for rock music are highly correlated. Based on these results, you would expect that a young person would buy rock records, listen to a rock music station, or play rock music on his stereo. In this case the correlation is *negative:* the greater the age, the *less* preference for rock; the greater the preference for rock, the lower the age (although below a certain age—perhaps nine—this correlation probably would no longer hold).

A problem with the correlational method is that people tend to misuse it. Instead of looking at a correlation as a comparison between two things, they see it as a cause-effect relationship. For example, medical researchers once found a high correlation between cancer and milk drinking. It seemed that the incidence of cancer was

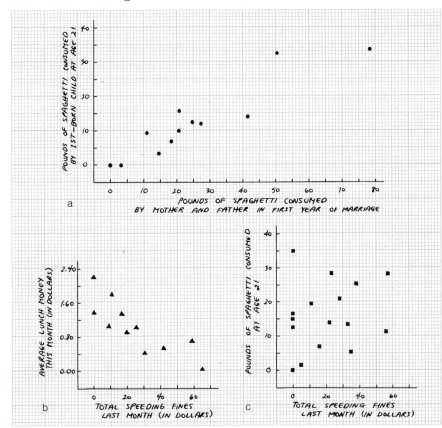

a

b

c

Figure 16.6

Graphs such as these, called scatterplots, reveal correlations between sets of data. (a) The data from twelve imaginary families reveal a strong positive correlation between the eating habits of the parents and the eating habits of their children. (b) Data from eleven imaginary individuals reveal a strong negative correlation between the amount of traffic violation fines and the amount of spending money for lunches. (c) The data for sixteen imaginary people show no correlation between yearly spaghetti consumption and amount of traffic violation fines.

increasing in areas of the world (such as New England and Switzerland) where milk consumption is high, whereas cancer remained scarce in areas (such as Ceylon) where little milk is consumed. Many people assumed from this data that milk drinking somehow causes cancer.

When researchers analyzed this information further, however, they found that a third factor was involved. Cancer is a disease that generally affects people in middle age and after. The areas of high cancer incidence are all areas where the standard of living is high and people have relatively long life spans, whereas people live much shorter lives in the poorer areas that have less cancer. Milk drinking and cancer are related, but only because a fairly high standard of living is required for both of them.

Thus, a correlation between two things may indeed indicate a cause and effect, but it may very well be due to some other factor that is causally related to them both. In order to determine whether a cause-and-effect relationship does exist between highly correlated data, investigators may have to turn to experiments.

Experimentation

Although experimentation is the core of scientific investigation, experiments are not the exclusive property of scientists in laboratories. You and people around you are performing experiments all the time. Some experiments, such as those described in detergent commercials, are fairly obvious: A comparison of the results of washing with the advertised brand to washing with Brand X shows that Our Brand gets clothes whiter and brighter.

Other everyday experiments are less obvious. For instance, if your television suddenly loses its picture in the middle of the detergent commercial, you might perform an experiment to see what will cause the set to work again. You might shake it, bang it, turn all the knobs, and so on. These may not seem like experiments when you are performing them, but, in fact, any attempt to discover a cause-and-effect relationship is a form of experimentation.

The only difference between your experiment with the television and a scientific experiment in the laboratory is that in a formal experiment the researcher goes to more trouble to control all the factors that might be involved, and he keeps careful records of everything he does and observes. Usually a scientist sets up an artificial situation so that he can arrange the components of his experiment and control the way they interact.

Experimentation may occur in a natural setting if the researcher is able to exert some control over the situation. Suppose, for example, that a psychologist is requested to find out what causes some restaurant patrons to tip more than others. First, the experimenter visits a restaurant during the busy dinner hours and makes some simple observations of the factors that could affect tipping behavior. He notes immediately that there is a correlation between

Figure 16.7

This series of drawings depicts a correlation between the woman's sadness and the man's anger. But is one causing the other? Not necessarily. Correlation does not imply causation. It is possible that the woman's sadness is causing the man's anger; it is possible that his anger is causing her sadness; and it is also possible that they are both responding to a third factor.

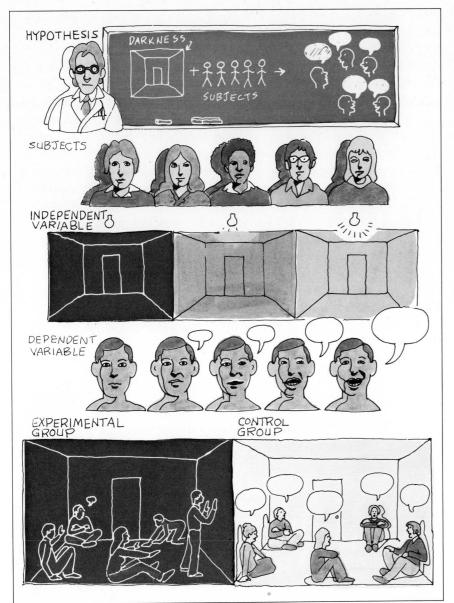

HYPOTHESIS

DARKNESS

SUBJECTS

SUBJECTS

INDEPENDENT VARIABLE

DEPENDENT VARIABLE

EXPERIMENTAL GROUP

CONTROL GROUP

Figure 16.8
The components of an experiment. The experimenter hypothesizes that complete darkness will encourage strangers to talk to one another. Using college students as subjects, he controls amount of light as the independent variable and measures amount of talking as the dependent variable. He performs his experiment by placing a group of subjects in a totally dark room and tape-recording what happens. In addition to this experimental group, he uses a control group, which is placed in an identical room but with normal lighting conditions. The results obtained from the control group give him a standard against which to compare the results from the experimental group. (Psychologists who performed this experiment found that their hypothesis was not confirmed. The strangers in the dark room talked less than those in the lighted one.)

the quality of a customer's clothing and the size of tip he leaves. The experimenter feels fairly confident that this correlation is a result of the fact that wealthy people can afford to tip more, and he turns to other possible factors that are of more interest—the position of the table, the time spent waiting for service, and so on. After these observations, he notices a strong correlation between the amount of smiling a waitress does and the size of the tips her customers give her. He forms a *hypothesis,* or supposition: Smiling causes tipping. He decides to test the hypothesis by performing an experiment.

In order to understand how scientific experimentation works, it is necessary to become familiar with certain terminology. Psychologists refer to the people or animals they are observing as *subjects*. In this experiment the subjects are the customers in the restaurant. The term *variable* is used to refer to any factor that is capable of change. In this experiment the variables are amount of smiling and amount of tipping. Further, psychologists distinguish between two types of variables, depending on whether they are controlling or observing the changes in the variable. The factor that is deliberately controlled is called the *independent variable* (in this case, the amount of smiling); the factor whose change (perhaps) depends on the independent variable and is allowed to change freely is called the *dependent variable* (the amount of tipping).

In scientific experimentation, the investigator manipulates the independent variable to see if or how the dependent variable is affected. Thus, in this experiment the psychologist might instruct the waitresses working in one section of the restaurant to smile all the time. Then, at the end of the day, he can count their tips and discover whether they made more money than on previous nights. If so, it may seem like evidence that his hypothesis is right; however, he still would not be sure if the increase is really due to the smiling or if, perhaps, it is just the result of a lucky day or of the customers having seen him talking to waitresses and thinking they were getting special treatment.

To eliminate such doubts, he would have to divide his subjects into two groups: a control group and an experimental group. A *control group* is a group of subjects that has the same characteristics as the subjects being tested (the *experimental group*) and that is given the same treatment. The one exception is that the independent variable is not applied to the control group. In this particular experiment, the control group would have to consist of a number of customers served by waitresses who work like the first group and are given some sort of fake instructions. The exception would be that the control group's waitresses are not given the instruction to smile.

If, in adding up the daily tips of the two groups, the experimenter finds that the smilers collected significantly more money, he could conclude that his hypothesis is sound: Smiles do bring more tips. (The truthfulness of this statement has never been tested experimentally, however.)

STATISTICS AND WHY THEY MATTER

After the experimenter has collected his data (whether by simple observation, a correlational study, or an experiment), how does he interpret the data he has gathered?

Researchers find it most useful to collect data in the form of measurements that can be analyzed by *statistics*. In an observational study of walking, a researcher might count the number of each of his walking types to see if certain kinds of walking are more common at certain times of the day. In a correlational study he might compare measurements of IQ and school grades.

Statistics are mathematical summaries of such data. They are used to put the data in a concise form that can be evaluated and reported. There are two main kinds of statistics: *descriptive* and *inferential.*

Descriptive Statistics

Descriptive statistics are used to reduce a mass of data to a form that is more manageable and understandable. Even though there may be a large amount of data and even though it may vary a great deal, descriptive statistics allow the experimenter to say something about it. In summarizing test scores, for example, descriptive statistics are useful in determining such factors as the average, or most representative, score; the differences between other scores and the average score; and the relationship between the average score on one test compared to the average score on another test.

Suppose a researcher gives 47 questions about anxiety to a group of fifty gas-station attendants and that each question can be answered "Yes, I am anxious about this at times" or "No, I never worry about this." After adding up all the scores, he finds that they form a *distribution.* Some of the gas-station attendants worry about many things; others worry about fewer things. No one worries about more than 36 things, and no one worries about less than 11. Most of them indicate worry on about 21 items. If the researcher then wants to compare this group's responses to the questionnaire with those of another group (dentists, for example) that answered the same questions, he can take the distribution of scores of both groups and find out what the *average* performance of each group is. By comparing the averages he can then determine how different the two groups were in the number of things they worry about. An average tells something about the level of performance of the whole group.

Distributions and Averages   There are many ways in which data can be distributed, and there are many ways to compute an average. The choice of the best kind of average depends on the nature of the distribution.

A common type of distribution in a large sample is the *normal distribution,* sometimes known as the "bell curve" because of its shape. Examples of such distributions are shown in Figure 16.9. In this distribution most of the scores are bunched together in the middle and the rest trail off evenly on either side. Obviously, the average is the score that lands right in the middle. One common way to compute this average is to add up all the scores and divide by the number of scores included, thus giving the *arithmetic mean.*

Notice that in these cases the arithmetic mean is also the score that occurs most often and the score that divides the distribution in half. These scores are not always the same in other kinds of distributions, however. In these other cases, the arithmetic mean may be quite misleading.

For instance, if you are told that the average income of the employees at a plastics company is $8,700, what does this figure mean? If $8,700 represents the mean income of the employees, you

Figure 16.9

Examples of statistical distributions and averages. (a) The distribution of the scores from an imaginary group of gas-station attendants on an imaginary questionnaire. (b) The distribution of the scores of an imaginary group of dentists on the same test. Note that these distributions are similar in range but different in their averages. Compare the difference between these distributions to the difference between the distributions on page 395. (c) The distribution of incomes in an imaginary plastics company. Note that the shape of this distribution is completely different from the shapes of the others. Note also how the locations of the mean, median, and mode vary in this distribution.

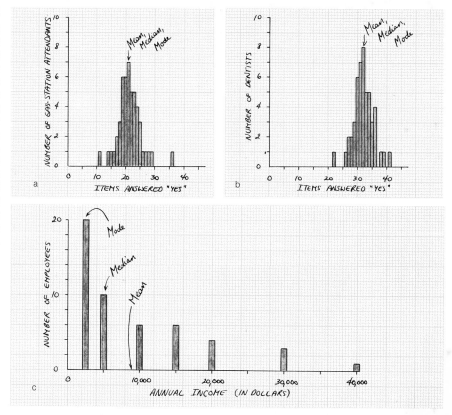

may find that the president of the company earns $40,000, pays seven top executives $20,000 or $30,000, and employs seven managers and salesmen at $10,000 or $15,000. Meanwhile the thirty people who actually run the machines earn $5,000, or less. In this case, then, the mean gives a distorted picture of the true income situation at the plant—no one makes $8,700, some people make considerably more, a lot of people make considerably less.

In this case, a more representative average would be the *median*—the score that falls in the exact middle of the distribution. In the plastics company, the median income is $5,000. Half the employees make more than $5,000, and the other half make less. An even more revealing figure would be the *mode,* the score that occurs most frequently. Because more employees make $2,500 than any other salary, it would be reasonable to say that the average income is only $2,500—rather a comedown from $8,700.

Variability The mean, median, and mode are three ways of summarizing the general trend in a set of scores or figures. But knowing the average still does not tell you how widely the scores or results are distributed—you still want to find out their *variability*. If everyone at the plastics company earned the same salary, there would be no variability in the salary figures, but because salaries range from $2,500 to $40,000, their distribution shows high variability from the average. Measures of variability tell the researcher how

394

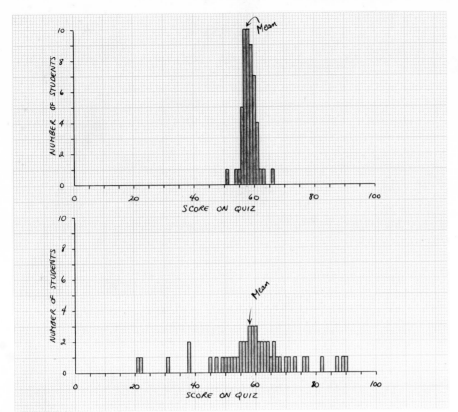

Figure 16.10
Two imaginary distributions of the history-quiz scores of fifty students. Note that these two distributions have the same average but different ranges. Note also that the general shape of the distribution is the same as that of the two distributions on page 394 and of the idealized curve on page 361 (Chapter 15). These are all called normal distributions.

closely clustered or widely spread out his distribution of scores is. Two distributions that have the same average but different variabilities are shown in Figure 16.10.

Variability is usually expressed in terms of the *standard deviation*—a number that indicates the extent to which figures in a given set of data vary from the mean. If you know, for example, that the mean of a set of scores on a history quiz is 58 and the standard deviation is small—say, 2—then you can expect almost all the scores to be very close to 58. About two-thirds of the scores will be within 2 points of the mean, so most of the scores will be between 56 and 60. Suppose, however, that the scores are widely spread, with a standard deviation of 17, for example. Now, although there are more scores around 58 than anywhere else, scores much higher and lower than this figure are common, too. By knowing the mean, you know what score a person was most likely to have obtained; by knowing the standard deviation you know whether to expect the actual scores to vary from the mean.a little or a great deal.

Inferential Statistics

Descriptive statistics are often not enough. You need to know what statistics mean and how trustworthy they are. Computations can be performed on descriptive statistics to answer such questions. These computations are called *inferential statistics.*

Psychologists use inferential statistics to try to determine whether

all heads
9 heads
1 tail
8 heads
2 tails ||||| |||||
7 heads
3 tails ||||| ||||| ||||| |||||
6 heads
4 tails ||||| ||||| ||||| ||||| ||||| ||||| ||||| |||
5 heads
5 tails ||||| ||||| ||||| ||||| ||||| ||||| ||||| ||||| ||||| |||
4 heads
6 tails ||||| ||||| ||||| ||||| ||||| ||||| ||||| |
3 heads
7 tails ||||| ||||| ||||| ||||| ||||| ||||| |||||
2 heads
8 tails ||||| ||||| |
1 head
9 tails ||
all tails

Figure 16.11
The distribution of outcomes of two hundred tosses of ten pennies, showing a normal curve. On the average, heads and tails turn up an equal number of times, indicating that there is nothing abnormal about these particular coins. Note that this distribution has the same normal shape as several of the other distributions shown in this chapter (except that it is turned on its side).

Figure 16.12
The researcher and inferential statistics. At first, this researcher infers that he is about to find another head like the one he encountered on page 385. This inference is improbable, however, because the new data show a much higher frequency of pyramid shapes than the original sampling produced. As it turns out, the researcher's inference is indeed wrong. He should have interpreted the overabundance of pyramid shapes as a significant difference.

their experimental results might be due primarily to chance or whether the data does, indeed, seem to show some significant pattern or relationship. The influence of chance on research results is studied in light of *probability theory.* Probability is a complex topic in mathematics and psychology, and only a few of its applications will be described here.

Statisticians have worked out methods for determining the probability and predicting the outcome of many different events. It is common knowledge, for example, that in tossing a coin the chance of getting heads or tails is 50 percent.

But what are the chances of getting ten heads in a row? It is possible to calculate these odds and find out that there is a little less than one chance in a thousand. If you were flipping a coin and got ten heads in a row, you might begin to suspect that there is something strange about the coin. This is exactly the kind of logic that is used in inferential statistics.

Such probability calculations are frequently used to evaluate the results of psychological experiments. Suppose, for example, you conduct an experiment on ESP and you want to know whether to trust your results. In your experiment, you have various people guess which of five symbols appears each time a card is turned over in another room. For each card, chances are one in five that a subject will guess correctly. If you have your subjects guess 100 cards, the rules of probability dictate that a person will get roughly twenty cards right out of the hundred. Some will get a few more, others, a few less. The question is, how many more than twenty does a person have to guess correctly before you decide that he has ESP? Could he get thirty by chance? Fifty? He *could* get any number, but, using the laws of probability, it is possible to compute that he would get thirty right fairly often but fifty, almost never.

Such unusual results are described as *significant differences*—a difference that is so unlikely that it must mean something. In the ESP experiment, if anyone guessed fifty cards correctly, you might reasonably say that a significant difference exists between him and the rest of your subjects, who guessed around twenty cards correctly. (Real ESP experiments never get such extreme results, but the logic is the same.)

Inferential statistics are mathematical calculations of the odds against something happening by chance. If results do show a significant difference, the psychologist is encouraged to continue his line of research and try to verify that his results are meaningful.

WRITING AND READING RESEARCH ARTICLES

Research projects, and the results obtained from these projects, would be of little value if no one but the researcher himself ever heard about them. Research psychologists regularly report their findings by writing articles for scientific journals, and they read the reports of others in order to enhance their scientific knowledge.

Because research articles are of great potential value for many people, and because they include such an extensive variety of subject matter, the scientific community has devised a specific style, or plan, for the writing of such articles. The benefits of a uniform style of reporting are that it provides the researcher with a convenient and logical format for organizing and presenting his research and that it provides the reader with an immediately recognizable means for obtaining information.

In reading the following description of how to write research articles, keep in mind that most scientific journals use this format, and any time you do research and wish to write a report of your findings, you will find this information of value.

Components of a Research Article

Beginning students are often put off and confused by the forbidding conciseness and technical terminology of research reports. The purpose of this section is to bring scientific reporting out of the realm of the mysterious by making the plan and some of the terms familiar.

Research reports have six components: an *abstract,* an *introduction,* a description of the *method* used, a summary of the research *results,* a *discussion* of what the results mean, and a list of *references.*

Abstract   An abstract is a brief summary of the project. Summaries used to be placed at the end of reports, but there are now so many journals to read that people find it useful to have a summary at the beginning of each article. A person can read an abstract quickly to decide whether he is interested in this particular research and to determine whether he wants to read further. A few sentences are usually enough to acquaint the reader with the nature of the project. The abstract is not the place for a detailed presentation; it merely tells the reader what the rest of the report is about.

Introduction   In introducing your report, you should state your original question and your reason for asking it. Explain the problem in detail, particularly those aspects you find of special interest. You may want to briefly review the results of similar research in the past history of the field or to relate your observations to another field of study. In general, you tell the reader what it is you are trying to do.

Method   What procedures and techniques did you use to answer the question you asked? What kind of equipment did you use? What was the experimental setting like? Whom did you choose as subjects, and how did you choose them? What did you tell them? Describing your method tells your readers how you went about your investigation.

In this part of your report it is important to give full details on how you conducted your investigation and what variables you considered. Other investigators may want to check your results by repeating your investigation themselves. If a method of research is duplicated exactly as reported and the results are not the same, something is wrong. The error may result from misinterpretation of the research report. Or the second researcher may find that the first researcher had not controlled for all the possible influences on his subjects. To be trustworthy, a piece of research must be able to be *replicated*—it must be able to be duplicated exactly and yield the same results.

A psychological research report usually contains a number of symbols that stand for certain commonly used terms. For example, E is used to designate the experimenter, and S represents the subject(s). An example from the ESP experiment might be: "S told E that he wanted to change his mind about the last card."

Results   Perhaps the most important part of your report is the section describing your results—the answer you got to your question. This is where you present your data. Results are usually presented in the form of tables and graphs as well as being stated in prose. Both descriptive and inferential statistics based on the data would be included here. In your ESP study, for example, you might state what the average number of correct guesses was for each person, how often people hesitated, how confident they said they felt, and so on. You might also include charts comparing the scores to the age and sex of the subjects. Finally, you might include calculations showing the probabilities involved in obtaining your results.

Discussion   What do your results mean? If, in your ESP study, you found that all the people whose scores were significantly different from chance were females over the age twenty, you might want to speculate on why you got this result. If no one scored significantly better than chance in your ESP research, you will have to conclude that you found no evidence for ESP. But you may want to compare your results with those of other experimenters who have found evidence for ESP and discuss possible reasons why your results differed from theirs.

References   Whenever you make use of the information or ideas of others, you should acknowledge the sources of these ideas in your report. For example, if you have consulted a book or article on ESP in order to compare your results with someone else's, you should cite the author's last name and the date of the source directly after your mention of these other results (as you would with a footnote). You can then provide a complete list of references (or bibliography) at the end of the report. By citing references you not only give credit where credit is due, but you also lend authority to the statements you have made and you provide your readers with access to the information you used.

WRITING REVIEW PAPERS

A review paper is an essay about the present scientific knowledge in a particular subject. Creating one involves reading, thinking about, organizing, and writing down what other people have discovered about a question. This work is worth doing for several reasons: It sharpens your own knowledge, it provides insights, and it makes you aware of the most useful ways of doing things. Also, it gives you experience in understanding scientific methods, in being critical, and in dealing with various kinds of research, from case studies to controlled experiments. Finally, your work may contribute something to scientific knowledge.

No single experiment can answer a major question. To answer such questions, it is necessary to look into what a number of people have discovered about small aspects of the overall question. By putting all these stray bits of information together, you may be able to become an expert in a particular area and to come up with an interesting and significant answer. Thus, you may be able to develop valuable ideas simply by studying the discoveries, insights, methods, and mistakes of others.

Becoming familiar with an area of research requires a few basic skills. These skills include knowing how to locate sources and making use of a library, as well as being able to evaluate a research article.

Using the Library

The search for information cannot begin until the sources of information are located. Most public libraries and all university libraries contain all the references you need; the problem is how to discover what exists and where to find it.

The librarian is likely to be your best source when you set out to find the written material related to your topic of investigation. The place to begin your search is the library card catalog. Books are classified alphabetically both by title and by author, and they are further classified according to subject matter. Therefore, it is not necessary to know a title or an author in order to find out what has been written on a subject. Also, most cards contain a brief summary of the information contained in the book. So if you look under the heading in which you are interested, you are likely to find plenty of useful references to begin your search.

You may, in fact, find too many references this way and not know how to choose among them. One good way to guide your search is to use the bibliography section of some book you already know to be good. A *bibliography* is a list of books and journal articles that the author has used to obtain the information he has written about. Magazine and journal articles also have lists of references, and many books (such as this one) have lists of suggested readings. Usually you can get a lead on the best sources of information from such lists.

Making Use of Resources

The most recent and most accurate sources of information available in the library are the many periodicals, or journals. If you are researching a particular question dealing with psychology and have not already obtained the names of some good articles, the place to start looking for articles relevant to your topic is in an index to psychological literature. There you will find brief descriptions of numerous articles, some of which will undoubtedly be related to your field of study. The *Psychological Abstracts* is a periodical that serves as such an index.

Current information in a generalized format can be found in such popular weekly and monthly magazines as *Time, Newsweek, Harpers,* and *Atlantic.* These publications try to present important research in an interesting and readable manner. *Time* and *Newsweek* focus on recent psychological events, but they also occasionally have long articles providing an overview of a particular area of psychology, such as biofeedback or dreaming. *Harpers* and *Atlantic* tend to carry longer, more in-depth articles on controversial issues, such as IQ testing or the effects of war on soldiers, and their pieces are often written by the psychologists involved in the research. The articles in these popular magazines are catalogued in the *Reader's Guide to Periodical Literature*, a valuable reference that can be found in most libraries.

Specialized information on psychological research can be found in *Scientific American* and *Psychology Today*. At least one article in each issue of *Scientific American* has information of psychological significance, and almost all articles in *Psychology Today* describe psychological findings.

Professional information, written for and by practicing psychologists, is contained in hundreds of specialized journals, but a good place to try is the *Psychological Bulletin*, a monthly journal that contains only review papers, not reports of original research. These articles provide good surveys of important topics in all areas of psychology. Another periodical, the *Annual Review of Psychology*, contains summaries of the research that has been done in each particular field during a given year. It is a valuable source for finding out the current state of knowledge in such areas as motivation, memory, psychotherapy, and so on.

A handy aid for all sorts of purposes is the *Encyclopedia of Human Behavior*, a two-volume reference book that covers all the major aspects of psychology, psychiatry, and mental health. It contains entries for terms, concepts, theories, and important personalities in the field.

THEORY AND PROOF

So far this chapter has described methods of research—observing, correlating, experimenting, reporting, thinking, and writing. But what does this all add up to? What is the long-term goal?

The world around you is in constant change. Everything it contains, including humans and their behavior, is in a continual process of growth and decay. People change as they grow older; the ideas you held as a child are not the same as those you hold today. And those you will hold in the future will be different still. That is the duty and the privilege of being human. You learn, you change, and you grow.

You, and everyone around you, are trying to understand the world you find yourself in. You build a picture, or *theory*, of the way things are, and you use it as long as it works. When it fails, you change it.

Scientific research works in the same way. Scientists do not believe that they have any final answers, or that they ever will. But they do believe that their understanding of the world can be made better. Scientists are always asking questions: Is the world like this? Do people behave like that? Does this method work? Does that way of thinking help? When the answer comes back "yes," they are pleased; the picture they have now seems more accurate. But they do not decide that the picture is final and that they can stop asking questions. It is always possible that the next question will produce a "no." Then the picture will have to be changed. In this way, a theory is only a picture to be used until someone disproves it. There is no proof—only disproof.

Every person's job, whether he is a scientist or not, is to continue this process to form the best picture of the world he can. But when his views or ideas are no longer correct, he must be equally willing to change them. He must take his cue from the scientist, who constantly checks his theories and models against the real world and tries to improve his methods so that he can come closer to the truth.

In every society certain theories become so widely believed that they resist disproof. In America, people have become used to such ideas as "A woman's place is in the home," and "Children should be seen and not heard." Many other such popular beliefs are not stated so explicitly, such as common ideas about the responsibilities of government or man's ability to control nature. It is only when change becomes a bad word that popular myths assume the status of "truth" through the strength of repetition.

Growth means change; human development depends on being prepared to revise old ideas and behaviors when they become useless and invalid. The improvement of the world "picture" begins with yourself. By maintaining an open mind and a willingness to change, by correcting the faults in your "theories," and by constantly testing your improved picture against the changing world around you, you can not only enrich your own life but also contribute something to humanity's chances for survival.

Figure 16.13

If you look at this figure from a distance or blur your vision of it in some other way, you will see a single unbroken image. This exercise illustrates how your own eyes and brain are engaged in a scientific endeavor: the creation of a simple and useful picture of the world from complex and often confusing information. The image is of the Greek letter Ψ (psi), which is often used by psychologists as a symbol for their discipline.

A conventional representation of the psi symbol appears on page 406 in an illustration of a different aspect of the scientific endeavor.

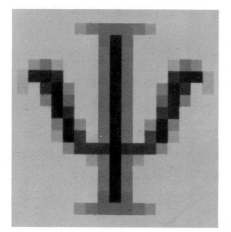

SUMMARY

1. The first step in conducting a research experiment is to formulate a question that contains no hidden assumptions about the possible answers.

2. Data are the pieces of information collected in a scientific investigation. In any investigation, only a sample, or representative segment, of all the possible data can be collected.

3. The person gathering data invariably influences it in some way. His attitudes dictate what aspects of the data he attends to. Also, subjects may behave differently than normal if they know they are being studied.

4. At the least, research involves simple observation. It is difficult and challenging to design good methods for observing and measuring complex behaviors.

5. A correlation indicates the degree of relatedness between two sets of data. Correlations may be positive or negative. Correlational studies are misused when people interpret correlations as cause-and-effect relationships.

6. The experimental method involves deliberate variation and precise observation of some of the factors involved and careful control of the rest. The factors that the experimenter varies are called the independent variables; the factors he observes for change are called the dependent variables. A control group is a group of subjects for whom the independent variables are held steady.

7. Statistics are mathematical computations on numerical data. They are used to put the data in a meaningful form that can be evaluated and reported.

8. Descriptive statistics are ways of briefly describing a mass of data. A distribution shows how often all the possible scores occur. The average score in a distribution may refer to the mean (the sum of all the scores divided by the number of scores), the median (the score that falls in the exact middle of the distribution), or the mode (the score that occurs most frequently in the distribution). The standard deviation is a statistic that indicates how much variability there is in a distribution.

9. Inferential statistics are mathematical calculations of the odds against something happening by chance. Odds are figured according to probability theory. A significant difference is one that is so unlikely that it must mean something.

10. Research reports have six components: an abstract, an introduction, a description of the method used, a presentation of the results, a discussion of what the results mean, and a list of references.

11. One can become an "expert" in a research area by reading, thinking about, organizing, and writing down in a review what other people have discovered about a question.

12. Scientific theories can never be proved—they can only be disproved. People must be willing to change their own personal theories in order to grow and develop as individuals.

ACTIVITIES

1. Measurement is the assignment of numbers to observations. Psychologists face many problems in trying to measure behaviors and feelings. For example, how might the following factors be measured? (1) the number of people in a room; (2) height; (3) the proportion of votes a candidate will receive; (4) hunger; (5) love; (6) liberty. What makes each phenomenon difficult or easy to measure? What can you predict from this exercise regarding the difficulties of measuring such things as personality and intelligence?

2. With a pad of paper and pencil, watch television commercials for several evenings, paying particular attention to those advertising such products as toothpaste, headache remedies, detergents, and

others that claim their product has been "proven more effective." Take notes as you watch, jotting down the "statistics" the advertisers use to support their claims. Often, the statistics used in advertising have been manipulated in various ways to present a distorted version of the facts. How many fallacies can you spot in the commercials you watch? Compare and discuss your results with others in your class.

3. You wish to determine whether or not a young child can be taught to love cauliflower. Would you use the method of simple observation or would you need to design an experiment? What would your independent and dependent variables be? What controls would you use? Could you develop a theory from this experiment, if it turned out to be valid? How far could you generalize your findings?

4. Several theories are presented below. How could you attempt to disprove each one? Are there any that could not be disproved?
   a. A person will remember an unfinished task.
   b. Love reduces hate.
   c. You can raise blood pressure by making a subject anxious.
   d. Motivation increases learning.
   e. Making a rat hungry will cause him to require less training to find his way through a maze.

5. Select a particular area of psychological investigation that is of interest to you. Go to a main branch or university library and by utilizing the card catalog, bibliographical references, and journals or magazines, see how far your research takes you. You may find that, like looking up a word in the dictionary, one thing leads to another, which leads to another, and so on.

6. Look through a popular magazine such as *Time, Newsweek,* or *Psychology Today.* Read an article about a scientific experiment and try to determine if the results presented correspond to the data given. What approach to obtaining data was used? Did the experiment contain a control group? What were the dependent and independent variables?

7. Based on the information provided in this chapter, design your own research experiment. If you should decide to carry out your design, write up a research report according to the style presented in the chapter and present your findings to the class.

8. Using the mean, median, and mode, devise some fake "statistics." Present your "facts" to family members, classmates, and friends (who are not taking a psychology class). Did your classmates spot the fallacies more quickly than the other subjects?

9. Take ten pennies, a sheet of paper (graph paper, if you have any), and a pencil. Put the numbers 0 through 10 along the bottom of the sheet, spaced evenly apart. Then toss the coins, all at once. Count the number of heads and make a mark (or fill in a square) above the appropriate number on the paper. Toss the coins again and again (fifty to one hundred times), each time making another mark or

filling in another square to indicate how many heads came up. In this way, you will generate a distribution. Does your distribution show a normal curve?

10. Using a watch with a second hand, or a stopwatch if you have one, count how many seconds it takes for different people to tell you what they were doing exactly twenty-four hours ago. Plot the results in the same manner as you did for the coins. Try to get scores for as many people as the number of times you tossed the coins, then compare the two distributions.

SUGGESTED READINGS

AGNEW, NEIL, and SANDRA PYKE. *The Science Game: An Introduction to Research in the Behavioral Sciences.* Englewood Cliffs, N.J.: Prentice-Hall, 1969. A nontechnical book for the introductory student or curious layman about "the continuity between everyday truth-seeking activities and the methods of science."

DETHIER, VINCENT. *To Know a Fly.* San Francisco: Holden-Day, 1963 (paper). This book is a personal and witty description of the author's research on the appetites of houseflies. (The results of his investigation are referred to in Chapter 5.) This book describes the experience of obtaining those results.

DUSTIN, DAVID S. *How Psychologists Do Research: The Example of Anxiety.* Englewood Cliffs, N.J.: Prentice-Hall, 1969. Designed for beginners in psychology, this book discusses how a number of psychologists—each representing a different approach—do different kinds of research on the same topic—anxiety. Each chapter describing a particular line of research is followed by a chapter that evaluates the contribution of that research to solving the problem.

HUFF, DARRELL. *How to Lie with Statistics.* New York: Norton, 1954. An easy-to-read and thoroughly enjoyable book about how people use statistics to "prove" anything they want to prove. This book is loaded with useful and practical information—and lots of surprises.

KOESTLER, ARTHUR. *The Case of the Midwife Toad.* New York: New American Library, 1971 (paper). Koestler presents a well-documented account of the mystery surrounding a highly respected Austrian scientist's suicide, committed when his findings of half a lifetime of research were being harshly questioned. A fascinating and revealing description of the little-known inner world of scientific investigation.

SARBIN, THEODORE, and WILLIAM COE. *The Student Psychologist's Handbook: A Guide to Sources.* Cambridge, Mass.: Schenkman, 1969. A practical guide to the gathering of resources and the preparation of research papers. Excellent material on how to use the library.

WHALEY, DONALD, and SHARON SURRATT. *Attitudes of Science.* Behaviordelia, Inc., P. O. Box 1044, Kalamazoo, Michigan, 49005. Although the information in this manual is presented in a highly clever and humorous manner, it is nevertheless designed to teach the scientific method to serious students of psychology. Strongly recommended for those who plan to continue the study of psychology.

Bibliography

Chapter 1

Alexander, Franz, and **Sheldon Selesnick.** *The History of Psychiatry.* New York: Harper & Row, 1966.

Biderman, A. D., and **H. Zimmer.** *The Manipulation of Human Behavior.* New York: Wiley, 1961.

Eysenck, H. J. *Uses and Abuses of Psychology.* Baltimore: Penguin, 1953.

――――. *Sense and Nonsense in Psychology.* Baltimore: Penguin, 1957.

――――. *Fact and Fiction in Psychology.* Baltimore: Penguin, 1965.

Fincher, C. A. *A Preface to Psychology.* New York: Harper & Row, 1964.

Havemann, Ernest. *The Age of Psychology.* New York: Simon & Schuster, 1957.

Itard, Jean. *The Wild Boy of Aveyron.* George and Muriel Humphrey (trs.). New York: Appleton-Century-Crofts, 1962.

Metzner, R. *Maps of Consciousness.* New York: Macmillan, 1971.

Miller, George. *Psychology: The Science of Mental Life.* Baltimore: Penguin, 1962 (paper).

Roback, A. A. *A History of American Psychology.* New York: Collier, 1964.

Sargent, D. S., and **K. R. Stafford.** *Basic Teachings of the Great Psychologists.* New York: Dolphin, 1965 (paper).

Singh, J. A. L., and **Robert Zingg.** *Wolf-Children and Feral Man.* Hamden, Conn.: Shoestring Press, 1966.

Watson, R. I. *The Great Psychologists: From Aristotle to Freud.* Philadelphia: Lippincott, 1968.

Wilhelm, Richard, and **C. Baynes** (trs.). *I Ching.* Princeton, N.J.: Princeton University Press, 1967.

Chapter 2

Arnheim, Rudolf. *Art and Visual Perception: A Psychology of the Creative Eye.* Berkeley: University of California Press, 1954 (paper).

Geldard, Frank A. *The Human Senses.* New York: Wiley, 1953.

Gibson, E. J., and **R. D. Walk.** "The Visual Cliff," *Scientific American,* 202 (1960), 64–71.

Gregory, R. L. *Eye and Brain.* New York: McGraw-Hill, 1966 (paper).

Hansel, C. E. M. *ESP: A Scientific Evaluation.* New York: Scribner's, 1966.

Held, R., and **W. Richards** (eds.). *Perception: Mechanisms and Models.* San Francisco: Freeman, 1972.

Hochberg, Julian. *Perception.* Englewood Cliffs, N.J.: Prentice-Hall, 1964 (paper).

Koestler, Arthur. *The Roots of Coincidence.* New York: Random House, 1972.

Koffka, K. *Principles of Gestalt Psychology.* New York: Harcourt Brace Jovanovich, 1963.

Kohler, I. "Experiment with Goggles," *Scientific American,* 206 (1962), 62–68.

Ostrander, Sheila, and **Lynn Schroeder.** *Psychic Discoveries Behind the Iron Curtain.* Englewood Cliffs, N.J.: Prentice-Hall, 1970.

Rhine, Louisa E. *Hidden Channels of the Mind.* New York: Apollo, 1961 (paper).

Wald, G. "The Receptors of Human Color Vision," *Science,* 145 (1964), 1007–1016.

Worrall, Ambrose, and **Olga Worrall.** *Explore Your Psychic World.* New York: Harper & Row, 1970.

Chapter 3

Adams, Jack A. *Human Memory.* New York: McGraw-Hill, 1967.

Bruner, Jerome S., Jacqueline J. Goodnow, and **George A. Austin.** *A Study of Thinking.* New York: Wiley, 1956 (paper).

De Bono, Edward. *New Think: The Use of Lateral Thinking in the Generation of New Ideas.* New York: Basic Books, 1968.

_____. *The Mechanism of Mind.* New York: Simon & Schuster, 1969.

Ghiselin, B. (ed.). *The Creative Process.* New York: New American Library, 1952 (paper).

Haber, R. N. "How We Remember What We See," *Scientific American,* 222 (1970), 104–112.

Halacy, D. R., Jr. *Man and Memory.* New York: Harper & Row, 1970.

Hunter, I. M. *Memory: Facts and Fallacies.* Baltimore: Penguin, 1964 (paper).

Koestler, Arthur. *The Act of Creation.* New York: Macmillan, 1964.

Neisser, Ulric. *Cognitive Psychology.* New York: Appleton-Century-Crofts, 1967.

Norman, Donald, and Peter Lindsay. *Human Information Processing.* New York: Academic Press, 1972.

Stromeyer, C. F. III. "Eidetikers," in *Readings in Psychology Today.* 2nd ed. Del Mar, Calif.: CRM Books, 1972, 357–361.

Chapter 4

Aaronson, Bernard, and H. Osmond. *Psychedelics: The Uses and Implications of Hallucinogenic Drugs.* Garden City, N.Y.: Doubleday, 1970.

Beers, C. W. *A Mind That Found Itself.* Garden City, N.Y.: Doubleday, 1908.

Bucke, Richard. *Cosmic Consciousness.* Rev. ed. New York: Citadel Press, 1970.

Chaudhuri, H. *Philosophy of Meditation.* New York: Philosophical Library, 1965.

Custance, J. *Wisdom, Madness and Folly.* New York: Farrar, Strauss & Giroux, 1952.

Estabrooks, G. (ed.). *Hypnosis: Current Problems.* New York: Harper & Row, 1962.

Faraday, Ann. *Dream Power.* New York: Coward, McCann & Geoghegan, 1972.

Foulkes, David. *The Psychology of Sleep.* New York: Scribner's, 1966.

Gazzaniga, M. S. "The Split Brain in Man," *Scientific American,* 217 (1967), 24–29.

Grinspoon, L. *Marijuana Reconsidered.* Cambridge, Mass.: Harvard University Press, 1970.

Herrigel, E. *Zen in the Art of Archery.* New York: Pantheon, 1953.

Hilgard, E. R. *Hypnotic Susceptibility.* New York: Harcourt Brace Jovanovich, 1965.

Huxley, Aldous. *Brave New World.* New York: Harper & Row, 1932 (paper).

_____. *Doors of Perception.* New York: Harper & Row, 1970, originally published, 1956.

Kleitman, N. *Sleep and Wakefulness.* Rev. ed. Chicago: University of Chicago Press, 1963.

Luce, Gay Gaer, and Julius Segal. *Sleep.* New York: Coward, McCann, 1966 (Lancer paperback).

Narajano, C., and R. Ornstein. *On the Psychology of Meditation.* New York: Viking, 1971.

Ornstein, Robert. *The Psychology of Consciousness.* New York: Viking, 1972.

Shor, R. E., and M. T. Orne (eds.). *The Nature of Hypnosis.* New York: Holt, Rinehart and Winston, 1965.

Tart, C. T. (ed.). *Altered States of Consciousness.* New York: Wiley, 1969.

Thompson, Richard F. (ed.). *Physiological Psychology.* San Francisco: Freeman, 1971.

Weil, Andrew. *The Natural Mind.* Boston: Houghton Mifflin, 1972.

Weil, Andrew, et al. "Clinical and Psychological Effects of Marijuana in Man," *Science,* 162 (1968), 1234–1242.

Chapter 5

Arnold, M. *Emotion and Personality.* New York: Columbia University Press, 1960.

Azrin, N. H. "Pain and Aggression," *Psychology Today,* 1 (May 1967), 27–33.

Delgado, J. M. R. *Physical Control of the Mind.* New York: Harper & Row, 1969.

Dethier, V. G. "The Hungry Fly," *Psychology Today,* 1 (June 1967), 64–72.

Eibl-Eibesfelt, I. *Ethology: The Biology of Behavior.* New York: Holt, Rinehart and Winston, 1970.

Holst, E. von, and U. von St. Paul. "Electrically Controlled Behavior," *Scientific American,* 206 (1962), 50–59.

Lorenz, Konrad Z. *King Solomon's Ring.* New York: Crowell, 1952.

_____. *On Aggression.* New York: Harcourt Brace Jovanovich, 1966 (paper).

McGaugh, J., N. M. Weinberger, and R. L. Whalen (eds.). *Psychobiology.* San Francisco: Freeman, 1967.

Olds, James. "Self-Stimulation of the Brain," *Science,* 127 (1958), 315–323.

"Probing the Brain," *Newsweek,* 77 (June 21, 1971), 60–67.

Selye, Hans. *The Stress of Life.* New York: McGraw-Hill, 1956.

Tinbergen, N. *The Study of Instinct.* New York: Oxford University Press, 1951.

Wooldridge, D. E. *Machinery of the Brain.* New York: McGraw-Hill, 1963.

Worrall, Ambrose. *Miracle Healers.* New York: New American Library, 1968.

Zimbardo, Philip, et al. *The Cognitive Control of Motivation.* Glenview, Ill.: Scott Foresman, 1969.

Chapter 6

Barber, T. X. (ed.). *Biofeedback and Self-Control.* Chicago: Aldine-Atherton, 1970.

Engberg, L. A., et al. "Acquisition of Key-Pecking Via Autoshaping as a Function of Prior Experience: 'Learned Laziness?' " *Science,* 178 (1972), 1002–1004.

Fischer, K. W. *The Organization of Simple Learning.* Chicago: Markham, 1973.

Honig, W. H. (ed.). *Operant Behavior: Areas of Research and Application.* New York: Appleton-Century-Crofts, 1966.

Reynolds, G. S. *A Primer of Operant Conditioning.* Glenview, Ill.: Scott, Foresman, 1968.

Sahakian, William S. *Psychology of Learning.* Chicago: Markham, 1970.

Skinner, B. F. *Walden Two.* New York: Macmillan, 1960 (paper).

_____. *The Behavior of Organisms.* New York: Appleton-Century-Crofts, 1961.

_____. *Beyond Freedom and Dignity.* New York: Knopf, 1971.

Chapter 7

Baldwin, Alfred L. *Theories of Child Development.* New York: Wiley, 1967.

Bandura, A., and R. H. Walters. *Social Learning and Personality Development.* New York: Holt, Rinehart and Winston, 1963.

Bellugi, U., and R. Brown (eds.). *The Acquisition of Language.* Chicago: University of Chicago Press, 1970.

Bowlby, J. *Child Care and the Growth of Love.* 2nd ed. Baltimore: Penguin, 1965.

Fischer, Kurt W. *Piaget's Theory of Learning and Cognitive Development.* Chicago: Markham, 1973.

Flavell, John H. *The Developmental Psychology of Jean Piaget.* New York: Van Nostrand, 1963.

Furth, Hans. *Piaget and Knowledge.* Englewood Cliffs, N.J.: Prentice-Hall, 1969.

Gardner, R. A., and B. T. Gardner. "Teaching Sign Language to a Chimpanzee," *Science,* 165 (1969), 644–672.

Kohlberg, Lawrence. "The Child as Moral Philosopher," *Psychology Today,* 2 (September 1968), 25–30.

Sears, Robert, Eleanor Maccoby, and Harry Levin. *Patterns of Child Rearing.* New York: Harper & Row, 1957.

Warren, R. M., and R. P. Warren. "Auditory Illusions and Confusions," *Scientific American,* 223 (1970), 30–36.

Chapter 8

Albert, E. "The Roles of Women: A Question of Values," in S. M. Farber and R. H. L. Wilson (eds.), *The Potential of Women.* New York: McGraw-Hill, 1963, 105–115.

Andreas, Carol. *Sex and Caste in America.* Englewood Cliffs, N.J.: Prentice-Hall, 1971 (paper).

Bem, Daryl J., and Sandra Bem. "We're All Nonconscious Sexists," *Psychology Today,* 4 (November 1970), 22–26, 115–116.

Bird, Caroline. *Born Female: The High Cost of Keeping Women Down.* New York: Pocket Books, 1969.

Blos, P. *On Adolescence.* New York: Free Press, 1962.

Douvan, E., and J. Adelson. *The Adolescent Experience.* New York: Wiley, 1966.

Erikson, Erik. *Childhood and Society.* New York: Norton, 1950.

———. *Identity, Youth and Crisis.* New York: Norton, 1968.

Friedenberg, Edgar Z. *The Vanishing Adolescent.* Boston: Beacon, 1959.

———. *Coming of Age in America: Growth and Acquiescence.* New York: Knopf, 1963.

Hoffman, M. *The Gay World: Male Homosexuality and the Creation of Evil.* New York: Basic Books, 1968.

Horner, Matina S. "Fail Bright Women," *Psychology Today,* 3 (November 1969), 36–38, 62.

Keniston, Kenneth. *Young Radicals: Notes on Committed Youth.* New York: Harcourt Brace Jovanovich, 1968.

Kinsey, Alfred, W. B. Pomeroy, and C. E. Martin. *Sexual Behavior in the Human Male.* Philadelphia: Saunders, 1948.

———. *Sexual Behavior in the Human Female.* Philadelphia: Saunders, 1953.

Masters, W. H., and V. E. Johnson. *Human Sexual Response.* Boston: Little, Brown, 1966.

Mead, Margaret. *Male and Female, A Study of Sexes in a Changing World.* New York: Morrow, 1949.

Opie, J., and P. Opie. *Children's Games in Street and Playground.* New York: Oxford University Press, 1969.

Silberman, Charles E. *Crisis in the Classroom: The Remaking of American Education.* New York: Random House, 1970.

Chapter 9

Aronson, Elliot. *The Social Animal.* New York: Viking Press, 1972.

Brown, Roger. *Social Psychology.* New York: Free Press, 1965.

Freedman, J. L., J. M. Carlsmith, and D. O. Sears. *Social Psychology.* Englewood Cliffs, N.J.: Prentice-Hall, 1970.

Fromm, Erich. *The Art of Loving.* New York: Bantam, 1970 (paper).

Goffman, Erving. *The Presentation of Self in Everyday Life.* Garden City, N.Y.: Doubleday, 1959.

Hall, E. T. *The Silent Language.* New York: Fawcett World Library, 1959 (paper).

———. *The Hidden Dimension.* Garden City, N.Y.: Doubleday, 1969 (paper).

Jourard, Sidney M. *The Transparent Self.* New York: Van Nostrand, 1964 (paper).

Rogers, Carl, and Barry Stevens. *Person to Person: The Problem of Being Human.* Lafayette, Calif.: Real People Press, 1967.

Schachter, Stanley. *The Psychology of Affiliation.* Stanford, Calif.: Stanford University Press, 1959.

Slocum, Joshua. *Sailing Alone Around the World.* London: Rupert-Hart-Davis, 1948.

Toffler, Alvin. *Future Shock.* New York: Random House, 1970.

Chapter 10

Allport, Gordon. *The Nature of Prejudice.* Garden City, N.Y.: Doubleday, 1954 (paper).

Deutsch, Morton, and M. Collins. *Interracial Housing: A Psychological Evaluation of a Social Experiment.* Minneapolis: University of Minnesota Press, 1951.

Fanon, Frantz. *Black Skin, White Masks.* New York: Grove Press, 1967 (paper).

Garfinkle, Harold. *Studies in Ethnomethodology.* Englewood Cliffs, N.J.: Prentice-Hall, 1967.

Grier, William H., and P. M. Cobbs. *Black Rage.* New York: Basic Books, 1968.

Halsell, Grace. *Soul Sister.* New York: World Publishing, 1969.

Janis, Irving. *Victims of Groupthink.* Boston: Houghton Mifflin, 1972.

Kanter, Rosabeth. "Communes," *Psychology Today,* 4 (July 1970), 53–57, 78.

Mackay, Charles. *Extraordinary Popular Delusions and the Madness of Crowds.* New York: Farrar, Straus & Giroux, 1932.

Schlesinger, Arthur M., Jr. *A Thousand Days.* New York: Fawcett World Library, 1965 (paper).

Sherif, Muzafer, et al. *Intergroup Conflict and Cooperation: The Robbers Cave Experiment.* Norman, Okla.: Institute of Group Relations, 1961.

Styron, William. *The Confessions of Nat Turner.* New York: New American Library, 1968 (paper).

Chapter 11

Adorno, T. W., et al. *The Authoritarian Personality.* New York: Norton, 1969 (paper).

Bem, Daryl. *Beliefs, Attitudes, and Human Affairs.* Belmont, Calif.: Brooks/Cole, 1970.

Cohen, A. R. *Attitude Change and Social Influence.* New York: Basic Books, 1964.

Dichter, Ernest. *Handbook of Consumer Motivations.* New York: McGraw-Hill, 1964.

Festinger, Leon. *A Theory of Cognitive Dissonance.* Stanford, Calif.: Stanford University Press, 1957.

Klapper, J. T. *The Effects of Mass Communications.* New York: Free Press, 1960.

Lifton, Robert Jay. *Home from the War.* New York: Simon & Schuster, 1973.

McGuire, W. J. "A Vaccine for Brainwash," *Psychology Today,* 3 (February 1970), 36–39, 63–64.

McLuhan, Marshall. *Understanding Media.* New York: McGraw-Hill, 1964 (paper).

Reisman, D., N. Glazer, and R. Denney. *The Lonely Crowd.* New Haven, Conn.: Yale University Press, 1953 (paper).

Rosenthal, Robert. *Experimenter Effects in Behavioral Research.* New York: Appleton-Century-Crofts, 1966.

Zimbardo, P. G., and E. B. Ebbesen. *Influencing Attitudes and Changing Behavior.* Reading, Mass.: Addison-Wesley, 1969.

Chapter 12

Adler, Alfred. *What Life Should Mean to You.* New York: Putnam, 1959 (paper).

Frankl, Viktor. *Man's Search for Meaning.* Boston: Beacon Press, 1962.

Freud, Sigmund. *A General Introduction to Psychoanalysis.* Joan Riviere (tr.). Garden City, N.Y.: Garden City Publishing Co., 1943.

Fromm, Erich. *Escape from Freedom.* New York: Holt, Rinehart and Winston, 1941.

_____. *Man for Himself: An Inquiry into the Psychology of Ethics.* New York: Holt, Rinehart and Winston, 1947.

Hall, Calvin S. *A Primer of Freudian Psychology.* Cleveland: World Publishing Co., 1954.

Hall, Calvin S. and Gardner Lindzey. *Theories of Personality.* 2nd ed. New York: Wiley, 1970 (paper).

Jung, Carl G. *Memories, Dreams, Reflections.* Anna Jaffe (ed.). Richard and Clara Winston (trs.). New York: Pantheon Books, 1963.

Maslow, Abraham. *Toward a Psychology of Being.* New York: Van Nostrand, 1968.

_____. *Motivation and Personality.* 2nd ed. New York: Harper & Row, 1970 (paper).

Perls, Frederick S. *Gestalt Therapy Verbatim.* Lafayette, Calif.: Real People Press, 1969.

Rogers, Carl. *Client-Centered Therapy.* Boston: Houghton Mifflin, 1951.

_____. *On Becoming A Person.* Boston: Houghton Mifflin, 1961.

Skinner, B. F. *Science and Human Behavior.* New York: Macmillan, 1953.

_____. *Beyond Freedom and Dignity.* New York: Knopf, 1971.

Chapter 13

Alvarez, A. *The Savage God: A Study of Suicide.* New York: Random House, 1970.

Bateson, Gregory. *Steps to an Ecology of Mind.* San Francisco: Chandler, 1972.

Fenichel, Otto. *The Psychoanalytic Theory of Neurosis.* New York: Norton, 1945.

Jordan, Thomas E. *The Mentally Retarded.* 3rd ed. Columbus, Ohio: Merrill, 1972.

Kaplan, Bert (ed.). *The Inner World of Mental Illness.* New York: Harper & Row, 1964 (paper).

Kisker, George. *The Disorganized Personality.* New York: McGraw-Hill, 1964.

Laing, R. D. *The Divided Self.* Baltimore: Penguin, 1959 (paper).

_____. *Sanity, Madness, and the Family.* Baltimore: Penguin, 1970 (paper).

Levant, Oscar. *The Memoirs of an Amnesiac.* New York: Bantam, 1966 (paper).

Lorenz, Sarah. *Our Son, Ken.* New York: Dell, 1969 (paper).

Maher, Brendan. "The Shattered Language of Schizophrenia," in *Readings in Psychology Today.* 2nd ed. Del Mar, Calif.: CRM Books, 1972, 549–553.

Rabkin, Leslie (ed.). *Psychopathology and Literature.* San Francisco: Chandler, 1966.

Rank, Otto. *The Trauma of Birth.* New York: Brunner, 1952.

Rosehan, D. L. "On Being Sane in Insane Places," *Science,* 179 (1973), 250–258.

Silverman, J. "When Schizophrenia Helps," *Psychology Today,* 4 (September 1970), 62–65.

Stone, Alan, and Sue Stone. *The Abnormal Personality Through Literature.* Englewood Cliffs, N.J.: Prentice-Hall, 1966.

Wheelis, Allen. *The Desert.* New York: Basic Books, 1970.

Chapter 14

Back, Kurt W. *Beyond Words: The Story of Sensitivity Training and the Encounter Movement.* New York: Basic Books, 1972.

Berne, Eric. *Games People Play.* New York: Grove Press, 1964.

Caplan, Gerald. *Principles of Preventive Psychiatry.* New York: Basic Books, 1965.

Fitts, William H. *The Experience of Psychotherapy.* New York: Van Nostrand, 1965.

Frankl, Viktor. *Man's Search for Meaning: An Introduction to Logotherapy.* New York: Clarion, 1970.

Gellman, I. P. *The Sober Alcoholic: An Organizational Analysis of Alcoholics Anonymous.* New Haven, Conn.: College and University Press, 1964.

Goffman, Erving. *Asylums.* Garden City, N.Y.: Doubleday, 1961 (paper).

Golann, S. E., and C. Eisendorfer (eds.). *Handbook of Community Mental Health.* New York: Appleton-Century-Crofts, 1972.

Greenblatt, Milton, et al. (eds.). *Drugs and Social Therapy in Chronic Schizophrenia.* Springfield, Ill.: Charles C Thomas, 1965.

Haley, Jay (ed.). *Advanced Techniques of Hypnosis and Therapy.* New York: Grune & Stratton, 1967.

Jarvik, M. E. "The Psychopharmacological Revolution," *Psychology Today,* 1 (May 1967), 51–59.

Lindner, Robert. *The Fifty-Minute Hour.* New York: Bantam, 1954 (paper).

Lowen, Alexander. *Physical Dynamics of Character Structure.* New York: Grune & Stratton, 1958.

Moreno, Jacob. *Psychodrama.* Vol. 1. Boston: Beacon, 1946 (paper).

Perls, Fritz, R. F. Hefferline, and **P. Goodman.** *Gestalt Therapy.* New York: Dell, 1965 (paper).

Raush, Harold L., and **Charlotte Raush.** *The Halfway House Movement: A Search for Sanity.* New York: Appleton-Century-Crofts, 1968.

Rogers, Carl. *Client-Centered Therapy.* Boston: Houghton Mifflin, 1951.

Rolf, Ida P. *Structural Integration.* Available from The Guild for Structural Integration, 1776 Union St., San Francisco, Calif., 1963.

Schofield, William. *Psychotherapy: The Purchase of Friendship.* Englewood Cliffs, N.J.: Prentice-Hall, 1964 (paper).

Skinner, B. F. *Beyond Freedom and Dignity.* New York: Knopf, 1971.

Szasz, Thomas. *The Myth of Mental Illness.* New York: Dell, 1967 (paper).

_____. *The Age of Madness.* Garden City, N.Y.: Doubleday, 1973 (paper).

Wheelis, Allen. *Quest for Identity.* New York: Norton, 1958 (paper).

Yablonsky, L. *The Tunnel Back: Synanon.* New York: Macmillan, 1965.

Chapter 15

Anastasi, Anne. *Psychological Testing.* 3rd ed. New York: Macmillan, 1968.

Buros, O. K. (ed.). *The Fifth Mental Measurement Yearbook.* Highland Park, N.J.: Gryphon Press, 1959.

Fitts, P. M., and **M. I. Posner.** *Human Performance.* Belmont, Calif.: Brooks/Cole, 1967.

Herrnstein, Richard. "I.Q.," *The Atlantic Monthly,* Vol. 228, No. 3 (1971), 43–64.

Hoffman, Banesh. *The Tyranny of Testing.* New York: Crowell-Collier Press, 1962.

Holt, Arthur. *Handwriting in Psychological Interpretation.* Springfield, Ill.: Charles C Thomas, 1965.

Holtzman, W. H., et al. *Inkblot Perception and Personality.* Austin: University of Texas Press, 1961.

Rosenthal, Robert, and **Lenore Jacobson.** *Pygmalion in the Classroom: Teacher Expectation and Pupils' Intellectual Development.* New York: Holt, Rinehart and Winston, 1968 (paper).

Chapter 16

Bachrach, A. J. *Psychological Research: An Introduction.* 2nd ed. New York: Random House, 1965.

Dustin, David S. *How Psychologists Do Research: The Example of Anxiety.* Englewood Cliffs, N.J.: Prentice-Hall, 1969.

Hampden-Turner, Charles. *Radical Man: The Process of Psychosocial Development.* Garden City, N.Y.: Doubleday, 1971.

Sarbin, Theodore, and **William Coe.** *The Student Psychologist's Handbook: A Guide to Sources.* Cambridge, Mass.: Schenkman, 1969.

Snellgrove, L. *Psychological Experiments and Demonstrations.* New York: McGraw-Hill, 1967.

Winthrop, H. "Cultural Factors Underlying Research Outlooks in Psychology," in J. F. Bugenthal (ed.). *Challenges of Humanistic Psychology.* New York: McGraw-Hill, 1967.

Glossary/Index

(Italic numbers refer to illustrations and captions)

A

AA (Alcoholics Anonymous), 341–342, *341*

abnormality, 305–309. An ambiguous and controversial term. It is often applied to any significant deviation from the average or from the majority. It is also applied to attitudes and behaviors that are inappropriate or maladjusted to a given society or culture. *See also* disturbance, mental.

Abramson, Michael, 254

accommodation, 162–163, *163, 169, 177, 179.* According to Piaget, the adjustment of one's schemes to fit newly observed objects and experiences. *See also* assimilation.

achievement test, 368–369. An instrument for measuring how much an individual has learned in a given field or area.

actualization. *See* self-actualization.

adaptation, 32. In sensation, an adjustment of the sensitivity of sensory receptors in response to prolonged stimulation.

addiction, 323–326, *324, 325,* 342. Physical dependence on a drug; it is produced by an altered physiological state in the body of the user. Addiction can occur only with depressant drugs.

adjustment, 307. The process of achieving a satisfactory relationship between oneself and one's environment. In such a relationship, one's needs are met and one is able to deal adequately with stress.

Adler, Alfred, 290–291, *290,* 300

adolescence, 187–194. The stage of human life lasting from the onset of puberty until biological maturity is attained.
  intellectual development, 194
  physical changes, 188–189
  sexual behavior, 189–191
  social development, 191–194

adrenal glands, 111, *111,* 112. The pair of endocrine glands, located above the kidneys, that secrete adrenalin.

adrenalin, 111, 112, 114–115, *115.* The hormone, secreted by the adrenal glands, that serves to mobilize the body for intense action, such as fleeing from danger or fighting for one's life.

advertising, 263, *265, 266*

affective reaction, 317–318. A type of psychosis in which individuals are subject to excessive and inappropriate mood states of elation or depression. *See also* depressive reaction; manic reaction.

afterimage, *44*

aggression, 173–174, *173*

Agnew, Neil, 405

aikido, 92

Albee, Edward, *307,* 328

"Albert," Watson's experiment on, 132–134

Alcoholics Anonymous (AA), 341–342, *341*

alcoholism, 323–324, *324,* 325, 341–342. The chronic use of alcohol to the extent that its use damages an individual's health, his ability to work, or his social relationships.

Alinsky, Saul, 255

Allport, Gordon, *303*

alpha patterns, *86, 92*

Altamont (Calif.), *244*

altered states. *See* consciousness, altered states of.

Alvarez, A., 328

ambivalence, 188. The experiencing of conflicting feelings.

American Red Cross, 267

American Sign Language, 165, *165*

Ames, Adelbert, *45*

Ames room, *45,* 46. A specially designed room for the study of visual illusions. The room appears to be rec-

E

physiological basis of, 111–116
Wundt's theory of, 18–19, *19*

encounter group, 342–344, *342, 343.* A small group formed for the purpose of promoting personal growth and improving interpersonal communication of its members through intensive experiences.

Encyclopedia of Human Behavior (Goldenson), 401

endocrine system, 106, 111, *111.* The system of glands that secrete hormones into the bloodstream in order to regulate the internal activity of the body.

endomorphy, 11–12, *11.* One of the three body configurations identified by Sheldon; a tendency to be round, corpulent, obese. *See also* ectomorphy; mesomorphy.

engineering psychology, 20, 21. The application of psychological methods to engineering problems. Engineering psychologists are involved in making environments and devices more suited to the characteristics of the humans that use them.

England, *264*

environment
heredity and, 123–124, *123, 124*
intelligence and, 365–367

epilepsy, *82,* 83, 109. A disorder involving disturbances in the electrical activity of the brain, characterized by convulsions that usually end in loss of consciousness.

Erikson, Erik, 182–183, *182, 183,* 194–195, *197, 198,* 201, *301*

erotic. Pertaining to sexual matters; sexually arousing.

escape, 142, *142.* Performing a behavior that terminates an aversive stimulus or removes the organism from it.

Escher, M. C., *48*

estrogen, 111. The female sex hormone, secreted by the gonads, that regulates sex drive and the physiological changes that accompany maturity.

ethology, 119–123. The study of human and animal behavior from a biological point of view; the study of the behavior patterns of animals in their natural environments.

evolution, 119. The continuous genetic adaptation of organisms (or of entire species) to their environment.

existentialism, 299, *299,* 300. In psychology, the study of human behavior from the viewpoint of free will. Existentialists maintain that human action is the result of choice and is not determined by forces over which the individual has no control.

exorcism, 14–15, *14.* The practice of techniques expected to free an individual from possession by evil spirits. Such practices have in the past included prayer, sacrifice, starvation, and bloodletting.

experimental group, *391,* 392. In an experimental situation, the group of subjects to whom the independent variable is applied. *See also* control group.

experimental psychology, 21. The study of psychology by means of measurement and experimentation as opposed to other methods of investigation.

experimentation, 390–392, *391.* The process of carrying out certain operations under controlled circumstances for the purpose of testing a hypothesis, proving a law, or discovering unknown relations, laws, or effects.

expertise, leadership and, 240

extinction, *133,* 134, *136,* 137–138, *137.* The gradual disappearance of a conditioned response. Extinction can occur because of repeated presentation of the conditioned stimulus without the unconditioned stimulus or because of the witholding of reinforcement.

extrasensory perception, 46–48. The ability to gain information by some means other than the ordinary senses (such as taste, touch, hearing, and vision).

extraversion, 289. According to Jung, the tendency toward being outward, objective, practical, and sociable. *See also* introversion.

eye contact, 209, 224, *224*

Eysenck, H. J., *6,* 25, *381*

F

Fabun, Don, 77

facial expressions, 209, *209*

faith-healing, *114*

family
Adler's view of, 291
Fromm's view of, 292
Rogers' view of, 295–296
in social development, 185, 191–192

family therapy, *20,* 344, *344.* Group therapy involving all members of a family.

Faraday, Ann, 98

Fast, Julius, 229

fear, 117–118, *118*
in childhood, 184
conditioning of, 132–134
desensitization of, 339–340, *339*
of success, 195–196, *196*

feature extraction, 55, 56, *56,* 59. The identification and analysis of specific features of sensory input.

feedback, 146–147, *146.* Information received after an action as to its effectiveness or correctness. *See also* biofeedback.

feral children, 7–9, *8.* Children who have been separated from human contact and have survived in the wilderness.

Festinger, Leon, 261–262

fetus, 157–158. The unborn child during the last six months of pregnancy.

figure-ground, 40–41, *41.* The division of the perceptual field into two distinct parts, one being the object or objects, the other the background or space between objects.

firing, 104, *105.* The transmission of chemical-electrical impulses by a neuron.

Fitts, P. M., 381

fixed action pattern, 120, *121.* A stereotyped pattern of movements that is characteristic of a species.

fixed-interval schedule, 140, *141.* A schedule of reinforcement in which a specific amount of time must elapse before reinforcement can be obtained.

fixed-ratio schedule, 140, *141.* A schedule of reinforcement in which a specific number of correct responses is required before reinforcement can be obtained.

flagellants, 9

flatworms, memory experiments with, 60

flexibility, *71, 71.* Readiness, when necessary, to modify old attitudes, strategies, or patterns of behavior or to adopt new ones.

forgetting, 64, *65*

frame of reference, 292. A background or context against which judgments are made.

Köhler, Wolfgang, 72, 384, *384*
"Kubla Kahn" (Coleridge), 72, *73*
Kuder Preference Record, 370, *371*. A type of vocational interest test that measures a subject's responses against those of persons engaged in various vocations.

L

La Rouchefoucald, *220*
La Salpêtrière, *17*
Laing, R. D., 179, 329, *352*
laissez-faire family style, 192. A family "structure" in which parents make no rules of behavior, make no demands on their children, and voice no expectations of them.
Landon, Alf, 384-385
language, 67
    development of, 165-167, *165*
    in feral children, 8-9
    in impaired children, 145
    see also communication
Lashley, Karl, 60
law, and insanity, 307
Lawick-Goodall, Jane van, 126
lay analysts, *334*
laziness, learned. *See* learned laziness.
Le Bon, Gustave, 10
leadership, 240-242, *241*
learned helplessness, 149-150, *149*. A state resulting from prolonged periods of pain and suffering during which one's actions to gain relief are futile. It is characterized by apathy, inaction, and a resignation to endure whatever befalls one.
learned laziness, 149-150. A state of inability to act, resulting from the early and prolonged experience of having one's needs and desires fulfilled without action on one's own part.
learning, 129-153. A lasting change in knowledge or behavior that results from experience, training, or study.
    by conditioning, 131-143
    in feral children, 8-9
    fetal, 158
    by imitation, 143-144, 160, 173-174, 185
    infant, *158*, 160-162, *162*
    perception and, 41-43, *42*
    of skills, 143-145
    of strategies, 148-150

learning theory, 299
Leavitt, Harold J., 239, *239*
Lennon, John, 291
lens, 33, *33*. A flexible, transparent structure in the eye that focuses light on the retina by changing shape.
lesbians, 196-198, *197*
lesion, 111, *111*. The destruction, either accidental or intentional, of bodily tissue or of an entire organ.
Lewin, Kurt, 342
library, use of, 400
lie detector. *See* polygraph.
life instinct, 284. Freud's term for those drives, such as hunger, thirst, and sex, that maintain individual survival and the propagation of the species.
Lifton, Robert Jay, 277
Lilly, John, 179
Lincoln, Abraham, 297
Lindner, Robert, 353
Liszt, Franz, 74
Literary Digest, 384-385
lobes. The divisions of the cerebral cortex. There are four pairs of lobes, with one of each pair located in each cerebral hemisphere. *See also* frontal lobes; occipital lobes; parietal lobes; temporal lobes.
lobotomy, prefrontal. *See* prefrontal lobotomy.
Locke, John, 79
long-term memory, 59-60, *59*. Information storage that has unlimited capacity and lasts indefinitely.
Lorenz, Konrad, 122, 126, 127, 167, *167*
love, *190*, 191, 224-226, *225*, *226*
    development and, 167-169
    Freud's view of, 194
    Fromm's view of, 293-294
Lowen, Alexander, 353
LSD, 94-96, *95*. An extremely potent psychedelic drug that produces hallucinations and distortions of perception and thought.
Luce, Gay Gaer, 99
Luria, A. R., 77
lynchings, 243

M

Machiavelli, Niccolò, 242
Machiavellian techniques, 241-242, *242*. Techniques of social interaction based on manipulation and extreme pragmatism. The techniques are so named because they reflect the use of power and strategy similar to that outlined by Niccolò Machiavelli in his classic book *The Prince.*
Mackay, Charles, 25
MacQuarrie Test for Mechanical Ability, *369*
Magritte, René, 67
maladjustment. *See* abnormality.
Malcolm X, 255
Malgott, R., 153
mandala, *288*
manic reaction, 317-318. A psychotic reaction characterized by extreme elation, agitation, confusion, disorientation, and incoherence.
manic-depressive reaction, 318
Mao Tse-tung, 272
Marceau, Marcel, *208*
marijuana, 94-96, 323. The dried leaves and flowers of Indian hemp (*Cannabis sativa*) that produce an altered state of consciousness when smoked or ingested.
martial arts, 92-93
Marx, Karl, *291*
Maslow, Abraham, 296-298, *296*, *299*, 300, 303, 308
mass behavior, 9-10, *10*, 243-245, *244*
    see also groups
master-slave relationships, 246
Masters, William, 189
masturbation, 190. The achievement of sexual satisfaction by manual or mechanical stimulation of the genitals.
maturation, 159-160, *161*, 188, 189. The internally programmed process of physical and psychological growth and development.
maturity, 189, 194-195. The end result of physical and psychological growth.
Maupassant, Guy de, 73
May, Rollo, 225-226, 303, *351*
McGaugh, J., 127
McGill University, *93*
McGinniss, Joe, 277

pupil, 33, *33*. The opening in the iris that regulates the amount of light entering the eye.

pursuit rotor, *146*

Pyke, Sandra, 405

R

race, and intelligence, 366–367, *366, 367*

racism, 243, *247*
see also discrimination; prejudice; segregation

random sample, 385–386,*385*. A sample that gives an equal chance of being collected to every piece of data within the scope of the research.

rapid eye movements, 86. The rapid back-and-forth motion of the eyes during one stage of sleep. *See also* REM sleep.

ratio schedule, 140, *141*. A schedule of reinforcement in which a number of correct responses must be made before reinforcement can be obtained. *See also* interval schedule.

rational-emotive therapy, *350*

rats, experiments on, 109–110, *109, 110*, 111, *111, 135, 141*

reaction time, 18. The time between the presentation of a stimulus and the production of a response.

Reader's Guide to Periodical Literature, 401

recall, 62–64,*62, 63*. The type of memory retrieval in which a person actively reconstructs previously learned information.

receptors, 29, 38, *38*, 104, *104*. Specialized cells in the skin, or in a sense organ, that are sensitive to particular types of physical stimulus.

Rechy, John, *210*

recognition, 62. The type of memory retrieval in which a person is required to identify an object, idea, or situation as one that he has or has not experienced before.

recombination, 72. In problem solving, mentally rearranging the elements of a problem in order to arrive at a novel solution.

Red Cross, American, 267

reference groups, 237, *237*. The groups with which a person identifies.

referred pain, 39. The sensation of pain in an area away from the actual source; most commonly experienced when pain is internal.

reflexes. *See* grasping reflex; rooting reflex.

regression, 287. A return to an earlier stage of development or behavior; it is utilized primarily when the person is threatened or in a stressful situation.

rehearsal, 57–58, *58*. Repetition of information or behavior to be learned. Rehearsal prolongs the retention of material in short-term memory and helps the transfer of material from short-term memory to long-term memory.

reinforcement, 135–143. Immediately following a particular response with a reward in order to strengthen that response.
    conditioned, 139
    negative, 142
    positive, 137
    schedules of, 139–141, *141*

relatedness, 291–292. According to Fromm, the feeling that one is part of humanity and nature.

reliability, 358–359, *359*. The ability of a test to give the same results when given to the same person under the same circumstances on several different occasions. *See also* validity.

religion
    in Jung's theory, 289
    mental illness and, 14–15

REM sleep, 86–87, *86*, 94. The period of sleep during which the most active and vivid dreaming occurs.

Repin, I. E., 55

replication, 398. Repetition of an experiment and achievement of the same results.

representational thought, 164. The ability to imagine things that are not physically present.

repression, 64, *65*, 286–287. The exclusion from conscious awareness of a painful, unpleasant, or undesirable memory.

research, approaches to, 383–402
    asking questions, 383–384, *384*
    correlation, 388–390
    experimentation, 390–392
    observation, 386–388

    reporting on, 397–399
    samples and data, 384–386
    use of statistics in, 392–397, *394, 395, 396*

research articles, 397–399

resistance, 336. In psychoanalysis, the patient's opposition to the attempts of the therapist to bring repressed thoughts into consciousness.

response, 129–130. A unit of behavior. An action. *See also* conditioned response; unconditioned response.

response chains, *144*, 145. Learned responses that follow one another in sequence, each response producing the signal for the next.

response patterns, 145. The grouping of simple responses or response chains into complex skills or activities.

retardation. *See* mental retardation.

reticular activating system, 106, *106*. A network of nerve cells in the brain that regulates wakefulness, alertness, and attention.

reticular formation, 106, *106*. That portion of the old brain that first receives signals and that controls the reticular activating system.

retina, 33, *33*. The innermost coating of the back of the eye, containing the light-sensitive receptor cells.

retrieval, 61–64. The process of obtaining information that has been stored in memory. The two types of retrieval are recall and recognition.

retroactive interference, 64. The hampering of recall of newly learned material by recall of previously learned material. *See also* proactive interference.

Reuther, Walter, *237*

review papers, 399–401

"Revolution" (Lennon and McCartney), 291

reward, 135–137, *138*, 160
    in child-rearing, 175
    in socialization, 185
    in token economies, 340–341
    see also reinforcement

rhesus monkeys, experiments with, 167–169, *168*

Rhine, J. B., 47

Richards, Whitman, 51

rigidity, 70–71. The inability to modify or discard strategies, attitudes, or behavior patterns when necessary.

rod, 33–34, *33*. A type of receptor in the retina that is sensitive to low-intensity light, but not to wavelength differences. The rods are particularly useful in night vision. *See also* cone.

Rogers, Carl, 294–296, *294, 295,* 297, 303, 337–33⁸, *343,* 353

role confusion, 195. According to Erikson, confusion of one's own sense of self with what others expect and imagine one to be.

role playing, 343–344. A technique in which a person acts out a role that is not his own. It is sometimes used in psychotherapy.

role-taking, 174. In cognitive-developmental theory, imagining oneself as another person and assuming his attitudes and point of view to determine how he would behave in given circumstances.

roles, 210–211, *210, 212.* Behaviors and attitudes that characterize and are expected of a person because of his particular position or status. Simple, hard-to-change patterns of behavior.
   in groups, 238, *238*
   social, 206–207, 246, *247*
   see also sex roles

Rolf, Ida P., 353

Rolfing, 353. A form of psychotherapy, developed by Ida Rolf, involving manipulation of muscles in such a way that one experiences bodily release.

Roosevelt, Eleanor, 298

Roosevelt, Franklin D., 384–385

rootedness, 292. According to Fromm, the feeling that one belongs in a family, community, and society of others; a feeling of brotherhood.

rooting reflex, 158–159, *158.* In newborn infants, a reflexive motion of the head and mouth that occurs in response to a touch anywhere near the mouth; movement is toward the source of the touch.

Rorschach, Hermann, 372

Rorschach Inkblot Test, 372–373, *372, 374.* A projective test in which the subject is shown ten inkblots of varying shape and color and is asked to give his interpretation of each one.

Rosenthal, R., 381

Roszak, T., 201

Rousseau, Jean-Jacques, 73

Rubin, Theodore, 329

Rudolph, M., 51

rule, 68. In cognition, a complex unit of thought stating a relationship between two or more concepts.

Russell, Bertrand, 384

S

sacrifice, personal, 235–236, *236*

Saint Catherine of Sienna, *14*

Salinger, J. D., 201

sample, 384–386, *385.* The small portion of data, out of the total amount available, that a researcher collects.

sanguine, 5, *6.* According to early theory, the personality temperament characterized as "cheerful" or "warm-hearted." It was thought to result from an excess of blood, one of the four humors.

Sarbin, Theodore, 405

Sargent, D. S., 25

Sartre, Jean Paul, *212,* 299, *300*

SAT. *See* Scholastic Aptitude Test.

satiation, 116–117. The complete gratification of a need or desire; the temporary elimination of a drive.

Schachter, Stanley, 114–115, *115, 116,* 216

schedules of reinforcement, 139–141, *141*

scheme, 162–165. According to Piaget, a cognitive and behavioral framework for dealing with experiences.

schizophrenia, 85, 314–317, *315, 316, 317.* Any of a group of psychoses primarily characterized by disturbances in cognitive processes. A schizophrenic's thoughts, emotions, and perceptions are confused and disconnected.

Scholastic Aptitude Test (SAT), 368. A widely used college placement test.

school, 186–187, *186*
   see also teachers

School and College Ability Test (SCAT), *364*

Schumann, Robert, 73

Scientific American, 401

scientific method, 17–19, *383*

sea slug, learning in, 130

secondary sex characteristics, 188

sedatives, 323

Segal, George, *307*

Segal, Julius, 99

segregation, racial, 251–252

selective attention, 54–56, *55,* 59. Focusing one's awareness on a limited set of sensory information out of the total amount one is receiving.

self, 294–296, *295.* According to Rogers, one's experience of oneself, one's actions, one's thoughts, and one's feelings, in relation to others. *See also* identity; self-concept.

self-actualization, 296–298, *296,* 308. The process of realizing one's potentialities.

self-concept, 211–212, *212.* The way in which a person views himself; a person's knowledge and understanding of himself or herself. *See also* identity.

self-esteem, 182, 188–189, 223. An objective respect for or favorable impression of oneself.

self-fulfilling prophecy, 273–274, *273,* 365. A belief, prediction, or expectation that operates to bring about its own fulfillment.

self-justification, 272–273. The need to justify one's attitudes and behavior.

Selye, Hans, 113

semicircular canals, 39, *39.* Three liquid-filled structures of the inner ear that respond to sudden movement and to changes in position. *See also* vestibular sense.

sensation, 29–39, 81, 104. The result of converting physical stimulation of the sense organs into sensory experience. *See also* sensory experience.
   in information processing, 53–56
   psychophysics, 30–33

senses. *See individual senses.*

sensitivity training, *342, 343*

sensory deprivation, 93–94, *93*

sensory experience, 30. The experience that occurs when a sense organ is stimulated.

sensory storage, 55, 57, *57,* 59. The momentary storage of sensory information at the level of the sensory receptors.

separation anxiety, 184. In infants, the fear of losing, or of being separated from, the mother.

Serebriakoff, Victor, 381

serial-position effect, *63*

set, 70–71. A habitual strategy or pattern of problem solving.

set, social, 192–193. A large, informal group of peers, composed of social cliques. Sets are usually arranged in a fairly rigid social hierarchy.

sex drive, 117

sex roles, 170–175, 185, *185,* 195–198, *195.* The complex range of behaviors, attitudes, and social rules that are considered appropriate to any individual because of his or her sex.
    cognitive-developmental approach to, 174–175, *174*
    Freud's theory of, 170–171, *171*
    social-learning approach to, 172–174, *172*

sexual behavior, 189–191

shadow, 290. Jung's term for the parts of the self that one hides from the outside world and from oneself.

shape constancy, 44. The tendency to perceive a particular object as always having the same shape, regardless of the angle from which it is viewed.

shaping, 144–145. A technique of operant conditioning in which the desired behavior is encouraged by first rewarding all acts similar to that behavior and then becoming increasingly selective, rewarding only those acts that closely resemble the behavior, and finally rewarding only the specifically desired behavior.

Sheldon, William, 11–12, *11*

Shirer, William L., 277

short-term memory, 57–59, *59.* Memory that is limited in storage capacity to about seven items and in duration to about twenty seconds.

Shriners, *234*

Siddhartha (Hesse), 281

sign stimuli, 120, *120,* 122, *122.* Environmental cues that trigger instinctive reactions or patterns of behavior.

signals, *136,* 138–139, *139.* In operant conditioning, behavioral cues that are associated with reward or punishment. *See also* conditioned reinforcer.

significant difference, *396,* 397. A difference so unlikely to have occurred by chance that it must mean something.

similarity, 40, *40.* In perception, an organizing principle that encourages elements to be perceived as belonging together because they share certain characteristics.

Singer, Jerome, 114–115, *115*

situational tests, 375–377, *376, 378.* A test that bases a prediction about an individual's performance in a real situation on his performance in a simulation of that situation.

size constancy, 44, *44, 45.* The tendency to perceive a familiar object as always being the same size, regardless of the distance from which it is viewed.

skills
    learning of, 143–145
    measurement of, 367–369

skin senses, 37–39, *38.* A general term for the various types of sensory information provided by the receptors in the skin. They include pressure, warmth, cold, and pain.

Skinner, B. F., 135–137, *135, 150,* 153, *299, 300,* 303

Skinner box, *135, 141*

Skylab, *232*

sleep, 85–90, 106
    alpha patterns, *86*
    dreaming, 87–90
    REM, 86–87, *86,* 94

sleep laboratories, *20,* 86

Slocum, Joshua, 216

smell, 37, *37*

Smith, Tommy, *235*

social approval, need for, 211, 251, 252, 261, 271–272
    see also conformity

social comparison, 217–218

social development, 185, 187, 191–194

social functions, 232, *232.* In groups, those functions directed toward filling the emotional needs of the members. *See also* task functions.

social influence, 257
    and attitude change, 268–269
    of authority, 267–269
    of peers, 269–272, *270, 271*
    persuasion as method of, 262–267

social interest, 291. Adler's term for one's feelings for others and one's innate tendency to work for the common good.

social-learning theory, 172–174, *172, 173.* A psychological approach based on the idea that personality develops as a result of learning—through imitation, modeling, reward, and punishment.

social psychology. The branch of psychology that studies social behavior. Social psychology is concerned with group behavior and with interactions between individuals and between groups.

social rules, 206, *206.* Any agreement among members of a society about how people should act in particular situations.

social workers, psychiatric, *334*

socialization, 184–187, 191–194, *195,* 248. The process of learning the rules of behavior of the culture in which one exists.

society, 206
    adolescents and, 187–188, 191, 193–194
    children and, 172, 185–187
    community mental health in, 347–350
    Fromm's views of, 291–292
    group conflict in, 245–248
    homosexuality and, 197
    individual development and, 9–10
    obedience in, 267–268
    sex roles and, 171–172, 195–196
    use of tests in, 366–367, 377–378
    see also socialization

sociogram, 238–239, *239.* A graph representing relationships within a group.

sociopaths, 321

somatosensory cortex, 106, 107, *107.* The portion of the parietal lobes of the cerebral cortex that is concerned with sensations from the skin, muscles, joints, and internal organs.

somatotyping, 11–12, *11.* A method developed by Sheldon for classifying individuals on the basis of their body configurations.

sound waves, 36

source, 264–265, *264.* The place, object, or event from which a given message originates.

Special Elementary Education for the Disadvantaged (SEED), *367*

species-specific behavior, 120. Behavior that is characteristic of a particular species of animal.

Spellbound, 89

spinal cord, 104–105, *104, 106.* The thick bundle of nerves running down the length of the back through the spinal column. Together with the brain it makes up the central nervous system.

Credits and Acknowledgments

We wish to extend special thanks to Steve Chain, who created the first drafts of most of these chapters; to Genevieve Clapp, Rick Ramage, and Frank Philip for their professional assistance; to Arlyne Lazerson for editorial help and contributions; to Dave Estrada for developing the Glossary/Index; to Martha Straley for proofreading; and to Rose MacDonald for typing. Special thanks are also extended to the following persons and sources for help in providing and developing graphics: Tandem Productions, Bill Bridges, Karl Nicholason, and John Dawson; Bonnie Weber for art production assistance; and Don Fujimoto for design assistance.

Chapter 1

2—John Oldenkamp/IBOL; 4—(*top*) Scala Fine Arts Publishers, (*bottom*) from the works of René Descartes; 6—Doug Armstrong; 7—From *Heads and Faces* by Nelson Sizer and H. S. Drayton, Fowler & Wells, 1895; 8—*The Wild Child,* © 1973 by F. Truffaut; 10—The Bettmann Archives, Inc.; 12—Karl Nicholason; 13—John Dawson; 14, 15, 16—The Bettmann Archives, Inc.; 17—Rapho-Guillumette Pictures; 18—The Bettmann Archives, Inc.; 20—(*left to right, top to bottom*) Steve McCarroll, Elizabeth Wilcox, Steve McCarroll (4), NASA, Jason Lauré, Costa Manos/Magnum Photos, NASA, Jason Lauré, Steve McCarroll (2); 24—John Oldenkamp/IBOL.

Unit I/26—Karl Nicholason

Chapter 2

28—Tom Suzuki; 33—John Dawson; 34—Steve McCarroll; 35—(*top*) Reproduced by permission of the author of the Dvorine Color Plates, distributed by Harcourt Brace Jovanovich, Inc. New York, (*bottom*) Tom Suzuki; 36, 37, 38, 39—John Dawson; 40—(*right*) After R. F. Street, *Teachers College Contributions to Education No. 481,* Columbia University, New York, 1931; 42—(*top*) Courtesy of Jerome Kagan, (*bottom*) John Dawson, after R. Held and A. Hein, "Movement Produced Stimulation in the Development of Visually Guided Behavior," *Journal of Comparative and Physiological Psychology,* 1963, Vol. 56, pp. 872-876, © 1963 APA and reproduced by permission; 43—Steve McCarroll; 45—(*top*) Philip Clark, (*bottom left*) photo by Robert Berger, reprinted with permission of *Science Digest,* © The Hearst Corporation, (*bottom right*) John Dawson; 48—Escher Foundation, Haags Gemeentemuseum, The Hague.

Chapter 3

52—© 1968 Metro-Goldwyn-Mayer, Inc.; 55—(*left*) Novosti Press Agency, photo from Alfred L. Yarbus, *Eye Movements and Vision,* Plenum Press, 1967; 56—From J. P. Guilford and R. Hoepfner, *The Analysis of Intelligence,* McGraw-Hill, 1971; 58—(*top*) Alastair McLeod, (*bottom*) Doug Armstrong; 59—(*top*) Terry Lamb; 61—(*left*) Courtesy of Bell Telephone Laboratories, (*center and right*) William Vandivert; 62—John Dawson; 63—(*top*) Doug Armstrong, after D. Elkind and J. Flavell (eds.), *Studies in Cognitive Development, Essays in Honor of Jean Piaget,* © 1969 Oxford University Press, reproduced by permission; (*bottom*) Alastair McLeod; 65—(*top*) Gillian Theobald, (*bottom*) Doug Armstrong; 66—Doug Armstrong; 67—Courtesy of Jasper Johns; 68—Gillian Theobald, after Edward De Bono, *New Think: The Use of Lateral Thinking in the Generation of New Ideas,* © 1967, 1968 by Edward De Bono,

published by Basic Books, Inc.; 70—(*top*) Werner Kalber/PPS; 71—(*top*) John Dawson; 73—Karl Nicholason; 75—(*top left*) Gillian Theobald, after Edward De Bono, *New Think: The Use of Lateral Thinking in the Generation of New Ideas,* Basic Books, Inc., 1968, (*right*) John Dawson, (*bottom left*) photo by Werner Kalber/PPS.

Chapter 4

78—Stephen Wells; 81—(*bottom*) Frank Jones; 82—John Dawson; 83—Philip Daly; 84—*The Three Faces of Eve,* © 1957 Twentieth Century Fox Corp., courtesy of the Museum of Modern Art Stills Archive; 85—Bill Buerge; 87—Joyce Fitzgerald; 88—Collection The Museum of Modern Art, New York, Mrs. Simon Guggenheim Fund; 89—(*top*) Courtesy Selznick Properties Corporation, (*bottom*) Richard Oden; 90—The Bettmann Archives, Inc.; 91—Peter Lloyd; 92—Philip Daly; 93—John Dawson; 95—Reproduced from *Triangle,* The Sandoz Journal of Medical Science, Vol. 2, No. 3, 1955; 97—Phillip Kirkland; 99—Terry Lamb.

Unit II/100—Karl Nicholason

Chapter 5

102—Rowland Scherman; 104—Doug Armstrong/John Dawson; 105—(*top*) John Dawson, (*bottom*) Doug Armstrong/John Dawson; 106—Doug Armstrong/John Dawson; 107—(*top left*) John Dawson, (*top right*) Doug Armstrong/John Dawson, (*bottom*) John Dawson, after Wilder Penfield and Theodore Rasmussen, *The Cerebral Cortex of Man,* © 1950 Macmillan Company; 108—(*top*) Doug Armstrong/John Dawson, (*bottom*) John Dawson; 109—James Olds; 110—(*top*) José M. R. Delgado, (*bottom*) Steve McCarroll; 111—(*top*) Courtesy Neal Miller, (*bottom*) Doug Armstrong/John Dawson; 112—Lorenzo Gunn/Gordon Menzie Photography; 114—Kenneth Murray/Nancy Palmer Photo Agency; 115—Karl Nicholason; 116—Sharleen Pederson; 117—John Dawson; 118—(*top*) John Dawson, (*bottom*) courtesy of R. A. Butler; 120—John Dawson; 121—Eadweard Muybridge; 122—(*top*) Thomas McAvoy, © Time, Inc., (*bottom*) John Dawson; 123—John C. Fentress; 124—Erik Hansen.

Chapter 6

128—Photo by Mike Gustadt; 130—Karl Nicholason; 131—John Dawson; 133—Karl Nicholason; 135—Steve McCarroll; 136—Karl Nicholason; 137—Bill Boyarsky; 141—(*top*) Alastair McLeod, (*bottom*) Steve McCarroll; 142—Karl Nicholason; 143—Steve McCarroll; 144—Bob Quittner/Photophile; 146—(*top left*) William MacDonald, (*bottom left*) Alan Mercer, (*right*) Robert Isaacs; 149—Commonwealth of Virginia; 150—Twin-Oaks Community.

Unit III/154—Art by Karl Nicholason; poetry from "Song For Boys and Girls" by Charles Angoff, *The Illustrated Treasury of Poetry For Children*, David Ross (ed.), copyright © 1970 by Grosset & Dunlap, Inc.

Chapter 7

156—Bill MacDonald; 158—(*top*) Ken Heyman, (*bottom left*) Bill MacDonald, (*bottom right*) Jason Lauré; 159—Ken Heyman; 161—(*top left, center, bottom left, bottom center*) Bill MacDonald, (*top right, center left, bottom right*) Steve McCarroll, (*center right*) Pamela Dalton; 162—Jason Lauré; 163—(*top*) Tom Suzuki, (*center*) courtesy of Mary Potter, (*bottom*) George Zimbel/Monkmeyer Press Photos; 164—Bill MacDonald; 165—Photos courtesy of R. A. and B. T. Gardner; 167—Thomas McAvoy, Time-Life Picture Agency, © Time, Inc.; 168—Harry F. Harlow, University of Wisconsin Primate Laboratory; 169—(*top*) Courtesy of Mary Potter, (*bottom*) Ken Heyman; 170—Terry Lamb; 171—Karl Nicholason; 172—Steve McCarroll; 173—Courtesy of Albert Bandura from A. Bandura, D. Ross, and S. A. Ross, "Imitation of Film-Mediated Aggressive Models," *Journal of Abnormal and Social Psychology*, 1963, p. 8; 174—(*top*) Bill MacDonald, (*bottom*) Burk Uzzle/Magnum Photos; 176—Ken Heyman; 177, 179—Courtesy of Mary Potter.

Chapter 8

180—John Oldenkamp/IBOL; 183—(*top left*) Stephen McCarroll, (*top right*) Bill MacDonald, (*bottom left*) Robert Smith/Black Star, (*bottom right*) Charles Harbutt/Magnum Photos; 184—Burk Uzzle/Magnum Photos; 185—(*top*) Rogier Gregoire, (*bottom*) Michael Alexander; 186—(*top*) Rogier Gregoire, (*bottom*) Michael Alexander; 187—(*left*) Reginald Jones, (*right*) courtesy of Vista; 188—Peter Hudson; 189—Michael Alexander; 190—(*left*) Peter Hudson, (*center*) Robert Isaacs, (*right*) Harry Crosby; 192—Rogier Gregoire; 193—Michael Alexander; 194—Victor Friedman; 195—(*top*) Charles Harbutt/Magnum Photos; 197—(*top*) Stanley Davis, Art Director; Carol Corbett, Copywriter; Robert M. Klosterman, Account Supervisor; 198—(*top left*) Jane Bown, (*top right*) John Oldenkamp/IBOL, (*bottom left*) Educational Development Center, (*bottom right*) Harry Crosby.

Unit IV/202—Karl Nicholason

Chapter 9

204—John Oldenkamp/IBOL; 206—(*top*) Karl Nicholason, (*bottom*) Ken Regan/Camera 5; 207—Doug Armstrong, after T. Burns, "Non Verbal Communication," *Science Journal*, 1964; 208—W. Gordon Menzie; 209—(*top*) Karl Nicholason, after A. E. Sheflin, 1964, (*bottom*) Michael Sexton, *Who Is the School?*, © 1973 The Westminster Press, used by permission; 210—Karl Nicholason; 212—(*top*) Steve McCarroll, (*bottom*) art by Karl Nicholason; 213, 215—John Dawson; 216—Art Institute of Chicago; 217—UPI Compix; 219—John Dawson; 220—Karl Nicholason; 221—Pete Robinson; 222—Photo by Joe Molnar; 223—Arthur Sirdofsky; 224—Art by Karl Nicholason, text from *Collected Poems by Sara Teasdale*, © 1915 by Macmillan Publishing Co., Inc., renewed 1943 by Mamie T. Wheless; 225—(*top left*) Michael Alexander, (*top right*) James Pickerell;

courtesy Vista, (*bottom left*) Alan Mercer, (*center*) Harry Crosby, (*bottom center*) Don Rutledge, courtesy Vista, (*bottom right*) Harry Crosby; 226—Karl Nicholason.

Chapter 10

230—Craig Head/Photophile; 232—NASA; 234, 235, 236, 237—UPI Compix; 239—(*bottom*) After Harold J. Leavitt, "Some Effects of Certain Communication Patterns on Group Performance," *Journal of Abnormal and Social Psychology*, Vol. 46, 1951; 241—Henri Cartier-Bresson/Magnum Photos; 242—Karl Nicholason; 243—John Oldenkamp/IBOL; 244—(*top*) Burk Uzzle/Magnum Photos, (*bottom*) Bill Owens/BBM Associates; 245—United Press International; 247—Karl Nicholason; 248—Courtesy of Jane Elliott; 249—UPI Compix; 250—From M. Sherif and C. W. Sherif, *Social Psychology*, Harper & Row, 1969; 251—Courtesy of Antelope Valley Press, Lancaster, California; 252—Edward W. Pearson, Operation Bootstrap; 253—(*top*) By permission of Metro-Goldwyn-Mayer, (*bottom*) by permission of Twentieth Century Fox; 254, 255—Courtesy of CBS Television Photo.

Chapter 11

256—UPI Compix; 258—(*top*) Adapted from J. J. Jenkins, W. A. Russell, and G. J. Suci, "An Atlas of Semantic Profiles for 360 Words," *American Journal of Psychology*, 71 (1958), p. 690, (*bottom*) from J. M. Jones, "Psychological Contours of Black Athletic Performance and Expression," a paper prepared for Physical Education Symposium on Race and Sport, Slippery Rock State College, Slippery Rock, Pennsylvania, June 19-23, 1972; 261, 264—Karl Nicholason; 265—Courtesy Medical World News; 266—Courtesy Department of the Army; 270—(*top*) Doug Armstrong, (*bottom*) William Vandivert; 272—Marc Ribaud/Magnum Photos; 273—Karl Nicholason; 274—Courtesy Department of the Army.

Unit V/278—Karl Nicholason

Chapter 12

280—John Oldenkamp/IBOL; 283—Culver Pictures, Inc.; 285—Phillip Kirkland; 287—The Granger Collection; 288—"Mandala of Evolution" by Dion Wright, photographed by Al Nomura; 290—The Granger Collection; 291—Courtesy of Erich Fromm; 293—Phillip Kirkland; 294—John Oldenkamp/IBOL; 295—Phillip Kirkland; 296—(*top*) Ted Polumbaum, (*bottom*) Phillip Kirkland; 299—Karl Nicholason; 300—(*top*) Ted Polumbaum, (*bottom*) UPI Compix; 301—(*top*) Photo by Lotte Jacobi, courtesy of W. W. Norton & Company, (*bottom*) Clemens Kalischer; 302—Courtesy of W. W. Norton & Company; 303—Courtesy of Gordon Allport.

Chapter 13

304—John Oldenkamp/IBOL; 306—Karl Nicholason; 307—*Who's Afraid of Virginia Woolf,* © 1966 Warner Brothers; 309, 310—Ignacio Gomez; 311—A Stanley Kramer Production, © 1953 Columbia Pictures Industries, Inc.; 312, 313—Ignacio Gomez; 314—The National Gallery of Art; 315—(*top 3*) Otto Billig from "Structures of Schizophrenic Forms of Expression," *The Psychiatric Quarterly*, Vol. 44, 1970, (*bottom 3*) courtesy Al Vercoutere, Camarillo State Hospital; 316—The

Minneapolis Institute of Arts; 317—Bill Bridges; 318—(*left*) John Oldenkamp/IBOL, (*right*) Gene Brownell; 319—Constantine Manos/Magnum Photos, Inc.; 320—Karl Nicholason; 322—John Oldenkamp/IBOL; 324—Karl Nicholason; 325—Ian Berry/Magnum Photos, Inc.; 326—Robert Van Doren.

Chapter 14

330—Bob Van Doren; 332—Courtesy Margaret Howard, from "Art Productions of a Gifted Adolescent with a Dissociative Reaction," I. Jakab (ed.), *Psychiatry and Art*, Vol. 1, S. Karger, 1968, pp. 86-91; 333—John Oldenkamp/IBOL; 336—Karl Nicholason; 337—Cliff McReynolds; 339—Steve McCarroll; 340—Costa Manos/Magnum Photos; 341—County of Los Angeles Health Department, Alcoholism Rehabilitation Center; 343—(*left*) H. Lee Pratt, (*right*) Michael Alexander; 344—John Oldenkamp/IBOL; 345—(*top left*) Eric Aerts, (*top right*) John Oldenkamp/IBOL, (*bottom*) Bill Bridges; 347—I. Jakab, "Art and Psychiatry, Their Influence on Each Other," *Psychiatry and Art*, Vol. 2, S. Karger, 1969, p. 96; 348—Richard Balagur/Nancy Palmer Photo Agency; 349—Ron Thal; 350—(*top*) Courtesy of Albert Ellis, (*bottom*) Hugh Wilkerson; 351—(*top*) Courtesy of Victor Frankl, (*bottom*) courtesy of Rollo May; 352—Pantheon Books; 353—Courtesy of Karl Menninger.

Unit VI/354—Karl Nicholason

Chapter 15

356—Construction Tom Gould, photography Steve McCarroll; 359—(*top*) Ron Sherman/Nancy Palmer Photo Agency, (*bottom*) Jane Bown; 360—Karl Nicholason; 362—Photo by John Oldenkamp, by permission of Houghton Mifflin Company from Terman and Merrill Stanford-Binet Intelligence Scale; 363—Photo by Werner Kalber/PPS; 364—(*left*) Reproduced by permission of Cooperative Test Division of Educational Testing Service, (*right*) from the *Army General Classification Test,* First Civilian Division, Form AH, © 1947 Science Research Associates, Inc., reprinted by permission; 366—Adrian Dove; 367—Robert Isaacs; 368—(*left*) Courtesy U.S. Department of Labor; 369—Copyright © 1925, 1953 by T. W. MacQuarrie, reproduced by permission of the publisher, CTB/McGraw-Hill, Del Monte Research Park, Monterey, California, all rights reserved; 370—(*top*) Courtesy Stanford University Press, (*bottom*) from *Strong Vocational Interest Blank Manual,* 1966 and 1969 revision, by permission of Stanford University Press; 372—Kurt Kolbe; 373—(*top*) Karl Nicholason, (*bottom*) © C.P.S., created by L. and S. Bellak; 374—From R. C. Burns and S. Harvard Kaufman, *Kinetic Family Drawings, An Introduction to Understanding Children through Kinetic Drawings,* Brunner/Mazel, Inc., 1970; 376—United Airlines Photo; 378—Stephen Wells.

Chapter 16

382—John Oldenkamp/IBOL; 384—John Dawson; 385, 387—Karl Nicholason; 389—Alastair McLeod; 390, 391—Karl Nicholason; 394, 395—Alastair McLeod; 396—(*bottom*) Karl Nicholason; 406—Steve McCarroll.

Cover design and illustration—Don Fujimoto

435